THE DEVELOPMENT OF INDUSTRIAL RELATIONS IN BRITAIN, 1911–1939

Studies in the Evolution of Collective Bargaining at National and Industry Level

RODGER CHARLES

Routledge
Taylor & Francis Group
LONDON AND NEW YORK

First published in 1973 by Hutchinson Ltd

This edition first published in 2025
by Routledge
4 Park Square, Milton Park, Abingdon, Oxon OX14 4RN

and by Routledge
605 Third Avenue, New York, NY 10158

Routledge is an imprint of the Taylor & Francis Group, an informa business

British Library Cataloguing in Publication Data
A catalogue record for this book is available from the British Library

ISBN: 978-1-032-81770-5 (Set)
ISBN: 978-1-032-84648-4 (Volume 9) (hbk)
ISBN: 978-1-032-84707-8 (Volume 9) (pbk)
ISBN: 978-1-003-51454-1 (Volume 9) (ebk)

DOI: 10.4324/9781003514541

The Development of Industrial Relations in Britain 1911–1939

Studies in the evolution
of collective bargaining
at national and industry level

Rodger Charles, S.J.

HUTCHINSON OF LONDON

HUTCHINSON LTD
3 Fitzroy Square, London W1

London Melbourne Sydney Auckland
Wellington Johannesburg Cape Town
and agencies throughout the world

First published March 1973

This book has been set in Baskerville type, printed in Great Britain on smooth wove paper by The Camelot Press Ltd, London and Southampton, and bound by Wm. Brendon of Tiptree, Essex

ISBN 0 09 112310 0

To the memory of my father
CLARENCE RODGERS CHARLES (1904–1955)

Contents

PART TWO THE WHITLEY COMMITTEE, REPORT AND SCHEME, 1916–39

Acknowledgements

This book has been many years a-writing. It is, indeed, my second attempt (the first was *Man, Industry and Society* published in 1964) to provide an account of the essential logic and philosophy of British industrial relations as they can be traced in the acts and the attitudes of the men who established the system upon which the Industrial Relations Act 1971 has now been imposed. Next to the benefactors of the English Province of the Society of Jesus who supported me during the years of study and the superiors who tolerated my interest in these matters, my main thanks are due to Mr. Allan Flanders, formerly Senior Lecturer in Industrial Relations at the University of Oxford and Fellow of Nuffield College. He supervised the major part of the doctoral research on which the book is based. It was a privilege to work closely with one who has done so much to enable the study of industrial relations in this country to reach maturity. At crucial points over many years it was he who provided me with the help, the guidance and the stimulus I needed in pursuing my own interests in this field. Whatever merit my work has owes a very great deal to him and I am delighted to be able to record my appreciation. To Alan Fox, too, Lecturer in Industrial Sociology at the University of Oxford and Fellow of the Oxford Centre for Management Studies, who supervised the last stages of my research, my thanks, as also to Professor E. H. Phelps Brown, Professor of Labour Economics at London University and to Mr. Arthur Marsh, Senior Research Fellow in Industrial Relations at St. Edmund Hall, Oxford, who were my examiners. The latter gave me much help in preparing for publication and has been good enough to write a foreword.

In collecting materials for research one inevitably relies a great deal on the assistance and co-operation of their guardians. I should like therefore to extend my thanks firstly to Mr. E. Brown, T.U.C. Librarian, Mr. Peter Pryer of the Department of Employment Library and Miss D. P. Black of the Registry of the same. Without the latter's assistance in guiding me through the Lab. 2 category of P.R.O.

documents I would have been very lost indeed. To her and to the numerous assistants in the Public Records Office who sorted and transported hundreds of files I express my gratitude. To the librarians at Nuffield College, Oxford, the Bodleian, the British Museum (especially the State Paper Room and Colindale) and to the London School of Economics, my thanks, too, for access to the Webb Collection. I was also much helped by the librarians in the reference sections of the Southampton and Manchester Public Libraries and by the staff of the *Southern Evening Echo* for access to the file of the *Hampshire Independent* which was not available at Colindale. The assistants in British Transport Historical Records Department proved most helpful also.

Individuals and officials of trade and other organisations were in almost every case co-operative. Mr. O. S. Whitley allowed me access to the Whitley family papers; and Lord Citrine, Lord Esher, Mr. J. K. Macara, Professor H. A. Turner and Mr. C. H. Edwards (Coleg Harlech Librarian) answered letters and requests for information, as did Mr. R. Gregson, General Secretary of the N.U.B.S.O., Mr. J. R. Heron, Assistant Secretary (Industrial Relations) of the British Footwear Manufacturers' Federation, Mr. T. George, Secretary of the Iron and Steel Wire Manufacturers' Association, Mr. H. Ratcliffe, Secretary of the Wrought Hollow-ware Trades Employers' Association, Mr. P. A. Leech, Executive Officer of the Chemical Industries Association, and Mr. S. Chapman, former Secretary and Director of the same, Mr. J. Jones, Secretary of the Bradford Dyers' Association and Mr. J. A. Peel, Secretary of the National Association of Unions in the Textile Trades, and Mr. G. H. Clarke, Contracts Manager of Hadens.

For permission to dig in records, minutes and files and/or for first-hand information of one kind and another I am indebted to Mr. W. R. Hanks and Mr. Ernest Crackle, Secretary and Chief Clerk of the British Spinners and Doublers' Association, Mr. J. C. Neale, Secretary of the employers' side of the Cement Manufacturing Industry J.I.C., Mr. A. J. Kean, O.B.E., formerly of the Blue Circle Industrial Relations staff, Mr. J. Bottomley, Director of Albright and Wilson, Mr. L. Williams, National Secretary of the T.G.W.U., Mr. T. H. Pike, Employers' Secretary of the Electrical Cablemaking Industry J.I.C., Mr. B. W. Burraway of the Industrial Relations Department of the National Association of British and Irish Millers, Miss Iris Conway, Secretary of the Heating and Domestic Engineering J.I.C., Mr. L. Green, General Secretary of the Heating and Domestic Engineering Trade Union, Mr. Roger Heaton, Executive Director of the

Hosiery and Knitwear Trades Employers' Federation, Mr. G. J. Lumb, Secretary of the Paint, Varnish and Lacquer Industry J.I.C., Mr. W. A. Lambert, Secretary of the Southern Section of the Employers' Federation of Papermakers and Boardmakers, Mr. Arthur Baker, now retired, formerly a Director of Bowaters, Mr. N. J. Perrot, Acting Secretary of the Quarrying Industry J.I.C., Mr. R. J. Simons, Industrial Relations Director for the Western Region of British Railways, Mr. R. R. Catty, Employers' Secretary for the Silk Industry J.I.C., Mr. L. L. Matthews, Secretary to the Tin Plate Manufacturers' Federation, Swansea, Mr. E. S. Booth, Director of the Wool and Allied Textile Employers' Council, and Mr. K. E. Abbs, Employers' Secretary of the Gas Industry J.I.C.

Getting this book to and through the press has had its problems. I am especially indebted to Mr. John Atkinson of Hutchinson for his efforts in its regard, and also to my secretary, Mrs. Susan Horton, for her assistance with the Index.

Foreword

by ARTHUR MARSH

Until the doubts of the 1960's assailed the conduct of British industrial relations it was common form to assert that we were the happy possessors of a voluntary system of exceptional maturity and sophistication. Indeed, our methods of handling industrial relations issues were, well into the 1950's, hailed as a major achievement of British culture and commonsense, a model to the world withheld from foreigners as a result of their lack of self-discipline and unhealthy dependence on labour legislation.

Times change. Poor industrial performance, a conviction that this has been hampered by strikes and by inflation induced by collective bargaining, pressures for incomes policies and, among other factors, the ambitions of a politically significant group of lawyers to assert their own notions of industrial equity and justice over those of conciliators, arbitrators and other proponents of industrial peace, have combined to erode the public confidence in such voluntarism. The Industrial Relations Act 1971 and its attendant legal institutions are now designed to provide for us the ground rules which it was once the pride of employers and trade unions to develop for themselves. To doubt the need for such a legal framework is currently no sign of grace. The clearmindedness of the advocate and of the judge are now required to underpin the shabby compromises, the bumblings and the evasions of the voluntarist.

The clouds which closed in upon our hitherto much-lauded system of industrial relations were visible on the horizon long before the lawyers gathered in the later 1960's to scatter the sceptics and command the vision of the righteous. Traditional voluntarism has been in decline for some time in the eyes of a considerable section of the population before the establishment of the Donovan Royal Commission on Trade Unions and Employers' Associations in 1965; indeed apprehension that our system had developed fundamental weaknesses was the principal reason for the Commission's existence. Belief in the virtues of self-regulation had declined along with the sagging prestige of the trade unions who were its principal protagonists. Ironically, it was the unions who were the first to turn away the modified form of voluntarism which the Commission put forward in 1968, leaving the field open for the most drastic excursion into legalism ever experienced in British industrial relations.

During the four years which have elapsed since the Donovan Report it has become increasingly evident that the sympathy of most, if not all, of its members for a continuation of voluntarism, would have presented Labour politicians with a difficult package to sell, even if trade unions had acted differently. The Donovan view that extensive legal intervention in the industrial relations system was likely to be ineffective if incautiously applied, and that the existing system, guided in the direction of greater formality, ought to be given another chance, was the kind of conclusion acceptable to most industrial relations specialists. It was not equally acceptable to those on the fringe of such activity or to those for whom industrial relations had no immediate concern. Voluntarism had made fewer friends than it once tended to claim.

It is too early yet to say whether the legalisms of the Industrial Relations Act will stand the test of time. Two things can be said with certainty. Whatever the future holds, the tide of voluntarism will never again cover the shore as completely as it did under the benevolent doctrine of legal abstention enshrined in the Trade Union Act 1871 and the Trades Disputes Act 1906; nor will the spirit and practice of voluntarism give up without a struggle. It will not be easy either to return to the past or to determine what elements of legal restraint will be acceptable for the next generation.

The justification for this excursus into recent industrial relations history is that this history forms the living background into which Dr. Charles' book is to be fitted. In one sense it is a penetrating analysis of what happened in the past, of that period in which our industrial relations system was formerly said to have 'matured'; in another sense it is an attempt to formulate a theory of the necessary conditions for the growth of rules and understandings through which trade unions and employers can, by their own efforts, regulate their mutual interests in industrial relations.

It may seem odd to the reader that such a book has not appeared before. Had a similar study been available to the Donovan Commission it is possible that its implicit defence of voluntarism might have been reinforced by the possibility of demonstrating that, given confidence in voluntarism, persistence and the initiatives of individuals and groups, answers to industrial relations problems can be seen to emerge. It is also possible that, in addition to its grasp of the need for procedural norms, the Commission might have evolved, as an alternative to the fragile general thesis of the 'two systems' of formal national agreements and unstructured, informal workplace bargaining, a more specific approach to the problems of different industries which would have captured the imagination and soothed the fears of the British public about the perils of voluntarism.

But no serious study of the period 1911–39 capable of being used in this way did exist during the Donovan period. The two best studies of the development of collective bargaining then available, Professor Phelps Brown's *The Growth of British Industrial Relations*[1] and *A History of British Trade Unions since 1889*, by Professor H. A. Clegg, Alan Fox and A. F. Thompson,[2] dealt with much earlier periods, the one being concerned with studying development against the background of the period 1906–14 and the other ending in 1910.[3] Can it be concluded that our failure to be curious about collective bargaining development between the wars was a by-product of our self-satisfaction about the British industrial system, a determination to ensure that the *lares* and *penates* of voluntarism were not violated by the prying eyes of investigators? I believe that, in part, such hesitation was indeed an unconscious product of voluntarism itself. Voluntarism has for more than a generation been a reason for the slow development of the study of industrial relations. In private matters accepted to be in the public interest there is no cause to pry; nor, where the arcane mysteries rely so much on personal contact and subtle, unspoken understandings is there much that can be revealed. What can be revealed may, however, affect the relationships between the negotiating parties, and possibly for the worse. In such circumstances the kind of scholarship which can produce an informed opinion can be regarded as a dangerous business.

The presence of informed opinion about our industrial relations system in the 1960's may or may not have made the continuation of voluntarism more likely. But it would have compelled those wishing to venture into the unknown to be more politically circumspect. It is not necessary to accept Dr. Charles' thesis that there are forces in British society which turn industrial relations conflict into co-operation if the ideologies and prejudices of the past can be cleared sufficiently to allow employers and trade unions to keep pace with changing

[1] Macmillan, 1959. [2] Oxford University Press, 1964.

[3] I. G. Sharp's *Industrial Conciliation and Arbitration in Great Britain*, Allen and Unwin, 1950, may perhaps also be placed in a similar category. I have omitted it for the reasons that it was substantially completed in 1939–40 and that its approach was too sectional and formally descriptive to constitute a true study of overall collective bargaining growth.

economic and social realities; nor is it necessary to accept that the norms for the voluntary development of collective bargaining in the 1970's would necessarily be those which he enunciates for the 1920's and 1930's. Any theory of voluntary development for the future could as he suggests scarcely avoid the need to take into account the requirements of the state in relation to productivity and incomes policy. But it is at least hopeful that, looking back on what appeared to the parties on the two sides of industry as a period of turbulence between the two world wars, progress can be detected. What has been done in the recent past could surely be done again.

The Development of Industrial Relations in Britain 1911–1939 is, I believe, an important book. It is also a scholarly one, written against a background of exhaustive detail gleaned from the documents of the period. There can be few sources which Dr. Charles has failed to investigate in pursuit of his general theme—the evolution of collective bargaining at national and industry level. An omission from his bibliography is G. D. H. Cole's *Workshop Organisation*, shortly to be reprinted by Hutchinson in this group of volumes about industrial relations. While it is understandable that Dr. Charles should have regarded this work as outside his brief, it points to an aspect of his studies which might have been given greater significance, particularly in view of subsequent development in workplace bargaining. The achievement of his book remains nevertheless an impressive one which will, I hope, stimulate other scholars to venture into that relatively unexplored and so vital area for the future of British industrial relations, the growth and dynamics of collective bargaining.

A. I. Marsh

St. Edmund Hall
12 June 1972

Introduction

(i) THE STUDIES IN QUESTION

The central institution of the British industrial relations system is the collective bargaining process. In this book, the evolution of that process, and hence of industrial relations, is traced through the most significant joint attempts made by trade unionists and employers to understand and improve it during the period in question. These attempts were through the Industrial Council (1911–13), the Whitley Committee, Report and Scheme (1916–39), the National Industrial Conference (1919–21) and the Conference on Industrial Reorganisation and Industrial Relations (1928–9). In the 1930's, the only significant extension of these initiatives was in the continued work of the Whitley Councils. The impact of the slump did not encourage new departures.

This group of conferences and committees has not previously been seen to fit readily into the development of the collective bargaining pattern in this country. Indeed, when I began my researches there was some difficulty in deciding how they should be regarded according to existing concepts and terminology. No previous attempt had been made to see them as part of a single line of thought and development although the Industrial Council, the N.I.C. and the C.I.R.I.R. have been linked as attempts at industrial self-government or industrial parliaments and the N.I.C. and the C.I.R.I.R. as essays in national economic consultation. Only the Whitley Councils had consistently been seen as a genuine contribution to the development of collective bargaining; even here there had been disagreement about the nature of this contribution. Clay[1] for example saw them as improvements in the organisation of collective bargaining only, adding nothing to our understanding of how we could improve the temper of industrial relations generally. Richardson[2] suggested they were something more, since they also involved joint consultation. He also distinguished the Whitley scheme from the Industrial Council, the N.I.C. and the C.I.R.I.R.

These accounts appeared to do less than justice to the facts. The Councils and Conferences possessed a common theme in that they

[1] H. Clay, *Problems of Industrial Relations and other lectures* (London 1929), pp. 143 ff.

[2] J. H. Richardson, *Industrial Relations in Great Britain* (London 1938), pp. 132 ff.

were each attempts by the parties to collective bargaining, with or without outside help, to work together in establishing the norms governing their relationship; they therefore assumed that the interests of capital and labour in industry could somehow be reconciled, however fumbling and imprecise their approach to the problem might be. In dealing with the traditional questions of collective bargaining, questions affecting wages and conditions, they favoured putting these within the context of improved co-operation and as their circumstances permitted, extending their scope to a much wider range of subjects. Herein lay a difficulty. Because they did not confine themselves to the immediate needs of wages, hours and conditions, they clearly had moved over into that category which the language of industrial relations knew as 'consultation and co-operation'.[1] This category has been seen traditionally as not only distinct from, but opposed to, that of collective bargaining. It is true that the value of the distinction, or its relevance, has been increasingly questioned over the years but it is also true that there has been and is no detailed and agreed theory of collective bargaining which satisfactorily allows for the inclusion within it of those matters which were once considered proper to consultation and co-operation. An examination of the work of the Councils and the Conferences, however, reveals a pattern of norms growing out of the traditional theory and practice of collective bargaining which spans the gap between bargaining and consultation/co-operation. These norms, detailed below, form the framework of the analysis which this book presents.

(ii) THE TRADITIONAL VIEW OF COLLECTIVE BARGAINING

The traditional theory of collective bargaining grew out of a conflict theory of industrial relations. Hugh Clegg,[2] referring to the government's attempts to encourage consultation during and after the 1939–45 war, pinpointed this fact. In contrasting collective bargaining with consultation it posed exactly the nature of the problem of anyone trying to account for the Councils and Conferences as part of the evolution of collective bargaining. The government, he noted,

> emphasised the difference between collective bargaining and joint consultation. Collective bargaining was appropriate to the narrow

[1] Hence the title of the Oxford doctoral thesis on which this study is based was 'National consultation and co-operation between trade unionists and employers in Britain 1911–39'.

[2] *A New Approach to Industrial Democracy* (Blackwell 1960), p. 36.

> area in which the interests of management and workers conflict; joint consultation was to be used in the wide area in which these interests coincided.

Conflict therefore had been seen as the keynote of collective bargaining. Bargaining was the means for agreeing truces and temporary pacts rather than an instrument for readjustment of temporary difficulties in a context of overall co-operation. Consultation on the other hand had co-operation as its keynote.

In the early 1950's Allan Flanders[1] suggested that the distinction was rather in the incidence of responsibility; after collective bargaining, this lay with both sides, while after consultation it lay with management only. Phelps Brown,[2] writing rather later, had begun to have doubts about the value of the distinction at all and the Research Papers of the Donovan Commission were even more sceptical.[3] The fact was that the realities of industrial relations in the 1950's and 1960's did not bear out the distinction. At an earlier period of industrial relations the conflict theory was reasonably well justified by the facts since a total divergence of view existed between labour and employers on the nature of the economic process. This divergence gave the two sides completely different ideas on the right approach to industrial relations, trade unions and collective bargaining. By degrees the divergence of view hardened into fixed attitudes which remained impervious to the changes which, however slowly, were removing the basis of the conflict theory. Meanwhile that theory had been hallowed by the authority of those who had written on the subject of industrial relations so that, in the way of these things, it seemed the last word had been said.

(iii) THE ORIGINS OF THE TRADITIONAL VIEW

The origins of the traditional distinction between bargaining and consultation lay in the social conflicts of the nineteenth century. That trade unionism and collective bargaining were born of conflict is one of the commonplaces of British history.[4] The aim of the wage-

[1] *Trade Unions* (London 1952), p. 132.

[2] *The growth of British industrial relations* (London 1959), p. 64.

[3] *Royal Commission on Trade Unions, etc.*, Research Papers 1 and 2 (part 1), paras. 57–63 and 83–8 respectively.

[4] S. and B. Webb, *History of Trade Unionism* and *Industrial Democracy* (London 1920 editions). H. Clegg, A. Fox and A. F. L. Thompson, *A History of British Trade Unionism since 1889* (Oxford 1964), and Phelps Brown, op. cit.

earner through trade unions was to obtain for himself security, decent wages and conditions.[1] The social and economic philosophy which ruled until the 1880's, and beyond, taught that wages, conditions and security were in the gift of the laws of supply and demand in a world of free trade and that any attempt to interfere with these laws was undesirable. The most that could be conceded, and that under protest, were the Factory Acts and the provisions of the Poor Law.[2] The Webbs showed how real was the conflict. Victorian society was totally unable to see that the unions were seeking in the only way open to them to secure rights which, for all but the wage-earner, were regarded as inviolable. Even when in the last twenty years of the century the economic theories on which the original opposition to unions was based had been superseded, and when it was agreed, at least among the experts, that their functioning was tolerable, those same experts were almost totally blind to the problem of effective demand.[3] Without an assurance that full employment was to be the norm, the unions could not be expected to be other than suspicious and defensive; there was no welfare state to tide them over bad times. The struggle of the unions in the nineteenth century was dictated less by socialist fervour than by the desire to see human standards established. They had tradition on their side. Until the 1820's it was accepted that the courts had the obligation to regulate the conditions of labour.[4] This was swept away in the high tide of *laissez faire* but the idea that since work was a human undertaking it should be appropriately rewarded was so deeply based in the common consciousness that temporary setbacks could not eradicate it. It was this instinct which provided the British labour movement with its inspiration; Marxism, or any other related 'ism', only began to have an impact in the 1890's, and then it was and remained peripheral. A respect for conciliation,[5] for negotiation, for proper procedures, for finding justice within the British system of law and politics was what marked and has continued to mark its main stream of thinking and action.[6] But it has been made to fight every bitter inch of the way. The attitude of the judiciary[7] summed up the prejudices and the an-

[1] Webb's *Industrial Democracy*, pp. 173 ff., 279 ff., 324 ff., 430 ff., 766 ff.

[2] In the 1890's concern with the conditions in the sweated trades led to the Lords Committee and by degrees to the Trade Boards Act of 1909. J. H. Clapham, *An Economic History of Modern Britain* (Cambridge 1938), pp. 427–8. The first Bill to provide the right to work or maintenance was introduced into Parliament in 1908.

[3] See below, pp. 87–8. [4] Webbs, *History*, p. 65.

[5] Phelps Brown, op. cit., pp. 126 ff. and 141 ff.

[6] See below, pp. 38, 47 ff., 90, 115 footnote, 230 ff., 266 ff., for example.

[7] A. V. Dicey, *The Law and Public Opinion in England* (London 1963), etc. Webbs, *History*, pp. 64 ff., 247 ff., 363 ff. Clegg, Fox and Thompson, op. cit., pp. 305 ff.

tagonism of educated society which persisted despite the demolition of the economic theories which once, superficially at least, justified it.

Mainly because of the obstacles placed in their way, the growth of unionism and collective bargaining was slow and uneven. There were but 2·5 million trade unionists in 1910; one-third were miners and the rest mainly in cotton, metals, engineering and the building trades. Collective bargaining affected one in five workers to some degree but it was limited in scope, local in coverage and possessed of little in the way of permanent machinery. Only in isolated cases did it extend to national agreements and then only on disputes procedures and certain conditions of work.[1] Until 1914 the work of the unions continued uphill all the way and even after the war, though the unions and collective bargaining had at last found a permanent and accepted place in the life of industry and the nation, they were still working in a context of economic thought and policy which gave them little hope; nor was their acceptance by any means total, politically and industrially; there were many hangovers of older attitudes.

The emphasis meanwhile continued to be on the duty of workers to co-operate and produce more, but there was no effective national economic policy to secure full employment or effective planning for social security. Indeed, there was a positive aversion to thinking in this way. The exhortation to co-operation was accordingly not as convincing as it might have been and, added to the residual antagonism to effective unionism, there was little enough incentive for the unions to think positively. The degree to which they none the less did so remains a remarkable tribute to their leadership. Nor were there lacking counterparts among the employers who showed similar vision. Meanwhile the trade union and labour movement in general refused to accept the implications of orthodox economic arguments however powerless they were to disprove them. They lost the battle time and time again but they won the war in the end. It was the recruitment of the trade unions behind the Labour Party which gave it its mass strength and, though it was Keynes who showed the way, and the conditions of national unity which existed during the 1939 war which provided the opportunity, it was the existence of the Labour Party as an alternative government which in the event made full employment and the welfare state inevitable.

[1] Clegg, Fox and Thompson, op. cit., pp. 466 ff. Clapham, op. cit., pp. 319 ff. Phelps Brown, op. cit., pp. 279 ff., and the *Report on Collective Agreements*, etc., S.P. 1910, XX.

(iv) THE REASONS FOR THE PERSISTENCE OF THE TRADITIONAL VIEW

Until the acceptance of national responsibility for full employment through control of the economy and until the advent of the welfare state it seemed reasonable enough to see industrial relations as an arena for conflict between contending social philosophies and consequently for conflict to be the keynote of collective bargaining. But the welfare state and the national policy for full employment have been with us for over twenty years; whatever the deficiencies of both it does not seem reasonable to claim that industrial relations today exist in the same context as they did up to the 1939 war. The fact is that neither in theory nor in practice have industrial relations kept pace adequately with the changing economic and social realities and needs of the time. It would seem that they have not done so because of the ideologies and prejudices bred by the past difficulties and still reflected in the language and the concepts of industrial relations have failed to adjust to meet the new realities and needs. On the other hand, twenty to thirty years is a short period in which to overcome an intellectual and emotional heritage built up over a century and still dominating much of our social and cultural life.

Ideologies were hardening before the 1914 war. Certain sections of labour were becoming increasingly susceptible to the appeal to violent or revolutionary solutions as they became soured by long awareness of injustice unrelieved. Socialist influence on some unions became evident in the 1890's,[1] and the conditions in the South Wales coalfield in the early twentieth century produced and fed the fervour of a group of Marxist Syndicalists whose impact on the whole of the movement was to be out of all proportion to its numbers. Guild Socialism and workers' control appealed to the same exasperation and the accession of able propagandists like G. D. H. Cole to the ranks did not encourage better understanding of or improvements in collective bargaining. It encouraged the illusion of more radical changes. That these views were in fact embraced by only a few is not the point. They were numerous and influential enough to confuse the issue and divert energies. On the employers' side those in mining and engineering refused before the 1914 war to take a more positive attitude towards unions and collective bargaining; they failed to learn the lesson that the railway directors and many of those in shipping and dock transport had learned and their

[1] Clegg, Fox and Thompson, pp. 291 ff.

refusal was to have an emphatic and unfortunate effect on the future of industrial relations in this country because it indicated a set attitude which was to continue after the war. The extremists on either side of industry showed little interest in adapting the system of collective bargaining to meet the changing needs of the time. They were well satisfied with the conflict theory if only in terms of keeping the enemy at bay. For neither was there any real future in trying to work out the full logic of their collective bargaining relationship and improving it to their mutual advantage.

Only slowly has the serious study of industrial relations gained acceptance as an academic discipline at university level; what serious literature there existed before the first world war reflected its uncertain role and status. Those who did take it seriously were on the whole out of sympathy with the system of profit-making and private ownership in industry. Where opponents of the unions turned their attention to industrial relations it was usually to attack them in general or particular or to suggest that the only alternative to the conflict theory was one which involved a unitary concept of the industrial relationship.[1]

The Webbs were by far the most considerable writers and thinkers on the subject of industrial relations and they showed in their two great works a profound understanding of the real strengths as well as the real weaknesses of collective bargaining in the existing system of industrial ownership and control; but their view of the nature of bargaining was narrow and they were more concerned with replacing the system than improving one of its institutions. The truce in war, the conflict theory, were norms of such institutions as far as they were concerned.[2] In the Introduction to the 1920 edition of *Industrial Democracy* they referred the readers to their *A Constitution for the Socialist Commonwealth of Great Britain* for their plan of how things should develop,[3] so far away had they moved from that basis in historical reality which had given their early works their value.

In terms of output and influence G. D. H. Cole must be ranked with the Webbs. But his eyes were even more firmly fixed on the far horizons

[1] 'A unitary system has one source of authority and one focus of loyalty . . . suggests a team analogy . . . the team stands alone, its members owing allegiance to their own leaders but to no others.' Research Paper 3 of the *Royal Commission on Trade Unions*, etc., 1966, p. 3. A good example of the unitary concept is to be found in P. S. Bagwell, *The Railwaymen* (London 1963), p. 413, quoting a railway manager.

[2] Bargaining is the modern compromise between diametrically opposed views, *Industrial Democracy*, p. 218. They found the quotation from the *Report of the Royal Commission on Labour* apt; it likened industrial conflict in the well-organised trades to war. Ibid., p. 221.

[3] Page xvii.

of socialism. Collective bargaining was acceptable in the context of war between the two sides, as a truce on the way to workers' control.[1] The Whitley Councils could do nothing to remove the deadlock; the main task was the abolition of the wage system.[2] There was 'no possibility of reconciling the claims and interests of opposing classes' through the C.I.R.I.R.[3] Men like Clay and Richardson were much more circumspect and cautious but they had little contribution to make to the development of a workable theory. The views of the T.U.C. developing from Gosling's address to it in 1916 through the Report by Citrine on Trade Union Structure in 1927 and the involvement with like-minded employers in the C.I.R.I.R. were much more perceptive and relevant. But a contribution to theory from this quarter was less spectacular and received less consideration. Cole scorned the C.I.R.I.R. as he had scorned Whitleyism. In the event it was the conflict theory based on the nineteenth-century practices which prevailed.

(v) THE CHALLENGES TO THE TRADITIONAL VIEW

It has become increasingly obvious that the concept of bargaining as advanced by the Webbs and based upon the experience of the nineteenth century was too narrow to account for the real nature of the industrial relationship.[4] A bargain is a transitory economic transaction whereas the process of negotiation which is central to industrial relations, though concerned with economic issues among other things, is more like a system of law-making, or a pattern of diplomacy and politics than that of the transitory market-place haggling which the Webbs envisaged. It is a lasting relationship which requires of its nature an attempt to reach lasting agreements and the development of procedures for interpreting and varying agreements and the scope of their interests. The considerations weighing upon the parties are more complex than the parallel with bargaining allows and they can introduce into their negotiations any matter on which it seems to them good to negotiate. Looking at the system of industrial relations as a whole it would appear then that the central institution may be better described as 'collective

[1] *The World of Labour* (London 1915 edition), p. 286.

[2] *Chaos and Order in Industry* (London 1920), pp. 118 ff.; also *Memorandum on the Causes of Industrial Unrest*, 1919, see below, p. 230.

[3] *Étude du statut de la production et du rôle capital* (Brussels 1938), p. 68.

[4] Allan Flanders, 'Collective bargaining: a Theoretical analysis', *British Journal of Industrial Relations* (March 1968). The works cited in this article indicate the range of the questioning.

negotiation' and 'bargains' better referred to as 'agreements'. The narrow, purely economic concept of collective bargaining then does not do justice to the facts. Nor does the conflict theory.

The men who developed the system, in this period of 1911–39 especially, were working on the assumption that they could in fact reconcile the claims of labour and capital in industry. What they sought was some means of realistic co-operation, that is to say, co-operation which did not assume a unitary concept of their relationship. Accepting that they represented different interests, they entered into agreements, as do parties to legal contracts, so that they might better serve those interests. Not that they made the mistake of seeing the collective agreement as comparable to the legal contract. They saw it as binding, not *legally* but *morally*, in so far as it was truly representative of the interests concerned and provided them with adequate means for interpreting and applying it.

This sort of co-operative bargaining[1] which we can call contractual co-operation, can only be developed where there is no ideological objection on the part of unions to employers and vice versa. The two sides must accept each other as legitimate representatives of legitimate interests. On this basis the way is open for full negotiations and effective agreements. Contractual co-operation is in fact the true ethos of British industrial relations.

The factors which have militated against the full acceptance and the free application of contractual co-operation have been discussed at some length. Ideological objections by a small but influential minority on both sides have had their influence. The lack of interest until after the 1939 war in the possibility of full employment and a comprehensive social security system provided the unions with no real incentive to co-operation. In a full employment, social security state, co-operation for better industrial performance is demanded by the logic of the situation. There will always be areas and industries in which poor employment opportunities and the threat of redundancy make it difficult to secure ready acceptance for such co-operation. Such areas are of national concern and must be handled accordingly. But the overall demands of a complex modern industrial economy in the context of socially responsible government policies indicate the need for co-operative collective bargaining born of self-interest and based on equal rights. Seen in retrospect the Conferences and the Councils between 1911 and 1939 were trying to establish the right psychological, organisational and economic policies and attitudes out of which such co-operation could grow.

[1] The same as that noted by many writers on industrial relations, e.g. Chamberlain and Kuhn, *Collective Bargaining* (New York 1965), pp. 425 ff.

(vi) THE DEVELOPMENT OF THE NORMS OF COLLECTIVE BARGAINING

One of the strengths of the traditional system of industrial relations in Britain is that it has been developed by the men most concerned with its day-to-day operation to meet what they have considered to be the real needs of the parties and in ways they have found appropriate in changing circumstances. This is another way of saying that voluntarism has been the basis of the system. Making a virtue of necessity in the first instance, unions and the employers accepted that the law should be invoked on specific issues of public interest such as those currently covered by the Factories Acts and by safety regulations.[1] But both sides clearly preferred the voluntary principle, believing that in the desire and ability of the parties to industrial relations to organise and regulate themselves lay the key to administering industrial relations in a free society. Granted that the tradition was established because the economic theory and political circumstances of the time would allow of no other, there is much to recommend such a principle in its own right and governments over the years intervened in ways calculated to improve and strengthen the system based on it while allowing the parties to determine its shape and character. The system has always had defects because of the pressure of economic conditions and of the failure of the community and industry to adjust to new conditions. But the fundamental principle is sound.

The Councils and Conferences were in this tradition. They looked to voluntarism first and sought government support to strengthen it. They consisted in the main of men active in the administration of industrial relations and they assembled, with or without official encouragement, to deal with the problems of their time as they saw them. They built upon existing structures and organisations. Nor did they make the mistake of thinking that the industrial relations system which they preferred was beyond criticism. On the contrary, they assembled to try to correct defects which they knew were obvious. They possessed the distinction of being in their time the only nationally significant groups of employers and trade unionists which tried to work out norms for industrial relations and attempted to improve institutions associated with them.

[1] 'The method of legal enactment' was one tried by some unions from the first: Webbs, *Industrial Democracy*, pp. 247 ff. There was little sympathy for their efforts among leaders of opinion and legislators. Ibid., p. 250.

Considered as a series of interlinked developments, with a common aim and inspiration, certain general trends, rules and norms affecting collective bargaining can be discerned, which they either specifically isolated and set out consciously to put into practice, or which were implied in their activities. To these, different Councils and Conferences gave different emphasis according to their circumstances and according to the pressures of the time. They stand nevertheless together and underpin each other.

The norms which were developed affected both procedural and the substantive issues in collective bargaining.[1] *Procedural* provisions govern the attitudes of the parties to each other, their authority, the means whereby agreements are made, applied, interpreted or varied and by which other matters not specifically dealt with in agreements can be handled. *Substantive* provisions govern rates of wages, hours and conditions and the standard by which adjustments are to be made in such agreements (*how* they are to be made is a procedural issue). Procedural and substantive issues may be distinguished as primary or secondary, the distinction between them being mainly one of logic. Such secondary norms are of great importance and indeed, without agreement on them, industrial relations remain primitive at best. The full range of norms set out here is that which is derived from the work of the Councils and Conferences as a whole. It is also set out in logical rather than historical sequence.

The primary procedural norm

The trade unions and employers involved in the Councils and Conferences reserved the right to strike or lock-out but accepted each other as equals in their right to exist in industry and to negotiate on wages, hours and conditions through well-integrated, well-organised machinery so that the needs of those subject to agreements were fully and adequately represented at all times and at all levels. Such organisation and such attitudes ultimately provided a basis for productivity bargaining in industries where it is relevant but the pre-conditions for its development were not present in this period. The Whitley Committee saw the possibility of a link between productivity and wage increases but was unconvincing on how this was to be achieved. The C.I.R.I.R. was nearer the mark but still lacked a full understanding of how to maintain the high level of employment which alone allows of the

[1] On the procedural-substantive distinction see Allan Flanders, *Industrial Relations: what is wrong with the system* (London 1965), pp. 5 ff.

general development of the productivity bargain. Despite these failings in social attitudes and national policy which made it difficult to realise it in practice, the fundamental attitude of the parties to each other in the Councils and Conferences was marked by the desire, not to perpetuate conflict, but to find a means of co-operating on the basis of equal rights and self-interest. Given that the first requirement in any negotiation is that the parties decide their attitude to each other and to the negotiation, this desire to co-operate out of self-interest and saving the right to strike or lock-out may be designated the primary procedural norm, the contractual co-operation norm. It presupposes: (i) Mutual acceptance of the equal right of unions and management to exist and look after their own interests in industry; they accept each other as representing legitimate interests. (ii) Mutual acceptance of the equal right of each side to negotiate on all matters affecting industrial relations and industrial performance up to and including where relevant what we now call productivity bargaining. (iii) Acceptance of the moral obligation to observe agreements made and administered in accordance with these norms plus those which follow from them and are listed in the following sections.

Secondary procedural norms

A number of secondary norms are associated with the primary norm of co-operation. These are first the *organisational norm*: full organisation of both sides from local to national level through permanent, well-integrated and organised machinery which makes effective voluntarism possible because confidence in the machinery assures the observance of agreements. In their various ways all of them looked to a completion of this voluntary pattern in individual industries by some form of national organisation with responsibility for the whole system, based again on consent, saving the right to strike but helping to avoid needless strikes and helping the process of conciliation and arbitration where possible. In the case of the National Industrial Conference and the Conference on Industrial Reorganisation and Industrial Relations, the overall national body was given wider consultative and representative powers too.

Secondly the *interpretation and application* norm governs the way in which the problems arising from the attempts to put agreements into practice are handled. It also allows of the introduction of matters arising but not covered by agreements. In the absence of effective agreement on this norm collective bargaining remains ineffectual, even disruptive.

Closely connected with these two secondary norms is that covering the *codification* of agreements, i.e. the need for setting out in formally printed statements the procedures for handling negotiations at all levels, the parties to them and the exact terms of the agreements reached and in operation as they affect each class of worker in each trade, area and region. The codification norm only has full effect if the other norms are in operation. It is in fact an automatic conclusion from agreements on those norms as the experience of the Whitley Councils will show. It is possible to agree on codification where the other norms are not totally accepted but this is less likely to happen and when it does it is less effective.

Primary substantive norms

There are two primary substantive norms: the *minimum wages and conditions norm* and the *adjustment norm*.

There is hardly any need to stress the importance of the *minimum wages and conditions norm*; that agreement should be first reached on *minimum* wages and conditions for the lowest paid is important because of their human implications and because without agreement here the building up of a proper wages and conditions structure is not feasible. In its turn a proper structure is essential if procedures are to work smoothly. Clearly it is impossible for unions and employers to agree on satisfactory norms unless social attitudes support the idea of adequate minima and the necessity for a full employment policy with all that it entails. Historically, employers and unions have been prepared to take the existing scales and differentials as the basis of such agreements. More sophisticated criteria will have eventually to be used and some progress has been made towards evolving them. The question of a national wages policy also arises as does that of the proper use of arbitration and conciliation within this framework so established. But these depend for their relevance and effectiveness on a collective bargaining system which embodies the norms here outlined.

Once there is agreement on the minimum wages and conditions norm sound wages structures and comprehensive substantive agreements can be developed so that procedures are relieved of the burden of conflicts on fundamental questions of principle. Procedures also need to be relieved of a further burden: that of running disputes on the standards governing adjustments in minimum wages and conditions. Here the right of the unions to strike and of employers to stand their ground can be invoked but many strikes and disagreements which neither side wants can be avoided if care is taken beforehand to specify intervals between readjustments and the norms governing such requests. For the rest, the need to agree on the criteria governing such adjustments remains one of the great unresolved problems of our system.

Secondary substantive norms

Once minimum wages and conditions are agreed and the norms governing adjustment are accepted, the essential issues affecting wages are covered. But bargaining restricted to such essentials, and those affecting basic conditions, is hardly satisfactory. Conditions in the basic sense cover issues such as overtime and payment for special tasks; more broadly they include health, pensions, safety, holidays with pay, redundancy, education and welfare. More important still, substantive issues embrace wages and conditions not only statically but *dynamically*; on the presumption or acceptance of co-operation they become linked to positive improvements in productivity, which may be initiated even by the unions themselves. The *Whitley Report* and the C.I.R.I.R. especially saw the need for such further development in theory. In practice in so far as anything like efficiency was seen as a legitimate interest of the unions in the Whitley Councils, for example, it was considered to be distinct from wage issues; the 'productivity bargain' was not envisaged. But on health, pensions, redundancy, welfare, holidays with pay and education some progress was made as we shall see, again through the Whitley Councils.

(vii) THE STUDY OF COLLECTIVE BARGAINING THROUGH THE COUNCILS AND CONFERENCES

The Councils and Conferences did not all deal with all the norms, nor were those with which each did deal considered with the same seriousness or effectiveness. These differences of interest and emphasis can be explained in terms of the evolution of the Councils and Conferences and the influences at work on them. To understand the evolution therefore it is necessary to consider:

(1) *The origins of each Council or Conference*
the situation leading to it, current problems of industrial relations and current ideas on them and their solution.

Particular influences encouraging it and affecting its form, individuals, organisations, ideas, the extent of government participation and initiative.

(2) *The work of the Council or Conference*
aims, membership, organisation and function, theory and practice.

(3) *The assessment of the Council or Conference*
as an answer to the problems of industrial relations at the time according to the soundness of its diagnosis of their nature, the adequacy of the remedies put forward, the degree of seriousness in their application and their success in practice.
As a contribution to the evolution of the norms and institutions of collective bargaining.

PART ONE

The Industrial Council 1911–13

I
The origins of the Industrial Council

(i) THE CIRCUMSTANCES OF ITS APPOINTMENT

The trend of opinion in the face of industrial unrest

In the summer of 1911 the country experienced a wave of strikes in the shipping, dock transport and railway industries. Such an event would have been significant by any standards but the industries affected in 1911 had not previously been among those which were strike prone[1] and the impact which the transport strikes had on the life of the big cities was more than ordinarily alarming. One of the areas most badly affected was Manchester–Salford and it was the experience of the disruption caused in all industries throughout the Manchester region that led Sir Charles Macara to put before the Lord Mayor of Manchester a plan for an Industrial Council. Macara[2] was 'the best known man in the cotton world'[3] at a time when cotton was the most important of Britain's export industries.[4] The Council was set up in October but it was first suggested in July and its development can be traced from the transport strikes of that summer. The idea behind it

[1] The miners (by far the most strike prone), the cotton operatives and the engineering/shipbuilding workers claimed that distinction. In the fourteen years in the period 1893 to 1908 when the number of days lost through strikes was in the region of 10 million days or more these three groups accounted for approximately two-thirds of the number. *Reports on Strikes and Lockouts*, etc., for 1908, 1909, 1910. S.P. 1909 XLIX, 1910 LVIII, 1911 XLI.

[2] *Charles Wright Macara*, 1845–1929. Born Edinburgh; moved to Manchester when seventeen years old. There he married into the Bannerman family and became a partner in Bannerman's (Spinners and Manufacturers) in 1886.

[3] C. Watney and J. Little, *Industrial Warfare* (London 1912), p. 117. Macara was President of the Cotton Spinners 1894–1914 and of the International Federation of Cotton Spinners, which he formed, 1904–15. See his autobiography, *Recollections* (London 1921). Also W. H. Mills, *Sir Charles Macara* (Manchester 1917). He wrote several books on industry and industrial relations which were widely read in their time, e.g. *Social and Industrial Reform* went through eight editions 1918–20.

[4] Its exports were valued at £120 million per annum in 1911–13, twice that of its nearest rival. B. R. Mitchell and P. Deane, *Abstract of British Historical Statistics* (Cambridge 1962), p. 305.

was not original. The Industrial Alliances of the 1890's had attempted to find an answer to economic and industrial relations problems through co-operation at national level.[1] The Industrial Union of 1893–4 and the National Industrial Association of 1900 were efforts to induce the co-operation of unions and employers in improving overall industrial relations.[2] Attempts at national conciliation and arbitration through some sort of Council had been suggested before[3] and had been thwarted, largely as a result of the objections of employers. That a plan which contained elements of all these formerly rejected suggestions should now in 1911 be accepted was due to its author's considerable personal standing, increasing awareness of the need to do something about industrial relations after the experiences of the summer, and the development of attitudes and possibilities since the 1890's. Great strikes in coal mining areas were one thing; great strikes which resulted in looting and riots in big cities, a situation of 'general' strike in several of them, shortages of food, movement of troops and a paralysis of the nation's rail network were another. More and more it became clear that public opinion was convinced of the need for a more conciliatory attitude to basic demands for union recognition, bargaining rights and minimum standards of work and pay. The employers, as a whole, wanted to work with the unions;[4] an increasing number realised that the best way to handle the inevitable problems that go with employing labour was to work with them. There was certainly no desire on the part of the unions to challenge the existing industrial and social structure. Even after his experience in the eye of the storm of 1911–13, Askwith could state that 'solid common sense, the real desire to work in general harmony governed the basic relations between employers and employed'.[5] The calling of the Council then was of a piece with the tradition and development of British industrial relations. Addressing its first meeting[6] Buxton could assert that, whereas a few years before it would have been premature, its existence now was essential. Though

[1] Phelps Brown, op. cit., pp. 137 ff., Clegg, Fox and Thompson, pp. 194 ff., J. H. Clapham, op. cit., pp. 271 ff. M. H. Mackworth, *D. A. Thomas Viscount Rhondda* (London 1921), pp. 101 ff. *Final Report of the Royal Commission on Labour*, 1894, S.P. 1894, XXXV, Appendix VIII.

[2] Clegg, Fox and Thompson, p. 176. T. B. Johnston, *Industrial Councils and their possibilities* (Manchester 1919), pp. 1 ff.

[3] *Royal Commission on Labour* and loc. cit., para 315, and Appendix V and VII. Phelps Brown, p. 186, and Clegg, Fox, Thompson, p. 265.

[4] Ibid., discussing the situation after Taff Vale, p. 362.

[5] *Industrial Problems and Disputes* (London 1919), p. 129.

[6] *Industrial Council. Notes on the proceedings of: October 26th, 1911 to June 10th, 1912* (Ministry of Labour, 331. 11), p. 6.

in the light of events it appears that Buxton least of all truly believed this, the phrase contained a certain truth. The British system of industrial relations had been evolved in response to actual needs. The problems of 1911 were being met in the same way and it was agreed some new departure was needed. Those among the employers who were for the *status quo* were increasingly isolated from their fellow employers and from those who would otherwise have been their natural allies. The mining, railway, shipping, docks and engineering industries had always been strongholds of those who objected to trade unionism. The events of 1911–13 were to change this pattern to a large extent.

Employers in the mining industry were organised into the Mining Association, formed in 1854 to keep an eye on legislation affecting the industry; all the main districts were affiliated.[1] Though the attitudes of the owners in the various areas differed widely, mineowners as a whole were distinguished by their opposition to any change or improvement suggested by the unions. They could not prevent trade unionism growing but they could and did make its growth and its work as difficult as possible. The Railway Companies' Association had done its best over the years to oppose the unions' attempt to get Parliament to act in improving employment and safety standards.[2] The Companies had effectively opposed trade union recognition in most areas and the discussions persisted in this opposition even after the settlement of the 1911 strike.[3] The Shipowners possessed in their Federation a staunch defender of 'Free Labour'. There was a venom in their opposition especially to trade union leaders which remains astonishing.[4] The dock authorities were connected with the Federation in organisation and in spirit; the ownership of the docks was a vast complicated network; it differed from port to port and there was little inclination among employers generally to federate locally or nationally. The docks were to some extent competitive and systems of ownership ranged from municipal to the most fragmented of private companies;[5] the resulting

[1] J. R. Raynes, *Coal and its Conflicts*, (London 1928), p. 291.

[2] P. S. Bagwell, *The Railwaymen* (London 1963), pp. 112–13 (Railway Regulation Act 1889) and 154–5 (Select Committee on Railway Servants—Hours of Labour), for example.

[3] *R.C.A. Minutes*, 1st December and 6th December 1911. In considering the request of the House of Commons for a meeting between the directors and the unions great care was taken to avoid taking a 'step in the direction of recognition'.

[4] The treatment handed out to J. H. Wilson was particularly harsh. Sir Walter Runciman, *Before the Mast and After* (London 1924), pp. 261–70. L. H. Powell, *The Shipping Federation* (London 1950), pp. 5 and 26. Tom Mann, *Memoirs* (London 1967 edition), p. 207. J. H. Wilson, *My stormy voyage through life* (London 1924 passim).

[5] Powell, op. cit., p. 65, and *Report of the Court of Enquiry concerning Transport Workers* (The Shaw Report), S.P. 1920, XXIV. Minutes of Evidence, pp. 38 and 46–9.

complications and the exceptional fluctuations of activity to which the trade was subject were largely responsible for the poor labour conditions in the industry; the state of the lower ranks of dock labour had been a cause for comment over many years.[1] Among dock employers standards varied. The Port of London Authority, under Devonport's leadership, was a byword for its intransigent attitude to unions and attempts to improve standards. It fought every attempted advance and spent hundreds of thousands of pounds in combating improvements in safety regulations.[2]

Finally, the engineering employers had formed a national Federation to combat the unions on the current issues of overtime, machine manning and general management prerogatives. Since engineering attitudes have had considerable effect on the development of British industrial relations and its traditions of collective bargaining, it is necessary to understand them in some detail even though in this period the engineers were not involved in the conflict.

The Amalgamated Society of Engineers, the main engineering union, was formed in 1850, at the height of Victorian prosperity and individualism. It embodied that individualism in the narrowness of its craft interests. The intention of ending redundancy, for example, 'dominated the policy of the Society'[3] and in this quest it set out to prevent all systematic overtime and piecework in the 1850's. There was a lock-out on the issue in 1852, the employers representing it as a 'manning' dispute. The 'manning' issue was one very close to the A.S.E.'s heart. Only very slowly did it, in the 1890's, accept the need to make common cause with the new grades of labour whom it saw rather as rivals than allies. It remained fragmented and sectional down to 1914 and the employers were able to use the disunity of the wage earners to their own advantage.[4]

The Engineering Employers' Federation was the spearhead of the employers' 'counter-attack' of the 1890's; it came into existence in 1895–6. A year later there was a lock-out on the demand of the unions for an eight-hour day though the issues were blurred by the recent wage disputes in some districts.[5] The resulting agreement[6] was a typical

[1] The degrading conditions of life and labour to which the dockers were subject were blamed by the Shaw Enquiry for the industry's industrial relations (*Report*, ibid., paras 28–9). See below, p. 44 and footnote.

[2] Ibid., *Minutes of Evidence*, especially pp. 7–8. Bevin's testimony.

[3] J. B. Jefferys, *The Story of the Engineers, 1880–1945* (London 1945), p. 32.

[4] Ibid., pp. 136 ff., and B. Pribićević, *The Shop Stewards Movement and Workers Control* (Blackwell 1959), pp. 29 ff.

[5] Over seven million working days were lost in it. Jefferys, op. cit., pp. 140 ff. Clegg, Fox and Thompson, pp. 161 ff.

[6] Jefferys, op. cit., p. 147. Clegg, Fox and Thompson, p. 167. A. Marsh, *Industrial Relations in Engineering* (London 1965), pp. 73 and 250.

product of the conflict theory. Trade unions were accepted by the employers and were given bargaining rights but they were hardly regarded as the legitimate representatives of legitimate interests; they were rather an enemy within the gate who had to be tolerated. The resultant procedures were primitive and substantive issues of the greatest importance to the men (overtime, manning) were claimed by the employers as issues affecting management prerogative and for their decision alone. The full effects of these attitudes were seen again in 1922 and have had their influence to the present day.

The coalmining, railway, shipping and docks industries all figured prominently in the disputes of 1911–12. In two of them (railways and shipping) the influence of the more belligerent employers was restrained and, in the third, docks transport, most of the main ports, with the exception of London where Devonport dominated, reached what in the circumstances was a generally satisfactory agreement. In the fourth, mining, initiative remained with hard-line owners despite the efforts of employers in federated districts to adopt a more conciliatory tone.

Public opinion in 1911–12 had little sympathy with the attempt to counter trade unionism in the industries concerned or to limit its industrial ambitions too narrowly and was generally on the side of moderation. It was the pressure exerted by the House of Commons which led to the railway owners agreeing to discuss matters at issue with the unions[1] and Bagwell records how annoyed the press was generally with the attitude of employers in the industry.[2] The House of Commons[3] supported the English coalowners against their more intransigent Scots and Welsh counterparts in their attempt to get a satisfactory settlement with their unions. *The Economist* was not the only journal of opinion to comment on the 'wholly unsatisfactory state of industrial relations in the industry'[4] and to point out that the extremists did not represent the attitude of the men. The House did all it could to get Devonport to agree to adopt a more reasonable approach to the London dockers but was defied; those who spoke in the House in his favour were few and did not reveal themselves in a good light.[5] In some vague and confused way it was accepted that the desire to work in general harmony of which Askwith spoke should be given practical expression; accordingly when Macara came to canvass

[1] 31 H.C. Deb. 5S, 22nd November 1911, cols. 1254 ff.

[2] Op. cit., pp. 298–9.

[3] 35 H.C. Deb. 5S, cols. 1723 ff. and 2104 ff., 19th and 21st March 1912.

[4] 30th March and 12th April 1912.

[5] 41 H.C. Deb. 5S, cols. 1083 and 1105 ff., 23rd July 1912.

support for his idea he found in many quarters a ready response to his hopes that national conciliation could achieve what, in its day, local conciliation had achieved. When the appointment of the Industrial Council was announced *The Statist* of 14th October noted that the approval of the new policy 'is so general that it was calculated to give a stimulus to business'.

The nature of the unrest

The industrial strife of 1911 came at the end of a period of a decade or more of comparative industrial peace. The employers' insistence on wage cuts during the depression which was beginning to be felt late in 1907 and continued until 1909 led to strikes in the engineering, shipbuilding and cotton textiles trades.[1] The railwaymen had threatened a national strike in 1907 and continued to be discontented with the conciliation scheme set up as a result of the threat.[2] The miners were unhappy also with the working of the Eight Hours Act which had brought to a head many other problems concerning the industry.[3] In all this the mood of the trade unionists was marked by a new militancy in support of points of principle, especially in so far as they were concerned with the notion of a minimum wage.

It was the same sort of determination to see that certain primary substantive norms were accepted which had led to the decline of the conciliation boards and the challenges to the sliding scale.[4] Strikes and lock-outs on such issues had the air of set-piece battles between enemies who had weighed the issues and knew the other's strength. The characteristic of the conflict of 1911 on the other hand was that it was spontaneous, to some extent reckless, and certainly poorly organised. Hence though by the summer of 1911 there had been a strike and lock-out in progress in parts of the South Wales field for more than eight months, it was not this but the action of Havelock Wilson of the

[1] Between 1899 and 1907 there were on average some 2·5 million days lost each year. In 1908 the figure was ten million and the average 1908–1911 was nearly eight million, *Report on Strikes*, etc., 1911, S.P. 1912–13, XLVII. The shipbuilders' dispute was from January to June 1908, the engineers' February to September and the cotton workers' September to November 1908. *Report on Strikes and Lockouts*, etc., 1908, S.P. 1909, XLIX. Phelps Brown, pp. 311 ff., and Clegg, Fox and Thompson, pp. 433 ff.

[2] Ibid., p. 423. Bagwell, pp. 262–88.

[3] Clegg, Fox and Thompson, p. 463. *Report on Strikes*, etc., 1909, S.P. 1910, LVIII.

[4] Phelps Brown, op. cit., pp. 134 and 141. Webbs, *Trade Unionism*, pp. 338 and 511. Clegg, Fox and Thompson, p. 101, but see also p. 203.

Seamen's Union in calling out his members on 14th June which was to prove the more significant.

Wilson alone among the leaders of the trade union movement connected with sea transport had realised the time was ripe. Sexton doubted the chances of success;[1] Mann admits to no more complicity in the starting of the strike than 'being kept informed' of progress in planning it.[2] Gosling asserted that 'it was Wilson who actually set fire to the heather . . . we were all saying he could not possibly succeed'.[3] The emphasis on luxury at sea epitomised in the *Olympic*, which arrived at Southampton on her maiden voyage on 3rd June, the approach of the Coronation which was to take place on 22nd June and the general upturn of trade after the comparatively slack preceding years, placed the union in a strong position strategically and psychologically, though Wilson alone seemed to have realised this fully. The strike in fact started before it was officially called. On 6th June the coal porters, one of the élite groups of dock workers, refused to coal the *Olympic* until they received a pay rise of one-third.[4] The seamen on the *Olympic* followed suit and on the 10th the seamen's unions were claiming that the liner could not get crew at the old rates; on the 12th there were reports of concessions.[5] The strike proper began on the 14th with the official calling out of the seamen and firemen: by the 16th twenty ports were reported affected to some extent, including Belfast, Cardiff, Bristol, Glasgow, Hull, Liverpool, Manchester, Newcastle, South Shields, Sunderland and Swansea. The list of demands was long,[6] but

[1] *Sir James Sexton Agitator* (London 1936), p. 214. [2] *Memoirs*, p. 208.

[3] *Up stream and down* (London 1923), p. 147. There had been attempts to form effective national and international transport workers' federations over the years, but with little success. The seamen acted independently of the other Transport Workers' Federation in 1911 and attempts at sympathetic action abroad came to little. See *The Times*, 10th June, and the *Shipping Gazette*, 16th June. Also Ben Tillett, *The London Dockers' Strike* (1911), E. J. Hobsbawm, *Labouring Men* (London 1964), pp. 215 ff., John Lovell, *Stevedores and Dockers* (London 1969), p. 148 and passim.

[4] *The Liverpoool Journal of Commerce and Shipping Telegraph* and *The Times*, 7th June 1911. *The Hampshire Independent* on the 10th observed that 'in all branches of waterside work there is a smouldering feeling of unrest'. That the strike should have started here at Southampton which the Royal Commission on the Poor Laws (S.P. 1909, XXXVII, VI, Section 21, par. 297) reported had no effective trade unionism (it had been replaced by free labour) is significant. Wilson congratulated the workers at the port on leading the strike, *Hampshire Independent*, 17th June 1911.

[5] *The Liverpool Journal of Commerce and Shipping Telegraph*, 10th and 12th June 1911.

[6] They wanted a Conciliation Board to consider, among other things, wages, manning scales, union representation, the Federation ticket and the Federation medical examination. *Report on Strikes and Lock-outs*, 1911, S.P. 1912–13, XLVII, p. 21. H. R. Hikins, 'The Liverpool General Strike', *Trans. of the Royal Hist. Soc. of Lancashire and Cheshire*, 1961, Vol. 113 (Liverpool 1962), p. 172, and Mann, *Memoirs* (London 1967),

as soon as it was clear that the initiative was with the strikers they were commuted into a simple wage claim with recognition of the union thrown in. Within a few days pay rises of something between 10s. and £1 a month were here and there being awarded.[1] The companies could well afford it. They had been making handsome profits, and it appeared in some ports that 'wages had not been altered for twenty years'.[2] Recognition of the unions, the abolition of the medical examination and the Federation ticket followed, piecemeal at first, later in wider and more comprehensive settlements.[3]

The dockers and port workers generally were next.[4] Here too Southampton led the way; it assumed the air of 'general revolt—even the White Star Laundry girls marched out in a body', said a surprised observer.[5] In Hull the strikers became so violent that it made Sir George Askwith wonder if the military would be needed and if the local territorials would be reliable.[6] Liverpool and Cardiff were to be in the grip of general strikes for considerable periods.[7] At Salford on 7th July two thousand wives and womenfolk of the dockers wound in silent protest through the streets in support of their men. Not for nothing, it was said, do women, some of them with children in arms, walk four or five miles in the burning sun over cobbled streets. Their banners told why they were there. 'Not mere alms but a living wage' and 'Our poverty is your danger'.[8] London was the last great port to erupt.[9] Although there had been rumbles since the beginning of

pp. 208 and 226, particularly emphasise the degrading manner of the medical examination. Nothing better illustrated the demand for better treatment as human beings which lay behind the strike of 1911 than the anger over it.

[1] *Shipping Gazette and Lloyds List*, 20th and 23rd June and 1st and 20th July. *Hampshire Independent*, 17th June 1911.

[2] *The Economist*, 29th July 1911.

[3] *The Liverpool Journal of Commerce and Shipping Telegraph*, 7th, 27th and 31st July. *The Times*, 11th July 1911. Specimen settlements in the *Report on Strikes and Lock-outs*, 1911, p. 140, Appendix II.

[4] The problem of dock labour had led to the previous big wave of industrial unrest in 1889. Casual labour was the root of the problem. *Report of the Royal Commission on the Poor Law*, S.P. 1909, XXXVII, VI, Section 21. W. H. Beveridge, *Unemployment a Problem of Industry* (London 1909), pp. 87–94, and E. Lascelles and S. S. Bullock, *Dock Labour and Decasualisation* (London 1924), Chs. 1 to 8.

[5] *Shipping Gazette*, 20th June 1911.

[6] Op. cit., pp. 149–50.

[7] Hikins, loc. cit., and *Report on Strikes and Lock-outs*, loc. cit., pp. 22 and 28 ff.

[8] *Manchester City News*, 8th July 1911.

[9] On 8th August there were over 100,000 affected in all departments of dock labour—from stevedores to van boys. All services of the port were disrupted and food supplies in the capital were short. The strikers straggled back to work 11th to 18th August, but the situation was still delicate with the railway strike intervening and the ship and dock owners ready to move blacklegs in to replace those dockers still out. Lovell, op. cit., pp. 168 ff. *Report on Strikes and Lock-outs*, loc. cit., pp. 23 ff. Phelps Brown, op. cit., pp. 322–3. Ensor, op. cit., pp. 430, 434, 437.

July it was early August before trouble really broke out. That it overlapped the railway strike made the total situation more ominous, and there were also the heavy threats surrounding the passage of the Parliament Act to add to the tension in the capital. Lloyd George was to point out to the House on 16th August[1] that those among the strikers and trade unionists who were advocating violence were no worse than the extreme Unionists who for weeks had been using the language of revolt and the threat of violence. Throughout this wave of strikes it was the spontaneous anger of the ordinary and often the unorganised lowest-paid worker which was most evident. The role of the unions initially was limited.[2] In many cases they came in simply to try to organise and give form to an existing tumult of protest. Nowhere was the essential energy of the strike wave better demonstrated than in the origin and development of the railwaymen's contribution which came last of all in mid-August. It was at Liverpool, where the combined activity of the seamen and the dockers had reduced the city to a standstill, that the strike took hold first, though inevitably the railwaymen had been to some extent involved in the troubles at all ports where they were enmeshed in the transport work of the docks. Finally at Liverpool the goods porters, the poorest-paid workers[3] of 'the stingiest company of the lot',[4] the Lancashire and Yorkshire Railway, made demands which they had not the wildest hope of seeing fulfilled. Their union advised them to submit their claim to arbitration,[5] but the company started making preparations for 'free' labour after the notice expired whereon the men came out at once. The railwaymen maintained throughout that they could have managed without the aid of the union;[6] Segar, who appeared before the Royal Commission

[1] 29 H.C. Deb. 5S, col. 1960.

[2] Askwith, op. cit., p. 177, emphasised that the official union leadership was taken by surprise by the outburst.

[3] According to the *Earnings and Hours of Labour Enquiry* (Railway service in 1907) (S.P. 1912–13, CVIII, p. iii) porters (goods), labourers, platelayers and porters (coach and traffic) were earning less than 22s. a week in that year—some of them much less. Fifty per cent of all adult male railwaymen were getting less than 24s. a week (ibid., p. 2). Rowntree (*Contemporary Review*, October 1911, using figures given by Bowley in a lecture referred to) said 23s. 6d. was the essential minimum for a family of five—the 'average' family. The criteria used are extremely stringent: there was no allowance for amusement, newspapers, tobacco, alcohol or subscriptions to any organisations.

[4] G. Blaxland, *J. H. Thomas: a Life for Unity* (London 1964), p. 67. The railway shopmen at Horwich were also agitating at the same time and on 3rd August refused to work under the existing conditions. *Liverpool Weekly Post*, 5th August.

[5] Hikins, op. cit., p. 184.

[6] *Report of the Royal Commission on the Railway Conciliation and Arbitration Scheme 1907*. Evidence, S.P. 1912–13, XLV, q. 5046.

as their main spokesman, was an A.S.R.S. member, but few who followed him were.[1] When, as a result of the flood of demands and the spontaneous strikes on all lines throughout the country, the unions' national leaders, meeting at Liverpool, decided to call out their members nationally if their demands for immediate recognition were not met, they were recognising a *fait accompli*. They had little knowledge and less control of what was going on.[2]

'The main cause of the strike epidemic', one Liverpool newspaper noted, 'is a bread and butter issue, a living-wage question.'[3] The vastness of the scale of poverty had long been known and commented on; the studies by Booth, Rowntree, Chiozza Money and Masterman had left no doubt in the public mind about its reality.[4] 'It is time', wrote Rowntree, 'for England to grasp the fact that there are today millions of people belonging to her working classes, who, if they spent every penny they had, would still be underfed and inadequately clothed'.[5] With thirty per cent of the adult male workers in this social group earning less than 25s. a week this is not surprising; it is reckoned they and their dependents numbered eight million all told.[6] Nor was there any doubt as to what the cause of the poverty was. It was not sickness, old age, unemployment—or technical change. It 'can hardly be too emphatically stated that of all the causes which have been brought to our notice, low wages are far the most important'.[7] Money had fallen in value since the turn of the century. This was a factor in the unrest but one that has no doubt been overestimated.[8] There was

[1] Ibid., qq. 8961–3.

[2] As the G.S. of the A.S.R.S. put it, 'there was no telling what any particular hour may bring . . . no use to name particular lines where unrest prevails . . . it is general and it affects all lines', *Daily Chronicle*, 14th August 1911. The reports of the Special meetings held at Liverpool on 15th August, etc., contain William's statement to the effect that he was 'not notified by the men of these disputes, neither have I received copies of the programmes submitted', *A.S.R.S. Report*, 1911.

[3] *Liverpool Weekly Post*, 19th August 1911: H. Quelch (in his *Introduction* to Tillett, op. cit.): 'This strike is purely economic in its origin and nothing more or less than a revolt against conditions which had become intolerable.'

[4] Charles Booth's *Life and Labour in London* was based on research done in the 1880's. B. S. Rowntree's *Poverty—a study of Town Life* came out in 1902, L. G. Chiozza Money's *Riches and Poverty* in 1905, and C. F. G. Masterman's *The Condition of England* in 1909.

[5] *Contemporary Review* article quoted above.

[6] Sidney Pollard, *The Development of the British Economy* (London 1962), p. 27.

[7] A. L. Bowley and A. R. Burnett Hurst, *Livelihood and Poverty* (London 1915), p. 42.

[8] The fact of the fall was commented on at the time, Askwith, p. 177, and the strikers themselves certainly mentioned it. Its exact size would seem to have been in the region of 5 to 10 per cent (Pollard, op. cit., p. 25). The likelihood is that even had the cost of living remained stable the lower paid would have gradually realised that they were not getting enough. The primary poverty that went with regular wage-earning could

evidence that a demand for positive improvement rather than a consciousness of the need to regain lost ground was the keynote of the protest. It was a better-educated working class, it was to some extent conscious of its political deprivation, it had been affected by socialist propaganda and it had been goaded by the constant attacks on trade unionism and denial of bargaining rights.[1] It was not so much the rise in the cost of living as the insistence that they be given the right of the security of a living wage which inspired the lower paid; 'not mere alms but a living wage' was the slogan on the placards of the women of Salford. For too long the notion that wages, any wages, were somehow the fruit of the munificence of employers had been built into the Victorian moral consciousness and at best the workers could expect only the benefits of a selling price sliding scale. Over the past twenty years it occurred to an increasing number that the human needs of the wage-earner required a different approach. Work at decent wages was more and more demanded precisely as a right and not a privilege.

The temper of industrial relations

It is in this context—the basic economic drive behind the strikes, and the limited contribution made to their leadership by the unions—that the consideration of the extent of syndicalist influences has to be made.[2] Taken literally, syndicalism stood for the abandonment by trade unionism of all conciliation and lasting agreements with employers.[3] As a doctrine it had been preceded by another, Industrial Unionism,[4] American in origin, which urged the earners to realise their political power through the normal means and once they had that power, make industrial unionism the only form of social organisation —replacing Parliament and the political state. Industrial Unionism

hardly be explained away in terms of the 1s. or 2s. in the pound rise in the cost of living.

[1] Askwith, op. cit., pp. 348–55, *Daily Mail* series 'What the workers want', 1912. C. Watney and J. Little, op. cit., passim.

[2] Phelps Brown, op. cit., p. 320. Ensor, op. cit., p. 438. Marwick, op. cit., p. 41. Askwith, op. cit., pp. 146, 177, 348–50. Watney and Little, op. cit., p. 34. Webbs, *History*, p. 667. G. Dangerfield, *The Strange Death of Liberal England* (London 1961 edition), pp. 207 ff. E. Halévy, *A History of the English-speaking people*, Epilogue, Vol. II (London 1934), pp. 433 ff. E. V. Sires, 'Labour unrest in England 1910–1914', *Journal of Economic History*, 1955. For specific references to syndicalist action in the strikes: Hikins, loc. cit., p. 170, and *Newcastle Daily Journal*, 20th June 1911.

[3] Pribićević, op. cit., pp. 10 ff. [4] Ibid.

and syndicalism were in their turn to be succeeded by Guild Socialism,[1] self-governing Guilds for each industry to be established by non-revolutionary but unspecified means, an idea that was in vogue from 1912 and received ardent support from G. D. H. Cole.

For the moment, however, it was syndicalism which was currently in favour. Syndicalism rejected any attempt to compromise with employers; instead, through a revolutionary industrial movement, direct action in the General Strike, capitalism would be overthrown. Few who adopted this doctrine seemed to have understood it and fewer still, in so far as they presumably understood it, meant it.[2] To accept it seriously while refusing to realise that it could only end in violence and bloodshed was to say the least naïve. A convinced Syndicalist would have welcomed the opportunities for violence and disorder that the strike offered. In fact there was little or none, save what could be ascribed to the mindlessness of mobs. Tom Mann, the completely convinced Syndicalist if such a person existed, appealed to the strikers at Liverpool to return to work when the situation was at its most critical.[3] Far from relishing its role as the co-ordinator of the mass rising of the wage slaves, the Strike Committee was regretful of having been 'saddled with the responsibility' for handling the railway strike too. What violence there was which made the headlines in the national press was caused not by the strikers but by the hangers on and the mobs attracted by the confusion of the mass strikes and rallies.[4] There were only isolated incidents in which strikers were identified as arsonists or instigators of violence and where this happened[5] it was peripheral and against the wishes of the mass of strikers and their leaders. In fact it would seem that in so far as the American and continental doctrines did have an impact at this time, they merely served to put a sharper edge on a militancy generated by the spontaneous anger of the lower-paid workers and they in no way affected the aims or the methods of the strikes which remained within the normal limits of union activity even if the sheer scale and spontaneity of the outbreak posed new problems.

[1] S. T. Glass, *The Responsible Society* (London 1966).
[2] As the debate at the T.U.C. 1912, *Report*, pp. 271 ff., revealed.
[3] In the appeal of the strike committee of which he was leader. *Liverpool Weekly Post*, 12th August.
[4] On the Liverpool disturbances of 14th and 15th August when two were shot dead. Mann, op. cit., p. 220, and Hikins, loc. cit., p. 186. Also *Correspondence on the Employment of the Military* during the strike, S.P. 1911, XLVII, p. 5. On that at Llanelly on 19th July when six died see *The Times*, 21st August 1911, the Home Office Report.
[5] A steward on the *Canada* was prosecuted at Liverpool for arson. *Liverpool Journal of Commerce*, etc., 4th July 1911.

The only centre in which it seemed that trade unionism had been seriously influenced by new doctrines was South Wales.[1] There was, as it turned out, little economic justification for the action of the Cambrian men at the Ely Pit; they earned a good wage when forced back to work on the employers' terms.[2] The crudity of the approach of the coalowners of South Wales to the human problems of their industry deprives them of any sympathy for having been unfairly pilloried in this instance; the development of the field was undertaken with a total disregard for social costs and the state of industrial relations in the area could hardly have been worse. The only consideration that had moved the developers of the coalfield had been quick profits.[3] They were now reaping the whirlwind. The owners were not as a class 'more liberally educated than the workers' . . . 'we do not do wisely to commit hundreds of thousands of workers to the charge of ill-educated men'.[4] They were noted for their opposition to the unions. Sir William Lewis, the 'last of the great industrial barons',[5] was the dominant figure in their councils and the sworn enemy of trade unions.[6] The South Wales owners put up the toughest opposition to the Minimum Wages Act of 1912 just as they had been tougher than any other area in applying the Eight Hours Act[7]—a fact which is not entirely explained away by the more difficult conditions of the field. Ironically, the man on whom the anger of the miners was now centred, Thomas, head of the Cambrian Combine, was the only type who offered the industry, and the South Wales section in particular, a solution to the long-term problems. He was an excellent business organiser and realised the value of working with the unions.[8] He was ahead of his time with those schemes for the rationalisation of the industry which were then, as they have been since, its only hope.[9] But he was unfortunately one of the wielders of 'masses of capital' whom the Marxist element among the miners loved to hate. The question is whether the activities of these extremists on the whole helped or

[1] R. Page Arnot, *The South Wales Miners* (London 1967), pp. 168, 176 and 375.

[2] The sticking point of the Cambrian men had been for a minimum wage of 6s. 9d. a day. Though forced to return on the owners' terms 'no case was known of a collier who had received less than 6s. 9d. a day in the Ely pit' and most had 'earned big wages at the "tonnage rate" ', ibid, p. 267.

[3] E. D. Lewis, *The Rhondda Valley* (London 1963), p. 103.

[4] *Report of the Commission of Enquiry into the Industrial Unrest, Area No. 7*, S.P. 1917–18, XV, p. 19.

[5] M. H. Mackworth, op. cit., p. 118.

[6] Clegg, Fox and Thompson, op. cit., p. 171.

[7] E. W. Evans, *The Miners of South Wales* (Cardiff 1961), p. 194.

[8] Mackworth, op. cit., pp. 103 and 118.

[9] Clapham, Vol. 3, pp. 162 and 220. Pollard, op. cit., p. 5. G. C. Allen, *British Industries and their organisation* (London 1958), pp. 50 ff. Lewis, op. cit., p. 103.

hindered the long-term cause of the miners that they were concerned to help. The Cambrian Combine dispute raised the question of the minimum wage and the train of events set in motion in 1910–11 resulted in the Act of the following year. Against this must be set the effect of *The Miners' Next Step*[1] and the extra bitterness generated by the extremists had on the future development of industrial relations in coal. The pamphlet in question was produced in the winter of 1911–12 by the Unofficial Reform Committee of the Cambrian Lodge and was published in 1912. It advocated deliberate hostility to the owners, efforts to make the collieries unremunerative and the ultimate taking over of the industry by the miners. The debate at the 1912 Congress showed how limited was the acceptance of such a view. In the House of Commons Stephen Walsh,[2] a miners' M.P., pointed out that the union as a whole had repudiated it. But it provided the enemies of trade unionism with all the ammunition they needed just the same[3] and they never tired of using it to create a scare; for many it was an unfailing standby down into the 1920's.

It seems reasonable to suggest, in fact, that the militants did more harm to the cause of the miners, indeed of the whole trade union movement, than they did good. The miners had built up one of the strongest trade unions by the efforts of men who were Liberals or I.L.P. in politics.[4] Alexander MacDonald (1821–81) was a pioneer of Parliamentary action and a Liberal M.P. Ben Pickard (1842–1904), leader of the Yorkshire miners, was also a Liberal M.P. He and Thomas Ashton (1844–1927) had built the Federation up into the formidable force it now was.[5] Their toughness in pursuing their aims of an eight-hour day and a living wage had not required any socialist philosophy, only a sense of the dignity of work and a determination to see it recognised. The miners were a considerable power in industry and in the land. There were in the region of one million men engaged in mining; there was not a more strongly organised group of workers in the country or one which was more conscious of its wrongs, and more determined to see them righted. Everything about the miner's life heightened his sense of togetherness and his sense of power in pursuit of what he regarded as, and which mainly were, reasonable aims. The geographical isolation of most mining centres from the rest of the

[1] Reprinted in K. Coates and T. Topham, *Workers' Control* (Panther 1970).

[2] 35 H.C. Deb. 5S, col. 2104.

[3] It was much appealed to in 1912. See *Industrial Council. Notes on the Proceedings of*: 5th March 1912. Arnot, op. cit., pp. 169, 176, 326 and 376. H.C. Deb., loc. cit., cols. 1766 and 2104.

[4] On this period of trade unionism in mining see Webbs, *History*, pp. 300 ff.

[5] On the Federation, Clegg, Fox and Thompson, pp. 99 ff.

community, the dangerous nature of the work, the natural loyalties of the team underground, the pit, the village—all these were summed up in the democratic and vigorous life of the union.[1] No work force, no union, needed less the extra spur of socialist militance, especially when it was so erratic and confused. But it was here that syndicalism took firmest hold. It was the miners who took the lead in forming that vast and futile organisation, the Triple Alliance,[2] whose effect on the fears of one section of the community and the illusions of another was to have such unfortunate effects down to the National Strike of 1926.

The attitude of the employers in the various industries to the new situation was varied—but the fact that Macara was able to get such wide support for his scheme showed that those who simply dug their heels in and refused to rethink the position were becoming more and more isolated. Their thesis, which amounted to a rejection of the co-operation norm, was increasingly being rejected by educated and responsible opinion at large.

The shipowners were one of the first groups to show cracks in their defences. The writ of the Federation did not run in all ports and all companies to the same extent and the diehards were soon outflanked; Sir Walter Runciman was among those who had long advocated a more reasonable approach and it was his time to triumph.[3] The railway directors and their doyen, Lord Claud Hamilton especially, were made of sterner stuff. They even persuaded a Royal Commission that they really could not accept trade unionism because the special disciplinary needs of the industry could not permit it.[4] That Lord Claud,[5] who had not changed his opinions on the unions since the Sheffield outrages of 1868, should dominate the counsels of a major industry is an indication of the problems faced by those who wished to improve industrial relations. An ex-Guards officer, Lord Claud really believed he could treat the men with the same paternalism with which a good regimental officer treated his troops. He insisted that he found no unrest among the railwaymen, nor did the other directors of the railway companies.

[1] G. D. H. Cole, *Labour in the Coalmining Industry During the War* (Oxford 1923), pp. 7 ff. B. Webb, *Diaries, 1912–24* (London 1952), p. 207. K. G. C. Knowles, *Strikes* (Oxford 1952), pp. 164 and 186. W. Citrine, *Men and Work* (London 1964), pp. 132 and 195.

[2] G. R. Carter, 'The Triple Alliance of Labour', *Economic Journal*, September 1916. *The Labour Year Book*, 1915. Bagwell, op. cit., p. 307. The railwaymen and the transport workers were the other members of the Alliance, whose constitution was not approved until 1915.

[3] Runciman, op. cit., pp. 261 ff. Wilson, op. cit., p. 123.

[4] *Report of the Royal Commission on the Railway Conciliation and Arbitration Scheme 1907*, S.P. 1911, XXIX, i, paras 51 and 52.

[5] Born 1843. Son of the 1st Duke of Abercorn; Harrow and Grenadier Guards. In 1872 joined the Great Eastern, Chairman in 1893; M.P. 1865 and 1910.

The unions were controlled by socialist agitators, unrepresentative of the men, fomenting unrest, ruining the country and requiring to be dealt with most firmly.[1] Indeed, had he not been 'taking the waters' at Harrogate when the settlement was made, things would have turned out differently. He accused those concerned in this settlement of having acted *ultra vires* and for this had to apologise to the Royal Commission. With such a man at their head it is not surprising that the Royal Commission could be persuaded to support the objection of the railway directors to the unions; he was a formidable personage. He and the railway directors could have appealed to the economic difficulties of the industry as the main ground of their opposition and they had the promise of the government that they could expect a rise in rates to compensate them for any rise in wages that the granting of bargaining rights would cost them.[2] But this was not their appeal; their appeal was to the incompatibility of railway employment and trade unionism. It was an appeal without logical or factual foundation and hence beyond rational refutation. Railway management as a whole did not have a high reputation for competence in any aspect of its job so that it is not surprising that it too should fail in its understanding of the industrial relations situation. Critics were scathing about the accuracy and adequacy of the statistical information upon which railways operations were costed. The showing of the directors and management during the crisis of 1911 and the subsequent Royal Commission only served to underline the justification for these criticisms.[3] But there were among the leaders of the industry a group of men who were showing a greater sense of realism than Lord Claud and his like. Three in particular stood out at this time: they were G. H. Claughton (1856–1921), Chairman of the L.N.W.R., Sam Fay (1856–1953), General Manager of the Great Central, and Sir W. 'Guy' Granet (1867–1943), General Manager of the Midland. Their backgrounds were varied. Claughton was an Old Etonian and his twenty years of service as agent to the Earl of Dudley were, as he was later to testify when a member of the Whitley Committee,[4] such as to convince him

[1] Evidence before the Royal Commission, loc. cit., qq. 10,010 to 10,376. How firmly is clear from the attempt of the employers to get the government to employ soldiers to operate the railways during the 1911 strike. They did get some sort of a promise but it was exaggerated by them and the government disclaimed their interpretation of it. *The Times*, 17th August 1911, and 29 H.C. Deb. 5S, col. 2045 ff.

[2] *The Statist*, 25th November 1911.

[3] A. E. Kirkus, *Railway Statistics* (London 1927), pp. 1 and 16. K. H. Johnston, *British Railways and Economic Recovery* (London 1949), p. 92. *The Statist*, 9th September 1911. *The Economist*, 7th October 1911. Lucy Masterman, *C. F. G. Masterman* (London 1939), pp. 208 and 214.

[4] See below, p. 98.

of the reasonableness of unions and the value of collective bargaining. Fay had started life as a clerk with the London and South West Railway and Granet, educated at Rugby and Balliol, had been called to the Bar, then in 1900 became secretary of the Railway Companies' Association. It was Granet who made the threat of the use of the military during the 1911 strike, but he showed a more promising frame of mind as the strike went on. He was in on the discussions on 19th August and later he, with the other two named, went as emissary from the R.C.A. to the unions.[1] He was among those railway directors who, by 1914, were convinced that direct negotiations with the unions should be normal practice; the initiative taken in this direction was thwarted by inter-union squabbles.[2]

In the dock transport industry it was Lord Devonport[3] who was the bastion against any positive improvement in the collective bargaining system. The strike was, as he saw it, on an issue 'on which no compromise is possible'.[4] He has been accused not without justification of wanting to crush the unions;[5] it is probably truer to say that he wished to prevent any growth in the strength or in their effective power in bargaining.[6] Devonport was proud of his achievement in 1912; so too were those who attended the Lord Mayor's banquet in that year; they gave him long and appreciative applause, he noted with some satisfaction.[7] Despite the change detectable in public attitudes, especially as reflected in the Commons, there was still a great deal of lingering support for men like Devonport and Hamilton who stood on 'principle' against the trend of the times. Whatever technical elements of right may have been on Devonport's side in the 1912 conflict, the effect of the strike was to make more difficult that rationalisation of the structure of industrial relations and collective bargaining in the port which was needed. Lack of organisation had made it very hard to find out what the dockers wanted when on strike.[8] The defeat of the unions in 1912 made sure that the organisational weaknesses would be perpetuated. The employers had fought to keep unionism and bargaining weak; they could hardly in future complain when the men were uncooperative and machinery worked badly.

But Devonport was by no means typical of dockowners and mana-

[1] Blaxland, op. cit., p. 76. *R.C.A. Minutes*, 1st and 6th December 1911.

[2] Blaxland, op. cit., pp. 85–6.

[3] *Hudson Kearley*, 1856–1934, formerly Lloyd George's Parliamentary Secretary at the B.O.T. in 1908, now Chairman of the Port of London Authority.

[4] Autobiography, *The Travelled Road* (London 1924), p. 175.

[5] E. J. Hobsbawm, *Essays in Labour History* (London 1964), p. 216.

[6] Askwith, op. cit., p. 223, and Lovell, op. cit., p. 201.

[7] Op. cit., p. 186.

[8] Askwith, op. cit., pp. 148–50 and 158.

gers. In London there were many who were opposed to his policies.[1] It so happened, however, that his position of dominance was practically unassailable and he had plenty of supporters. In other ports there were men like Booth, a 'new type of employer' according to Sexton.[2] Among the mineowners too there were many who were opposed to the attitude of the South Wales section.[3] Events, however, contrived to leave the general situation in the hands of the hard-liners. To the mineowners and the engineering employers was to fall the honour of being the last to relinquish the views that made the 1911 conflict inevitable and which have had a destructive effect on British industrial relations down to today.

(ii) INFLUENCES ON THE COUNCIL AND ITS WORK

Government patronage

Faced with a problem of industrial unrest which was new and alarming, the government was intent on showing it was doing something; 'time was against deliberation, the public wanted action'.[4] It was the government which called the Council into being and it was the government which controlled its destinies, but it was the pre-existence of Macara's plan, and his own assiduous canvassing of support for it, which enabled him to present it as a viable scheme with the support of the country and the House of Commons. The original letter was sent to Behrens on 10th July. The *Manchester Guardian* and the *Yorkshire Post* took it up at once[5] but it was from the first a matter of coaxing the government to do anything about it.[6] Barnes[7] asked a question in the House on the matter on 17th July and the Prime Minister's answer indicated that he required to be convinced of the need for the scheme and support for it. Hence throughout July and August 'the idea was widely canvassed by Macara and was approved by municipalities . . . engineers, shipowners, spinners, railway companies, co-operatives and most labour leaders and representatives of almost every branch of industry'.[8] A list of supporters was forwarded to Asquith.[9] The

[1] See Gosling's testimony in the *Industrial Council. Notes on the Proceedings of:* 18th June.
[2] Op. cit., p. 223.
[3] Below, p. 64. Davies' insistence during the meetings of the Council on the menace of socialism rang hollow even to the other employers. *Notes,* etc., 5th March.
[4] Askwith, op. cit., p. 180. [5] Mills, op. cit., p. 114.
[6] Ibid., p. 117, and Macara, *Recollections,* p. 170. [7] 98 H.C. Deb. 5S, col. 692.
[8] *The Times,* 10th August 1911; C. Macara. *The Industrial Council,* London (no date), p. 6, reprint of an article in the *Financial Review of Reviews,* October 1911, together with correspondence on the Council. [9] Ibid., p. 14.

industrial situation was discussed again in the House on 14th August,[1] the day before the national railway strike was announced. The meeting that took place at the Board of Trade between the government representatives and the employers on the one hand and of the trade unions on the other on the following day was overshadowed by the outbreak of the strike and it was a month before anything more was heard of the Council. A Board of Trade *Memorandum* on the subject was circulated in September[2] and on 10th October the *Memorandum* announcing the establishment of the Council and the list of members was made public. It was the familiarity of the idea of conciliation and the clear need for some new initiative which enabled Macara to convince so many people that a scheme of national conciliation would work.

As it turned out the government did little but bring the Council into being, though that in itself was significant enough; at the time there was no other way of establishing such an organisation. The need to appoint members to serve on it was another inevitable result of the situation, however unfortunate the effects of such procedure appeared to be to some and however much it hindered its effectiveness. There were personal jealousies involved as a result of non-selection according to Macara.[3] And no government-appointed body was likely to have the full confidence of industry that was needed if it was to do its work. On the other hand, in setting up the Council and allowing it, as it did, practically to work out its own terms of reference, the government started more than it thought it had started and most of the useful work of the Council—above all its work on the *Report on Industrial Agreements*—was done as a result of the freedom of manœuvre allowed it.

The advocacy of Sir Charles Macara

Macara had been largely responsible for the drawing up of the Brooklands agreement which had ended the twenty weeks' strike of 1892–3.[4] This agreement[5] is of interest in that it showed remarkable sophistication for its time, although failure to achieve agreement on the adjustment norm led to periodic and prolonged dispute. His part in its evolution, however, and the effort he made over the years in making

[1] 29 H.C. Deb. 5S, col. 1544.

[2] B.O.T. Records B.T. 20/25, B.T. 21/4 and B.T. 13/49.

[3] Below, p. 58.

[4] Clegg, Fox and Thompson, pp. 116–17. Mills, p. 87, *Report on Strikes and Lock-outs*, 1892, S.P. 1894, LXXXI, i. The strike began on 7th November 1892, and not until 25th March 1893 was work resumed. In the first stages only 45,000, by the end 200,000, were directly or indirectly affected.

[5] It is reproduced in the 1910 *Report on Collective Agreements*. See Mills, p. 94, also.

a success of it gave him good credentials in the move to form an Industrial Council. His original idea was for the establishment of an advisory body of trade unionists and employers working with a new government department for labour affairs.[1] The trade unions and employers were to act as arbitrators without powers of compulsion in case of deadlock in disputes in the staple trades.[2] In the process of its establishment and work it assumed rather a different role.

The mention of the department of labour affairs to which the Council was to be an adjunct highlights the lack both of a government labour policy[3] and the means of carrying one out. The inadequacy of methods for dealing with industrial relations problems had been evident since the early 1890's at least, though the attempts to establish an independent Labour Department had so far failed. The Commercial Branch of the Board of Trade, however, was set up in 1893 and it was possessed of a Labour Department and a Commissioner for Labour in H. Llewellyn Smith, together with a staff of thirty or forty.[4] Its main work was the collecting of statistics but even this was regarded by some as an unwarranted interference by the government. The Conciliation Act of 1896 gave the government a more positive role in that the Board of Trade had the authority to intervene in strikes to try to get a settlement. This only formalised a practice which was already familiar. Gladstone had intervened in the 1893 mining strike and the Parliamentary Secretary to the Board of Trade had done the same in the boot and shoe trades dispute of 1895. Powers under the Act, however, not only gave the Board much more scope through its normal working but allowed also that the President of the Board of Trade would be able to develop it in more startling ways if he chose. When Lloyd George and Winston Churchill were successive Presidents in 1905–10 they did just that.[5] It was Lloyd George also who encouraged Askwith in his role as conciliator as well as himself intervening in major disputes. In 1909 he appointed Askwith the Comptroller General of the B.O.T. Commercial Department[6] and his continuing involvement in the work of conciliation led him to concentrate more and more on it. He was accordingly appointed Chief Industrial Commissioner and Chairman of the Industrial Council in 1911.[7] Whether such a Commissioner would have been appointed but for the establishment of the Council is not clear.

[1] *The Industrial Council*, p. 5. [2] Ibid., p. 6.

[3] Askwith, op. cit., p. 351, is especially emphatic about this lack.

[4] V. L. Allen, *Trade Unions and the Government* (London 1960), pp. 49 ff.

[5] Buxton, the next President, however, was less interested; he would not help the seamen get a hearing from the employers. *Industrial Council Enquiry into Industrial Agreements, Evidence*, S.P. 1913, XXVIII, q. 3492.

[6] Allen, op. cit., p. 53. [7] Below, p. 61.

2

The Industrial Council

(i) MEMBERSHIP

The Board of Trade Memorandum of 10th October 1911[1] gave the names of those who were appointed to the Council. Some of them had been involved in the initial round of talks on 15th August, but not all; likewise some of those who had been then involved were not in this group, which consisted of, on the employers' side, George Ainsworth, Chairman of the Steel Ingot Makers' Association and President of the Cleveland Ironmakers' Association, Sir Hugh Bell, President of the Iron, Steel and Allied Trades Federation, Mr. G. H. Claughton, Chairman of the L.N.W.R., W. A. Clowes, President of the London Master Printers' Association, J. H. C. Crockett, President of the Incorporated Federated Associations of Boot and Shoe Manufacturers of Great Britain and Ireland, F. L. Davies, Chairman of the Board of Conciliation for the Coal Trade of Monmouthshire and South Wales, T. L. Devitt, Chairman of the Shipping Federation Limited, Sir T. R. Ratcliffe Ellis, Secretary of the Lancashire and Cheshire Coal Owners' Association, F. W. Gibbins, Chairman of the Welsh Plate and Sheet Manufacturers' Association, Charles Macara, President of the Federation of Master Cotton Spinners, A. Siemens, Chairman of the Executive of the Engineering Employers' Federation, R. Thompson, past President of the Ulster Flax Spinners, and J. White, President of the National Building Trades Employers' Federation.

The trade union representatives were Thomas Burt, M.P., General Secretary of the Northumberland Miners' Association, former President of the T.U.C. and Parliamentary Secretary to the Board of Trade, Thomas Ashton, Secretary of the Miners' Federation of Great Britain, C. W. Bowerman, Secretary of the Parliamentary Committee of the T.U.C. and the President of the Printing and Kindred Trades Federation of the U.K., F. Chandler, General Secretary of the Amalgamated Society of Carpenters and Joiners, J. R. Clynes, Organising Secretary

[1] *Ninth Report of the Proceedings under the Conciliation (Trade Disputes) Act*, 1896, S.P. 1912–13, XVII, Appendix II.

of the National Union of Gas Workers and General Labourers, Harry Gosling, President of the National Transport Workers' Federation, Arthur Henderson, M.P., Friendly Society of Ironfounders, J. Hodge, General Secretary of the British Steel Smelters, Mill, Iron and Tinplate Workers' Amalgamated Association, W. Mosses, General Secretary of the Federation of Engineering and Shipbuilding Trades, W. Mullin, President of the United Textile Factory Workers' Association, E. L. Poulton, General Secretary of the National Union of Boot and Shoe Operatives, A. Wilkie, M.P., General Secretary of the Shipconstructors and Shipwrights Association, and J. E. Williams, General Secretary of the Amalgamated Society of Railway Servants.

Buxton[1] was to tell them that they were chosen 'because you were known by the positions you held to be representative men'. Appointment by the government in this way had its problems. It was given by Macara as one of the reasons why the Council was not successful.[2] That it was not in any way elected by those it was intended to serve was clearly a defect. On the other hand the traditions of the time did not allow of reference to the T.U.C. by the government on such matters[2] and there was no comparable organisation for the employers. There was a positive aversion among most firms for any such concerted action, 'the average firm which is Federated does not welcome the idea of any further measure of co-operation other than that it may voluntarily choose to embark on'.[4] If anything was to be done it had to be done by appointment. The results were not without merit.[5] The iron and steel trades, cotton, building, the printers, boot and shoe industry and Welsh tinplate were on the whole distinguished by the thoroughness of their unionism and collective bargaining.[6] Among the employers,

[1] In his speech to the first meeting of the Council, 26th October 1911, *Notes on Proceedings*, p. 8: at least one man approached did not accept, Will Thorne of the Gasworkers and Chairman of the T.U.C. He refused because he saw the troubles of the time as the responsibility of the employers. *Labour Leader*, 20th October 1911.

[2] Letter to Asquith, 30th April 1912, published in *The Industrial Council*. The letter here referred to is on p. 13. See also Askwith, op. cit., p. 180.

[3] The G.F.T.U. (*Labour Leader*, 20th October 1911) complained about the way the Council had been appointed and dismissed it as a 'packed jury'. At the 1912 Congress Tillet complained that the T.U.C. had not been consulted (*Report*, p. 191). On the other hand the T.U.C. refused to give evidence before its enquiry into agreements 'in as much as four members were serving on the Council'. *Report of the Enquiry into Industrial Agreements*, S.P. 1913, XXVIII, p. 3.

[4] Watney and Little, op. cit., p. 240.

[5] 'Able cautious individuals', B. C. Roberts, *The Trade Union Congress* (London, 1958), p. 250. 'An impressive membership', V. L. Allen, *Trade Unions and the Government* (London 1960), p. 54. 'Excellently chosen', *The Economist*, 14th October 1911.

[6] The Brooklands agreement mentioned above, p. 55, footnote. A. Fox, *A History of the National Union of Boot and Shoe Operatives* (London 1958), pp. 227 ff. W. E. Minchin-

it was the more moderate sections of mining interests, Lancashire and Northumberland, which had members; the South Wales Conciliation Board, which represented at least the hopes of conciliation, was present too. The Shipping Employers and the Railways had been to the forefront of the troubles of 1911, but, as we have seen, were among those where the solid front of opposition to unionism had broken or was breaking. The engineering employers were represented also. They and the South Wales coalowners were to prove in the long run the most recalcitrant.

The trade unionists on the Council were all of them basically moderates. Clynes[1] and Gosling[2] it is true had been identified with the movement to organise the general and transport workers and therefore had been ranked with the agitators in recent years but their participation in the Council underlined that they identified with the traditional aims and methods of the trade union movement. Of the rest, Wilkie had been involved in the National Industrial Association[3] which was an earlier attempt to get some kind of Industrial Council into being. Henderson's trade union career marked him out as a moderate and his career as a politician, especially in so far as he could influence the industrial wing of the movement, was to confirm it. He was to be the labour advocate of the 1919 Industrial Conference.[4] Burt[5] and Ashton[6] were among the older-style trade union leaders in mining—militant in industrial policy within the accepted limits but not identifying with the more ideologically motivated elements developing. Chandler, Hodge, Bowerman and the others were in the same mould.

ton, *The British Tinplate Industry* (London 1967), pp. 125 ff. A. Pugh, *Men of Steel* (London 1951), pp. xi–xiii. R. W. Postgate, *The Builders' History* (London 1923), pp. 380 ff.

[1] *J. R. Clynes*, 1869–1949. National Organiser of the Gas Workers since 1891 and M.P. 1906–31. The Gasworkers were one of the unions infiltrated by socialism, Clegg, Fox and Thompson, pp. 57 ff. and 293 ff. In his *Memoirs* (London 1937), p. 103, Clynes emphasised how bitterly he felt at this time.

[2] *Harry Gosling* (b. 1861), General Secretary of the Lightermen's Union. He was 'normally a mild man and possessed of great integrity' (Lovell, op. cit., p. 198).

[3] Clegg, Fox and Thompson, p. 176.

[4] *Arthur Henderson*, 1863–1935. District and later General Organiser of the Friendly Society of Ironfounders, 1892. Labour Party Executive 1904–35. M.P. 1903–35 with brief intervals. Though the Ironfounders were one of the oldest and most conservative unions, Webbs, *History*, p. 200. H. Fyrth and H. Collison, *The Foundry Workers*, Manchester, 1959, p. 125, note Henderson's declining popularity after 1903 as a result of his moderation.

[5] *Thomas Burt*, 1837–1922. Liberal M.P. 1874–1918. See above, p. 57.

[6] Thomas Ashton took upon himself in the 1911 Cambrian dispute to issue a personal denunciation of the strike leaders in Rhondda (Arnot, *South Wales Miners*, p. 256).

(ii) PURPOSES

The *Memorandum* of 10th October 1911 stated that the Council was established for the purpose of

> considering and enquiring into matters referred to them affecting trade disputes and especially of taking suitable action in regard to any dispute referred to them affecting the principal trades of the country or likely to cause disagreement involving the ancillary trades or which the parties before or after the dispute are themselves unable to settle.

It was thought desirable that

> the operation of the Board of Trade in discharge of their duties under the Conciliation Act of 1896 should be supplemented and strengthened and that effective means should be available for referring such difficulties as may arise in a trade to investigation, conciliation, or arbitration as the case may be.

This supplementation and strengthening was to be provided by the Council. However, Buxton[1] stressed that 'the last thing' he desired was 'to lay before you a cut and dried scheme'. Reflecting on these things the Council decided that it would meet in February, June and November of each year and that its Chairman, Askwith, should have power to call meetings at any time for consultation. Council members would act in a juridical capacity and not as advocates. The Chairman[2] reviewed the potentialities of the Council and saw them as follows:

(i) It could give its opinion, privately, on cases referred to it.
(ii) It could ascertain the facts of a case referred to it if requested and make recommendations, privately and of course not binding, to each side.
(iii) It could do as in (i) or (ii) but on the previous understanding that the recommendations and opinions would be published.
(iv) It could be formally requested by the parties to a dispute to decide a question on the understanding that they bound themselves to accept the decision.

[1] At the first meeting of the Council on 26th October 1911, *Ninth Report*, loc. cit., p. 119.
[2] Ibid., p. 120.

(v) The Board of Trade or the government could refer a case to it under special circumstances.

(vi) It could consider other matters, apart from particular disputes, which the Government or the Board of Trade might refer to it with a view to obtaining a representative opinion on specific points.

This range of functions set out in the official *Report* and presumably accepted by the Board of Trade whose Chief Industrial Commissioner[1] was the Chairman of the Council presumably also represented the official policy. If that was so, a government which wished to use it properly could achieve a great deal through it in establishing facts and anticipating any possible outbreaks of unrest, conciliating and finding possible ways of resolving difficulties. No reference was, however, made to that new government department for labour affairs with which Macara's original idea had been linked. It was to take the impact of war to convince the government that a Ministry of Labour was a necessary or desirable proposition.

(iii) THE WORK OF THE COUNCIL

Organisational details for the Council were not worked out with any clarity in the first instance because of the experimental, not to say confused, nature of its intended role. The operation was conceived initially by analogy with that of local conciliation boards and though Askwith's list of possible roles for the Council clearly moved it into a different order of activities the original concept of *ad hoc* informal meetings very largely remained. When, at its first meeting on 26th October, it found that a dispute had already been referred to it by the Corporation at Newport, Monmouthshire,[2] a subcommittee of Davies, White, Gosling and Williams, under Askwith as Chairman, was appointed to handle the matter.

Newport Docks Dispute, 1911

The dispute involved Houlders, a shipping company, and the dockers at Newport; the point at issue was the dockers' claim to be paid piece

[1] See above p. 56 and Askwith, op. cit., p. 179. B.T. 21/4: letters (i) of 13th September 1911, concerning the proposal to form an industrial Council presided over by a Chief Industrial Commissioner, (ii) of 27th October appointing Askwith to that post.

[2] *Ninth Report of the Proceedings under the Conciliation Act*, loc. cit., p. 94. *Industrial Council. Notes on the Proceedings of:* Meeting of 26th October 1911.

rates when loading general cargo. There had been an arbitration on the matter in May 1910.[1] Sir David Harrell had ruled that a generous day rate was preferable, and this despite the fact that 'all other ship-owners whose ships take general cargo from Newport are satisfied with the universally accepted and recognised rates' provided there was sufficient supervision.[2] Since there were twenty-six other companies apart from Houlder's using the port the insistence of the latter on its point of principle, even with the backing of an arbitrator who was trying to be generous to the men while preserving the position of the owners, was remarkable. Trouble had followed whenever Houlder boats were in dock and Newport Town Council, one of those canvassed by Macara in the late summer, was tired of having to meet the cost of keeping the peace. It therefore asked the Council to do something about it.

The previous history of the dispute makes it clear that the Council was dealing with a local conflict which had origins not so much in an honest difference of opinion or failure of communication but in a bitter and protracted struggle determined by personalities and 'principles' which defied conciliation because conciliation assumed some readiness to compromise. Houlder's sticking point when the Council intervened seemed unreasonable. The unions were later to show themselves no less unreasonable. It was one of those disputes which were beyond conciliation; only the surrender of one of the parties, or its petering out through the exhaustion of both of them, could end it.

At first the Council's efforts seemed to bring success. The two sides were brought together but after three weeks they broke off the talks. It did not appear to the unions at least that the Council had failed. On the contrary they addressed a very appreciative letter to it.[3] The whole Bristol Channel area was now in support of the dockers' demand and they got from Houlders the same agreement they had with the other companies; Askwith's intervention on 15th December secured this but now the strikers refused to work with anyone who had been employed by Houlder during the strike. The private battle between the firm and the strike committee went on and it was not until in late January when the National Transport Workers Federation issued a statement disowning the strikers[4] that the dispute fizzled out. Askwith contrasted his own success with that of the Council's failure.[5] In fact

[1] *Eighth Report under the Conciliation Act*, S.P. 1911, XIII, pp. 37–40.
[2] *South Wales Daily Argus*, Saturday, 18th November 1911.
[3] *South Wales Daily Argus*, 20th November. *Notes on the Proceedings*: letter of 16th December 1911.
[4] *South Wales Daily Argus*, 6th, 8th and 10th January.
[5] Op. cit., p. 182.

his success, if that it was, may have owed much to the earlier intervention of the Council. The dispute broke out again, this time with the unions clearly to blame. Further conciliation failed to produce a settlement.[1] In the end the dispute died of exhaustion.

The Cotton Trade Dispute, 1911

This dispute involved the North East Master Cotton Spinners and Manufacturers' Association and the Northern Textile Trades Federation.[2] In order to compel a group of operatives at Accrington and Great Harwood to join the union, the Federation threatened to strike at the factories concerned and met a counter threat of a lock-out by the employers. On 27th December 1911, since neither side would give way, the lock-out involving 160,000 operatives began. In order to prevent a glut of yarn the Master Spinners' Association, of which Macara was Chairman, soon advised its members to work short time. The Council was never called in to attempt to settle a dispute which was precisely of the sort with which it had ostensibly been designed to deal. Instead, Askwith personally acted as conciliator and on 19th January an agreement was reached. In effect, the issue was frozen for six months and Askwith asked that at the end of that period to give his judgement on it. He did and it was indecisive.[3] Askwith unaccountably asserts that Macara was 'the Chairman of the employers who decided on a lock-out'[4] and other writers on the matter have presumably taken his word for it.[5] In fact, Macara was not Chairman of the Association concerned but of the Federation of Master Cotton Spinners in Manchester, the relevant Chairman being Wilkinson Hartley.[6]

The incident revealed neither Macara's lack of confidence in the Council, nor his duplicity, as some have suggested. The account of the proceedings of the Council meeting on 14th February and 4th March show that he was angry that the matter was not referred to it.[7] He later suggested that the reason for the non-reference of the dispute may have been personal pique on the part of those not elected

[1] One John Macauley, General Manager of the Alexandra Docks, *South Wales Daily Argus*, 1st January 1912.

[2] *Report on Strikes and Lock-outs 1911*, loc. cit., p. 28; *Ninth Report under the Conciliation Act*, p. 7, and *The Economist*, 30th December 1911.

[3] *Report on Strikes*, p. 178. Askwith, op. cit., p. 192.

[4] Op. cit., p. 182. [5] Allen, op. cit., p. 55, and Phelps Brown, op. cit., p. 341.

[6] *Cotton Year Book*, 1912: W. Haslam Mills, op. cit., p. 85. *Ninth Report under the Conciliation Act*, p. 113.

[7] *Industrial Council. Notes on the proceedings of*: loc. cit., 14th February and 4th March 1912.

to the Council.[1] The government and the Board of Trade had power to refer it as he pointed out with some asperity when the excuse was given that this power did not exist.[2] Yet Askwith did not refer it when it came to him. He tackled the matter on his own. The dispute was on the most intractable of all issues and it was incapable of being resolved by conciliation or arbitration. Askwith's deliberations after six months' cooling off brought no result. The dispute was beyond his or anyone's power to resolve satisfactorily.[3]

The miners' strike, 1912

On 29th September 1911 a joint meeting between the miners and the coalowners on the minimum-wage issue resulted in deadlock. On 6th October, the miners reasserted their demand for an individual minimum wage on a district basis. The English Conciliation Board section of the owners seemed prepared to accede but were forced by the Scottish and Welsh sections to refuse, and on 20th December it became clear that the owners would not further discuss the matter and that none of the districts would be offered an individual minimum wage.[4] A strike ballot was decided on by the miners and if the required two-thirds majority was received, notices should take effect from the end of February 1912. The vote was four-to-one in favour of the strike. The unions and the employers met on 7th February but the South Wales owners made it clear that they were not prepared to discuss the minimum wage and withdrew from the talks. The rest reached no agreement, but the unions expressed the desire for further talks if the owners wished them, provided that the same point—an individual minimum—was accepted to be the point at issue. Nothing was done for two weeks and no one seemed to have any suggestion to offer as the nation rolled inexorably towards a stoppage in an industry employing a million men with the whole of the industrial economy at its mercy. This was a situation tailored for the Industrial Council if ever there was one. On 20th February, Askwith reconvened it and suggested 'that in the interests of the community they should consider whether the position should not be clearly put before the government'.[5] He did not think that the owners and the miners

[1] Letter to Asquith, 30th April 1912: *Industrial Council*, p. 14.

[2] The powers were among those outlined by Askwith and listed above, p. 60, as Macara pointed out in the same letter.

[3] Askwith, op. cit., p. 192.

[4] R. Page Arnot, *The Miners*, Vol. 2, pp. 79 ff. and 90 ff.

[5] Op. cit., p. 202.

would appreciate a direct approach though he clearly thought the Council had it in its power to make it. A communication to this effect from the Council met with an immediate response[1] and a meeting took place between the Prime Minister, the Foreign Secretary, Sir Edward Grey, the Chancellor, Lloyd George and the President of the Board of Trade, Sidney Buxton, on one side and four officials of the Miners' Federation on the other. 'There followed the longest series of declamatory speeches and explanations, without any business being done, I have ever heard. The Ministers had no particular plan in mind. They did not propose that the parties should resume conferences or consider the questions with experienced business men . . . but seemed to be very interested in hearing for the first time some of the difficulties of the miners' lives and their proposals.'[2] With *The Times* in the background trying to convince the nation that the whole thing was a Syndicalist revolt on the lines of *The Miners' Next Step*,[3] further meetings were held. Asquith was showing himself acutely aware of the issues and in a series of meetings from the 27th to the 29th with the special delegate conference of the M.F.G.B. proposals were worked out which would enable the principle of the district minimum for individuals to be settled by negotiation in each district, disputed cases to be settled by the decision of government representatives. The miners were dubious on the latter point and were sticking out for a specific minimum in any case. The owners, with the exception of the South Wales and Scottish areas, were for accepting the government plan. There was not only breakdown but deadlock.[4] The mines came to a halt on 1st March 1912; only the safety men remained at their posts and no coal was cut or wound.

The efforts of the last ten days of February seemed to have exhausted the powers of the Cabinet and there was a lull until, again, the Industrial Council urged further attempts to bring the two sides together. On 4th March,[5] it had decided to meet each day until there were signs of something stirring and on the 5th, at the suggestion of Henderson,[6] a deputation of Askwith, Macara, Bowerman, Gosling, Henderson and Thompson called on the Cabinet to enquire if negotiations were going to be reopened.[7] Yet again, the government responded to the initiative and met the Miners' Executive on the 6th. The Council

[1] *Tenth Report under the Conciliation Act*, S.P. 1913, XIX, p. 6. *Industrial Council. Notes on the Proceedings of:* 4th March 1912.
[2] Askwith, op. cit., p. 204.
[3] Page Arnot, *South Wales Miners*, p. 286.
[4] Page Arnot, op. cit., p. 289.
[5] Letters of Macara to Asquith, 20th March 1912, *Industrial Council*, p. 12: *Notes on the Proceedings of:* 4th March.
[6] *Notes*, 5th March.
[7] *Notes*, 6th March.

now adjourned and the next series of negotiations between the miners and the government and the owners went on. Both the owners and the unions were adamant on their main points and the government had in the end to impose upon both a Bill which gave a district minimum wage to be decided by a joint board, disputes being subject to adjudication by the Chairman. The Council was not called on again in any capacity after the deputation of 5th March.

What would have happened in the course of the dispute, if the Council had not urged the government to take new initiatives on 20th of February and 5th March, is clearly a matter for speculation. It is beyond doubt, however, that its efforts were decisive in getting those initiatives moving at those times and in those ways. This in itself was no small achievement. The miners were not displeased with the outcome. On 15th March, the miners' representatives noted that 'whatever may develop in the end, we at any rate have no cause to complain, as workmen's representatives. I think Mr. Lloyd George has shown special anxiety that we should come out of this, at any rate, the miners shall come out of it, in a favourable light.'[1]

Askwith seemed to think that the Council could have made a better attempt at settlement than the Cabinet Committee.[2] Asquith's excuse for not using it further was that the deputation on 5th March 'did not find themselves able to take further action'[3] and that in any case the Council needed the approval of both sides before it could take further action or intervene. Macara's answer was that the Prime Minister was wrong on both counts. Correspondence with Askwith which he enclosed proved the first point,[4] while the official account of the proceedings of the Council proved the second.[5] Nor was Macara certain that the Chief Industrial Commissioner had done all he could have done in using the Council.[6] He, Macara, was held responsible for its failings by those who had supported him in getting it established as he had already had occasion to point out to the Council.[7]

[1] Page Arnot, op. cit., p. 301. [2] Op. cit., p. 212.

[3] Letter of M. Bonham Carter to Askwith on the Prime Minister's behalf, 26th April 1912, reproduced in *The Industrial Council. Notes on the Proceedings of:* p. 12.

[4] Letter of 30th April, ibid. The actual correspondence is not reproduced.

[5] *Ninth Report under the Conciliation Act*, Appendix II, loc. cit., see above, p. 60.

[6] *Industrial Council*, p. 11. Letter of 30th March 1912.

[7] *Notes on Proceedings*, 4th March 1912.

The London Dock strike of 1912 and the Report of the Enquiry into Industrial Agreements

The London Dock strike of 1912 began on 23rd May and quickly affected the whole port.[1] The dockers' case was weaker than it had been in the previous year, the determination of the Port Authorities much greater. Mr. Asquith was away on holiday at the beginning of the crisis and the Chief Industrial Commissioner was asked if he would preside at an enquiry into the dispute, but refused, saying that it would serve no purpose. He did, however, suggest a short list of those who might serve and Sir Edward Clarke undertook to make a Report. This appeared with admirable speed but did not impress Devonport. Buxton's suggestion of a Conference was rejected by Devonport also.

The Industrial Council, still in being but not called upon, met on 12th June and discussed the strike. It helped to crystallise its conviction, already apparent in previous discussions, that the key issue was effective organisation for collective bargaining. It therefore suggested that it should undertake an enquiry into the keeping of industrial agreements, an inability to do which was one of the Devonport charges against the dockers.[2] This suggestion was forwarded to the government and on the 13th accepted.[3] The terms of reference of the enquiry were as follows.[4] The Council was to enquire:

(1) What is the best way of securing due fulfilment of industrial agreements?
(2) How far, and in what manner, industrial agreements which are made between representative bodies of employers and workmen should be enforced throughout a particular district?

Though they had no power to call witnesses and though they were

[1] *Report on Strikes and Lock-outs*, 1912 (S.P. 1914, XLVIII). *Report on the Present Dispute*, etc. (S.P. 1912–13, XLVII) and Lovell, op. cit., Chapter 7. In so far as there was a simple issue in the strike it was the determination of the unions to have the N.T.W.F. as the sole negotiating body for the dockers and the determination of Devonport to prevent this. Above, p. 53.

[2] *Industrial Council. Notes on the Proceedings of:* 12th–13th June. The discussion in the Council particularly on these two days is very interesting in showing the degree of consensus that existed despite the inevitable clashes of personality and principle.

[3] Ibid., 13th June 1912. It was accepted by a government 'dimly aware they were in a mess'. Askwith, op. cit., p. 234.

[4] *Tenth Report under the Conciliation Act*, Appendix II, p. 84.

by no means of one mind on all issues,[1] they went about their task with an admirable thoroughness. Two thousand employers' associations and trade unions were circularised, thirty-eight meetings were held and ninety-two witnesses heard.[2] Activity such as this, carried on by a group with none of the advantages of a truly official enquiry, testifies to an extraordinary determination and depth of conviction.

The *Report* was issued on 24th June 1913. As to the first of its terms of reference it found that the difficulty lay not in getting agreements observed but in making agreements of an adequate kind, and providing them with means of interpretation, application and adjustment or revision which would ensure that disputes arising out of confusion or frustration did not normally occur. The complaint of some employers and their allies at the refusal of the unions and their members to keep agreements was in fact a non-issue.[3] It was not this which caused disputes so much as the absence of, or defects in, agreements themselves. The *Report* underlined that many agreements were made in times of stress and anger at the end of confused and embittered disputes and that in any case it was much harder to make sure that the agreements were really representative of the wishes of those on whose behalf they were signed than were normal agreements between principals. What was needed was a way of making agreements which eliminated such problems as far as possible and there was no doubt about how this was to be done:

> where agreements are the outcome of properly organised machinery for dealing with disputes, they are, with very few exceptions, loyally observed by both sides . . . the value of efficient organisation as a means of securing due fulfilment of industrial agreements is very clearly demonstrated by the experience of the different trades of the country.[4]

[1] The *Industrial Council. Notes on the Proceedings of:* reflect this throughout; the *Evidence* given before the enquiry S.P. (1913, XXVIII, qq. 17,221to 17,247) contains a typical exchange between Gosling, Devitt and Laws. The *Memoranda* attached to the *Report of the Enquiry into Industrial Agreements* show the same conflicts. Below, p. 72, footnote.

[2] *Report of the Enquiry into Industrial Agreements,* ibid., p. 4.

[3] As noted the P.L.A., whose actions led to the suggestion by the Council that it should undertake this enquiry, had chosen this point of criticism of the unions. The enquiry's conclusions showed that the P.L.A.'s policy was misguided throughout. The employers had tried to ease out or split the unions (Clegg, Fox and Thompson, op. cit., p. 71. Lovell, op. cit., p. 189) and they had refused to federate to facilitate negotiations (Askwith, op. cit., p. 224), they were therefore of such a mind as to prevent the conditions in which adequate agreements could be drawn up. The Report is an indictment of the industrial relations system at the docks.

[4] *Report of the Enquiry into Industrial Agreements,* paras. 7 and 18.

Properly organised machinery prevents the hurried making of vague agreements after angry confrontation. There is need for machinery designed to provide continuous negotiation on all appropriate issues. This is not spelled out but it is implied in the *Report*'s logic. Fixed periods for the running of agreements on substantive issues (what the *Report* calls agreements 'resulting from the working of machinery'), these it did spell out in so many words. It also pointed out the need for adequate means of readjusting agreements and getting decisions on all matters of dispute.[1]

To ensure collective bargaining of this kind the *Report* suggested that, subject to a Board of Trade enquiry, an agreement made by a substantial group of workers and employers in any one district should be made applicable to all in the district,[2] provided that a stated period of notice was agreed on by both sides for arranging adjustments and that there should be no stoppage of or change in any matter affecting the agreement until the issue in question had been investigated. The problems of such legislation are discussed in greater detail below.[3] Given the difficulties on primary substantive norms which had been increasingly in evidence before 1911, it is hardly likely that action along these lines would have been very effective. But the linking of the recommendation with the principles which lay behind the Fair Wages Clauses in government contracts[4] is a useful indication of the way the Council was thinking—in terms of some kind of agreed minimum based on what was paid by the best employers; in this sense it accepted the minimum wages and conditions norm. The recommendation is important in another respect—it underlined the need for a national labour policy. The government, as the Council saw the matter, had to set out its principles on this subject; it suggested that the most fundamental was to give the fullest support of the law to the existing voluntary methods of wages and conditions determination. Despite the practical difficulties its implementation faced, and despite too the fact that without the right sort of economic policy it was likely to be futile, the recommendation underlined that positive support of trade unionism and collective bargaining could no longer be denied. The idea that industrial relations were based on 'mutual consent' also occurs in the *Report*.[5] Gosling[6] was to say that through the work of the Council he became for the first time aware that this mutual consent was central to the system. The Council mentioned it in the *Report* in the context of the

[1] Ibid., paras. 7, 43–4 and 46–7.

[2] Para. 61. The Council also considered the question of monetary penalties for non-observance of agreements but did not recommend this.

[3] pp. 205 ff.

[4] *Report of the Enquiry into Industrial Agreements*, para. 55.

[5] Ibid., para. 36.

[6] *Up and down stream* (London 1937), p. 188.

need to get agreements respected. This could best be done by relying on mutual consent and moral obligation. It implied in other words the acceptance of those assumptions upon which co-operative bargaining is based. When the parties to the industrial relationship have accepted each other in good faith as the legitimate representatives of legitimate interests they can negotiate agreements which they can abide by and co-operation out of self-interest is possible.

The value of the *Report* at the time was very great and it retains a great deal of that value. Like the Council it was ignored by the government.[1] All that the former had done since its appointment had been done at its own initiative and insistence. The *Report* was published in July 1913 and though the Council was only reappointed for 1912–13 it never apparently went formally out of existence.[2] Its inglorious career and its passage into oblivion simply confirmed that the government had never taken it seriously and had only been cajoled into creating it because of the exigencies of 1911 and the persistence of Macara.

[1] The *Report of the T.U.C. Congress 1913*, pp. 223 and 239 ff., recorded the trade unions' rejection of it too. It was not a good time to mention to the unions the possibility of the further intervention of the law in their affairs.

[2] The reappointment is noted in the *Tenth Report under the Conciliation Act*, loc. cit., p. 4. See below, p. 72.

3

The Council assessed

(i) AS AN ANSWER TO THE PROBLEMS OF INDUSTRIAL RELATIONS IN 1911

The Industrial Council was conceived as an answer to the problems of industrial relations current in 1911 which were fundamentally the result of the pressures of economic necessity, aggravated by the lack of proper negotiating and conciliation procedures. The Council was set up on the assumption that these problems could be solved by a national level conciliation board just as, in a previous generation, local conciliation boards had been seen as an answer to the local problems. This assumption misunderstood both the fundamental nature of the problems it faced and the role of conciliation in helping to solve them. The irrelevance of national conciliation in removing the causes of the industrial unrest—mass poverty and the growing refusal of the wage-earners at the lower end of the scale to tolerate it any longer—is self-evident. But even had the means to abolish mass poverty existed and had been put into practice, the immediate role of such an organisation as the Council was not national conciliation, which can only work even in theory as a final stage when the structure of collective bargaining and conciliation in individual industries is complete and smooth-working. Most of the industries affected by the strikes of 1911–12 were not of this kind. Where there was effective negotiation there were attitudes among the employers and the unions which prevented satisfactory agreements being reached on fundamental procedural and substantive norms. And without these conditions, which would make the work of the conciliator possible, the Council had little or no role. It did have a limited success on one occasion, during the 1912 mining strike, but of all the industries which needed to find agreement on fundamentals before pinning its hopes on conciliation, mining was the most obvious case.

The main practical significance of the Council is that it helped to consolidate the mass of moderate opinion—which was ultimately as predominant on both sides of industry as it was in the country generally—behind the belief that the main immediate task was to give the maximum possible encouragement to collective bargaining and the trade unionism on which it depended. The legislation it recommended to this end would no doubt have failed; but that the *Report* did recommend this means as a way of encouraging the growth of effective collective agreements underlines the importance it attached to such agreements and, perhaps more important, emphasised that government could no longer simply hold the ring but had to have a positive and forceful policy for industrial relations in support of voluntarism.[1] The advance marked by its recommendations is clear when these are compared with those of the Royal Commission of twenty years before. The *Final Report* of the latter[2] appreciated that it was through trade unionism and collective bargaining that the system could be improved but it did not include forceful recommendations for their support. All that it could do was to recommend improved means of conciliation; hence the main result of the *Report* was the Conciliation Act of 1896—useful in itself but concerned with palliatives in times of crisis rather than positive measures for improving industrial relations. The shift of emphasis in the Industrial Council's *Report* caused some of its members a certain regret. One, not surprisingly an engineering employer,[3] was nostalgic for the days when the employers were at 'liberty to come to terms mutually satisfactory to the individuals concerned'.

While the unions and collective bargaining were regarded by many as a necessary evil at best, it was not possible for the *Report*'s recommendations to be given effect. The war however changed things. In the copy of the *Notes on the Proceedings* of the Council that was kept in the Ministry of Labour files there is a note to H. J. Wilson from another official dated 10th October 1914. It gives an outline of the Council's work and emphasises that it was never officially disbanded. The note was clearly a response to an enquiry concerning the Council's possible value in war. It was not in fact reactivated but the nation was soon forced to accept that the attitudes and the recommendations of the Council were the only way to secure that industrial co-operation needed for an all out war effort.

[1] Watney and Little, op. cit., p. 235, saw the giving of the task to the Council as in itself 'the abandonment of *laissez faire*' a decision which 'may one day come to be recognised as the most important development in economic matters in this country in the last fifty years'.

[2] S.P. 1894, XXXV, paras. 90–8, 288–91 and 363–8.

[3] Alexander Siemens, Memorandum No. 3 to the *Report of the Enquiry into Industrial Agreements*, loc. cit.

(ii) AS A CONTRIBUTION TO THE EVOLUTION OF THE NORMS AND INSTITUTIONS OF COLLECTIVE BARGAINING

The Council in its work and its *Report on the Keeping of Agreements* concerned itself with five of the norms outlined in the introduction. It did so with differing degrees of comprehension and effectiveness. It dealt most thoroughly with two of the procedural norms, co-operation and organisation.

The fact that the unions' and the employers' representatives worked together in the Council was proof that they wished to accept each other as the legitimate representatives of legitimate interests. They accepted also their mutual right to negotiate and the obligation to abide by agreements. They accepted the contractual co-operation norm at a time when, in some industries at any rate, ideologies on both sides were hardening. The Council, said Gosling, was 'one of the first bodies to appreciate' that if industrial relations are to work to the satisfaction of all concerned 'there must be an attitude of friendliness and tolerance, that collective bargaining must be based on the principle of mutual consent'.[1] The Council gave practical expression to the co-operation norm in accepting its logical conclusion, the full organisation of both sides for effective collective bargaining, *the organisation norm*. It did not go a stage further and recommend national collective bargaining because this was beyond the scope of the possible at the time. Its existence and the role it thought it could fill, however, indicated that, even within a voluntary framework, some form of National Council covering the whole of industry was needed as a Court of Appeal. What it thought it could do and how it thought it could do it were misguided. But the belief that a properly ordered industrial relations system requires some kind of national court seems to be a demand of simple logic. The point was made by the Whitley Council in its *Fourth Report*[2] and in its deliberations it referred to the work of the Council. In the 1970's we are still aware of the need though confused as ever as to how to fulfil it. The Industrial Council was the first significant joint body of industrialists which reasoned out the need. The principles on which it did so remain valid.

A third procedural norm to which it gave some attention was that

[1] Op. cit., p. 188. *Industrial Council. Notes on the Proceedings of:* for 4th February are interesting in this regard.

[2] Below, pp. 101–2 and 221–2.

governing the *interpretation and application* of the agreements; it was insistent that without clauses in agreements allowing for the proper procedures for this purpose to be set up and followed, the keeping of agreements was difficult if not impossible.

As pointed out in the introduction, the effective establishment and working of procedures, which stem from the co-operation norm, depends to a large extent on the support of public policy for full employment and high wages. In 1911 there was no hope of this being realised. The laws of economics were assumed to be free of the control of governments and those laws decided the level of both employment and the wages and conditions that should prevail. And if this approach undermined procedures, it was much more effective in preventing the meaningful support of the idea of a minimum wages and conditions norm or an adjustment norm in the sense detailed. On the other hand, the reference in the Report on Agreements[1] to the Fair Wages Resolutions of the House of Commons and the suggestion that this standard should be that by which to judge the local agreements supported by law, showed that the Council was aware of the need for a *minimum and fair wage* as the basis of a proper industrial relations system. Similarly the emphasis in the *Report* on the need for agreement on the periods for which agreements should run[2] underlined an important element in the *adjustment norm* though the much more important one, the standard by which such adjustments should be judged, was inevitably ignored.

[1] Para. 55. [2] *Report*, paras. 42–4.

PART TWO

The Whitley Committee Report and Scheme 1916–39

4
The origins of the scheme

(i) THE COMMITTEE: THE CIRCUMSTANCES OF ITS APPOINTMENT AND ITS WORK

The needs of reconstruction

The 'two nations' were very much in evidence in 1914. Seventy-five per cent of the working population, some 15·6 million wage-earners, were 'the main core of the working class as understood by contemporaries'.[1] This 'class' was, as Marwick observes, always the *object* of enquiries; the middle and upper classes were *subject*. Politically this vast economic and social grouping had no effective parliamentary voice. Fifty-eight per cent of adult males had the vote in 1910; they returned 650 M.P.s of whom just over forty were supported by the Labour Representation Committee;[2] many of the Liberal M.P.s were either 'Labour' or labour backed, but not in any way that made the Liberal Party conscious first of its duty to look to their interests. The two main parties were unaware that 'the unrest of the working class is of far greater moment than imperial or constitutional questions'.[3] It was Ireland and the privileges of the Lords which dominated politics in the period immediately before 1914. 'So far as the government was concerned, ministers were immersed in constitutional struggles; they had little or no labour policy. The members of the government were strangely outside and ignorant of the labour movement of the country or any personal knowledge of labour leaders.'[4] When seeking the co-operation of the T.U.C. in the 1915 Congress, Lloyd George spoke as if to a foreign power appealing for aid, 'without you our cause is lost . . . with you victory is assured'.[5] The gap between the nations was one the basic needs of war demanded should be bridged. The first attempts to bridge it were in the name of expediency, not idealism,

[1] A. Marwick, *Britain in the Century of Total War* (London 1968), p. 38.
[2] D. E. Butler and J. Freeman, *British Political Facts 1900–1960* (London 1964), p. 122.
[3] *The Statist*, 19th August 1911. [4] Askwith, op. cit., p. 351.
[5] *Report* quoted in the *History of the Ministry of Munitions*, London, 12 vols., 1918–22, etc. (Henceforth 'H.M.M.'), Vol. 4, pt. 1, p. 37.

as was acknowledged. In introducing the Whitley Report to the House of Commons in 1917, Montagu was later to say: 'We have passed through a lot of history in dealing with the labour question during the war. We began in old Board of Trade spirit in which you govern labour for the good of labour on behalf of labour but keep labour at a distance.'[1] By 1917, labour was asking for and getting an executive function and its co-operation was being sought for as a matter of course. Barnes, in introducing the reports of the Commissions on Industrial Unrest, put his finger on it. Labour wanted to take part in the community 'as partners rather than as servants',[2] and indeed by 1917 Labour had been incorporated into the government of the country. Henderson was in the War Cabinet, Hodges was the Minister of Labour and Clynes shortly to be Food Controller; several other Labour representatives occupied minor posts.[3]

In the early days, however, the labour interests were, as before, outsiders in the Councils of the nation. For all that, once preliminary uncertainties had been resolved, the response of the unions to the war was complete and immediate. From August 1914, there was unparalleled peace in industrial relations[4] despite the fact that until the onset of war an upheaval threatened which would have rivalled that of 1911–12. Engineering and building, sectors not affected in the previous years, were stirring in 1913. The London building lock-out in 1914 lasted six months and would probably have led to a national conflict if the war had not intervened. There was a threat too of action by the Triple Alliance industries in support of the railwaymen and the Scottish miners. The byword had been 'wait until the autumn'.[5] All this was forgotten once war was declared, but it was not long before the unions began to wonder if they had done the right thing. The cost of living soared and there was suspicion of unequal sacrifice. From now until the end of the war, the feeling that they had been cheated and that sacrifices had been distributed unfairly at home was the root of the labour unrest. As early as February 1915, Askwith[6] was warning that 'unless something is done to correct the view that contractors are entitled to make unlimited profits, the workmen would claim corresponding freedom and they had never been in a better position to

[1] 95 H.C. Deb. 5S, col. 595. [2] S.P. 1917–18, XV, *Recommendations* (4).
[3] H. Pelling, *A Short History of the Labour Party* (London 1965), pp. 38–9.
[4] H.M.M., Vol. 1, Pt. 2, p. 36.
[5] Askwith, op. cit., p. 356. See *Eleventh Report under the Conciliation Act*, S.P. 1914, LXXIX. Halévy, op. cit., p. 478. Lloyd George, *War Memoirs*, London 1938, Vol. 2, p. 1141. *The Times*, 22nd and 23rd July 1914. W. A. Orton, *Labour in Transition* (London 1921), pp. 3 ff.
[6] H.M.M., Vol. 1, pt. 2, p. 69.

enforce their demands'. The British Association's *Report*[1] and the *Reports* of the Commissions of Enquiry[2] confirmed that this feeling of having been cheated through profiteering and rising prices remained the main cause of labour bitterness.

The result of the impact of sudden demand at the outbreak of war was predictable enough; 'profits rise first, then prices, then wages'.[3] The question was not whether profits would rise; this was inevitable. It was whether that rise could be moderated and whether sufficient care could be taken to see that the community reclaimed from those who made large profits, an equitable share through taxation.

There were three kinds of transactions or business dealings through which profiteering was possible; the first was through the making of munitions or the supply of war materials of any kind, the second was through supplying the needs of the home population, the third was through the supply of capital. The alleged profiteering from the first two were confused in the popular discussions; that possible through the third was largely ignored.

The trade unions in the munitions industries and in engineering, which was the central one in this group, had been from the first under pressure to relax their restrictive trade practices to facilitate the war effort. They were slow to do this. 'The fear of dilution was the fear that the future of the craft was in jeopardy and with it protective measures against unemployment';[4] this is how the official *History* saw the opposition. The engineers did not see why they should relax their practices while the employers maintained theirs,[5] until, that is, the armaments contracts were shared out among other firms or the skilled workers who were out of work moved to the areas where they were needed. This the employers resisted. There was much criticism of the unions for their narrow-mindedness; there was little of the employers for theirs. It was also recognised by many that until the unions were given some guarantee that the profits of firms benefiting from the provisions of the Treasury Agreement were curtailed it would not be fair to expect the unions to accept them. Indeed, it is doubtful whether the Agreement would ever have been signed by the unions if such a *quid pro quo* had not been assumed. What came of it was too

[1] A. W. Kirkaldy (ed.), *Labour, Finance and the War* (London 1916), pp. 21, 22, 29, 32 especially.
[2] Survey of the *Reports* made by George Barnes, S.P. 1917–18, XV.
[3] T. J. Kiernan, *British War Finances and their Consequences* (London 1920), p. 98.
[4] H.M.M., Vol. 4, pt. 1, p. 31.
[5] Dilution of work was just as difficult as dilution of labour. See Gerald Stoney's address to the British Association in 1916 reported in *Engineering*, 8th September 1916; also H.M.M., Vol. 1, pt. 1, pp. 99 ff.

little and too late.[1] In the meantime, firms quoting for contracts were allowing 'not only for the costs of immediate production but for more or less hypothetical increases in wages and costs of materials'.[2] The firms who jealously guarded their privileges as armament suppliers aimed to make 'as much profit as they could out of the troubles of the Empire'.[3] And firms were being given grants for the extension of premises, and improvement of machinery and methods, which most of them made quite clear they regarded as straight gifts.[4] Other suppliers of government needs apart from the munitions firms were finding profits unrestricted; those made in clothing and meat were even embarrassing to their beneficiaries.[5]

The rising costs of munitions may have offended the wage-earner's sense of justice; but it was the cost of the necessities of life that really affected him.[6] As late as 19th July 1915,[7] Runciman was defending the right of a business man to make whatever profit he could. True he was defending the right of the wage-earner to do the same, but by that time effective restraints had been placed on the freedom of the wage-earner to make the selfish best of his position. In the meantime, it has been reckoned that the effect of the free market in shipping accounted for one half of the increase in retail prices in 1915–16;[8] Bonar Law admitted in the House of Commons that shipping profits were enormous.[9] Only very slowly were controls introduced.[10] The government had to be cautious. There was in the first months the illusion that the war was to be a short one. Even when it became clear that it was to be a long war, its scale and nature presented problems never before faced; answers had to be worked out the hard way. In retrospect it seems that strong measures would have been tolerated earlier. McKenna 'tasted general popularity' for the first time when he introduced a tough budget late in 1915.[11] He demanded sacrifices that were without parallel in the history of the country and he found himself popular for doing so.

[1] H.M.M., Vol. 1, pt. 2, pp. 69 ff. The proposal was to operate the armaments firms on the same principle as the railways. The firms rejected the proposal; similarly they rejected the idea of profit-sharing (ibid., p. 77).

[2] Ibid., pt. 1, p. 80. [3] Stoney, loc. cit. [4] H.M.M., pp. 103 ff.

[5] E. M. H. Lloyd, *Experiments in State Control* (Oxford 1923), pp. 31 and 157.

[6] A debate on the subject in the House of Commons took place on 11th February 1915: 69 H.C. Deb. 5S, cols. 755 ff. It was admitted that coal had risen 14 per cent, sugar 72 per cent, wheat 72 per cent and meat 6 to 12 per cent since the beginning of the war. [7] 73 H.C. Deb. 5S, cols. 1208 ff.

[8] S. J. Hurwitz, *State Intervention in Great Britain* (New York 1949), p. 189.

[9] 69 H.C. Deb. 5S, col. 793. [10] A. Marwick, *The Deluge* (London 1965), pp. 171 ff.

[11] Stephen McKenna, *Reginald McKenna* (London 1948), p. 245.

Firmness in controlling the free market in the supply of munitions and of the necessities of life was lacking. It was, if anything, even more lacking in the control of the finance of the war. The standard authority finds it 'hard to resist the view' that the government was too much influenced by purely banking advice,[1] advice that is from those who had most to lose from restraints. It was in fact not until 1917 that the government took steps to lower the interest rate,[2] steps which had been in its power to take much earlier.

The slowness of the government to tackle the problems of the free market contributed to the profiteering which was undoubtedly a feature of these first three years of war. More important, the unions were convinced that this was the case. On the other hand, it is certain that as a result of full employment and the opportunities for bonus work and overtime, there was less pauperism and a higher standard of living for the working population as a whole in the war years than ever before.[3] This was an advantage bought at high cost in terms of fatigue and overwork and it represents more a condemnation of the previous poverty and quality of life of the people than anything else. But it was a fact nevertheless and one of those by-products of the need for total national co-operation in war which was to have such effects in other directions. In the light of the emphasis often placed on the scale of war-time unrest, it is well to remember that the number of days lost through industrial action in 1915–18 was by pre-war standards small—in 1915 3 million, in 1916 2·5 million, in 1917 5·9 million and in 1918 6 million.[4]

The sense of national unity was shown in other more startling ways also. Here the effect of labour's other contribution to the war made its greatest impact. The privileged element in the two nations had previously had, in its own eyes at least, no cause to be grateful to the less privileged. The alacrity with which the ordinary people rallied to the colours in 1914[5] and the bravery with which the volunteer armies of 1915–16 performed changed all that. Relics of the old prejudices were slow to disappear, as the furore on the 'drink question' in 1915 indicates.[6] The charges laid against the shipbuilding, transport and

[1] E. V. Morgan, *Studies in British Financial Policy 1914–1925*, p. 32. See Kiernan, op. cit., pp. 90 ff.

[2] Kiernan, op. cit., p. 95, and Morgan, op. cit., p. 111.

[3] W. H. Beveridge, *British Food Control* (Oxford 1928), pp. 20 and 334. This despite the fact that in the first three years of the war rates of wages lagged behind the rising cost of living. A. L. Bowley, *Prices and Wages in the United Kingdom* (Oxford 1921), p. 106.

[4] *Twelfth Report under the Conciliation Act*, S.P. 1919, XIII, 1, p. 25.

[5] By March 1916 2·5 million men had volunteered for the armed forces, A. J. P. Taylor, *English History 1914–15* (Oxford 1969), p. 20.

[6] *Return to an order of the House of Commons . . . for a copy of the Report and Statistics on bad time keeping in the Shipbuilding, Munitions and Transport Areas*, S.P. 1914–16, LV., H.M.M., Vol. 4, pt. 2, pp. 44 ff.

munitions workers by an officious Director of Naval Equipment were, it was later revealed, almost entirely without foundation and what foundation they had would never have justified the degree of outrage that was evidenced at this supposed dereliction of duty by the lower classes. It was fed by the prejudices of what Montagu called 'the naked Tory mind'.[1]

By 1916, however, this was not the dominating note in national public opinion. It was the war as 'the great leveller' which was found most impressive. A speech by Walter Long on this issue in February 1916 was regarded by many as very significant of the rethinking that was going on.[2] The courage of the volunteers in the battles of 1915–16 was making the 'comradeship of the trenches' cause for questioning the older prejudices at home. Reconstruction was in the air. A small Cabinet subcommittee on reconstruction problems was set up in March 1916[3] to be replaced in March 1917 by something more grandiose, a Reconstruction Committee of Cabinet Ministers with Lloyd George as Chairman.[4] In addressing its first meeting on 16th March 1917, he spoke of a chance that had not been given 'to any nation before, not even by the French Revolution' to reconstruct itself.[5] Hammond's paper on the subject of reconstruction in June 1917 echoed those sentiments[6]—'the note of 1815 was of despair; the note of 1917 is a note of hope'. Industrial relations were one of the objects of reconstruction. In the unlikely setting of a gathering of the Institute of Mechanical Engineers, Michael Longridge appealed for a situation in which 'employer and employed shall live in peace and work together for the glory of our native land'.[7] It was in this atmosphere that the Whitley Committee was set up, worked and reported.

The demand for workers' control

The effect of industrial unionism, syndicalism and guild socialist ideas on trade union policy 1911–14 was not very profound, serving rather to add bite to traditional policies than to replace them. The railwaymen had been in favour of nationalisation since the 1890's in order to get better conditions rather than to advance the cause of theoretical

[1] Quoted in Lloyd George's *Memoirs*, p. 199.
[2] See *Public Opinion*, 25th February 1916. [3] Rec/1/40, March 1916.
[4] It was replaced in August 1917 by a fully-fledged Ministry of Reconstruction. *Report on the Work of the Ministry of Reconstruction*, S.P. 1918, XIII. Passfield Papers (Reconstruction Papers), 1916–18, Part A, fols. 1–1133. The latter reveal how ill-organised and ineffective it all was.
[5] Rec/1/41. [6] Rec/1/40/795. [7] *Engineering*, 27th April 1917.

socialism. Then in 1912–14 this was changed to a demand that it should be accompanied by workers' control in some form. The radicals were given a boost during the war as they spoke for the rank and file against not only a government but a union leadership which it seemed to them was more concerned with keeping the railways running than with the needs of those who ran them. At the end of the war the unions, and the N.U.R. in particular, were strong in their demand for nationalisation with workers' control.[1] The miners, who like the railwaymen had been demanding public ownership of the mines long before 1911–13, were less affected by the desire for workers' control until the war years; afterwards it formed part of their post-war programme.[2] During the first two years of the war the South Wales miners presented the major problem of industrial relations. They showed their contempt for war time legislation by defying it and ultimately the industry was taken over by the government for the period of the war.[3] But if the more considerable threat came from the miners, it was the engineers who caught the imagination and the headlines in a more specific way as they became identified with the demand for workers' control. Not unnaturally, in the light of these trends, there was a substantial fear in some quarters that the end of the war would lead to a real challenge to the existing order. Some acceptable alternative must be found. The Whitley Councils provided it.[4]

The centre of the agitation was Clydeside. The reasons for the ferment of ideas and plans in this area are deep and complex.[5] A syndicalist-inspired amalgamation committee movement organised by shop stewards[6] had been active before the war and though the war put a stop to it the rising discontents of early 1915 once more gave it impetus.

[1] Pribićević, pp. 4 ff. Bagwell, pp. 238, 304, 372.
[2] Pribićević, pp. 7 ff. Arnot, Vol. 2, p. 184, and G. D. H. Cole, *Labour in the Coalmining Industry During the War* (Oxford 1923), p. 70.
[3] The South Wales area in December 1916, the rest of the industry in February 1917. R. A. S. Redmayne, *The British Coal Mining Industry during the War* (Oxford 1923), pp. 62 and 88. Cole, op. cit., pp. 47 ff., 60 ff., and Arnot, Vol. 2, pp. 169 ff.
[4] See below, pp. 85 and 112 ff.
[5] R. K. Middlemass, *The Clydesiders* (London 1965), pp. 18 ff. W. R. Scott and J. Cunnison, *The Industries of the Clyde Valley during the War* (Oxford 1924), pp. 138 ff. In 1911 over half the population of Glasgow lived in houses with one or two rooms only (H.M.M., Vol. 4, pt. 2, p. 43). The high proportion of dispossessed Highlanders and immigrant Irish in the city's population did not help to ease the situation; nor did the slump in the shipping industry in 1907–10. The stress of war, the growth of the engineering industries and the influx of munition workers added extra pressures.
[6] The shop steward developed his role because of the primitive nature of workshop procedures. H.M.M. traces the origins of the power of the steward, Vol. 4, pt. 2, p. 40. See also Middlemass, op. cit., pp. 50 ff.

The shop stewards were the nerve and muscle of a strike there in February which involved some eight thousand and led to the formation of a Central Withdrawal of Labour Committee.[1] The Committee on Production soon had this strike under control and it was not until the shop stewards were able to use the deep-felt social grievances of the area that they really began to register. The trouble over rents in July and November 1915, gave them their first opportunity and they took it with both hands.[2] The problems of the Munitions of War Act—the enforcement of dilution in controlled establishments, the need for clearance certificates and the introduction of compulsory arbitration—produced many others.[3] So great was the simmering discontent that Lloyd George visited the area in December 1915—with disastrous results.[4] The New Year brought no immediate respite, but the Dilution Commission, co-operating with Kirkwood and Wheatley in working out an agreement which would satisfy government, management and unions on the details of each scheme, soon found a way round the real difficulties.[5] The deportation of several strike leaders and the restriction of the journalistic activities of certain individuals lowered the tension and after the first two months of 1916, the Clyde was comparatively quiet for the rest of the war.[6] Later in the year there was more trouble in the engineering industry—this time at Sheffield over the recruitment of skilled men. Since the first weeks of the war, key men had been 'badged'.[7] When conscription was introduced in January 1916 there was a threat to enlist all those under twenty-six who had been so 'badged' and it was out of the mistrust bred by this that the strike arose. The unrest at Barrow in March 1917 also developed over the exemption of skilled men now designated under a Trade Card scheme administered by the unions. The government was not satisfied with the scheme and wanted to replace it with a more direct method. According

[1] Middlemass, op. cit., pp. 58 ff. Scott and Cunnison, op. cit., pp. 139 ff. W. Gallacher, *Revolt on the Clyde* (London 1949), pp. 42 ff. D. Kirkwood, *My Life of Revolt* (London 1935) pp. 93 ff.

[2] Middlemass, op. cit., p. 61. *A Note on the 1915 Rent Strike*, Appx. to H.M.M., Vol. 4, pt. 2.

[3] H.M.M., Vol. 4, pt. 4, pp. 98 ff., and pt. 2, pp. 50 ff.

[4] Ibid., Vol. 4, pt. 4, pp. 101 ff. Middlemass, pp. 63 and 113 ff. Kirkwood and Gallagher, loc. cit. Pribićević, pp. 113 ff.

[5] Kirkwood, p. 116, and Middlemass, p. 66. Pribićević, p. 119. H.M.M., Vol. 4, pt. 4, pp. 116 ff., and Appendix XVIII.

[6] Between April and July 1916, the commission was kept busy; after August it had little or nothing to do. Scott and Cunnison, p. 153. H.M.M., loc. cit.

[7] H. Wolfe, *Labour Supply and Regulation during the War* (Oxford 1923), pp. 24 ff. and 42 ff. S. Pollard, *History of Labour in Sheffield* (Liverpool 1959), pp. 272 ff. H.M.M., Vol. 4, pt. 3, and Vol. 6, pt. 1, pp. 35 ff.

to Wolfe, the new scheme would have probably been accepted had not a move to extend statutory dilution of labour to private works also been made in the House at this time.[1] In fact it was the way in which one particular firm decided to use this extension of dilution to private work which sparked off the most widespread strike in May 1917. It began in Lancashire and it soon extended to the other major engineering centres.[2]

The possibility of post-war industrial unrest

As the war drew to a close, there were fears about the peace-time mood of labour;[3] concern to find an answer to workers' control was very much a concern to anticipate continuing post-war demands for such control. The outbreak of unrest in May 1917 brought to a head the fears of what might happen when peace came. It led to the establishment of the Commission on Industrial Unrest which worked in eight panels for various areas of the country. To it the findings of the Whitley Committee were transmitted before they were published. They found that the proposals of the *Report*, expecially those on the matters of workers' participation in the Councils, were generally welcomed.[4] If there was to be a challenge to the existing system of ownership and control of industry in the post-war years, as the increasing power of labour and its evident growth in self-confidence seemed to indicate, the proposals of the *Whitley Report* seemed to be the only antidote based as these were on the solid traditions of British trade unionism but marking a considerable advance over what before the war would have been regarded as an acceptable national policy.

(ii) INFLUENCES ON THE COMMITTEE AND ITS WORK

Wartime reflections on the industrial relations problem

The bitterness that was evident in the industrial relations situation in the conflicts of 1911–14 had already produced some measure of soul-searching among the more privileged sections of the community. Guild socialism in particular, was the product of middle-class intellectualism; there was also the remarkable phenomenon of the Agenda

[1] Op. cit., pp. 49 ff. [2] H.M.M., Vol. 6, part 1, pp. 102 ff.

[3] This is discussed in more detail below, pp. 99 and 115.

[4] Below, p. 113.

Club,[1] supported not only by John Galsworthy, A. A. Milne, Evelyn Wrench and Northcliffe but also by J. A. Hobson, Sidney Webb and Graham Wallas. The Romney Street group, which succeeded it, included Tawney and Cole as well as Hilton, Clay, Zimmern, Vaughan Nash and Philip Kerr;[2] all of them were active in the Reconstruction Ministry and its industrial relations section during the war. In the first weeks of the war, the Industrial League was formed[3] and in September 1915 came the first-ever attempt by a prestigious group like the British Association to examine the factors making for 'Industrial Harmony'. Thereafter, there came a torrent of ideas, suggestions, plans and hopes. The Engineers' Club of Manchester declared in September 1915[4] that individualism was played out and that the employers must learn to co-operate. But it was 1916 before the movement really got under way. In February 1916, Mr. Malcolm Sparkes put forward suggestions for an Industrial Council in the Building Industry;[5] in April, the *Caxton Magazine* carried an article on reconstruction in the printing trade from which a movement stemmed.[6] In May the Garton Foundation's *Memorandum* was being circulated and in September the National Alliance of Employers and Employed was formed.[7] In October, the Whitley Committee was set up and in December, the *Report on Reconstruction in the Iron and Steel Engineering and Shipbuilding Industries* was issued by a group of Scottish employers.[8]

The year 1917 brought no respite. In January and February, the Ilkley and Penscott conferences met.[9] In February, an Industrial Council was set up in the painting and decorating trade.[10] In March, the first *Whitley Report* was produced and presented to the Reconstruction Committee. In April, the pottery industry reviewed its industrial relations and took the steps leading to the establishment of the J.I.C.[11]

[1] Started by J. T. Thorpe (1875–1963), journalist and publicist, who from 1916 to 1934 was the drama critic of *Punch*.

[2] *Friends and Adventures*, Thorpe's autobiography (London 1931), pp. 147–70 and 176–8. E. Nixon, *John Hilton* (London 1946), p. 61. *The Other War* by Philip Kerr and others (London 1918).

[3] *The Industrial League and the Council Journal*, Vol. 1, No. 1, September 1918.

[4] *Engineering*, 26th November 1915.

[5] Garton Foundation: *Report on the Industrial Council for the Building Industry* (London 1919), pp. 12 ff.

[6] Federation of Master Printers' *Circular*, December 1917. Article on 'Betterment'.

[7] Pamphlet, *National Alliance of Employers and Employed: Origins, objects and ideals*, by Harry Duberry, October 1917.

[8] *Labour Year Book*, 1919, p. 247.

[9] Reports on the Conferences. Penscott, 17th and 18th February 1917, and Ilkley, 20th and 21st January 1917.

[10] *The Decorators and Painters Magazine*, 16th April 1917.

[11] *Report on the Establishment and Progress of Joint Industrial Councils*, H.M.S.O. 1923 p. 29.

In June–July the *Whitley Report* was being circulated.

Two or three of the contributions are of especial interest or merit; their efforts were made dispassionately and with due regard for all the factors involved, weighed in the balance of honest intellectual assessment and exposing the problems of the primary substantive norm and the impossibility of reconciling opposing views within the existing framework of economic thought and policy.

The discussion at the British Association in 1915 on the subject of 'The Problems of Industrial Harmony' provides a case study of the difficulties faced by those who attempted to grasp the nettle. Opening it Professor Kirkaldy,[1] an economist, stated that if only the two sides would see what economics were really about they would co-operate to produce the wealth out of which everyone's increased expectations could be satisfied. Sir Hugh Bell[2] then proceeded to show that the two sides had different views on what the lessons of economics were. He proved to his own satisfaction, but not to that of Professor Hobhouse another contributor, that he could not pay greater wages because the fund out of which he paid them was determined by prices. Hobhouse, expressed some surprise at the resurrection of such a thesis. The argument from the impossible had never particularly impressed labour however frequently it was used; and 'if prices limit wages, it is not less true that wages react on prices'. Head-on disagreement of this kind proved that

> each side is trying to convince the other of something that it is unwilling to see and, failing that, to push it somewhere it is unwilling to go . . . *there is a deep and perfectly genuine intellectual cleavage as to the meaning and the concatenation of the main factors of industry* let alone the difficulty of ascertaining those factors. . . . In other words there are *no clearly defined and generally accepted elementary principles of economic and industrial science; and therefore no one can speak with authority on the controlling forces which underlie any given situation.*[3]

The trade unionist refused to be convinced that he should put adequate wages and security second; the employer was honestly convinced that in calling for greater productivity first he was backed by reason, sound economics and common sense. The reason for their clash of opinion lay deep in the traditional dogmas of economics. Ricardo accepted the famous dictum of Say, that 'supply creates its own demand'. 'No man,' said Ricardo, 'ever produces but with a view

[1] A. Kirkaldy (ed.), *Credit, Industry and the War* (London 1916), p. 18.
[2] Ibid., pp. 36 ff. [3] Ibid., p. 60.

to consume or sell and he never sells but with the intention of buying another commodity; by producing he becomes either the consumer of his own goods or the purchaser and consumer of the goods of some other person.'[1] As Schumpeter points out,[2] Say's assertion was in fact the unjustifiable exaggeration of a propagandist rather than the careful statement of a precise thinker. Marshall saw through Mills' fourth fundamental principle ('demand for commodities is not a demand for labour') but he was still not able to admit that 'it was possible in normal circumstances to have a state of equilibrium below the full employment of capital and labour as a result of the defect of effective demand'.[3] Many criticised this emphasis of the traditional economics and were in their turn criticised. Whatever the defects of the critics, the fact is that 'the leaders of prevailing opinion completely failed to go into the matter [i.e. of saving-hoarding in depression], a fact which explains much in the recent history of economics'.[4] The importance of effective demand and the means of maintaining it in the real monetary economy as opposed to the neutral abstract world of economic theory was the key to many of the problems of the mature capitalist society. It was to become crucial in the 1920's.[5]

Because there was still this fundamental difference concerning the priorities in economic policy, the primary substantive norms remained in dispute and the role of the unions and collective bargaining could still be questioned. From time to time, as in the Garton *Memorandum,*[6] the need to give labour assurance of security and decent wages through effective demand is glimpsed.[7]

> . . . assured markets are essential for steady production . . . home demand depends first of all upon the general prosperity of the people. If confidence and credit are maintained and earnings are large, the increases in purchasing power will be reflected in the brisk demand for goods . . . it is obvious that labour cannot be fairly asked to remove . . . restrictions . . . unless some definite assurance is given against the evils (i.e. unemployment and insecurity) anticipated.

Yet in the end the conventional wisdom triumphs. The main obstacle to obtaining labour's co-operation is not the fear of insecurity but the

[1] D. Ricardo, *The Principles of Political Economy and Taxation* (Everyman 1965), pp. 192–3.
[2] J. A. Schumpeter, *History of Economic Analysis* (London 1963), p. 618.
[3] E. Eshag, *From Marshall to Keynes* (Blackwell 1963), p. 105.
[4] Schumpeter, op. cit., p. 1130.
[5] R. Skidelsky, *Politicians and the Slump* (London 1967).
[6] *Memorandum on the Industrial Situation after the War* (London 1916).
[7] Ibid., pp. 55 and 66.

desire for an improved status which some form of consultation will satisfy if it is linked with proper machinery for negotiating pay and conditions and adjusting differences.[1]

The practical recommendation of the Garton Foundation's *Memorandum* and those of the British Association's *Report* on unrest are remarkably similar.[2] Both assume the co-operation norm and both assume that the primary norms can be extended beyond those usually the concern of collective bargaining. Both mention the need for Councils at various levels as a means of implementing the organisational norm. The link between the recommendations of the Whitley Committee and the Garton Foundation's work was mentioned by some contemporary writers.[3] Balfour, one of its three trustees, was influential enough to get the Assistant Director of the Foundation[4] appointed to work in that capacity with the Reconstruction Committee.[5] However this may be, the fact is that when the *Whitley Report* was being prepared, the same sort of ideas were current in the press and the opinions of the interested people generally. Industrial relations could be improved if collective bargaining was improved in such a way that the greater degree of acceptance of labour's rights was given practical expression. There was little or no awareness on the other hand of the importance of expansionist economic policy in giving the unions the incentive to maintain wartime co-operativeness. Only in the by-products of the work of Penscott Conferences was a real practical concern with this problem evidenced. One of the results of Penscott was the formation of the British Association for Industrial Reconstruction which, among other things, sponsored a series of lectures in the British Museum. After one of them on 'Finance in relation to industry' Ernest Bevin rose up to ask a question.[6] Could not the Ministry of Reconstruction examine the effect of banking, the gold standard and credit on

[1] Ibid., pp. 67–8.

[2] *Memorandum*, pp. 79–84, and Kirkaldy (ed.), *Labour, Finance and the War* (London 1916), pp. 34, 42, 43, 44, 50.

[3] Colonel D. Carnegie, *The Promotion of Industrial Harmony* (London 1919), p. 14. B. G. De Montgomery, *British and Continental Labour Policy* (London 1922), p. 460. Lord Esher, responsible for the Garton Foundation, was in no doubt about it. *Journals and Letters*, edited Brett (London 1934–6), Vol. 4, p. 293. On the Foundation itself N. Angell, *After All* (London 1951), pp. 162 ff., and E. Nixon, *John Hilton* (London 1964), p. 60.

[4] The Assistant Director was John Hilton (1860–1943), later first Professor of Industrial Relations at Cambridge. Nixon, op. cit., pp. 121 ff.

[5] Balfour Papers 94719–292, letter of 6th August, making the request. Hilton was responsible for the drawing up of 'A study of trade organisations and combines in the U.K.', published as an appendix to the *Report of the Committee on Trusts*, S.P. 1918, XIII.

[6] A. Bullock, *Ernest Bevin*, Vol. 1 (London 1960), p. 71.

industry? Nothing came of the suggestion, but this was the crucial issue as the next years were to show. When, however, the government did get round in 1929 to appointing a Committee on Finance and Industry, Bevin was on it. For the moment the Cunliffe Committee was working on the problem of currency and foreign exchanges. Its recommendations looked back to 1914 rather than ahead to the 1920's; since economic policy in the 1920's was based on the recommendations of the Committee, this was to have lasting consequences.

In the late autumn of 1916 when the Whitley Committee assembled, these deep matters were hardly within the purview of those concerned to improve industrial relations. The consensus which had developed was summed up in the Garton Foundation's and the British Association's careful documents. The need was for the continuance of the war-time spirit in industrial relations and an improvement in the mechanism of collective negotiation to enable the wage-earners to enjoy a higher standard of living and a greater degree of control over the decisions affecting them. This consensus was accepted by the moderate trade unionists, the mass of trade unionists, that is, and it received confirmation in the events of the 1916 Trades Union Congress. Held in Birmingham, it fell to Neville Chamberlain as Lord Mayor of that city to welcome the delegates. He spoke of labour's right to be admitted to the counsels of the employers and to expect a higher standard of life from their labour.[1] Gosling, the President, expressed sentiments which he later was to note were hardly different from Chamberlain's.[2] The trade unions wanted precisely a right to share in the decision-making which affected them and they wanted also to get a better life for themselves. It was fitting that Gosling, who had been made aware of the need for the co-operative approach to industrial relations through his experience in the Industrial Council, should have had the privilege of speaking for the movement and voicing its ambitions which his life and ideas so closely reflected, and this at the moment when it was better realised than ever before that labour had a right to be treated as an equal in industrial and national councils. It was in this atmosphere, when the sense of national and industrial unity was greater than it had ever been, that the Whitley Committee was chosen and assembled.

[1] K. Feiling, *The Life of Neville Chamberlain* (London 1946), p. 61. *Report of the 1916 Congress*, pp. 50 ff.

[2] Op. cit., p. 130. The workers, said Gosling, were tired of war in industry. They wanted peace based on their rights, not to do the work of management and to sit on Boards of Directors, but to have an equal voice in all those matters which affected their day-to-day lives at work—their rewards for it, the conditions affecting it, the decisions governing it.

The war, industrial organisation and industrial relations

Industrial organisation was affected by the war in three main directions. Firstly, industry gained an experience of working co-operatively in the execution of government policy regarding materials, production of goods and distribution which was quite new to it; secondly the war brought a growth in the size of the business unit; finally direct government intervention and control affected technical, economic and organisational aspects of industry as well as collective bargaining, welfare and industrial relations.

The execution of government policy in industry as part of the war effort required that there be trade associations capable of acting as intermediaries; where none existed the government department concerned saw that one was created.[1] The growth in the size of business encouraged the same spirit of industrial self-government through larger integrated units. The number of actual mergers was small compared with the number of temporary or lesser associations.[2] In industries and firms directly under its control the government encouraged the development of new methods of production, of research, work organisation and economies of scale. The reduction of transport costs that came from the national organisation of both coal and railways was an obvious case of economy; it is reckoned that 700 million ton miles per annum were saved.[3] The modern electricity supply industry largely takes its origin from the wartime needs of industry and of the efforts of the Ministry of Munitions to supply them.[4] Whole new industries, ranges of products and methods were developed through state initiative as were better costings, factory layouts, production planning and use of by-products.[5] The Great War also 'put management on the map'.[6] It made both the personnel and the technical aspects popular as never before. The Ministry of Munitions had to lead manufacturers by the hand; it sold over 10,000 copies of the standard work on factory administration to firms with whom it was in contact on war work.[7]

[1] H.M.M., Vol. 7, pt. 1, p. 11. Appendix to the *Report of the Committee on Trusts*, loc. cit. E. M. H. Lloyd, op. cit., Ch. 27 and 28.

[2] Lloyd, op. cit., p. 351. See also Clapham, Vol. 3, Ch. V, and the *Report of the Committee on Trusts*, loc. cit.

[3] Redmayne, op. cit., p. 102, see also p. 271; and H.M.M., Vol. 7, pt. 1, p. 88. Pollard, p. 61.

[4] H.M.M., Vol. 8, pt. 3, pp. 92 ff.

[5] A. Marwick, *The Deluge*, pp. 226 ff. Lloyd, op. cit., pp. 391 ff. H.M.M., Vol. 7, pt. 1, pp. 35 ff. and 87 ff.: Vol. 8, pt. 1 (especially pp. 84 ff.) and pt. 4.

[6] L. Urwick and E. F. L. Brech, *The Making of Scientific Management* (London 1946–51), Vol. 2, p. 185.

[7] Ibid., p. 23.

Government action also spurred efforts on proper welfare and personnel policies helping to undermine the notion of economic man working what hours and under what conditions necessity required.[1]

The result of this complex pattern of influence was to encourage industry-consciousness and the notion of industrial self-government on the one hand, and on the other to underline that efficiency and a rational approach to the problems of industry went hand in hand with a humane personnel policy which met traditional demands of the unions more than halfway. But the logic of trade unionism was being accepted in more significant ways too.

Although as late as March 1916 Runciman[2] could still protest that unions could not be trusted to co-operate with their employers in matters confidential, concessions had already been made which outdated his objections. In two major respects the war from the outset guaranteed that the power of the unions, and that their value in the running of the industrial system, would be appreciated as never before. The one was the need to control wages and to get the co-operation of the unions in introducing new methods of production. The other was that the need for the government to, in effect, take over some industries for the duration of the war. In this they needed the co-operation of the unions as well as of the employers.

The working of the Committee on Production[3] ensured that the collective bargaining rights of the unions would be extended and secured and that legal enforcement of agreements and awards which the Industrial Council had asked for should not only be permitted but enforced. National agreements on wages, a thing unknown before the war, became standard. Almost as and perhaps more important, the cost of living sliding scale for the first time secured the recognition of the need to take the human factor into consideration in wage determination. The war therefore gave the unions the accepted positive

[1] The Health of Munition Workers Committee was in operation from early 1915: sixteen memoranda were issued by it. S.P. 1914–16, LV, and *Final Report*, S.P. 1918, XII. The 350,000 workers in the national factories and the nearly two million in the controlled establishment were directly affected by improvements in standards which would have taken decades in peace. H.M.M., Vol. 5, pt. 3, pp. 168 ff., and the factory inspectors' *Report* there quoted.

[2] Rec. 1/40. Reconstruction Committee Meeting of 24th March 1916.

[3] The Committee was set up on 4th February 1915, to consult 'with representatives of employers and workpeople' as to the best methods of increasing production, and to report accordingly. A full account of its work is in the *Twelfth Report of Proceedings under the Act*, S.P. 1919, XIII, I. Not all industries were subject to the Committee in the control of wages; the main ones outside its scope were mining, agriculture and transport, loc. cit., pp. 16 ff. But each of these was subject to state regulation of wages by other means.

right to represent the wage-earners and did something to link wages to human needs. The growth in trade union membership through the war was then considerable; there were twice as many members of unions in 1920 as there had been in 1914.[1]

The needs of adaptation to war needs in the workshops and factories further enhanced the role of the unions as representatives of the work-force. Settlement of the Clyde disputes was achieved through negotiation with the unions to obtain agreements that met their needs and those of their members. Government initiative favoured giving the unions an even greater part to play in administration of the war effort; but the Local Armaments Committees were curtailed by the action of the employers and the proposal to put employee representatives on the Boards of the national shell factories was also opposed by them.[2] In other industries which came directly under government control—railways,[3] mines,[4] shipping,[5] textiles[6] and building[7]—the rights of the unions were fully respected and indeed, in some, the unions were represented on the boards which ran them.

There was inevitably resentment at government interference.[8] The speed with which wartime decontrols were rushed through was an indication of it—nor were the unions unaware of the disadvantages as well as the advantages of state interference. The Munitions of War Act they had especially resented. For all that the total effect of war experience could not be eradicated. Through government interference industrial self-government had increased, scientific and professional management had received a boost, the cost of living standard of wage adjustment had been made popular, the possibilities of co-operation between unions and management had been emphasised and the unions were for the first time accepted as equals in the affairs of industry. All this would henceforth be part of the industrial consciousness and organisation, despite an inevitable reaction which would to some extent nullify it.

[1] *Twenty-second Abstract of Labour Statistics*, H.M.S.O. 1937, p. 137. G. D. H. Cole, *Organised Labour* (London 1923), pp. 77 ff. and Appendix 12 gives details of the amalgamation movement also encouraged by the war.

[2] H.M.M., Vol. 1, pt. 3, pp. 18 ff., and Appendix XIV and Vol. 2, pt. 2, pp. 72 ff.

[3] The railways came under state control under existing legislation as soon as war broke out, Bagwell, p. 346.

[4] Above, p. 83.

[5] *Report on the Work of the National Maritime Board*, S.P. 1920, XXI.

[6] *Memorandum* on the work of the Control Board for the woollen and worsted Industries: Ministry of Reconstruction, 1917 (M. of L. library).

[7] *Twelfth Report under the Conciliation Act*, loc. cit., p. 29. H.M.M., Vol. 5, pt. 1, p. 209.

[8] H. Clay, *The Problem of Industrial Relations* (London 1927), pp. 145–7. He points out that the resentment was evident before the war and the employers and trade unionists were resentful for different reasons.

5
The Whitley Committee, the First Interim Report and its reception

(i) THE COMMITTEE

The illusion that this was to be a short war meant that post-war problems were under consideration from the first few months of hostilities. As the months and years dragged on, the approach became more formal although when the Cabinet Subcommittee on Reconstruction Problems was set up in March 1916 there was no clear idea of what the problems might be and how they should be tackled. It was imagined that they would be mainly concerned with the supply of capital and the depreciation of currency; hence the concern of the Treasury.[1] The schemes for social reform were a later development. None the less, surveys were made in the first months of 1916 to consider the broader industrial and commercial results of the conflict and on 28th March Vaughan Nash addressed a letter to all departments telling them of the existence of the committee 'on the lines of the Committee on Imperial Defence' and asking them what plans they had made for the transition to peace.[2] By the end of May 1916, there were committees or projects for committees on a wide range of subjects from 'Demobilisation' to the 'Increase of the Home Grown Food Supply' and 'Public works Available for Execution at the end of the war'. The replies to the enquiry mentioned were already forming a positive pattern in which social problems were prominent. The Department of Education emphasised that a greater stress on education was needed if public well-being was to be secured and the Board of Trade was in consultation with the Chief Industrial Commissioner's Department on the question of securing industrial harmony and efficiency after the war.[3] The period, it must be remembered, was that in which a reassessment of industrial and national ideals was going on under the impulse of the 'comradeship of the trenches'. Not all those involved had been affected by the new mood; the question of labour representation on the Committee investigating post-war

[1] Passfield Papers, loc. cit., fol. 46, 'Notes on preparation for post war reconstruction'.
[2] Ibid., fol. 50. [3] Ibid., fol. 50.

industrial problems and prospects came up in March 1916. It revealed old-fashioned attitudes.[1] As late as September of that year, Montagu could submit a paper to the Cabinet suggesting that the domestic problems of reconstruction were all well under consideration.[2] The Whitley Committee was not at this time formed. On the other hand something was stirring. On 28th April Beveridge and Llewellyn Smith of the Board of Trade had been in consultation with Nash and Dale of the Reconstruction Committee on the question of 'the relationship of capital and labour'.[3] Nash had not given the matter much thought and though the Board's representatives suggested that some sort of small committee was needed, 'we were not at all ready for such a committee at the present time'. By October something had happened to change minds. Perhaps it was the tide of events, perhaps the publication of the various reports, especially the Garton *Memorandum*. A note by Montagu to the Reconstruction subcommittee had reminded it that 'subjects sometimes suggested in the press were suitable for its consideration'[4] and there is evidence that the subcommittee was seeking ideas from interested parties. On 7th September T. B. Johnston replied to its enquiry giving his suggestions for the improvement of industrial relations, noting that 'twenty-three years ago I conceived of a union of masters and men'.[5]

The committee itself was in the event instructed:[6]

1. To make and consider suggestions for securing a permanent improvement in the relations between employers and workmen.
2. To recommend means for securing that industrial conditions affecting the relations between employers and workmen shall be systematically reviewed by those concerned with a view to improving conditions in future.

One or two of the *Memoranda* sought from those concerned have survived.[7] The papers of the Committee itself shows that the members were aware and influenced by the work of the Garton Foundation, the British Association and the Report of the Scottish Iron and Steel trades.[8] Whitley himself had approached Malcolm Sparkes for an elaboration of his ideas.[9] The Welsh Tinplate Conciliation Board and

[1] Above, p. 92. [2] Cab./24/2 G (War) series 47–100 G 76, September 1917.
[3] Passfield Papers, loc. cit., fol. 93. [4] Rec. 1/40, 6th June 1916.
[5] Rec. 1/71, Part One. See above, p. 38.
[6] *Interim Report,* para. 2. *Report on the Establishment*, etc., p. 6.
[7] In the Ministry of Labour library 331.883, e.g. the Labour Co-partnership Association's observations. [8] See above, pp. 86 ff., and below, pp. 98 ff.
[9] Sparkes had outlined these in *The Venturer*, December 1916. The result of Whitley's enquiry was *The Memorandum on Industrial Self-government* drawn up by Sparkes while

later Joint Industrial Council was sure that the Councils were modelled on its work; they quoted the Chairman of the Committee to that effect.[1] The Committee did not include any official representation from the T.U.C. despite the increasing prominence of that body. The T.U.C. and the Employers' Parliamentary Association had already been in contact, at the former's initiative, 'for the express purpose of coming to an agreement in order to meet some of the problems arising out of reconstruction after the war'.[2] The Association had agreed and a meeting took place on 17th November 1916; Macara was present at it. Questions were raised however about the representative nature of the Association and talks were broken off; on 2nd April 1917 the E.P.A. wrote to say that it had merged with the F.B.I. and that was the end of the matter.[3] The T.U.C. for its part was clear on what was needed: a forty-eight-hour week, a 30s. minimum wage for adults, the recognition of full trade union rights and the provision by the state of unemployment pay were the kind of things they thought provided a basis for meeting the reconstruction problems. Perhaps the uncompromisingly specific demands of the T.U.C. were sufficient to put off the government from seeking its co-operation.

J. H. Whitley was a Yorkshireman, a member of the family firm of cotton spinners, S. Whitley of Halifax. As Chairman of the Ways and Means Committee of the House of Commons in 1911–14, he won golden opinions for his handling of the stormy debates of the period. A Liberal with a record of activity in local charities at home, a man with business interests and experience, it is very likely that the choice of Whitley for this post was the result of his 'known impartiality and capacity to control controversial discussions'. A shrewd, highly principled man, whose politics were strongly influenced by his fervent Congregationalism, there is nothing in his record to suggest that he was deeply interested in the wider social problems, their connection with the questions of industrial unrest and the desire for industrial reform.[4]

The secretaries were Arthur Greenwood[5] and H. J. Wilson[6] and, as

working with the Garton Foundation. See the *Report on the Industrial Council for the Building Industry*, p. 43.

[1] *Transcript* of the proceedings, 5th October 1917. *Report of the first meeting of the J.I.C.*, 7th March 1919.

[2] *Report of the T.U.C.*, 1916, p. 255.

[3] Ibid. and *Report* 1917, p. 136.

[4] *The Whitleys of Halifax*, Rowland Bretton (Halifax Antiquarian Society 1963) and duplicated *Memoir* by W. A. Davies, 1953.

[5] 1880–1959. Lecturer in Economics, Leeds University, and active in the W.E.A. Assistant Secretary of the Ministry of Reconstruction 1917. M.P. 1922–31.

[6] As Secretary of the Committee on Production he 'embodied the experience of the Board of Trade'. H. Clay, *The Problems of Industrial Relations* (London 1929), p. 149.

both Clay and Halévy pointed out,[1] the secretaries of such a committee have a considerable influence upon it. Wilson had been on Askwith's staff at the Board of Trade and had served as secretary to the Industrial Council. Greenwood was, Halévy suggests, something of a Guild socialist though his contribution to the Ruskin College conference hardly bears this out.[2] If Wilson can be counted strictly neutral, there is no doubt where Greenwood's sympathies lay. Of the four trade union members of the committee, F. S. Button[3] and J. R. Clynes were known moderates, Susan Lawrence[4] was a Fabian; and Robert Smillie,[5] considered by many to be the embodiment of miner's militancy. Of the employers' representatives Allan Smith, Chairman of the Engineering Employers' Federation, was, according to Citrine,[6] rather unimaginative and inclined to take the narrow view. No official of an employers' organisation, however senior, could afford to do other than represent the official view of his organisation and the engineering employers were notoriously hard in their attitudes. Sir George Carter, Chairman of the Shipbuilding Employers' and Managing Director of Cammell Laird's, was more imaginative and approachable, though no less firm in his opinions.[7] Sir George Claughton had been one of the railway directors who in the pre-war period had shown most awareness of the changing needs of the times; he had been a member of the Industrial Council. Ratcliffe Ellis[8] was a moderate in the stormy politics of mining; he too had been a member of the Industrial Council. The other members of the Council were mainly labour sympathisers; Mona Wilson was a National Insurance Commissioner; J. J. Mallon[9] of Toynbee Hall and J. A. Hobson,[10] briefly a member of the Labour Party, though he always remained Liberal at heart. S. J. Chapman,[11] Professor of Political Economy at Manchester and on the

[1] E. Halévy, *Revue d'economie politique*, 1919. Clay, op. cit., 149.
[2] *The Reorganisation of Industry*, Pigou, Greenwood and others (London 1916).
[3] Born Kent, 1873. Experience in local politics and industrial conciliation. A.S.E. executive 1913–17. Member of the Industrial Court 1919.
[4] 1872–1947. Cambridge graduate. Local politics. N.U.G.W. official.
[5] 1857–1940. Scottish Miners' President. Founder member of I.L.P. M.F.G.B. President 1912–21.
[6] Lord Citrine, *Men and Work* (London 1964), pp. 54 and 70. See below, pp. 252–3.
[7] Ibid., p. 54.
[8] 1892–1921. Educated at Wigan Grammar School; a solicitor whose legal work for the coalowners led to his appointment as secretary of the Association.
[9] Born 1880 M.A. (Manchester). I.L.P. and Fabian Society. Parliamentary correspondent *Labour Leader*, 1912–15.
[10] 1868–1940, born Derbyshire, M.A. (Oxon.). In a whole series of books from 1889 he challenged economic orthodoxy.
[11] Edited *Labour, Capital and the War* (London 1918), with contributions by Whitley, Clynes, Button, Lawrence, Lord Lever, Hugh Bell, etc.

British Association Committee which produced the report quoted and examined, was probably nearer to a neutral position.

The Committee first met on 9th November 1916,[1] and a smaller group was given the task of considering ways 'in which the committee might best proceed with their enquiry and to submit an agenda for this purpose'.[2] At a second meeting on 23rd November the subsequent *Memorandum* was accepted as a 'first survey of the position' and the full committee then turned its attention to the four specific points raised in that *Memorandum*,[3] namely:

(i) Means for ensuring the co-operation of labour on the constructive side of industry.
(ii) Existing organisations for joint continuous consideration of trade matters.
(iii) Means for improving these existing organisations.
(iv) Whether or not the state had a useful function to perform in assisting them.

Each of the members of the full committee was asked to submit suggestions on these matters in writing before 12th December in preparation for the third meeting on 11th January[4] and by this time they were in possession of a printed copy of the *Memoranda* submitted, together with the Chairman's minute summarising the general conclusions which the collective observations justified.[5] The *Memoranda* were interesting in that they gathered together the many strands in the trends of current thinking. Button was for Councils and Joint Boards at the various levels and acting in a consultative capacity. Carter took Gosling's address to the T.U.C. in that year as his starting point. Chapman tried to grapple with the economic implications of co-operation. Claughton, drawing on his experience as Lord Dudley's agent, was in no doubt that the essential temper of the British trade unionists was co-operative. Hobson took a more radical view of the nature of the problem; joint boards would not overcome the difficulty concerning profits and they might be harmful to public interest; the assumption of the British Association and the Garton *Memorandum*

[1] A 'register' of meetings and attendances M. of L. 331.883 shows that there were eight meetings on the *First Report*; attendances were uneven. Smillie was only at two, Smith at five, Claughton and Clynes at four.

[2] *Ministry of Reconstruction: Report* of second meeting of Whitley Committee (M. of L. 331. 883).

[3] Ibid. and the Whitley Committee *Memorandum* in M. of L. 331.883 which dates the meeting as 30th November.

[4] Ibid. [5] Ibid.

concerning co-operation as a matter of self-interest on both sides he did not accept. Ratcliffe Ellis refers to the Garton *Memorandum* more favourably and supports both its contention that inadequate participation was the biggest problem and its remedy of the three-tier councils. Smith predictably emphasised flexibility in wages, district rather than national agreements, the law of supply and demand and the need for workers to 'give of their best'. Mallon, in a *Memorandum* which was not incorporated into the printed format,[1] was concerned with problems of unemployment and maintenance of standard rates, with industrial parliaments and works committees.

Whitley's *Memorandum* summarises the views expressed. Joint conferences between labour and management are desirable on three counts. The first is that 'grave difficulties and strained relations' will be the result if the problems raised by the war in industry are not tackled by those who have an intimate knowledge of them. The second is that government departments are not able to deal with these problems as efficiently as the men directly concerned in the running of industry at all levels. The third is that there is no better way of enlisting the co-operation of the two sides in industry than by close association in determining common policy on immediate problems. The present time was best for setting up machinery because the end of the war would bring many opportunities for common action. There was a spontaneous move in this direction in industry itself—witness the *Report* of the Scottish Iron, Steel and Engineering industries—and though the subcommittee should not aim at providing any stereotyped scheme there was clearly a great deal it could do to enable different industries to set up their Councils.

Arising out of these *Memoranda* and his own summary of them, Whitley drew up a Minute which detailed definite propositions on which he suggested they could take action at the next meeting in the form of a *First Report* to the government. They were:[2]

(i) That in the national interest a sustained effort should be made to secure after the war both a permanent increase in the productivity of industry and a permanent improvement in the status of labour.

(ii) This purpose can best be attained by means of continuous co-operation between employers and employed in each industry with a minimum of government interference.

[1] It is in M. of L. 331.883.

[2] *Minute* attached to the *Memorandum* of the Committee, loc. cit. In fact it was to take four more meetings to get the *First Report* ready.

(iii) The government should be advised to propose without delay to the various trade organisations the formation of Joint Standing Councils of employers and employed where they do not already exist.

(iv) That the object of these councils should be indicated in general terms as for the regular consideration of matters affecting the progress and well being of the industry from the point of view of all those engaged in it and of the interest of the rest of the community, but that the methods should be worked out by the councils themselves.

(v) That the government's assistance should be limited in the first instance to an offer to provide chairmen and/or a secretary where it was so desired and to the circulation of information from industry to industry so that all should have the benefit of the experience of all.

(vi) That in larger industries district as well as national joint industrial councils should be formed.

From the *Memoranda* and from the *Minute* it emerged that the Committee was working on four assumptions in shaping its recommendations. The first was the awareness that peace was going to bring problems for the industrial system of which those met in war were only a foreshadowing. The second was that the positive recommendations—joint committees—were an extension of the best of the pre-war practices and that the spirit of co-operation in which they were intended to work reflected the attitudes of both sides. The third was that these joint committees had a function which went beyond the normal scope of collective bargaining and in particular that they would help to bring about the desired improvement in productivity. The fourth that national rather than local level organisation was to be stressed though provision was to be made for district organisation too. In the *Report* the three-tier structure was more completely outlined and emphasised. The close parallel between these assumptions and those of the British Association, the Garton *Memorandum* and speeches by Chamberlain and Gosling at the 1916 T.U.C. is clear. There was a definite reluctance on the other hand to become involved with the sort of problems which Hobson raised. The thinking of the Committee followed along well-tried lines that experience had shown could reduce, if not eliminate, conflict. The emphasis then was practical and, as Whitley's linking of productivity and the status of labour as the twin problems to be faced showed, the theoretical assumptions were in line with current orthodoxy. There was no conflict between the two sides as to productivity and, as to distribution, what conflict there was could be reduced through consultation.

These *Memoranda* and the *Minute* based on them were duly considered at the meeting on 11th January. Between then and 16th March inclusive (the First *Interim Report* was signed on 8th March) there were five more meetings. Details of these meetings do not seem to have survived, but the eventual *Report* is so clearly related to the *Memoranda* that they were obviously devoted to working out in greater detail the ideas there contained.

(ii) THE FIRST INTERIM REPORT AND THE NORMS OF COLLECTIVE BARGAINING

The Committee had been instructed to make and consider, not only suggestions for securing a permanent improvement in the relations between employers and employed but also means for ensuring the industrial conditions affecting the relationship between employers and employed could be systematically reviewed with a view to improving them in future. It was, then, a wide-ranging brief and the Committee found it necessary to make its *Report* in five separate documents. One of these, the most important by far, is the first interim, 'the' *Whitley Report*.[1] The last, the fifth, merely summarised the findings and recommendations of the other four. It contained the famous caveat by Clynes, Hobson, Lawrence, Mallon and M. Wilson welcoming the Councils if through them minimum conditions and common interests could be improved and forwarded. It welcomed, too, the tendency towards industrial peace, but warned that 'a complete identity of interests between capital and labour cannot thus be effected and that such machinery cannot be expected to furnish a settlement for the more serious conflicts of interest involved in the working of an economic system primarily governed and directed by the motives of private profit'.[2]

The *Second Report*[3] was based on a distinction which was found to be unnecessary so that it merges with the *First Report*; the *Supplementary Report on Works Committees*,[4] the *Third Report*, does not by definition concern us here and the *Fourth Report*, on *Conciliation and Arbitration*,[5]

[1] Signed 8th March 1917, S.P. 1917/18, XVIII.
[2] Signed 1st July 1918, S.P. 1918, VIII.
[3] It dealt with J.I.C.s in the less well-organised trades, was signed on 18th October 1917, and is in S.P. 1918, X.
[4] Signed 18th October 1917, S.P. 1918, XIV.
[5] Signed 31st January 1918, S.P. 1918, VII. See below, p. 222.

dealt with one aspect of the organisational norm only. It is important here only in so far as it shows that the Committee was aware of the need for a final stage arbitration beyond that provided by the industry. The *First Interim Report* then is our concern. In that *Report*[1] the Committee noted that it was firstly interested in

> the problem of establishing permanently improved relations between employers and employed in the main industries of the country, in which there exist representative organisations on both sides. The present Report accordingly deals more especially with these trades.

Wartime conditions helped them in their task; they offered:[2]

> a great opportunity for securing a permanent improvement in the relations between employers and employed, while . . . It is generally allowed that the war almost enforced some reconstruction of industry and . . . we have kept in view the need for securing in the development of reconstruction the largest possible measure of co-operation between employers and employed . . . that after the war the co-operation of all classes established during the war should continue and more especially with regard to the relations between employers and employed.

The factors in its favour, as the Committee saw them, were the awareness that something must be done to improve industrial relations, the necessity for reconstruction enforced by the war and the spirit of co-operation between the classes, especially in industry, evidenced during it. For securing this improvement:

> it is essential that any proposals put forward should offer the workpeople the means of attaining improved conditions of employment and a higher standard of comfort generally and involve the enlistment of their active and continuous co-operation in the promotion of industry; to this end the establishment for each industry of an organisation representative of employers and workpeople, to have as its object the regular consideration of matters affecting the progress and well being of the trade from the point of view of all those engaged in it, as far as this is consistent with the general interest of the community, appears to us necessary.

[1] Para. 3. [2] Ibid., para. 5.

These paragraphs 3 to 5 are the heart of the *Report.* They establish the end and purpose for which its recommendations are intended as well as, in principle, the means by which they are to be obtained. Collectively they recommend that in well-organised trades, the wage-earners should be provided with the means by which, in the spirit of 'co-operation established during the war', they may join in making industry more efficient and, in so doing, secure for themselves the better standard of living they seek. In other words the link between increased productivity and increased earnings is in principle appreciated and the Committee wished that it should be realised. It did not, however, see that the general conditions which would make it realistic for unions to share its enthusiasm were lacking, and the Councils did not begin to develop productivity bargaining. The *Report* continued:

7. With a view to providing means for carrying out the policy outlined above, we recommend that His Majesty's Government should propose without delay to the various associations of employers and employed, the formation of joint standing Industrial Councils in the several industries in which they do not exist, composed of representatives of employers and employed, regard being paid to the various sections of the industry and the various classes of labour engaged.
9. The Councils should meet at regular intervals.
10. The objects to which the consideration of the Councils should be directed should be appropriate matters affecting the several industries and particularly the establishment of closer co-operation between employer and employed. Questions concerning demobilisation will call for early attention.

Despite the emphasis on post-war problems the recommendations were long term with long-term improvements in mind. What exactly the committee was referring to in suggesting that some well-organised industries already possessed Joint Industrial Councils is not clear.[1] The phrase echoes one in Whitley's *Minute.*[2] It probably indicates no more than the confusion of the thinking behind it—a confusion compounded of a desire to say something new while not implying criticism of those who thought themselves 'well organised'. The fact

[1] The only J.I.C. in being at this time was the painters and decorators (*Garton Foundation Report on the Industrial Council for the Building Industry*, p. 45. The *Decorators and Painters Magazine*, 16th April 1917). If it is on this the statement was based, the Council was hardly a working model. The Committee regarded the organisation of some industries relevant (above, pp. 95–6).

[2] Above, p. 100.

is that it was for 'well-organised' trades that its recommendations were meant. The inference is that what was 'well organised' before the war was not good enough now.

> 12. The matters to be considered by the Councils inevitably differ widely from industry to industry as different circumstances and conditions call for different treatment, but we are of the opinion that the suggestions set forth below ought to be taken into account, subject to such modification in each case as may serve to adapt them to the needs of the various industries.
>
> 13. In the well-organised industries one of the first questions to be considered should be the establishment of local and works organisations to supplement and make more effective the work of the central bodies. It is not enough to secure co-operation at the centre between the national organisations; it is equally necessary to enlist the activity and support of employers and employed in the districts and in individual establishments. The National Industrial Council should not be regarded as complete in itself; what is needed is a triple organisation in the workshops, the districts and nationally. Moreover it is essential that the organisation at each of these three stages should proceed on a common principle, and that the greatest measure of common action among them should be secured.

Experience was to show that the problems of establishing this structure were very great; works committees required singularly favourable conditions. They were not considered seriously as part of the industrial relations structure in the majority of the J.I.C.s. District Councils also were in many cases superfluous, although in others it was the district rather than the national council which had the real power.

The scope of the work of the Councils is the subject of paragraph 16.

> 16. Among the questions with which it is suggested that the national councils should deal or allocate to district councils or works committees the following may be selected for special mention:
>
> (i) The better utilisation of the practical knowledge and experience of the workpeople.
>
> (ii) Means for securing to the workpeople a greater share in and responsibility for the determination and observance of the conditions under which their work is carried on.
>
> (iii) The settlement of the general principles governing the conditions of employment, including the methods of fixing,

paying and readjusting wages, having regard to the need for securing to the workpeople a share in the increased prosperity of the industry.

(iv) The establishment of regular methods of negotiation for issues arising between employers and workpeople with a view both to the prevention of differences and to their better adjustment when they appear.

(v) Means of ensuring to the workpeople the greatest possible security of earnings and employment without undue restriction upon change of occupation or employer.

(vi) Methods of fixing and adjusting earnings, piecework prices, etc., and of dealing with the many difficulties with regard to the method and amount of payment apart from the fixing of general standard rates, which are covered in paragraph (iii).

(vii) Technical education and training.

(viii) Industrial research and the full utilisation of its results.

(ix) The provision of facilities for the full consideration of inventions and improvements designed by workpeople and for the adequate safeguarding of the rights of the designers and workpeople.

(x) Improvement of processes, machinery and organisation and appropriate questions relating to management and the examination of industrial experiments with special reference to co-operation in carrying new ideas into effect and full consideration of the workpeople's point of view in relation to them.

(xi) Proposed legislation affecting industry.

These aims embraced *first* some of the traditional collective bargaining functions [(iii) and (vi)] though the linking of 'methods of fixing, paying and readjusting wages, having regard to the need for securing to the workpeople a share in the increased prosperity of industry' and the emphasis on security [(v)] marked a significant innovation. *Secondly*, they looked to the prevention of disputes by regular consultation and their speedy resolution if they developed. *Thirdly*, they hoped for the more active participation of the wage-earner by using his practical knowledge [(i) and (x)], his sense of responsibility [(ii)] and inventive powers [(ix)]. To this end they assumed that developments in the industry which affected them should be open to discussion with them [(x) and (xi)]. *Fourthly and finally*, they were concerned with education and research [(vii) and (viii)].

The four aims then were: (1) To put the normal collective bargaining functions in the context of security, increased production and an increased share in prosperity resulting. (2) The prevention of disputes and their easier settlement when they arose. (3) The more active involvement of the wage-earner at all levels and on all relevant subjects; this assumed the right of consultation on all matters affecting him. (4) The Councils were to encourage education and research.

It is not clear from the *Report* how the Councils related to existing collective bargaining structures.[1] From the fact that they were intended for well-organised industries and that it positively suggests[2] that District Councils could evolve out of existing negotiation machinery, it would seem that it was assumed that the National Councils would do the same, i.e. extend and improve the existing machinery. Paras 17 and 18 repeat once more the need to 'leave it to the trades themselves to form schemes suitable to their special circumstances', although the scheme should be put forward to the trade unions and employers generally and, at a suitable time, the general public. The possibility of government observers being at early meetings is mentioned in paras 19 and 20 and the necessity too of making sure that the Councils do not develop anti-social tendencies. Also:

> 21. It appears to us that it may be desirable at some later stage for the state to give the sanction of law to agreements made by the councils but the initiative in this direction should come from the councils themselves.

Repeating once again that this applies only in trades where 'fairly representative' associations on both sides exist, the *Report* presses the point[3] that it is

> 23. . . . our considered opinion that an essential condition of securing a permanent improvement in the relations between employers and employed is that there should be adequate organisation on the part of both employers and workpeople. The proposals outlined for joint co-operation through the several industries depend for their ultimate success upon there being such organisation on both sides; such organisation is necessary also to provide means whereby the arrangements and agreements made in industry may be effectively carried out.

[1] See below, p. 111. [2] Para. 14.

[3] A *Memorandum* surviving in the Ministry of Labour records, loc. cit., would seem to suggest that paras 23 and 24 are a later insertion; they appear almost verbatim as 'suggestions for new paragraphs'.

On the other hand, reflecting the fear that many trade unionists rightly had that any form of profit sharing was likely to bring with it suggestions of anti-unionism, as the deliberations of the British Association underlined:

> 24. We thought it well to refrain from making suggestions or offering opinions with regard to such matters as profit sharing, co-partnership, or particular systems of wages etc. It would be impracticable for us to make any useful general recommendations on such matters, having regard to the varying conditions in the different trades. We are convinced moreover that a permanent improvement in the relations between employers and employed must be founded on something other than a cash basis. What is wanted is that the workpeople should have a greater opportunity of participating in the discussion about the adjustment of those parts of industry by which they are most affected.

There is a great deal of wisdom in the reasoning of the first part of paragraph 24. The same cannot be said for that of the second. The contention that the permanent improvement looked for must be founded on something other than a cash basis is reminiscent of some of the rasher assumptions of the Garton *Memorandum*. To have suggested that good industrial relations were simply a matter of high wages would, of course, have been an error. But it was equally erroneous to suggest that the question of wages was so unimportant that the matter could be excluded from the pattern of considerations which provide the foundation of a good industrial relations system.[1] The co-operation norm without assurances on the primary substantive norms was not enough.

Of the last two paragraphs one is very apt, the other less so:

> 25. The schemes recommended in this *Report* are intended not merely for the treatment of industrial problems when they have become acute, but also, and more especially, to prevent their becoming acute. We believe that regular meetings to discuss industrial questions, apart from and prior to any differences with regard to them that may have begun to cause friction, will materially reduce the number of occasions on which, in the view of either employers or employed, it is necessary to contemplate recourse to stoppage of work.

[1] At a meeting in August 1917 at which the Ministry of Labour officials met to urge the *Report* on the members of A.S.L.E.F. it was made quite plain that the 'cash basis' was the most important thing. (M. of L., 331.883.)

If the collective bargaining system was to be improved, this was an important point; but in venturing

> 26. . . . to hope that representative men in each industry, with pride in their calling and care for its place as a contributor to the national well-being, will come together in the manner here suggested, and apply themselves to promoting industrial harmony and efficiency and removing the obstacles that have hitherto stood in the way.

—the *Report* made too evident the illusions of the time. The obstacles to harmony and efficiency were too deep-rooted and complex to be wished away by appeals to pride of calling and national well-being. In conditions of slump and unemployment which afflicted too many trades after the war they meant very little. The primary substantive norms had to be secured.

In summary: if we take the main points in the passages above quoted we find that, speaking of the industries in which 'Representative organisations of both sides exist', permanent improvement in industrial relations is to be achieved by making use of the circumstances of the time which have made co-operation possible and enforced reconstruction of industry. Proposals have to be such as to offer the workpeople improved conditions and a higher standard of comfort as well as enlisting their active and continuous support in the promotion of industry. Through three-tier Industrial Councils, the active participation of the wage-earners could be enlisted in the task of reconstruction, ensuring the greater productivity out of which the desired improved standard of living could be obtained and the active involvement of the wage-earner in all aspects of industrial life which affected him and to which he could make some real contribution. The Councils were not opposed to existing collective bargaining mechanisms and indeed the *Report* specifically states that strong organisation on both sides is the basis of everything. It did not however explicitly state how the existing collective bargaining mechanism could be meshed with the new three-tier structure. Yet there was nothing in it, as it stood in its original state as presented to the Reconstruction Committee, which encouraged the view that it wished to or would undermine the authority or the role of trade unionism and collective bargaining.

The *First Interim Report* of the Whitley Committee therefore intended to show how the wage-earner's claim for a better standard of living would be met from increased prosperity. This prosperity would in its turn be secured by getting his co-operation in the more effective reconstruction of industry. That participation involved getting his co-operation in the improvement of the existing methods and scope of collective bargaining and fully respected the rights and powers of free trade unionism. But it wished to attain that co-operation on a much wider range of matters affecting the technical and commercial well-being of the industry as well as the protection of the immediate interests of the trade union members.

Looking at the *Whitley Report* in terms of the norms laid down in the introduction, its recommendations covered most of them in whole or in part. Of the procedural norms, the *contractual co-operation* norm was the basis of the whole Whitley scheme. In building on the wartime spirit, it was building on an idea of equality between trade unions and employers in the industrial relationship which the war brought home as nothing else could have done. The two sides had been able to see each other as the legitimate representatives of legitimate interests, as co-operators in industry on the basis of self-interest. The exigencies of war ensured that they should. The war, on the other hand, also gave encouragement to those who rejected co-operation and wanted workers' control or nationalisation or both. They did not represent the mainstream of British trade unionism but the attraction of flashy slogans for the moment gave them real influence. There was no comparable reaction among the employers in wartime, but the hard conditions of the twenties were to show that those who spoke for the employers on labour matters were at heart at least as intransigent in the long run. Whereas the mainstream of British trade unionism thinking in the 1920's moved towards co-operation in a far more positive form than ever before, the employers who wished to reciprocate had to struggle against the tide of their own organisations.

The *organisation* norm was also specifically accepted and considerably extended and consolidated by the *Report*. Here too, it embodied the experience of the war in national bargaining—but it also emphasised the need for proper organisation at works, regional or district and national level and an intermeshing of the three. It emphasised that these must meet regularly and be standing, permanent organisations. Organisations of this kind far surpassed the normal standard of pre-war collective bargaining arrangements. The question of a Final Court of Appeal in industrial disputes was dealt with in the *Fourth Report*, but has its place here among the procedural norms too.

The *interpretation and application* norm was only mentioned by implication—for example in para 16 (iv) it emphasised 'issues arising' and the prevention and adjustment of differences; many of these come in fact from the need to interpret or apply existing agreements. The *codification* of agreements is likewise only mentioned by implication. As stressed before, it follows from a well-organised system, all the parts of which need to be present before codification makes real sense. The experience of the best of the Whitley Councils was that this was the case.

The *Report* emphasised the *minimum wages and conditions* norm in so far as it stressed the need to provide higher wages and good conditions. It is a little short on specifics for reasons mentioned above. It is specific, however, on the need to agree on the *norms for adjustment* [para 16 (iii)] though again it does not lay down the standards of that adjustment and for the same reason. The *Report* innovates, however, in the scope it gives to the development of the range of substantive agreements.

The full range of the substantive norms outlined in the same paragraph permitted the negotiation of fringe benefits, many matters that have since been the subject of legislation (redundancy, holidays with pay, improvements in safety and health provisions), as well as the more positive aspects of bargaining which we can see in retrospect may be said to contain the elements of the productivity agreement, although as already emphasised, the essential pre-conditions for its development did not exist. The *Report* however did indicate that there should be a wider range of agreements and that on many issues it should be possible to find a formula with which to link the demand for increased earnings with that for increased efficiency and productivity. Paragraph 16 above conjures up the vision of a collective bargaining system in which the efforts of the wage-earners are recruited in perfecting processes and techniques [sections (i), (vii), (viii), (ix) and (x)] while improving wages, hours and conditions in the context of increased security, prosperity and work satisfaction [sections (ii), (iv), (v), (ix), (x)]. All the main elements of productivity bargaining are here though lacking not only a credible economic and social context, but any real logical sequence in themselves. Yet as an insight into the development of a more mature and rational pattern of collective bargaining, the *Report*, and this paragraph in particular, has great value.

(iii) THE REPORT, THE RECONSTRUCTION COMMITTEE AND THE CABINET

The *Report* was passed to the newly formed Reconstruction Committee and approved by it in principle on 29th March,[1] though Mrs. Beatrice Webb, a member of the Wages and Employment Panel of the Recon-

[1] *Ministry of Reconstruction*, Rec. 1/41 Minutes of meeting, 29th March 1917.

struction Committee, was asked to draw up a *Memorandum* on the possible difficulties of promulgating the *Report*.[1] These she listed in some detail.[2] There was, she thought, no point in publishing such a *Report* unless it was part of a comprehensive plan for economic reconstruction. There was a danger that everything might be left to the industrial councils and that through them the government might escape its responsibilities especially in the matter of the restoration of pre-war practices. The Councils would also undermine the authority of trade unions by introducing profit-sharing schemes and they assumed too much about the possibilities of getting trade unions to work together. There were difficulties about the relationship of the Councils with existing collective-bargaining systems, about 'what was an industry', about majority votes deciding issues on such Councils and there was the danger that decision would be made binding on the whole of the industry by law.

Some of her objections make it possible to doubt whether Mrs. Webb had read the *Report* carefully, or, indeed, whether she had read it at all. It had made quite plain that it would *not* recommend the Councils to introduce profit-sharing schemes and that it had no intention of undermining the authority of trade unions; on the contrary it had insisted that without strong organisation on both sides nothing could be achieved.[3] To suggest that the result of the setting up of the Councils would be to do precisely what the *Report* said they should not do was a point of view that required substantiating. It is true that the *Report* was vague on the relationship of the Councils to the existing collective bargaining bodies and a clarification was asked of it on this point.[4] It revealed that Mrs. Webb's fears were groundless. The Reconstruction Committee replied to her objections in a document which took them point by point, revealing how little substance there was in them.[5] She had suggested that the railway and postal services, which had no collective bargaining system, might find the Councils useful; but the subcommittee wished the scheme to have far wider application than that.

[1] Rec. 1/41/50. The request was made on 30th March 1916. She notes in her *Diaries* (p. 87), 3rd June 1917, that she alone opposed the *Report*.

[2] Rec. 1/41/50.

[3] Above, p. 106.

[4] The *Report* was referred to the Wages and Employment Panel and Whitley was asked to attend its meeting on 24th April 1917 to discuss the matters raised (Rec. 1/41/64 and 66). The answers to the questions put to Whitley and Wilson were published as an Appendix to the *Report*. They made clear that fears regarding the supercession of collective bargaining and trade unionism were groundless. Relations between the J.I.C.s and existing machinery were for mutual arrangement. The Councils were to be formed of trade unionists and employer association representatives. Any binding powers would be freely agreed on. The restoration of trade practices was to be unaffected by the J.I.C.s.

[5] Rec. 1/41/58.

Mrs. Webb's own words are quoted to the effect that 'there may be a sphere in which a standing Council representing the employers' associations and all the trade unions connected with each industry might be generally useful in other industries and acceptable to the trade union world'. 'If this be so', comments the Reconstruction Committee, 'the case against the *Interim Report* falls to the ground as the Committee has not suggested any hard and fast scheme. The associations in an industry will determine the sphere of the Council for themselves.'[1] Far from the Committee's proposals weakening the trade union's their involvement in the councils would increase their effectiveness and authority. As to 'what is an industry', if it was such a problem 'the process of federation and amalgamation would not have proceeded as far as it has already'.[2] Industry knew what an industry was even though it could not define such an entity with complete precision.

As to the suggestion that the proposals are a leap in the dark, 'the suggestion of the *Report* is that certain machinery should be regularised, systematised and considerably extended. In one sense it is a normal development; in another sense it is a new development. It would for example bring within the range of discussion questions which previously were considered to be no affair of workpeople or were neglected altogether.'[3]

> In conclusion it may be pointed out that the subcommittee has tried to devise, in general terms, a plan which would give opportunities for satisfying the growing demands made by trade unions for a share in 'industrial control'. It is admitted that the plan is not without difficulties, but it is suggested that so far as the organised trades are concerned it is the only practicable plan for dealing with the problems referred to the subcommittee.

In this latter observation the Committee is surely right. Whatever the defects of the Committee's report, the recommendations were based on a respect for traditional practices and were shrewdly designed to make the most of wartime gains without seeking to suggest that the millennium was around the corner. They were in line with the current consensus and suggested a labour policy for the government and the nation which was a great advance on pre-war. Had it been grasped with both hands from the outset by the trade union movement as a whole, as some of the more energetic and realistic grasped it later, it is possible that the general pattern of industrial relations might have been changed.

[1] Rec. 1/41/58. Conclusion (ii). [2] (c) (i). [3] *Certain General Points* (ii).

From the Reconstruction Committee the *Report* went to the Cabinet on 2nd May 1917.[1] A month later, on 6th June, a further recommendation was made that it should be published. The Cabinet responded not by recommending publication[2] but

> in the first instance the Ministry of Labour should circulate the Report to the leading trade unions and employers associations and also to the Commissioners on Industrial Unrest, with a view to ascertaining their general attitude to the proposed industrial Councils at an early date.[3]

Accordingly, the Commissions of Enquiry, which were appointed on 12th June, and went to work between the 13th and 25th, put the recommendations of the *Report* before the witnesses. On 28th June Montagu introduced the *Report* in the House and on the 29th it was published.[4] The months of July, August and September passed without further official action beyond the circulation of the *Report* and the work of the Ministry of Labour in publicising and giving help in establishing the Councils where they were asked for that assistance;[5] in the meantime public reaction continued to be favourable. On 26th September Roberts, whether on his own initiative or not is unclear, presented his report to the Cabinet on the state of affairs regarding the Whitley scheme. The 'question for decision' according to him was as follows:

> . . . in view of the wide interest taken in the *Report*, especially as a result of the endorsement of it by the Commissioners on Industrial Unrest, it is desirable that the Cabinet should approve or disapprove at an early date the principle of the *Report*. If the Cabinet approve the principle there will not be any need of legislation and the actual

[1] A *Memorandum* by Montagu drawn up at the Ministry's request suggested the procedure to be followed—a series of small conferences with trade unions and employers and a firm promise that pledges on pre-war practices would be met. Rec. 41/53, 2nd May 1917.

[2] The government did not take much notice of the Reconstruction Committee even though Lloyd George was technically at its head. Only one report of any of the numerous subcommittees went before it: this was the *Whitley Report*. Passfield Papers, loc. cit., fol. 454.

[3] Report by the Minister of Labour (G. H. Roberts) dated 26th September 1917, on the attitude of employers and employed to the *Whitley Report*, Cab. 24/27.

[4] From Montagu's words it would have seemed that the government was fully committed to the support of the Councils as a positive policy. 95 H.C. Deb. 5S, col. 595.

[5] Roberts, loc. cit., p. 1.

carrying out of recommendations will rest with trade unions and employers' associations but it will be necessary for the Ministry of Labour to approach the different bodies concerned to arrange conferences, draft schemes and generally to take steps to ensure that the proposals receive full consideration. Further the establishment of Joint Standing Industrial Councils on the government's suggestion, although the basis of the councils will be voluntary, implies a degree of government recognition hitherto conceded to no industrial association and will be regarded as entitling the new organisation to a special position in relation to the government.

After reviewing the results of the enquiries made and the difficulties facing the Councils the memorandum concluded that:

> Briefly the recommendation of the *Whitley Report* is that the government should ask the existing association in each industry to organise themselves in such a way that they can adjust their difficulties and prepare for the period of reconstruction without troubling the rest of the community, and at the same time give the workers the opportunity for which they are asking of taking a part in shaping the conditions under which they work. If the associations do not respond, the recommendations fall to the ground; but in view of the body of opinion which has been collected it is very unlikely that an invitation from the government will meet with a refusal. It will be necessary however that the government should give some indication as to the functions and status of the Councils when formed.

To this end he suggests that the Councils be given an important role in handling problems relevant to transition to peace, that they be officially recognised as the consultative committees for the industry and that they be asked to undertake the extension of conciliation machinery where necessary and the setting up of the District and Works Councils for the scheme as in the *Report*. If it is granted that the principle of the scheme—that there is some common interest in each industry which requires an organ of expression—is sound, then there is no doubt that there is value in possessing in the main industries a representative machinery allowing adjustment of differences.

> If however the government proposes to adopt the *Report* it is desirable that it should do so promptly. The reports of the Commissions on Industrial Unrest have raised expectations which will

> easily turn to bitterness if disappointed and the wide circulation of the *Whitley Report* has prepared people's minds for action on the lines it proposes. Moreover the Commissioners' support of the *Whitley Report* is based quite as much in the need of industry during the war as on the problems which will confront it afterwards. The *Whitley Report* provides a great opportunity for reconciling the conflicting interests which are at present manifesting themselves in so many directions and of building up a permanent constitution for the great industries which will enable them to face the difficulties of reconstruction strong and united, instead of being engaged on internal warfare, which may otherwise be the case when peace comes.

On 5th October Addison, the Minister of Reconstruction, asked Hankey to 'bring up the *Whitley Report* at the Cabinet'.[1] On the 9th it was approved and on 20th October a new circular was sent to employers and unions asking them to implement the *Report*. On the 25th of the same month, 'we announced our official adoption of the *First Report* and expressed our hope that it would be carried into effect'.[2]

There is every indication that the reason for the government's support was expediency rather than conviction. Mrs. Webb's objections seem to have had great impact—perhaps these provided a required excuse. The government, on the other hand, was very concerned about the menace of industrial unrest which had, or seemed to have, connections with revolutionary interests and from that point of view the Councils served their purpose and their support had a practical use.[3] But one is struck by the contrast between Lloyd George's words at the first meeting of the reorganised reconstruction committee in March 1917,[4] those in which Montagu introduced the *Report* to the House, and the government's refusal to follow the Reconstruction Committee's recommendation as to procedure. This procedure

[1] *Four and a half years* (London 1934), Vol. 2, p. 435.

[2] Lloyd George, *Memoirs*, p. 1161.

[3] On 1st June 1917, just after the greatest period of wartime unrest, Barnes circulated a *Memorandum* to the Cabinet on the shop stewards' movement; he stressed that works committees on an elective basis are an antidote to extremist activities; he quotes the Hotchkiss Works, Coventry. He 'understands' that the *Whitley Report* recommends works committees. In August 1917 Lord Milner caused to be circulated to the Cabinet a *Report* by Professor E. V. Arnold of Bangor University in which it was said that 'the number of loyal and patriotic workers, once very large, is dwindling'. He accuses the Commissions of enquiry of missing the point. Barnes, in a rejoinder also circulated, scoffs at the fears and insists that the extremists have been rebuffed. Cab. 24/14/GT/897; Cab. 24/24/GT/1849 and Cab. 24/26/GT/2073.

[4] Above, p. 82.

would have introduced the scheme through conferences between the Prime Minister and leaders of industry. Even more striking is the slowness of the government to give the lead in introducing the Councils among its own employees.[1] The government had much else on its mind of course, but there is little doubt that the fullest propaganda advantage was taken of the *Whitley Report* in 1917–18 without any conviction as to its real value.

(iv) THE REPORT, THE PRESS AND INDUSTRY

In his report to the Cabinet Roberts asserted:

> The *Report* was received with great interest by the press. All the morning and evening papers devoted leading articles to it and published large extracts. The comments were all favourable, though some did not see in the proposals of the *Report* more than a suggestion for extending and improving conciliation machinery. The weekly press was in the main, equally favourable, but hostile criticism both of the practicability and of the desirability of the proposals was the line taken by the *New Statesman* and the *New Age*. The labour press, with the exception of the *Labour Leader*, was in the main favourable. The technical and the employers' organs were divided, the fear being expressed by some that the scheme of the *Report* would lead to undue interference with management.

The Times[2] on 3rd July spoke of the plan as sound and the Committee's observations of points of administration as full of good sense; it warned, however, against the men of bad will who would try to thwart it. For the *Morning Post* of 2nd July it was plain that anyone who had reflected on the lessons the war had taught must welcome it. The *Daily Telegraph* on 30th June was not blind to the difficulties of putting the *Report* into practice but expressed a fair hope that it could be done. The *Daily News* and the *Daily Chronicle* on the same day, 30th June, were enthusiastic; the former said it would not be surprised if this was not the most important seed sown by the war in this country. For the *Westminster Gazette* on the 29th the lesson was that employers had to wake up to the fact that their employees in future would require more consideration, treatment as human beings. The *Observer* of 1st July

[1] Below, p. 123 and footnotes.

[2] The reaction of the press was closely watched and the main comments collected for the Minister of Labour. Lab. 2/229/2469/12.

regarded the scheme suggested by Whitley as 'opportune and pertinent', the *Economist*, 7th July, hoped that the Councils would be set up without delay; the *Pall Mall Gazette* on the 29th congratulated the Committee on its work and the *Manchester Guardian* of the 29th also saw the advantages of the Committee's recommendations. The *New Statesman* was less sure; while welcoming on 7th July the abandonment of the idea that the employer was always right, it doubted whether the scheme would work; the *Nation* on 30th June had pointed out that something more radical was needed; the employer did not in fact own industry, the community did and should act accordingly. The *Labour Leader* gave the *Report* short shrift as Roberts noted.

The trade press was considerably more sceptical. *Engineering*, 13th July, saw the whole thing as a final subjection of industry to the control of the trade unions; the *Iron and Coal Trades Review* on the 6th of the same month saw a certain common sense in some of the proposals but also the possibility of the employers losing control. *Fairplay* was uncompromising; its opinion, expressed on 5th July, was that by the Council's 'control would be taken completely out of the hands of the employers'. The *Colliery Guardian* on the other hand was ready to see the scheme as necessary for the post-war convalescence of industry even though it was a little rigid. The *Cotton Factory Times* of 6th July exhorted those unions which could make use of it to do so; for itself, the cotton industry did not need it. The *Railway Review* of 13th July did not regard it as sufficient; the democratisation of industry was needed if the workers were to have new status. Taking a more optimistic view the *Daily Herald* of 7th July saw the Whitley Councils as a means for the unions to press their claims but futile if they were allowed to be merely conciliatory organisations.

The immediate reaction from the trade unions and the employers was a little unclear though tending on the whole to be more favourable than less. This turned out to be illusory and the true attitude seemed to have been more accurately reflected in the trade press. The vagueness of the *Report* itself at crucial points did not help. Nor was the situation eased by doubts concerning the exact status of the councils and their relationship with government and industry. The confusion was increased by the differing methods used in the official sounding of opinion.

When the decision to circulate the *Report* to the interested parties had been taken in June a letter was prepared to accompany the copy of the *Report* sent to each.[1] It stressed that post-war problems demanded the existence of some mechanism to ensure the discussion of those problems by those involved in industry. The proposals of the Whitley

[1] Cab. 24/27/ p. 323.

Committee were forwarded to obtain the opinion of industry on them and a reply was requested within a month. If it was eventually decided to adopt the *Report,* then each of the trades affected, and it was stressed that these were the well-organised trades, would be invited to discuss ways and means. Special officers were appointed to give any information and assistance required and they were ready and able to attend conferences on the matters involved, in London or the provinces. By the end of September, seven trade unions, three employers' associations and two joint conferences had invited the presence of these officers and five others had made application for their services.[1] The letter and the copies of the *Report* were forwarded to 146 trade unions, thirty-seven federations of trade unions, 107 employers' associations and federations. The T.U.C. parliamentary committee, the G.F.T.U., and the F.B.I. were also sent copies of the *Report* and by the end of September between 10,000 and 11,000 had been distributed.

Of the 209 organisations approached, 103 replied.[2] None opposed in principle, though five objected to the scheme being applied to their own industries, eighty-six expressly approved and twelve approved with reservations. The *Report* by Roberts mentioned that the Ministry's enquiries showed that the Builders, Painters and Decorators, China, Pottery and the Printing trade were already setting up, or had set up, Councils of the same general kind. Not surprisingly then the building unions which replied were on the whole favourable. These included the Operative Stonemasons, the Carpenters and Joiners and the Painters. The Pottery Workers, the Printers and the Iron and Steel Trades Confederation were favourable too. Textile unions were split. The Cotton Spinners were against, the Amalgamated Weavers and the General Union of Textile Workers for the scheme. According to the returns, the A.S.E., Railway Clerks, the N.U.R., A.S.L.E.F. and the N.T.W.F. were in favour, which would cast doubt on their reliability.[3] The responses of the employers also present some obvious and some less obvious features. The Building Trades Employers were in favour—but so was the Mining Association; the mining unions' attitude made it impossible to put the seriousness of the Association's resolve to the test. There was no reply from the Engineering Employers, despite the presence of Smith on the Committee. The Railway Companies Asso-

[1] Roberts, loc. cit., p. 1.

[2] Roberts, loc. cit., pp. 1–2. The details of the replies are given in an appendix to Cab. 24/27. 'Schedule of societies who have given their opinion on the proposals contained in the *Whitley Report.*'

[3] The A.S.E., of course, rejected the *Report.* Pribićević, op. cit., p. 38. So too did the railwaymen: above, pp. 83 and 117, and below, p. 121.

ciation sent no reply either; the Printers and Potters and the Cotton Spinners were in favour.

The T.U.C. circularised its affiliates on 24th July telling them of the receipt of the *Report*[1] and of its acceptance of the general terms of the recommendations embodied therein, which it said appeared to suggest that all machinery set up to deal with industrial differences between employers' associations and trade unions should be established on a voluntary basis and secured by mutual agreement. In the debate Bevin expressed surprise that the T.U.C. had no subcommittee on reconstruction keeping an eye on such matters. He suggested that without it the movement was missing a great opportunity.[2] Smillie, a member of the Committee, emphasised that the *Report* did not cover the industries which already had machinery for avoiding disputes;[3] it certainly did not apply to mining. In the event the *Report* was referred to a subcommittee. Congress appeared to have suspended judgement on the *Report* rather than accepting it positively as Roberts' report would suggest.[4]

The National Alliance of Employers and Employed welcomed the *Report* with enthusiasm.[5] The Federation of British Industries at this period saw itself as an organisation concerned with the general principles of industrial relations. It published on 3rd August 1917, its own *Recommendations* on the *Report*,[6] welcoming it, as its reply to the official enquiry also showed, but being cautious about works and District Committees which it said should only be allowed to develop in the light of need and experience. Its recommendations put emphasis on a representative National Industrial Council for all industry with councils for each industry and each trade section and each works within it. The reports of the reception of the Committee's proposal which came from the Commissions of Enquiry were encouraging. All the Commissions endorsed its general principles; that for the Yorkshire area did not mention it specifically but endorsed the general idea.[7]

[1] *Report of the T.U.C. Congress, 1917*, p. 183. [2] Ibid., pp. 226–7. [3] Ibid., p. 228.
[4] Ibid., p. 235. Roberts, in fact, was anxious concerning rumours that the T.U.C. had turned the *Report* down. *T.U.C. Report*, 1918, p. 88. The final verdict of the T.U.C. given in April 1918 was in favour, despite reservations.
[5] The *Objects* of the National Alliance of Employers and Employed make mention of them, though they note with concern that it was only designed for well-organised trades.
[6] *Recommendations on the Whitley Report*, F.B.I., 3rd August 1917.
[7] S.P. 1917–18, XV. The *Report* for the *North East* (p. 10) expressed itself 'thoroughly in accord with the underlying principles'; the *North West* (p. 22) put the *Report* before the leading trade unionists and employers and, though desirous of examining it at greater length, all were in cordial approval of the basic principles; *Yorks and East Midlands*, as noted, did not mention it specifically but (p. 4) endorsed principles in accord with it; *West Midlands* (p. 10) recommended that the *Report* be implemented; *London and the South East* (p. 6) saw the proposals as the natural line of development;

In July–September 1917, therefore, there seemed to be general acceptance of what the *Report* was trying to do and of the way it was trying to do it. Events were, however, to show that this was an illusion. It was as if the *Report* was, to both the majority of employers and trade unionists, a temporary diversion thrust upon them by the government and to whose general pieties they did not think it decent to give too discouraging an answer at the time.[1] The war had changed basic attitudes very little throughout the industry as a whole. The major unions, as we have noted, were demanding nationalisation and/or workers' control and were too conscious of the new-found power they possessed to seek to build up slowly on the foundations of pre-war and the more moderate wartime gains. The employers were, on the whole, still adherents of the more conservative views on industrial relations and economic policy and in the issue had no illusion about what would determine the pattern of industrial relations after the war. Government departments themselves were among the most reluctant to give effect to the *Report* and one of the most interesting results of its acceptance was the way in which, for the first time, the government as a major employer was compelled to work out its own labour policy.[2] It is beyond doubt that, for those who read it carefully and realistically assessed the situation, the *Report* offered the means of consolidating wartime gains and changes in the most effective way possible. Many of those in the union movement who poured such scorn upon it were hurting no one but the average trade unionist. Yet at the time the welcome, such as it was, given to it, was based less on an appreciation of its real merits than on a wish not to be too long diverted by disputing it. It was, to many who considered themselves abreast of events, not really worth the effort of lengthy refutation.

The *Reports* of the Ministry of Labour intelligence section early in 1918 are more revealing of true attitudes than the official enquiries.[3] In the Clyde district the Engineering and Shipbuilding Federation was very much on the defensive;[4] employers passively resisted attempts

the *South West* (p. 5) found it acceptable to the employers and wage-earners and the witnesses in *Wales and Monmouthshire* (p. 30) found that 'quite a large number' of 'employers and employed were in favour'.

[1] *Engineering*, which had on 13th July rejected the *Report*, was prepared to accept it on 19th October; it did so, however, with so many restrictions that it is clear the basic attitude was still opposition.

[2] In a paper for the Cabinet on the subject on 18th June 1918, Bonar Law was moved to point out what was involved 'assuming the government does accept the *Whitley Report*'. Cab. 24/5/213 21st June 1918.

[3] Ministry of Labour, 331.883. *U.K. M. of L. Intelligence section. Report on Trade Conferences 1918.*

[4] 2nd February 1918.

to get it put into practice, only the works committees, of a purely advisory nature, were considered favourably. From Manchester it was reported on 15th December 1917 that the publication of the *Report* and the government's acceptance of it had seriously prejudiced the policy of establishing joint industrial councils. The Engineering Employers' Federation in Birmingham approved of the *Report* on the dubious grounds that the industry they were in had had Councils since 1896. Sympathetic consideration was given by a group of trade unionists meeting in the same city, but they refused to consider a meeting with employers on the matter.[1] At Liverpool on 15th February there was some sharp questioning of Clay and others on why the government had not implemented the *Report* in the Post Office; in that city suspicion of both it and the government was the dominant mood. The Leeds Conference with the United Garment Makers expressed the opinion that the real problem was the hostile attitude of employers to the unions. Yet another in London with A.S.L.E.F. members proved that the *Report* was regarded by them with derision. The Hosiery Federation, representing nearly 30,000 employees in the trade, meeting at Leicester, approved as did a conference of bobbin manufacturers and another of electrotypers and stereotypers; worsted workers and those in the boot and shoe trade in the Leeds area were also generally in favour

In summary, it is true to say that 'the warmest reception of the first report came from more or less neutral quarters',[2] from those industrialists or trade unionists who for one reason or another were convinced that the change in attitudes was deep and real or from those few industries—building, pottery and printing—in which particular circumstances had given experiments akin to the Whitley Councils a toehold already. But the Whitley scheme was never accepted by industry as a whole and on any effective level as the basis for organisation or reorganisation of industrial relations. Nor was it fully accepted by the government, now or later, as the basis of an effective labour policy to be pursued with vigour.

[1] Ibid. Yet another *Report* (Rec. 1/71/2/7249) told of a conference on the subject at Manchester on 8th and 9th December 1917 and of a 'considerable body of opposition to the *Whitley Report* on the part of a section of the audience, composed principally of shop stewards. It is clear that the Ministry of Reconstruction will labour under considerable difficulties because of the suspicion with which the proposals of the government will be regarded.' The most bitter speech was from a wounded ex-soldier from Gallipoli who had had his pre-war job kept for him—at pre-war rates of 19s. a week.

[2] Fabian Research Department Memo No. 6. *The Whitley Reports and their application*, August 1918.

6

The Joint Industrial Councils scheme

(i) THE SCOPE OF THE SCHEME

The circumstances in which the Whitley scheme was set up, the nature of the industrial relations system it was concerned to improve, the report itself, the subsequent observations of its chairman,[1] its reception and the activities of the Ministry of Labour Industrial Councils Division in concentrating on the private and public utility sectors in establishing the Councils,[2] indicate that it was with the improvement of industrial relations in this sector, and above all in private competitive industry, that the *Report* was concerned. It was only after second thoughts that the Committee turned its attention to government departments and only after much pressure that Councils were set up here.[3] They were singularly successful in the Civil Service but they were

[1] 'Originally the Committee thought of what are called ordinary industrial relations.' Quoted by L. White, *The Whitley Councils in the British Civil Service* (Chicago 1933) p. 5.
[2] It was pointed out in the *Second Report* (loc. cit., para. 24) that the efforts of the Ministries had been confined to this area; it entered a plea for the Councils to be established in government service. On the difficulties of putting the *Second Report* into practice see the *Memorandum* by the Ministries of Labour and Reconstruction (S.P. 1918, XXII) and the *Report on the Establishment*, etc., pp. 13–14. The I.I.R.C.s were a stop-gap measure to meet difficulties. (*Report on the working of the Ministry of Reconstruction*, S.P. 1918, XIII.)
[3] Bonar Law, loc. cit., reminded his colleagues that as early as 18th December 1917 the House had been promised action. He referred to the pressures being brought to bear, especially by the Labour press, to this end. It is possible that fears about the loyalty of Civil Servants in the industrial troubles of 1918–19 gave the task an extra urgency. Setting up Councils in Industrial Establishments presented little difficulty. By October 1918 this was accomplished. The clerical and other sections were more difficult and it was July 1919 before the National Joint Council was established. There were fifty-four members distributed between the Post Office Association (10) the Civil Service Federation (5) and the smaller organisations on the employees' side; there were in addition some seventy separate councils for the various departments. White, op. cit., pp. 6 ff. and p. 40. *Report on the Establishment and Progress of J.I.C.s*, pp. 54 ff.

also applied with significant success in a group of private industries and public utilities which between them employed several times as many.[1]

The most significant area of experiment for the Whitley Councils was in fact 'ordinary' industry because it was here, where commercial considerations predominated, that the problem of industrial relations had to be solved, if solved it could be. It is with J.I.C.s in this sector that the following pages will be concerned.

The scheme was, of course, intended to improve industrial relations throughout the whole of organised industry. In fact few of the major trades adopted it even for a brief time. But enough did, and enough smaller but still significant industries did, to make their study return significant results concerning the effect of Whitleyism on industrial relations in the sector for which it was intended.

(ii) THE COUNCILS TO BE EXAMINED

There are three main difficulties to be faced in examining the way that the Whitley scheme worked in private industry and the public utilities. The first is that it is not easy to say exactly what a Whitley Council was in practice so great was the range of modification introduced in the J.I.C.s. For the purpose of this study it has been assumed that where an organisation had been set up in response to the *Report* and consciously based on its recommendations and where the organisation had practical effects on some aspects of industrial relations, there a Whitley Joint Industrial Council existed even if it did not handle primary substantive issues. The railway industry presents a typical problem. Its collective bargaining structure was reorganised before the Whitley Scheme was grafted on to it; the way that the scheme was applied to the industry was in any case unique. But the modifications introduced as a result of the scheme did have practical effect and did consolidate important aspects of collective negotiation and procedures. A much more important reflection is that it was the existence of the Whitley scheme, and the possibility of appeal to it, which enabled Lloyd George and J. H. Thomas to reach agreement on an industrial relations system for the reorganised railway structure

[1] The *Directory of J.I.C.s* 1920 lists some 300,000 in the Civil Service; in addition some 88,000 in industrial establishments and 6,000 employed by the Ministry of Works. At this time there were nearly three million covered by other J.I.C.s.

which would meet the needs of both sides. The second difficulty is that it is not possible to say with any accuracy just how many Councils operated effectively at any one time or over the whole period. The third is that even if the exact number was known and the records of all were carefully preserved, the examination of them would not necessarily yield meaningful results for a survey of this kind.

The lack of adequate statistics and records stems from the tenuous and brief existence of some Councils and the consequent lack or disappearance of records; it also owes something to the uncertain status of the Councils and the anomalies in their relationship with the Ministry of Labour,[1] in particular its lack of power over them in any way, the absence of a right representation on them and of any obligation to keep it informed of their activities. Its information at any one time was patchy, as it recognised,[2] and its records were accordingly incomplete. In fact, after 1933 it lost interest altogether and ceased to keep even the records it had kept hitherto.

The irrelevance of some of the Councils to a study of this kind is that they were so small that calling them industries for purposes of classification does not necessarily give them a significance in the present context. The building industry, with upwards of 800,000 employees when the Council was set up, and the seed crushing and compound cake industry, with its 2,000 or so, are clearly different kinds of animal—yet they both possessed J.I.C.s. Whatever the answer to the question 'What is an industry?' is, it does not make sense to consider the lessons of the experience of one in the same category as the other. On the other hand to decide what size an industry must be to enable it to rate as large enough to be significant and to be used as a basis of comparison, involves some kind of exercise in arbitrariness. If six-figure employment is too large a minimum, four figures would seem too small. A reasonable compromise perhaps then would be a minimum employment of 10,000. Furthermore, a clear picture of the working of the scheme can only come from an inspection of Councils which survived the period—but several other J.I.C.s which were significant in one way or another are also examined despite their early demise

For all practical purposes the establishment of J.I.C.s stopped after 1921; there were twenty formed in 1918, thirty-two in 1919, sixteen

[1] Discussed in greater detail below, pp. 256 ff.

[2] Official *Memoranda* in Lab. 2/1309/671 (parts one and two), contain data compiled to deal with questions about the Councils. They show how incomplete its information was. Official replies and publications were all well qualified with phrases like 'within the knowledge of the department'.

in 1920 and six in 1921—seventy-four in all.[1] Of these, seven were in the Civil Service or government industrial establishments so that to that date sixty-seven were possibles for our inspection. By 1923 the figure was sixty-two—allowing for seventeen Councils that went out of existence and twelve I.I.R.C.s which became full J.I.C.s. Among these sixty-two, which on average during 1919–39 employed some 2·05 million workers,[2] there was a group of twenty, each of which employed more than 10,000 (and in fact they accounted for more than 1·8 million of the 2·05 million) which survived the period. It is on these, and on four which did not survive but existed for a period in important industries, that our attention will be concentrated.

Table 1: *Employment in certain industries*

(a) Where the J.I.C. did not survive until 1939

Industry	*Approximate No. Employed*[3]
1. Building	800,000
2. Boots and shoes	215,000
3. Papermaking	60,000
4. Wool and allied	280,000
Total	1,355,000

[1] *Report on the Establishment and Progress of J.I.C.s*, pp. 26–7 and 31; these figures do not include the railway's industrial relations system which was partly modelled on Whitleyism; it has been included, as one Council, in this seventy-four. That an industry and J.I.C.s appeared in the Ministry's figures does not mean it had any effective existence as attempts to hunt out records from at least one trade association revealed.

[2] This figure excludes the 250,000 employed in maritime services which did come under a J.I.C. Powell, op. cit., p. 36. But industrial relations in shipping took a strange turn in the 1920's and they constitute a study on their own.

[3] The average employment is for the period of the existence of the Council in so far as it can be ascertained. The numbers given in the *Directory of J.I.C.s* for January 1920 and the *Bulletin of J.I.C.s*, July 1919, are used as a basis. The censuses of production 1924 and 1930–5 and of population 1931 have been utilised where possible though the census categories vary and they do not necessarily coincide with the industry's own view of its scope; other sources have been used where available (e.g. an article in *Unity*, January 1936, for municipal employments and public utilities). The figures of course refer to total employed in the industry, not to those in unions or represented on the Councils. The only real doubt concerning the approximate accuracy of the figures given is that for the Heating and Domestic Engineering J.I.C.; it does not appear as a separate industry on the Censuses and other sources suggest it employed something like 60,000–70,000; since the industry hardly employs this number today I have made a guess of what the correct figure should be.

(b) Where the J.I.C. was still in existence in 1939

Industry	*Approximate No. Employed*
5. Electrical cables	30,000
6. Cement	10,000
7. Chemicals	55,000
8. Docks	130,000
9. Electricity supply	55,000
10. Flour milling	25,000
11. Gas supply	100,000
12. Heating and domestic engineering	30,000(?)
13. Hosiery	110,000
14. Local authorities (manual workers)	160,000
15. Paint and varnish	25,000
16. Pottery	60,000
17. Printing	220,000
18. Quarrying	65,000
19. Railways	550,000
20. Silk	50,000
21. Soap and candles	30,000
22. Tinplate	25,000
23. Tramways	75,000
24. Water supply	30,000
	Total 1,835,000

The detailed industrial relations characteristics of the J.I.C.s are discussed at length in subsequent chapters. The characteristics given on pages 128–9 have been chosen to enable a general comparison to be made between the various types of industries concerned. Details of how the figures of *average employment* have been computed have already been given. The degree of *geographical concentration* varies widely even within the category. Cement manufacture, though mainly concentrated in one area, was and is spread throughout the country; tinplate and pottery on the other hand were highly localised. *Concentration of ownership* is not measured here with statistical exactness but simply to contrast the industries in which comparatively few firms controlled the majority of trade with those in which it was in the hands of very many. In Cable manufacture it was a group of some sixteen firms, in Cement one combine, the Associated Portland Cement Manufacturers and the British Portland Cement manufacturers, which controlled the majority of the output.[1] In Soap and Candles two large groups, Unilever and Hedley's, dominated, though others were not small;[2] in flourmilling Ranks and Spillers stayed ahead of the C.W.S., also large.[3] In heavy Chemicals I.C.I. was dominant after 1926 and in the railway transport industry only the four large groups existed after 1921. The *Growth* category indicates those whose product was in increasing demand, whether the demand was met in the main by increasing efficiency in the use of traditional methods (as in boots and shoes), by the shifting of resources (as in building), or in the improvement of organisation in some cases combined with the introduction of new materials, products or techniques (as in chemicals, hosiery and electricity). It contrasts with the category of comparative decline in which industries like pottery and railways found themselves.[4] The *sheltered industries* comprise those which were neither important export industries nor subject to sizable overseas competition at home. Well over half of those employed by J.I.C.s were in this category. *Protected by tariffs* before 1932 indicates a position of some privilege; general protection was not introduced until that year.[5] Dyestuffs, raw silk and vitrified pottery were so favoured. Boots and shoes came under the Merchandising Marks Act of 1925. Hosiery tried to obtain the same favour but failed. The measure could hardly in any case be considered an economically significant form of protection. *Average unemployment* figures were compiled from standard sources.[6]

[1] The C.M.A. were responsible for 90 per cent of the industry's output; Balfour Committee on Industry and Trade *Survey of the Metal Industries*, p. 304; P. L. Cook, *The Effect of Mergers* (Cambridge 1958), p. 90, shows 70 per cent of the cement trade controlled by the A.P.C.M.–B.P.C.M. group.

[2] Cook, op. cit., pp. 229 ff.; in the 1930's Unilever had half the capacity of the industry, Hedleys and C.W.S. most of the rest.

[3] H. V. Edwards in *Further Studies in Industrial Organisation* (London 1946), p. 44, shows Ranks and Spillers as controlling half the output in the 1930's.

[4] Pollard, op. cit., pp. 99 ff., 110 ff.

[5] F. Benham, *Great Britain under Protection* (New York 1941), pp. 25 ff. D. Abel, *A History of British Tariffs* (London 1945), pp. 27 ff.

[6] The *Twenty-second Abstract of Labour Statistics*, S.P. 1936–7, XXVI, the Annual Reports and other documents of the J.I.C.s and Mitchell and Deane, op. cit., p. 67.

Table 2: *Some characteristics of*

	1 Building	2 Boot/Shoe	3 Cables	4 Cement	5 Chemicals	6 Docks	7 Electricity	8 Flour Mills	9 Gas
Average number employed (000's) More than 200	x	x							
Between 100–200						x			x
50–100					x		x		
25–50			x					x	
Fewer than 25				x					
Manufacture/process		x	x	x	x			x	
Construction	x								
Service/transport						x	x	x	x
Extractive									
Industries with a marked degree of: geographical concentration		x		x					
concentration of ownership			x	x	x			x	
Based on skills requiring formal apprenticeship	x								
Growth industries	x	x	x	x	x		x		
Sheltered industries	x						x		x
Industries protected before 1932					x				
Average percentage unemployed 1919–39 (all industries 13%)	16	14	7	12	11	28	7	7	7
J.I.C.s dealing with wages and hours 1919–39			x	x	x	x	x	x	x
J.I.C.s extant 1939			x	x	x	x	x	x	x

the industries which had J.I.C.s

10	11	12	13	14	15	16	17	18	19	20	21	22	23	24
						x		x						x
	x	x												
				x	x		x	x	x		x	x		
x			x							x			x	
	x		x	x	x	x			x	x	x			x
x														
		x						x				x	x	
							x							
	x				x						x			x
								x		x				
x						x								
x	x		x	x		x	x						x	
x		x										x		
					x				x					
12	9	12	6	10	26	6	19	9	13	7	20	8	7	15
x	x	x	x				x	x		x	x	x	x	x
x	x	x	x		x	x	x	x	x	x	x	x	x	
Heating	Hosiery	Local Authorities	Paints/Varnish	Papermaking	Pottery	Printing	Quarrying	Railways	Silk	Soap/candles	Tinplate	Tramways	Water Supply	Wool

7

The establishment and organisation of the J.I.C.s

(i) THE ORGANISATION OF INDUSTRIAL RELATIONS BEFORE THE J.I.C.S

The Councils were set up in industries which had three distinctive traditions of organisation, or non-organisation, in industrial relations. There were those which had before the war an effective degree of collective bargaining, those which only developed one during the war and those which, even at the end of the war, still lacked one. What constituted an effective degree of collective bargaining before the war of course differed in one important respect from what constituted an effective degree of bargaining after it; before the war there were no national agreements on wages and hours, after it, national agreements were standard. On this understanding the industries can be classified as follows:

Table 3: *Organisation of industrial relations before the J.I.C.s*

Effective collective bargaining 1914	Effective bargaining developed 1914–18	Lack of effective bargaining in 1918
Tinplate	Wool and allied	Papermaking
Boots and shoes	Chemicals	Hosiery
Printing	Flourmilling	Silk
Railways	Soap and candles	Quarrying
Building	Paint and varnish	Cement
Docks	Cablemaking	Electricity supply
Heating, etc.	Pottery	Water supply
Tramways		Local authorities
Gas supply		

Industries with effective collective bargaining before 1914

The effectiveness and the nature of this coverage differed widely. The criterion is not 100 per cent membership of trade unions and a comparable organisation among employers, nor yet that agreements were comprehensive and affected the wages and conditions of work of the majority of the workers in the trade. It is rather that in some industries there was a distinct pattern of collective negotiations before 1914, a pattern which marked them off from other industries.

One industry which could in fact claim something like 100 per cent trade union membership was the *Welsh Tinplate and Sheet* trade.[1] Their Conciliation Board, which was much more than a Conciliation Board in the normal sense at this time, settled wages and hours and conditions with a thoroughness few industries could equal; procedural agreements and arrangements were also extremely thorough. The agreements[2] were subject to annual review and covered all rates and jobs in all foreseen circumstances; any matter of dispute arising out of interpretation or unforeseen circumstances was subject to conciliation by a group of six—three from each side—and decision by the Conciliation Board to which they reported. The *Boot and Shoe* operatives had also been among those who had made the Conciliation mechanism suit the needs of strong trade unionism. Though their attempts to force the issue in 1895 had failed they still possessed a pattern of local boards which decided many major substantive issues. By the outbreak of war the right to national negotiation, lost in 1895, was restored.[3]

The skilled *Printing* trades had been among the pioneers in the trade union movement and had a long tradition of collective negotiation. The exclusiveness of the crafts did not help the total effort to organise the industry and the Printing and Kindred Trades Federation formed in 1902 spent most of its time and energy trying to settle inter-union problems. There were more than 50,000 workers in the industry covered by agreements in 1910.[4]

The *Railway* managements had since 1911 conceded *de facto* recognition to the unions though the failure to grant the same *de jure* still rankled. In 1913, with the formation of the N.U.R., 300,000 of the

[1] W. E. Minchinton, *The British Tinplate Industry* (Cambridge 1957), p. 125.

[2] e.g. Welsh Plate and Sheet Manufacturers' Association. 'List of wages to remain in force until the 30th June, 1911.' (24th May 1910.)

[3] Clegg, Fox and Thompson, op. cit., pp. 200–1 and 454: Webb's *Trade Unionism*, p. 493, *Industrial Democracy*, pp. 186 ff. Alan Fox, *The National Union of Boot and Shoe Operatives* (Blackwell 1958), pp. 294 ff.

[4] Child, op. cit., p. 203.

326,000 railway trade unionists were under one banner. Government control during the war and the potential position of strength that the unions were in during it soon made their power actual; it was the first industry to get an all-round national increase in wages and by the end of the war the railwaymen were as militant as any.[1]

Building workers had a longer tradition of unionism and collective negotiation than the railwaymen but incidental factors had left them weak in the pre-war years. Unionism was by and large the privilege of the skilled men and even among them, it was reckoned that less than half of the bricklayers, masons and joiners were in their unions. It was nonetheless negotiations between the craftsmen and their employers which settled the district rates; conciliation procedures were linked through a system of local district and national boards.[2]

The *Dockers*, whose problems had figured large in labour and trade union history since the 1880's, had by 1913 won limited recognition and union rights in the main ports and the war strengthened their arm too. By 1919 some 85,000 of the 125,000 dockers were union members;[3] but the problem of casual labour still prevented any real progress in collective negotiations for the group as a whole. Though the Liverpool White Book was a good example of a comprehensive agreement covering workers in a particular docks its limitations were considerable.[4]

The *Heating and Domestic Engineering* industry was small but growing before the 1914 war; in 1904 the National Association of Master Heating, Domestic Engineering employers was formed to deal with trade and labour matters and from the first showed a preference for national rather than local negotiations on all save wages. The National Union of Employees appeared in 1910 and a national code of working rules was agreed on in 1910 though it was 1917 before the first national wages settlement was made.[5]

In two of the municipal employments—*Tramways* and *Gas Supply*—local unionisation and collective negotiation were well established in

[1] Bagwell, op. cit., pp. 309 ff. and 344 ff.; Clapham, Vol. 3, p. 326.

[2] R. Postgate, op. cit., pp. 369 ff.: Clapham, Vol. 3, pp. 324–5. *Report on Collective Agreements* (1934) H.M.S.O., pp. 344 ff., Clegg, Fox and Thompson, pp. 352 ff.

[3] *Report of the Court of Enquiry concerning Transport Workers* (The Shaw Report), S.P. 1920, XXIV, para. 9.

[4] The *Shaw Report*, Appendix 48, gives the details of the White Book. The questioning by Bevin (*Evidence*, p. 399) showed how its provisions could be evaded because of casual and boy labour. A. Bullock, op. cit., pp. 116 ff. and above, p. 32.

[5] *The story of the Association of Heating, Ventilating and Domestic Engineering Employers* (London, 1954, for private circulation) and the various Reports of the National Union of Operative, Heating, etc., Engineers, especially the Triennial Conference 1917 and Quinquennial 1936.

many main areas. The Gasworkers had a tradition of effective unionism and it was markedly militant. Local collective bargaining was well developed by 1914 but it was an award of the Committee on production in 1917 which first provided a national wages agreement.[1] The Tramwaymen likewise bargained locally in the main urban areas; again a Committee on Production award in 1918 gave them a national wage settlement for the first time.[2]

Industries which developed collective bargaining 1914–18

One of the distinctive marks of wartime negotiations was the growth of national agreements. This affected all industries, including those which before the war had possessed an effective degree of collective negotiation. But there was another group of industries in which the other incidental effects of war also produced the first effective pattern of negotiations in the industry as a whole.

The strength of trade unionism and collective negotiations in the *Wool and Allied Trades* was in the dyeing and finishing section in which, in 1913, about half of the 85,000 employees were unionised. In the other sections it was nearer one in ten out of 220,000. In this larger section such collective agreements as there were took the form of local piece lists.[3] The wool industry was one of those most profoundly affected by the war, being run at the end by a Control Board with statutory powers[4] and the needs of co-operating with the employers and the government on these matters encouraged the unions and the employers in the efforts at organisation so that by 1918 both were fully organised. But the war did little to improve the shaky wage structure. Basic rates were determined by an Arbitration Award one month after the J.I.C. was formed.[5]

Trade unionism and collective negotiation in the *Heavy Chemical* industry before the war was negligible though the nature of the work

[1] Clegg, Fox and Thompson, pp. 57–8 and 291. H. Clegg, *General Union* (Blackwell 1964), pp. 1, 4, 151 ff. Ministry of Labour *Memorandum*, Lab. 2/458/139/3/1921, 8th April 1921.

[2] Clegg, Fox and Thompson, op. cit., p. 331, and N.J.I.C. *Minutes*, 15th June 1921. Lab. 2/652/24.

[3] Clegg, Fox and Thompson, pp. 33–4, 184 and 455. Clapham, Vol. 3, p. 330.

[4] See above, p. 93.

[5] *Memorandum* on Working of the Control Board for the Woollen and Worsted Industry (Ministry of Reconstruction 1917). The *Woollen and Worsted Industry*—an historical study of the building up of existing wage structures (typescript in the Wool and Allied Trades Employers' Council files.)

and the poor conditions originally existing[1] had by 1914 convinced some employers in the trade that fair conditions were ultimately a better proposition. The eight-hour day and the annual holiday with pay were in operation by some.[2] During the war, the need to save time in unnecessary referral to the Committee on Production led to the employers approaching the unions to negotiate settlements and this established the pattern of national negotiations. Chemicals were another industry deeply involved in the war effort and conditioned to national organisation in the execution of munitions policy. A Chemical Employers' Federation was formed in 1918 for the purpose of handling the industry's labour matters and it was the Dockers and General Workers —Bevin's union—which was approached by them with a view to forming a J.I.C.[3]

In the *Flourmilling industry* before the war 'each miller paid what rate seemed fit to him and worked the number of hours he chose'.[4] The Flourmills Committee, through which the government co-operated with the employers in organising the trade for war needs and the essential supply of the home market, produced an industry consciousness which made the development of a national labour policy easier; early in 1918 the first national agreement—on hours—was developed from an award originally gained by Bevin for the south-western section of the trade.[5]

The *Soap and Candle Manufacturing industry*[6] was closely allied with the Chemical trades and like them became used to collective action in the war. It was Roscoe Brunner of the Chemical Employers whose advice led to the establishment of the Soap and Candle Trades Federation. Lever's was at the time and for all practical purposes the soap industry and the employment policies of the firm had been paternalistic and anti-union. It was however a Lever representative who was the first Chairman of the Council; the first wages agreement with the unions was signed in April 1918, that is before the negotiations for the formation of the J.I.C. had begun.[7]

[1] Dona Torr, *Tom Mann and His Times*, Vol. 1 (London 1956), p. 222.

[2] H. Bolitho, *Alfred Mond* (London 1933), p. 65.

[3] Information supplied by Mr. J. Bottomley of Albright and Wilson from a paper read before the Chemical Industries Association.

[4] Sir W. Norman Vernon of Spillers and Ex-President of the F.E.F. writing in *Unity*, November 1937.

[5] Bullock, op. cit., p. 86. *Milling* (Silver Jubilee of the F.E.F. and J.I.C. edition), May 1944.

[6] This later became the Soap, Candle and Edible Fats industry; the shorter title is used throughout.

[7] Notes supplied by Mr. Petrie of the Employers' Federation; on Lever's pre-war policy, Charles A. Wilson, *A History of Unilever*, Vol. 1 (London 1954), pp. 147 ff.

The *Paint and Varnish industry*[1] found also that the regulation of supplies during the war, and the awards of the Committee on Production, faced it with a new prospect. The recognition of the need for more effective negotiation machinery after the war had progressed far enough by the time the Whitley scheme was put to it that its acceptance was easy and indeed welcome.[2]

Electrical Cablemaking was in the hands of a very few firms in 1914 and its labour relations, while lacking in formal negotiations, were good and its wages and conditions were comparatively good. There was some delay in setting up the Council but this owed more to conflicting interests than organisational weakness. Agreement on wages and hours on a national basis had been reached by negotiation while the conflict over the formation of the Council was going on.[3]

The *Pottery industry* had shown a strong reluctance to unionise and to develop an effective negotiation system. What agreements there were before 1914 were more honoured in the breach than in the observance.[4] The unions had always preferred co-operation with the employers rather than negotiation on basic issues—perhaps the tradition of skilled men hoping to be masters was partly the reason.[5] Though the war strengthened the Pottery Workers' Federation, the wholeheartedness with which the Whitley scheme was embraced, and indeed the fact that a pilot scheme was in progress before Whitley,[6] was indicative of conditions and attitudes peculiar to the industry; the career of the Council confirmed their lack of realism which undermined any attempt to establish an effective negotiating pattern.

Industries lacking effective collective bargaining in 1918

The Ministry of Labour had power to set up Trade Boards or Interim Reconstruction Committees but since the voluntary principle was

[1] Paint, Lacquer and Varnish industry, to give it its full title.
[2] *Seventh Annual Report of the National Federation of Associated Paint Manufacturers* (1918) and the *Report on the Establishment*, etc., p. 40.
[3] The Balfour Committee *Survey of Metal Industries*, p. 304, remarks on the good tradition of Labour relations. Details of the national agreement of 1919 in the *Minutes of the J.I.C.*, 4th September 1919.
[4] W. H. Warburton, *Trade Unionism in the North Staffordshire Potteries* (London 1931), pp. 214 ff.
[5] Ibid., p. 187. Clapham, Vol. 3, p. 330. There had been schemes of Alliance with the employers on the Birmingham model in the 1890's as well as attempts at co-operative production. Warburton, op. cit., pp. 185 and 211.
[6] *Report on the Establishment and Progress of J.I.C.s*, pp. 28–30.

preferred, tried where it could to get full Councils established, putting pressure on the two sides to do so. In other cases the Councils appeared despite the initial inadequacy of organisation because for one reason or another individuals considered the effort at organisation for a Whitley Council worth while.

The *Papermaking industry* possessed in the National Union of Paper Millworkers the nucleus of a strong organisation with about 14,000 members in the growing industry in 1914 but the characteristics of the industry made it possible for the employers to stick to their belief that the individual mill owner could best deal with the labour problems independently. Even the experience of the war did not remove this conviction and it took the efforts of the more enlightened professional managers to bring about the necessary change of mind.[1] When the first steps to the formation of an industry-wide negotiation system were taken, a trade board was discussed and in the event it was an I.I.R.C. that was established.[2]

The *Hosiery* and the *Silk industries* were in a state of considerable disarray when the possibility of establishing a J.I.C. was broached. The former had once been a leader in the conciliation movement, but the Board had collapsed and the employers did not share the unions' enthusiasm for their revival,[3] partly because they were aware of the impossibility of getting rivals to accept the decisions of the Boards, partly because they preferred the freedom that absence of the Board gave them. The war did strengthen employers' organisations on a local basis as it enabled the unions to organise the fifteen or more scattered local associations into National Federations of the two main sections of the trade. The two sides were ready to set up a Council,[4] but defects of organisation, especially among the employers, made it difficult.[5] At the time it was a Trade Board rather than a J.I.C. which seemed likely.[6]

The *Silk industry* was in even worse case. It had been in decline since the middle of the nineteenth century and the artificial silk industry

[1] Before the war the unions were pushing for national negotiations; rebuffed by the Papermakers' Association Southern Section they approached Charles R. Seddon of the Northern area. It was his effort which led, against determined opposition, to the formation of the *Employers' Federation of Papermakers and Boardmakers*; it was 1919 before the Scottish employers were in. *1860–1960, 100 Years of Progress*, East Lancashire Paper Mills (Radcliffe) Centenary booklet. Arthur Baker: *The Employers' Federation of Papermakers and Boardmakers* (London 1953).

[2] *I.I.R.C. Minutes*, 17th October 1919. *Minutes* of first meeting of the J.I.C., 4th May 1921. Baker's pamphlet cited states that the Ministry of Labour was prepared as late as January 1919 to press for a trade board.

[3] F. A. Wells, *The British Hosiery Trade* (London 1935), p. 240.

[4] Ibid.

[5] *Report on the Establishment and Progress of J.I.C.s*, p. 37.

[6] See below, p. 142.

had not yet grown to a scale large enough to revive its fortunes. It was only agitation by the Ministry of Labour that something should be done to reorganise its relations that led to the first steps towards collective negotiations.[1] Even then, though five employers' associations and five trade unions were represented on the Council, they failed because between them they did not muster enough strength to make it effective.

The attempt to establish a J.I.C. in *Quarrying* was complicated by the fact that the industry had never considered itself as one industry but as several related sections. Only two of these—limestone and slate—had any effective tradition of bargaining. The difficulty for the unions in organising to present a united front for a J.I.C. was great enough but that of the employers was greater; their organisation had to be created from scratch.[2] The *Cement Making* industry, closely related to quarrying through its use of chalk and limestone as a raw material, had similar problems, but the presence of one big group—the A.P.C.M.-B.P.C.M.—made them easier of solution. Even so the possibility of a trade Board faced it as it faced quarrying, so poor was the state of organisation.[3]

Of the municipal and public utility employments, *Electricity, Water Supply* and the manual workers employed by *Local Authorities* were lacking in organisation. Electricity supply was an infant industry before the war and still in its early development after it. Neither its personnel nor its employers were organised for systematic national negotiation though the engineers and the E.T.U. had established some local agreements before the war. The general application of wage advances in the industry and the degree of control exercised over the trade by the Ministry of Munitions encouraged national trends but the problems of inter-union rivalry and of organising the mixed group of employers proved very considerable,[4] and but for the advent of the Council such organisation would hardly have taken place.

[1] Ibid.

[2] An address by E. J. Burt, who was largely responsible for creating it, to the first aggregate meeting of the National Federation of Granite and Roadstone Quarry owners (26th October 1927) details the main outlines of the struggle to cajole the various sections into the national organisation. The *Dept. Enquiry on Checkweighmen* (S.P. 1908, XI) showed the N.U.G.W. organising 1,300 of the 7,000 limestone quarry workers, according to Hartle of the union. The slate workers—mainly in North Wales—were strongly unionised. (Clegg, Fox and Thompson, op. cit., p. 212.) The dispute between Lord Penrhyn and the Quarrymen in the 1890's was prolonged and bitter.

[3] Cement manufacture, like quarrying, was located in rural areas and drew its labour and its standards of industrial relations from the ill-organised rural workers. Most of the cement workers were taken on by the day; only key men were regulars.

[4] 'Organisation of labour in the electricity supply industry', *The Labour Magazine* October 1925.

The vast range of employments constituted under 'local authority manual workers' and the great variety of conditions and places in which they were employed, combined with the weakness of unions and the previously localised outlook of the employers to make the problems of the J.I.C. in this field unusually great and complex and it was later emphasised that only the insistence and the intervention of the Ministry made it at all possible.[1] In *Water Supply* the variety of employments and employers was more limited and the question of organisation for the J.I.C. less complex; the fact that the Association in which the Metropolitan employees were organised was not strictly a trade union caused some difficulty but it was overcome without much delay.[2]

(ii) ATTITUDES TO THE J.I.C.S

As the account of the response of industry to the publication of the *Report* given above indicates, there was no widespread and spontaneous enthusiasm in industry in general for the scheme. Closer analysis of the pattern of response in particular industries which did take it up shows us that this was complex. It may be set out as follows:

Table 4: *Attitudes of various industries to the J.I.C.s*

Industries anticipating the Councils	Industries accepting them readily	Industries requiring persuasion by the Ministry
1. Painting and Decorating[3]	1. Chemicals	1. Cement
2. Building	2. Paint and varnish	2. Quarrying
3. Pottery	3. Soap and candles	3. Gas supply
4. Printing	4. Flourmilling	4. Water supply
	5. Tinplate	5. Electricity supply
	6. Heating, etc.	6. Hosiery
	7. Wool and allied	7. Silk
	8. Boots and shoes	8. Tramways
		9. Local Authorities
		10. Papermaking
		11. Electrical cables

[1] Below, p. 143. [2] *Report on the Establishment and Progress of J.I.C.s*, etc., p. 51.
[3] This Council merged into the Building Industry Council and is not listed on pp. 125–6, above.

The Docks and the Railways present a special case. They owed their J.I.C.s to the recommendations of the Shaw court of enquiry and the personal intervention of the Prime Minister negotiating with the union leaders.

Industries anticipating them

The Painters and Decorators Joint Industrial Council was set up in February 1917[1] and in May of the next year a Building Industrial Council was established. The influence of one individual—Malcolm Sparkes—on developments in the Building industry was probably decisive in setting it on the road that was to lead to the Guilds and the *Foster Report*.[2] The Pottery industry J.I.C. had origins which reflect even more vividly the wartime spirit. It was chosen by a group of enthusiasts as a suitable subject for an Industrial Council before the *Whitley Report* was published, although it was January 1918 before the Council had its first meeting.[3] The Printing industry's ambitions were more moderate and it waited until the general publication of the Whitley scheme and the official canvassing before bringing together, under the aegis of a Council, the various strands in the betterment movement the war had brought with it.[4]

Industries accepting them readily

The *First Whitley Report* had been concerned with the well-organised trades; the second with securing the same kind of three-tier industrial council organisation in the trades which did not possess adequate organisation for collective negotiation at the time. Because of the difficulties, in theory and in practice, that such a distinction led to, and because in particular of the suggestion that Trade Boards might

[1] p. 103, above.

[2] See below, pp. 198–9: Sparkes had been the Managing Director of a London firm of joinery manufacturers and therefore involved in the disputes in the industry in 1913–14 which were leading to a major lock-out in August of the latter year. A sincere Quaker, he was moved by this conflict to reflect on the industrial relationship. The result was his propaganda in favour of industrial Parliaments, and in particular his work with the *Garton Foundation* (above, p. 88), to this end. The Painters and Decorators set up their Council as a result of contact with Sparkes and through Sparkes the Building employers were persuaded to set up their Council. *Report on the Industrial Council for the Building Industry*, pp. 14, 45, etc.

[3] *Report on the Establishment and Progress of J.I.C.s*, etc., p. 29.

[4] Child, op. cit., p. 254.

be established as a means to the development of Industrial Councils, it was decided that the Ministry of Labour could go ahead in setting up Councils where this could be done right away. Where it could not, the Ministry of Reconstruction would encourage the establishment of an Interim Reconstruction Committee from such trade union and employer organisations as did exist with a view to strengthening both and setting up a fully fledged Industrial Council which could function on its own.[1] From 1st May 1919 the Reconstruction Committee came under the wing of the Ministry of Labour which from then on was responsible for the whole of the Whitley scheme.

In the period between the publication of the *Report* and the government's announcement of its acceptance, the role of the Ministry of Labour was to distribute the information required and to be prepared to answer queries. Once the formal acceptance of the *Report* by the government was made the special Industrial Council's division of the Ministry was set up to handle the tasks more efficiently. According to the *Report* the method was a gentle one,[2] but there is no little evidence that the semi-official nature of the Whitley scheme and the hangover of wartime direction gave its officers a power and an influence in the weakly organised trades which was not in their official brief. Especially effective was the free use of the threat of the possible establishment of a trade board if a Council was not set up.

The ease with which the Councils were established in some industries was clearly due to the effect of wartime organisation. The Board of Control for the Wool and Allied industries was wound up at the end of the war and its disappearance spurred negotiations on a Council which had been going on since late in 1917. It was not however until January 1919 that the Council met for the first time—the Scottish section of the trade having decided to work as an independent unit.[3] In the Boot and Shoe industry the Trade Advisory Committee and the close and the successful co-operation of the government with the industry during the war gave the J.I.C. introduction,[4] though it would seem that the employers were more enthusiastic for it than the men.[5] The extensive government control exercised over the Flourmilling industry through the Flour Mills Committee helped the realisation that labour relations after the war was over required different handling, but older habits died hard and it was apparently the approach of the

[1] *Memorandum* by the Ministry of Reconstruction or the Ministry of Labour on Industrial Councils and Trade Boards. S.P. 1918, XXII. *Ministry of Reconstruction, Report on the Work of the Ministry*. S.P. 1918, XIII, *Report on the Establishment and Progress of J.I.C.s*, etc., pp. 14 and 23. [2] Ibid., p. 23. [3] *Report on the Establishment and Progress of J.I.C.s*, etc., p. 37. [4] Ibid., p. 47. [5] Fox, op. cit., p. 403.

Ministry of Reconstruction which tipped the balance in favour of the scheme which then went forward without much difficulty.[1]

The Chemical employers, on the other hand, realised that labour relations in the industry required some positive organisation and philosophy after the war and the Wages Committee of the Federation required little assistance from the Ministry in setting up the Council.[2]

The Soap and Candle manufacturers were initially less ready to adopt the scheme—a fact which ties in with Lever's attitude to the unions and with the history of the Council in the early 1920's. But the approaches of the Ministry and the action of the Chemical employers made it hard to resist and pressure from the unions clinched it.[3] The Paint and Varnish trade were more positive. The local association agreed that 'the Whitley principles for the bringing together of capital and labour was for the country's good' and they went ahead to negotiate with the unions who were no less enthusiastic.[4]

The Heating and Domestic Engineering trade was equally attracted to the idea of the Council and required no urging, although the threat that they might be incorporated into the Building industry J.I.C. spurred their enthusiasm. This they wanted to avoid at all costs and their readiness to accept a Council was one way of doing so. On the other hand, they showed themselves also aware of the continuity of thought between their own pre-war approach to industrial negotiation and the ideas of the *Whitley Report*.[5] The Tinplate industry of South Wales was likewise convinced that it already had what it took to make an effective Whitley Council and was ready to adopt the scheme when approached.[6]

Industries requiring persuasion

Some trades which were weakly organised or concentrated in one or a small number of unions, lacked the effective will or means to set up

[1] *Milling*, 23rd March 1918, and 27th May 1944 (Silver Jubilee of the J.I.C. and F.M.E.F. edition).

[2] Mr. J. Bottomley's paper cited above and the *Report on the Establishment*, etc., p. 40.

[3] Notes supplied by Mr. Petrie. At a meeting between the Employers' Federation representatives and the Warehouse and General Workers' Union on 18th July 1918 the latter raised the matter; the J.I.C. met for the first time on 9th July 1919.

[4] *Seventh Annual Report* of the N.F.A.P.M. (1918), p. 57, and the *Report on the Establishment and Progress of J.I.C.s*, p. 40.

[5] *Report on the work of the Heating and Domestic Engineering J.I.C.*, January 1920.

[6] *Transcript of proceedings* of first meeting of J.I.C., March 1919. It is not quite clear if the Council was under way before the industry was approached by the Ministry, but in any case the predisposition to a Council was evident.

national structures without some pressure from outside, even though they had no ideological objection to Whitleyism or faced no complicated organisational problems. Others showed elements of ideological objection or faced serious difficulties in setting up national organisation.

The *Cement*, the *Hosiery* and the *Silk* trades come into the first category, their previous looseness of organisation making it difficult for them to organise as an industry, though they had no deep-set objection to so doing. Pressure from the Ministry in the threat of a possible Trade Board, and the efforts of Malcolm Stewart of the A.P.C.M., carried the *Cement* industry through the I.I.R.C. to the J.I.C.[1] Since during the war the unions in *Hosiery* had been seeking a revival of the conciliation boards and the employers were definitely awaiting the outcome of the Whitley Committee's work to see what was the best way to proceed, the industry's slowness in getting its Councils set up was not due to basic objection. But organisation on both sides was so poor that again a trade board was threatened. The Council 'was not exactly forced on the trade but it was made pretty plain at a meeting at Leicester that unless one was set up a trade board would be'.[2] The occasion on which the Ministry of Labour called together the two sides in the *Silk* industry regarding the possibility of a Council was 'the first time the two main interests had met together with a view to joint action for its benefit' and it was pointed out that the trade had developed haphazardly in all parts of the country and its conditions were not satisfactory. For this reason the possibility of a Trade Board was a real one.[3]

The *Quarrying, Local Authorities* manual workers and the *Papermaking* industries were not only ill-organised, they were not too convinced of the desirability of national organisation. The complexities of the *Quarrying* industry already referred to made its objections not unreasonable. The Ministry of Reconstruction persevered, making it clear that failing the establishment of at least an I.I.R.C. a Trade Board would be imposed. The I.I.R.C. had a brief and inglorious period of existence, the unions pressing for a J.I.C., the employers showing marked resistance to the organisation from the top that the situation demanded, a resistance only overcome by Ministry persistence and pressure.[4] Parochial

[1] The C.M.F. was first approached by the Ministry in 1918 about an I.I.R.C. or a trade board. The latter was a possibility until 1919. *Minutes*, C.M.F., November 1918 and March–September 1919.

[2] J. R. Allard in *Unity*, July 1936, Wells, op. cit., p. 240. The *Report on the Establishment*, etc., p. 37, makes it clear that the weakness of employers' organisation was the main trouble.

[3] *Annual Report* 1918–19 and *Minutes* of J.I.C. meeting, 17th January 1933.

[4] Address by Burt cited above, p. 164, and the *Report* of the proceedings of a Conference of Chairman, Vice-Chairman and Secretariat of I.I.R.C.'s Caxton Hall, 18th February

attitudes in the *Local Authorities* employment and the lack of effective organisation, especially on the employers' side, posed probably the biggest problem to the Ministry. The latter's action in calling conferences in some areas to get the District or Provincial Councils set up as the basis of the national organisation provided the Council in later years with a very good case for asserting that since the whole thing was the government's creation the government should give it whatever aid was needed to remain in being.[1] The organisational difficulties in *Papermaking* were largely overcome by the time that the Council was being considered, though they were still real enough. It was unwillingness rather than inability which made the organisation of the employers slow in the first instance. The unions were weaker and were insufficiently convinced of the employers' goodwill to trust a J.I.C. They preferred direct confrontation on traditional collective negotiation lines and with their attitudes. This also was an industry which progressed through threat of a Trade Board, an I.I.R.C. and finally a J.I.C. As it was no Council was established until May 1921 and it never really took hold.[2]

Industries which found themselves faced with major problems of organising nationally were five—*Electricity*, *Gas* and *Water Supply*, *Tramways*, and *Electrical Cablemaking*.

The problem in *Electricity Supply* was that the municipalities wanted directly elected representatives on the Council rather than their representation at one remove through the Incorporated Municipal Electrical Association. Though set up in 1919 it was 1921 before the Council was reconstructed to meet this demand.[3] There was the difficulty too of the representation of the wage-earners and the technical staffs.[4]

In the *Gas* industry the Gas Council which was set up during the war

1919. *Minutes* of the Quarrying I.I.R.C. Meeting, 1st April 1919. It was Jones of the N.Q.W.U. and Hartle of the N.U.G. & G.W., whose unions had developed collective negotiation in their sections, who pressed the matter of a full J.I.C.

[1] Ministry of Labour *Memorandum*, 16th April 1921, and *Notes* prepared for a deputation to the Ministry of Labour, 8th January 1926, indicate the reluctance with which the industry accepted the Councils. A *Memorandum* from the N.J.I.C. on 6th May 1927 bitterly contrasts the government pressure in 1917 with the neglect of the Councils ten years later (Lab. 2/278/112/43, Lab. 2/857/805/3 and Lab. 2/280/129/3).

[2] C. J. Bundock, *The Story of the National Union of Printing Bookbinding and Paperworkers* (London 1959), p. 412, would indicate that in 1918 the unions were anxious to have a J.I.C.; the subsequent delays and the advantages gained by straight union negotiation made it less desirable. At a meeting of the I.I.R.C. (*Minutes*, 17th October 1919) the Ministry of Labour representatives said that it was the poor state of unionisation and the refusal of the major union to have representatives of the general unions on the Council that were impeding progress.

[3] *Report on the Establishment and Progress of J.I.C.s*, p. 52.

[4] *The Labour Magazine*, October 1925.

proved unsuitable for handling the Whitley scheme, but it was not until the Federation of Gas Employers was set up that the J.I.C. could be established. The unions were well organised and there was no problem on their side.[1] The *Tramway industry* proved difficult from both the employers' and the trade unions' point of view and there was opposition to the Whitley scheme among the unions in particular. When to this is added the existence of inter-union rivalry it is not surprising that it took two years of negotiations to set up the Council.[2] In *Electrical Cablemaking* the problem first of all was that of the non-federated firms and the question of their representation on the Council in an industry which had been marked throughout its life by an unusual degree of cohesion among its comparatively small group of firms. There was rivalry among the unions too and the E.T.U. showed in the first months that it had objections to Whitleyism. As it was, the first meeting of the Council did not take place until September 1919.[3]

The special case of the railways and port transport

The hope of the Whitley Committee was to produce a scheme of industrial relations which would be applicable to the major industries which had shown themselves to be particularly strike prone before the war. Part of the mythology of its failure is that the Councils never succeeded in establishing themselves in any such trade. In fact it was the *Report* which enabled two of them—the railways and the docks—to rebuild their industrial relations system on a more satisfactory basis. It was also applied to the maritime services, though not with the sort of result anyone could have foreseen. To have influenced to a considerable degree the industrial relations systems of two of the four industries which in the immediate pre-war period had been so disturbed was no mean feat. That the intervention of powers outside industry was needed to effect this was entirely in accord with the *Report*. It was envisaged by the Committee,[4] and reflected in the procedure suggested by the Ministry of Reconstruction, that they should be put into practice on a voluntary basis, letting the individual industries work out their own destiny but with that degree of official encouragement which was required and was tolerable. In fact the establishment of the Councils in the industries in question was directly due to official intervention of very different kinds.

[1] *Report on the Establishment and Progress of J.I.C.s*, p. 52.
[2] Ibid., p. 54. [3] *Report* of first meeting, 4th September 1919.
[4] *Interim Report*, paras. 7, 18, 22, and Appendix Q.2.

The metamorphosis of the railwaymen's ambition between 1917 and 1921 remains one of the most startling developments in the industrial relations in this period. At their Annual General Meeting in 1917 they caught the mood of the moment and made demands for a 50 per cent share in management and state ownership of the industry.[1] They soon had the Report of the Select Committee on Transport to support part of their claim[2] and yet by 1921 they had abandoned both their ambitions and settled for a system of collective negotiation and conciliation which owed a great deal to the Whitley scheme. In 1919 the railwaymen, ably led by Thomas, won their main points against a government still controlling the railways,[3] but rapidly abandoning any pretence at managing the nation's affairs in the spirit of reconstruction. Thereafter Thomas and Lloyd George worked out a compromise which led to the abandonment of the idea of nationalisation and workers' control but secured for the railwaymen the consolidation of all their gains of the last seven years under the reorganised railways system. How this came about is described in great detail by Bagwell.[4] Whether it would have been possible to substitute consultation for nationalisation and/or workers' representation without the Whitley scheme being at hand to provide an acceptable alternative may be doubted. The collective bargaining system established after the 1919 strike was formally incorporated into the new system[5] and 'councils composed of officials and elected employees' with 'functions as designated in Clause 16 of the *Whitley Report*'[6] were to be set up at relevant levels. The railwaymen at last had a complete system of collective bargaining, set up in an atmosphere in which co-operation was possible and in the formation of which Whitleyism played a large part.

The Shaw enquiry, which began in February 1920, was the result of a dockers' claim which the employers had not rejected out of hand but which they had offered, in the spirit of the time, to refer to arbitration. During Macassey's summing up for the employers, Lord Shaw intervened to ask him if there was any hope of setting up a J.I.C. on Whitley lines.[7] Macassey was sure that such was too doctrinaire an approach.

[1] See above, p. 83.

[2] *Second Report* from the Select Committee on Transport, etc., 14th November 1918, S.P. 1918, IV, p. vii. 'It appears desirable that there should be unification of ownership not merely of management, [whether] the state or one large company is immaterial.'

[3] Bagwell, op. cit., pp. 375 ff.

[4] Op. cit., pp. 407 ff.

[5] See below, pp. 188 ff.

[6] Agreement 3rd May 1921, reproduced as an Appendix to the *Memorandum on the Railways Bill*, S.P. 1921, Vol. XXX, p. 3. Bagwell, pp. 409 ff., and Blaxland, pp. 157 ff. See below, p. 157.

[7] *Report of the Court of enquiry concerning Transport Workers* (The Shaw Report), S.P. 1920, XXIV, Evidence, p. 283.

Bevin for his part told the Committee that he and his union had given a favourable answer when approached by the Ministry in 1918 but that he found that nothing was done. Bevin's reasoning was that 'the foundation was the national centre and that you had to get the national centre right and then gravitate outwards and the branches would afterwards conform as near as possible to the centre'. It was with Bevin that the majority of the Shaw Committee agreed and as a result, in December 1920, a National Joint Council for the Port Transport industry was set up.

Given this pattern of influences in the formation of the Councils their growth cannot be ascribed to any single factor. In some cases it is clear that some sort of J.I.C. would have been set up with or without the Ministry's help. In these it was the determination of the two sides which led to the setting up of a Council even though the Ministry was ultimately involved. In other cases there was a disposition by one or both sides to set up a Council but the encouragement of the Ministry was needed too. Finally there were cases where a Council was eased into being—even against a degree of positive opposition, or at least positive unwillingness, by one or both parties. In so far as it seems possible to classify the Councils according to the main impetus for their formation Table 5 opposite attempts to do this. The difficult ones to identify are in that group in which, though there was a predisposition to set up a Council, Ministry intervention was needed. A primary and secondary cause has been given in these cases.

(iii) AIMS, MEMBERSHIP AND ORGANISATION OF THE J.I.C.S

Aims and membership

The first Interim Report of the Whitley Committee intended to show that by involving the participation of the wage-earner in the task of effective industrial reconstruction, the increased prosperity out of which his claim for a higher standard of living could be met would be provided. Participation would at once increase prosperity and improve the status of the worker. The suggestions of the Minister of Labour regarding the functions of the Councils were less sanguine

Report, para. 29, asserted that a perusal of para. 16 of the *Whitley Report* (above, pp. 104–5) 'would appear to bear directly on those problems the failure to solve which, in the direct relations between employer and employed, is as now reported by the court, a cause of serious conflict, difficulty, delay and loss'.

Table 5: *The main factors influencing the establishment of J.I.C.s*

	Joint effort of employers and trade unions	Employers more than unions	Unions more than employers	Official
Building	1			
Boots and shoes		1		
Cables				1
Cement		2		1
Chemicals	1			2
Docks			2	1
Electricity	2			1
Flourmilling	1			2
Gas				1
Heating	1			2
Hosiery				1
Local A.				1
Paint/varnish	1			2
Papermaking				1
Pottery	1			
Printing	1			
Quarrying			2	1
Railways	2			1
Silk				1
Soap			1	
Tinplate	1			
Tramway				1
Water supply				1
Wool and allied	1			2
	Primary 9 Secondary 2	Primary 1 Secondary 2	Primary 1 Secondary 2	Primary 13 Secondary 5

and show slightly more appreciation of the difficulties involved, but they remain for all that far-ranging. An analysis of these provides a guide to what the Councils in practice were intended to do since it was upon them that the objects and conditions of all but a few of the Industrial Councils were founded.

Their general purpose was to 'secure the largest possible measure of joint action between employers and workpeople for the development of the industry as a part of the national life and for the improvement of the conditions of all engaged in that industry'.[1] More specifically they had three main functions, according to their various constitutions: (1) To improve the existing methods and content of collective negotiation and conciliation within the traditional ambit of wages, hours and conditions; (2) To extend the scope of such negotiations to subjects relating to wages and hours but not previously contained in the average collective agreement; (3) To involve the unions in some way with the promotional, technical and organisational responsibilities normally connected with the management function at plant level or above.

Under the *first* of these can be included the regular consideration of wages (*Suggestions,* para. 2), the improvement of grievance procedures where they existed and their establishment where they did not (para. 4) and, because of its connection with the mutual interest in apprenticeship expressed in many agreements before the war, the 'supervision of entrance to and training for the industry' (para. 11). Under the *second* come attempts at regularising employment (para. 3), protection against industrial disease (para. 10) and co-operation with the education authorities in arranging education in all its branches for the industry (para. 11)—subjects near related to the traditional themes of negotiation but introducing a new emphasis. Under the *third* comes a list of functions of collective negotiation which were well beyond the normal scope of the process—securing the inclusion of employers and wage-earners in their respective organisations (para. 5), collecting statistics and information concerning the industry (para. 6), regularising production (para. 3), encouraging the study of processes of design and of research for the improvement of products (para. 7), enquiry into the special problems of the industry and the publication of reports on the same (para. 9), publicity (para. 13), the encouragement of the formation of District and Works Committees (para. 15), liaison with other J.I.C.s on matters of common interest (para. 16), representation to the government and other organisations (para. 13), and 'intimate and continuous' liaison between the Industrial Councils

[1] 'Suggestions prepared by the Ministry of Labour as to the constitution and functions of a National Joint Council', *Report on the Establishment and Progress of J.I.C.s,* Appx. 1.

and the various government departments (para. 12). In this connection the constitution refers to the Industrial Councils division of the Ministry of Labour. Such passages, and the energy with which the Ministry acted in the first two years, not unnaturally led those who responded to its blandishments to assume that the Councils were an intimate part of government industrial policy and could rely on government help if needed.

As was made plain in the *First Report* and emphasised in the answers to questions, the membership of the Councils was to be restricted to trade unionists and the chosen representatives of the employers and their associations.[1] In industries where there were no problems of inter-union rivalry and no problems of disagreement among the employers concerning representation the situation was straightforward enough. But not all industries were in this position.

In printing there was the question of the non-union house and the traditional difficulties with the newspaper industry; these were settled by compromise. The non-union house could not be directly represented in the J.I.C. but indirectly it could through the Federation; the Newspaper Society was allowed representation.[2] The Paperworkers' Union refused to countenance the presence on the Council of any representatives of the general unions and this they insisted on in face of all objections.[3] It was the inter-union rivalry among other things which led to the dissolution of the Council.[4] The Cablemakers faced in the first instance the refusal of the E.T.U. to co-operate[5] and then later on the problem of the Independent Cablemakers; the way that this latter problem was overcome was interesting. The C.M.A. were able to persuade the unions to work with them. The E.T.U. threatened to 'black' cable made by I.C.M.A. members and government departments were reminded of the Fair Wages Clause; manufacturers soon found they faced ruin if they did not conform to the Council's rates.[6]

The Chemical trades in the first instance faced a problem of rather a different kind—what the scope of its activities should be. The Soap

[1] See above, pp. 106 and 111–12. [2] Child, op. cit., p. 256.

[3] *Minutes* of I.I.R.C. meetings, 17th October 1919, 15th December 1920.

[4] The issues involved in the General Strike separated the smaller Amalgamated Society of Papermakers from the larger National Union, but the Council by that time had been weakened by the attitudes of both sides and it had no effective life after 1923–4. It gets a mention as a Court of Last Appeal in disputes in the agreement of 1926 but not in the next one, 1930.

[5] The E.T.U. announced that it had withdrawn from all J.I.C.s, including the Cablemaking industry's. It soon returned when it was made plain that only parties to the J.I.C. would have negotiation rights. *Minutes* of the J.I.C. meetings, 4th March and 21st April 1920. [6] Ibid., 16th March and 20th April 1921.

and Candle trades declined to come under its wing and went ahead to form its own Council.[1] The Fine and Pharmaceutical section of the trade managed to avoid both the larger organisation's embrace and the pressures of the Ministry to set up any effective alternative organisation.[2] In Electricity supply the immediate problem was to settle the dispute between the Electrical Power Engineers' Association (the technical grades union) and the Electrical Trade Union over membership of the Council. The former was not affiliated to the T.U.C. and the E.T.U. therefore objected to it being on the J.I.C. The employers wanted it to maintain its identity and remain on the Council. There is more than a little indication of political motivation on both sides and the E.P.E.A. was in fact to point out after the General Strike the lesson of what would have happened if the E.T.U. had organised, as it claimed to do, all switchboard attendants.[3] The upshot of the early difficulties was the formation of a separate National Joint Board for the E.P.E.A. negotiations with their employers.

The Local Authorities J.I.C. had to resolve the question of the Agricultural Labourers' Union which wished to be represented on the Provincial Councils but not on the national body.[4] In the case of the Waterworks J.I.C. difficulty over the status of one of the employees' organisations in the light of its non-affiliation to the T.U.C. was a stumbling block; after arbitration the union, which later became the National Union of Waterworks Employees, was admitted to the Council.[5] The Pottery J.I.C. at first restricted the workers' side to the craft unions, who even then were only reckoned to cover 35 per cent of the total employees; but later the general unions, the Clerks and the Commercial Travellers were also allowed representation.[6]

The size of the Councils varied considerably and the larger the industry or the more complicated its organisation the greater was the difficulty in providing for adequate representation without having an

[1] Information from *Notes* provided by Mr. Petrie concerning an address by Brunner to the employers in the Soap-making industry, 14th December 1917.

[2] *Minutes* of the Drug and Fine Chemicals Manufacturers' Association, 14th December 1917 to 5th June 1919; on 15th May 1919, the trade was protesting that the Trade Board with which the Ministry was threatening it was not what a well-organised trade like theirs wanted. On 5th June it was clear that there was a strong opposition inside the industry to a J.I.C.

[3] *Minutes* of N.J.B. meeting, 20th July 1928. A Ministry of Labour *Memorandum* of 8th January 1925 stated that many employers were opposed to a united front by the unions on one J.I.C. and preferred separate negotiations. Lab. 2/912/137/25.

[4] *Minutes* of a Conference between the National Council and the Provincial Councils, 15th September 1921. *Memorandum* of the Ministry of Labour, 16th April 1921. Lab. 2/278/112/43.

[5] *Report on the Establishment and Progress of J.I.C.s*, p. 51.

[6] Ibid., p. 30.

unwieldy number with which to deal. The largest of the Councils in terms of membership was that for the Building industry with its sixty members on each side and sixteen professional members in addition. Not for nothing was it called the Builders' Parliament. The Tinplate Council was also large but nothing like so large as the Builders; it had sixty-four members in all. At the other end of the scale was the Cement J.I.C. which only had fourteen members altogether. In so far as it is meaningful to talk of an average membership, it was in the twenty to forty range. For reasons of economy and also because of the difficulty that the general unions had in providing suitable members for all the Councils they sat on, many J.I.C.s agreed to reduce their numbers. In others a system of substitute members was introduced.

The extent to which the general unions were represented on the Councils has been accounted one of their characteristics.[1] For obvious reasons the industries in which the general unions organised were inclined to be weaker in collective bargaining and therefore were more likely to come within the scope of a scheme rejected by many strongly organised trades. But if at the end of the scale in the group of trades we are examining there was evidence that the appeal was to the less well organised, there was at the other a group in which a stronger union or unions, usually a Federation, dominated on the workers' side.

Some idea of the complexity of the organisation of the employees' side of the Councils in the case of the first group may be gathered from the chart depicting union affiliation in certain relevant J.I.C.s; as can be seen, the four named unions were with certain exceptions represented on each of the Councils; the 'other unions represented' cover practically the whole range of possibilities.[2] The situation represented by the chart is that obtaining when the Councils were set up. Amalgamations reduced the number of unions involved.

In contrast to the multiplicity of unions in Councils in these industries, there was another group where one large union or federation dominated—such as the Building Trades Federation, the Boot and Shoe Operatives, the Operative Heating and Domestic Engineering Union, the Federation of Hosiery Workers, the Printing, Bookbinding and Paper Workers, the Pottery Workers, the National Union of Railwaymen and the Association of Textile Unions. The Builders and the Printers were the only skilled unions with any major interest in the

[1] Bevin was on fourteen and the Chairman or Vice-Chairman of five of them.

[2] The Municipal Employees, the National Union of Public Works Operatives, the Labourers' Union, the National Union of Enginemen and Firemen, the Amalgamated Society of General and Municipal Workers were, for example, represented on many.

Table 6: *Representation of the main general unions on selected J.I.C.s*

Industry	National Union of General Workers	Dock Wharf and Riverside Workers	Workers Union	National Amalgam. Union of Labour	Other unions represented
Cables	x		x	x	4
Chemical	x	x	x	x	3
Electricity supply	x	x	x	x	4
Gas	x	x	x	x	3
Local authorities	x	x	x	x	5
Paint/varnish	x	x	x	x	1
Quarrying	x	x	x	x	2
Soap/ candles[1]	x	x	x		2
Tinplate	x	x			4
Water supply	x		x	x	5

J.I.C.s. Only the A.S.E. and that in but two industries—Tinplate and Electricity Supply—appears on the lists otherwise.

Compared with the difficulties of the unions in organising themselves for the Councils, those facing the employers were considerably smaller. The public utilities, because of the conflicting attitudes of the companies and the municipalities, were the main initial problem; the Cablemakers had a short tussle with the independent makers. For the rest, the needs of the Councils gave the spur to complete organisation where this did not exist. The Quarrying industry provides a good example of the effect that the need could have and the thoroughness with which the employers could meet it if they wished.

The National Councils

The frequency of meetings of the Councils was laid down in the model Constitution as being 'as often as necessary and not less than once

[1] The membership of the Council was adjusted in 1921; the N.U.G.W. had its membership reduced and the D.W.R. and the W.U. had members for the first time.

a quarter'. In practice the usefulness of the Council usually determined the frequency of the meetings. Few kept up the monthly meetings with which many had started. The N.J.I.C. in electricity supply was one exception; it did meet monthly throughout the inter-war years—with the exception of the summer break. So too did the Tramways and the Electrical Cablemakers. Other equally active Councils—for example the Flourmillers—held general meetings quarterly and left the everyday work of the Council in the hands of the executive or the specialist subcommittees. The Tinplate J.I.C., after its reconstruction to meet the complaints of the unions, decided to meet annually in full session and to leave the ordinary work of the Council to the joint standing committee of twenty-six which met monthly. At the other end of the scale were the Councils which met at intervals of months, even years. The Soap and Candle Trades J.I.C. managed but one meeting in 1930 and 1931 and with none at all in 1932 and 1933 when troubles were besetting it. As early as 1922 one of the Joint Secretaries was complaining that it seemed ages since a meeting was held.[1] The executive committee met irregularly and that at an interval of months rather than weeks. But infrequency of meetings was by no means a sign of crippling problems or the reluctance of some employers to take the Council seriously; the Cement J.I.C. met at intervals of six months or so after 1926; in the early 1930's this could extend to a year or more. Not all the Councils could find something regularly to deal with if they kept to scheduled meetings. The liaison officer who attended a Local Authority J.I.C. meeting in 1923 was moved to remark on the futility of the proceedings.[2] There must have been many such.

J.I.C. meetings were presided over by a Chairman or Vice-Chairman provided either by the employers' association or the trade unions. The model constitution says nothing of the alternating of the Chairmanship and practices differed. In the Flourmilling J.I.C. Bevin and Humphries alternated in the role until 1935; in Cablemaking, on the other hand, the Chairmanship was held by Atkinson of the employers, to everyone's satisfaction. In so far as the employers were more likely to be able to provide someone experienced for the post, this was inevitable. Where it was an outstanding man like Stewart of the Cementmakers Federation, the unions insisted that he continue when there were signs he wished to retire. Occasionally there were indications that the long domination of the employers' representatives was resented. In 1929 Rowan asserted at a meeting of the Electricity N.J.I.C. that they again

[1] Letter of 7th May 1922 to the Ministry of Labour Liaison Officer. It had in fact been a year since the previous meeting. Lab. 2/968/96/3.

[2] Memorandum of 12th July 1923. Lab. 2/278/103/5.

waived their right to the seat but would claim it next year, which they did.[1] Whatever the reason for the failure of some of the Councils to accept the alternation of the Chairman, it would seem that here was a relic of a way of thinking which the Councils were partly intended to eradicate.

Since voting on the Councils was by bloc and since no measure which failed to obtain a majority of both sides in its favour would be approved, there was no need for an equality of membership or number present from each side within the given quorum.[2] Much of the work was done by executives or subcommittees on conciliation, arbitration, education, wages and negotiating, apprenticeship; it was through committees of this kind that unwieldy national organisations could perform a useful function. Particularly in regard to wages and other controversial issues the use of specialist groups enabled the real problems to be isolated and wrangled over so that at least the issues were clear and the exact points of dispute properly understood by all concerned.

None of the Councils had anything like the staff that they needed if they were to fulfil their basic functions. Two only had so much as full-time secretaries—Flourmilling and Pottery—the rest made do either with joint secretaries or the secretary of the employers' association acting also as secretary of the Council. In July 1920 a Ministry of Labour Memorandum[3] on the staff deficiencies of the employers' side of the Electricity Council could be taken as a fair comment on all. The maintenance of such staffs on the other hand was an expensive business; the Pottery Council, which did things in style, had an annual budget which was originally £1,000 and which rose steadily through the years. Not unnaturally there were voices raised, especially from the union side,[4] about value for money they had provided.

The relationship between the National, District and Works Councils

Both the original *Report* and the model constitution of the Ministry[5] assumed that the national organisation would dominate in the three-

[1] N.J.I.C. *Minutes*, 19th April 1929 and 20th June 1930.

[2] The Building industry J.I.C. was an exception to this rule, hence the acceptance of the Foster Report with all its consequences, below, pp. 198–9.

[3] Lab. 2/672/118/29.

[4] Memorandum by the Ministry of Labour Officer, 15th December 1931. The issue was raised by Hollins of the Pottery Workers at the executive and general purpose meeting.

[5] *First Interim Report*, paras. 7 to 16. Above, pp. 148–9. Suggestions of the Ministry of Labour, Parts I and II, loc. cit.

tier scheme (or that at least all the other aspects of the Council's work would spring from it), and that all industries would use the three-tier scheme. But events were to show that some industries, in fact the majority, preferred to work by regions or districts and give the main power for organising the collective-bargaining structure to them with the National Council having a supervisory function or such functions as the Districts wished it to exercise. Arrangements had to be worked out by degrees in many industries, however, and the fact of having a national deliberative body in the first instance helped this consciousness to develop. The part played by District Councils continued to vary from industry to industry. In some they gradually declined in importance even to the point of disappearing altogether. The Works Committees, however, never emerged as an integral part of the scheme though some Councils made efforts to propagate them and in some industries they did play a useful part. The reason for the failure of Works Committees to establish themselves was linked with the failure of industry, even the J.I.C. industries, to appreciate fully and give effect to the co-operation norm. If attitudes determine organisations, in no part of the industrial relations structure are attitudes more important than at works level. Only when there is a genuine mutual respect for the equal rights of employers and unions and a determination to build up works committees which embody this respect do they avoid being anti-union or anti-employer devices. The sophisticated organisation and the enlightened leadership that this requires was in short supply then as now. Not surprisingly the industries in which Works Committees performed a useful function were those which showed more ability to accept the co-operation norm at other levels.

It was in the Public Utility industries that the place of the District Councils as the basis of the industrial relations and collective negotiation system in the industry was from the early days very clear. The *Electricity Supply* industry at the outset established thirteen such councils and they gradually worked out a pay structure satisfactory to both sides.[1] The N.J.I.C. ratified these agreements and changes were then applied nationally in accordance with variations in the cost of living. In 1921 the Districts were allowed direct representation on the National Council. In Gas the Regional Councils, nine of them, became the centre of the real power and activity in the industry, rationalising the pay structure which was then ratified by the National Council.[2] The

[1] *Minutes* of N.J.I.C. meetings, 16th April 1920, 12th May 1920, and 8th December 1922.

[2] Gas Supply N.J.I.C. *First Annual Report*, 1919–20. Ministry of Labour *Memorandum*, 8th April 1921, Lab. 2/458/139/3.

Local Authorities J.I.C. had sixteen District or Provincial Councils and the difficulty of direct representation on the National Council for the employers' associations (which were not national as the unions were), led to its reconstruction in 1921. The District Councils became the real centres of power though the National Council had overall surveillance and made recommendations on overtime and basic rates.[1] The Provincial Councils could act in major matters without reference to the national body; so the West Riding Council applied to the Ministry for arbitration without such reference.[2]

There were eleven district councils in operation in *Water Supply* and they worked out the details of pay structure, the N.J.I.C. having a role in other matters relating to collective negotiation—hours, holidays and the sliding scales.[3] The nine District Councils in the *Tramways* industry also had a large degree of autonomy. They graded wages and were empowered to negotiate better terms than provided in national agreements where they could.[4]

The *Cablemaking* industry was centred in London and Lancashire and District Councils were set up for these two areas in 1919. They met only when specific disputes were referred to them[5] and they had no part in the collective negotiation process beyond this. The ten District Councils in *Cement Manufacture* had the same role as those in cablemaking—interpreting national agreements and arbitrating in disputes. Because of the size of the industry in the Thames–Medway area as opposed to the rest of the country this District Council was by far the most important.[6] The *Paint and Varnish* industry was one with a strong tradition of district organisation, the National Federation of Employers, formed in 1911, being based on it. Six District Councils were set up; they provided a stage in the conciliation machinery and after a wage dispute in the London areas in 1929 they were allowed to negotiate rates above the nationally agreed scale though the scale remained the basis.[7] The Printing J.I.C. set up District Councils and organised an annual convention to which they sent delegates. The wage negotiations

[1] *Report* of Conference between the National Council and Provincial Councils, 15th September 1921. Also Ministry of Labour's *Memo* of 7th December 1921. Lab. 2/278/112/43.

[2] N.J.I.C. *Minutes*, 6th April 1923.

[3] N.J.I.C. *Minutes*, 1st July 1921. Industrial Court Award 679 of 26th July 1921.

[4] *Report on the Establishment and Progress of J.I.C.s*, p. 94. *Interim Report of the Constitution and Functions Committee*, 1st February 1926.

[5] For example, *Minutes*, 19th September 1923, 13th May 1925. Though they were not very frequently called on to exercise this function, when they did so the situation was usually an important one.

[6] Ministry of Labour *Memorandum* on the Cement Manufacturing industry, J.I.C. Lab. 2/811/532/5. N.J.I.C. *Minutes*, 6th January 1921.

[7] N.J.I.C. *Minutes*, 13th June 1930.

being in the hands of direct negotiators from unions' and employers' associations, the work of the District Councils was restricted to participation in conciliation procedures and the general discussion of problems at the Annual Convention.[1] The complex organisation of the quarrying J.I.C. embraced five sectional Councils for the five main products of the trade, each section represented on the National Council and each section having in addition area Councils within given regions. The sectional area Councils, in theory, settled rates and conditions with the approval of the central body; they also acted as local conciliation agents.[2] The *Woollen* industry was divided into four districts (Northern, West of England, Wales, Midlands) though in practice the North, employing 75 per cent of those in the industry, dominated.

The Railway and the Dock Transport industries adapted the principles of Whitleyism to their different needs. Under the reorganisation of the Railways in 1921 a Railway Council was established in each of the four regions; within each region there were five sectional councils and as many local departmental committees as were required. The Railway Councils themselves proved superfluous and under the reorganisation of the industry's industrial relations system in 1933 they were dropped. The Railway Staff National Council and a National Tribunal handled the final stages of negotiation after discussions between unions and companies on major substantive issues.[3] The N.J.I.C. for the Dock Transport industry had its equivalent of the District Councils in the Port or Area Committees which were concerned mainly with administering registration schemes and handling disputes on working rules and the application of national agreements.[4]

In another group of industries the J.I.C.s established District Councils but there is little trace of them performing any real function. So in the Chemical trades seven were established with a further one for the salt section. Originally given the power to work out agreements provided they did not affect other areas and provided also that those agreements were registered with the National Council, it was reported in 1922 that few were meeting regularly because there was nothing for them to do.[5] The Flourmilling Council orginally possessed sixteen District Councils and they were given a role in the conciliation machinery. Attempts were also made to involve them in the support of the technical education subcommittee's work but not very successfully. The rationalisation

[1] Child, op. cit., p. 257.

[2] Address of E. J. Burt, loc. cit., and a chart, 'Organisation of the Quarry Industry of Great Britain', published by the N.J.I.C., undated.

[3] See below, p. 189.

[4] Ministry of Labour *Port Labour Enquiry Report*, 1931. *Industrial Relations Handbook*, 1944.

[5] N.J.I.C. *Minutes*, 3rd April 1919 and 24th November 1922.

of the industry deprived them of any relevance; as was pointed out in the 1930's, the important decisions were increasingly made at the centre.[1] In Heating and Domestic Engineering no formal District Councils were established; the work of the National Council in fact became increasingly, and ultimately entirely, limited to the function of its Apprenticeship subcommittee.[2] That the Papermaking industry never established formal District Councils was the result of its general difficulties, likewise the troubled early years of the Soap and Candle Trades Council and its restriction to collective bargaining functions did not encourage sophisticated organisation. Collective negotiations at the local level were in the hands of the District Committee of the Federation and the unions; there were no District Councils of the J.I.C.

Finally, there was a group of industries which, because of their structure or location, did not require or could not support any formal district organisation. Tinplate, Hosiery and Pottery were so localised that any industrial council for them was a District Council. Silk was so weakly organised and so scattered that it could not have supported or organised a formal district organisation. At the deliberations of the National Council, however, everyone spoke or thought in terms of the various areas in which it was mainly centred—Brighouse, Macclesfield and Leek.

With regard to the responsibilities of the National Councils in encouraging workshop committees, some, not all, performed this function during the first flush of enthusiasm; few, very few, kept up the effort.[3] Some industries of course do not lend themselves to the sort of workshop organisation envisaged; the needs of the workers on a building site for example are vastly different from those of an engineering shop. The use of the language and concepts relevant to the Works Council was not all that helpful when what was wanted was a site committee. The weakness of the collective negotiating machinery and tradition in Silk and Hosiery would alone account for their lack of interest in this refinement; the same is true of Quarrying. In the Soap and Candle trades the dominance of Lever's and the suspicion of trade unionism that existed there made development of the sort of workshop committee Whitleyism envisaged a remote possibility from the first.

[1] N.J.I.C. *Fourth Annual Report*, 1923, p. 19, and *Fifteenth*, 1934, p. 9.
[2] As the Chairman noted in the *Minutes* of the Annual Meeting, 13th January 1931.
[3] Clay, op. cit., p. 166, mentions that the effect of the Councils in encouraging works committees had been beneficial. He does not, however, give any details. J. B. Seymour, *The Whitley Council Scheme* (London 1932), pp. 81 ff., considers one of the most obvious defects of the scheme was its failure to establish works committees effectively.

Of the Public Utility industries which mention in their J.I.C. minutes the question of works committees, Electricity Supply approved a draft constitution and circulated it,[1] as did Gas Supply where note was taken of the efforts made by the unions to ensure that all members of such councils were trade unionists.[2] The Tramways' J.I.C. approved the draft of a model constitution and as late as 1928 the reception of the minutes of some of the meetings of these works committees was recorded.[3]

The Cement Manufacturing industry not only encouraged the formation of works committees but gave them as such a place in the arbitration system.[4] There was initially on the other hand a suspicion that the committees were a lever to undermine the employers' authority and welfare committees were fostered to counter them.[5] In fact the two types of committee were able to work in harness and in harmony. In Flourmilling there was an attempt to make the committee an integral part of the machinery of collective negotiation and action. They were asked at one time to examine what could be done to relieve unemployment when trade was slack[6] but nothing more concerning the committees appears in the minutes thereafter. Not surprisingly the Pottery Council was one of the most active in trying to form workshop committees. As late as 1926 it was still, though less hopefully, urging their formation.[7] The Railway Act of 1921 provided for the equivalent of shop committees in the Local Departmental Committees and many of these were established though they never performed the role expected of them.[8]

The approach of other Councils to the question of completing the Whitley organisation by setting up works councils was at best half-hearted and perfunctory. The Chemical J.I.C. referred to the attempts being made to establish them[9] but after 1919 made no further mention.

[1] *Minutes*, 17th September 1920.

[2] Executive Committee *Minutes*, 23rd September 1920: a Ministry of Labour *Memorandum* of 15th March 1921 notes that there is very little reference in the Minutes of the Regional Councils to the question of works committees (Lab. 2/458/139/3); only two out of the ten make such reference and then only in general terms of well wishing. The *Gas World* of 11th June 1921 refers to the completeness of works organisation in the Gas Light and Coke Co.

[3] N.J.I.C. *Minutes*, 9th September 1920 and 19th January 1928.

[4] They handled disputes at first level. N.J.I.C. *Minutes*, 6th January 1921.

[5] Information supplied by Mr. A. J. Kean, O.B.E., who was connected with the Blue Circle Group industrial relations and welfare department at its inception in 1919 and until his retirement.

[6] N.J.I.C. *Annual Report*, 30th June 1921.

[7] *Report on the Establishment and Progress of J.I.C.s*, p. 74, and *Report* of the N.J.I.C. meeting, 1st May 1926.

[8] Frank Pickstock, *British Railways, the Human Problem* (London 1949), pp. 19 ff.

[9] N.J.I.C. *Report* of the Annual Meeting, 3rd April 1919.

The Cablemakers decided that they were optional, the Paint and Varnish J.I.C. put off the consideration of the matter until another time[1] and apparently never returned to it. The Papermakers thought that the matter should be left for decision at local level; the Tinplate Council that the existing workshop organisation was adequate[2] while the Wool and Allied trades after deliberating on the matter for a time, never got round to taking any action.[3]

[1] N.J.I.C. for the Electrical Cablemaking Industry *Minutes*, 8th October 1920, and Paint and Varnish J.I.C. *Minutes*, 18th September 1918.
[2] *Transcript* of the Conciliation Board Annual Meeting, 26th July 1918.
[3] N.J.I.C. *Minutes*, 22nd July 1919 and 7th January 1920.

8

Understanding the work of the Councils

As we have seen, it is extraordinarily difficult to define with precision the scope of Whitleyism. The problem arises again when the work of the Councils in practice is considered. This varied considerably. Not all of the Councils were the full collective bargaining agents for their industry; some of them dealt with the secondary procedural and substantive issues only. And in so far as they were the full collective bargaining agents their scope and success varied considerably too.

There are therefore problems of scope, content and classification. There are problems of methodology also. To understand the contribution of the Councils to the evolution of the norms outlined in the Introduction it is necessary to consider each within its historical and experiential framework. What they actually did, and the sequence in which they actually did it, is important in understanding how the framework of norms developed and what relative importance they assumed. This historical approach requires some initial inversion of the theoretical order of those norms. In the Introduction, it is pointed out that, from a theoretical and logical point of view, a model system of industrial relations according to the plan which, in retrospect, we can see the Conferences were trying to evolve, requires that the primary procedural norm, the co-operation norm, first be fully established. When it is fully accepted by both sides, they can approach the building up of the procedures and the making of substantive agreements with the frame of mind which best guarantees success. In practice, the initial concern of the Councils was not with the refinement of the primary procedural norm as a preliminary to perfecting their collective bargaining systems, but with the primary substantive issues. Success or failure here decided the comparative success or failure of those Councils which were strong enough to tackle the substantive issues effectively. Historical treatment, the treatment of their problems as they saw and experienced them, shows that given adequate organisation for effective bargaining it was the *attitude of mind* of the parties which determined their success in overcoming the substantive problems. If there were in the Councils the beginnings of an understanding of what the contractual co-operation norm involved, mutual acceptability and readiness to reach agreement on the basis of mutual rights and respect, there was a possibility that substantive problems would be solved by some compromise such as a sliding scale. The same is true of procedural problems; where there was a predisposition to take a positive view of the industrial relationship, adequate procedures could be worked out.

But consideration of the work of the Councils through the problems as they saw them also poses other difficulties with the theory of bargaining as laid down in the Introduction. First, that theory involves the acceptance of productivity-orientated collective bargaining which, in its turn, only makes sense when national economic policy aims at full employment and the public philosophy accepts the welfare state. Until the unions were convinced that the right to work or decent maintenance was accepted, they were fully justified in refusing to enthuse over productivity. The *Whitley Report* ignored this problem; only in the C.I.R.I.R. was there a realistic understanding of the need for a framework of economic policy that would make it reasonable to hope for union co-operation. An attempt therefore to analyse the work of the Councils on the assumption that anything like productivity bargaining made sense or was intended, would do violence to the facts. There were activities of the Councils, mainly ineffective it is true, that link up in theory with productivity bargaining. But none of them were connected in any way with a *quid pro quo* in terms of wages, hours and conditions. They were in a separate category which was that recognised as the proper role and concern of consultation.

There is a second difficulty in applying that classification. It is assumed that agreements are made in such a way that they are fully comprehensive and that the only disputes concern the question of interpretation and application. In fact few were comprehensive in this sense and many disputes were 'matters arising' with which agreements did not deal. In the following chapters all points of contention will be examined under the general category of *Procedures*; the evolution of the more sophisticated set of procedural norms will in that way be understood more clearly.

The work of the Councils has, therefore, to be examined industry by industry, and in each industry the significance of their work must be seen as they saw it. For obvious reasons the Councils which were the full bargaining agents for their industry were the most significant and in them the main problem, as it appears in their history, was that of agreeing on the primary substantive norms. They were by no means all as successful in overcoming their difficulties and the reasons for their failure and success indicated the importance of the attitudes of the two sides to each other, the importance of the primary procedural norm. The Councils which were not the full bargaining agents for their industry provide a separate category for examination as does the promotional, industrial efficiency and organisational work of the Councils as a whole. As the latter bore no relationship to the other functions the small effort in this direction may be considered collectively.

9

The J.I.C.s as full and efficient collective bargaining agents: agreements and procedures

(i) CEMENT MANUFACTURE

Primary substantive agreements

Under the J.I.C. the existing wage structure—compounded of pre-war district rates, plus wartime increases and the results of the arbitration award in 1919—was formalised in district agreements. Taking these district agreements as a base, rates could only then be varied in accordance with decisions of the National Council. For a period a cost of living sliding scale was in operation but after 1923 wages were stabilised and between then and 1939 the only adjustments were upwards, money wages rising from 14s. to 18s. a week according to area in this period.[1] A move to establish national minimum rates in the early 1920's did not succeed; recommendations on the matter were made by the N.J.I.C. but not enforced.[2] Given the Council's coverage[3] it very effectively regulated wages for the industry. Approved working rules were agreed in 1921 and they covered the standard working week of forty-seven hours for day and forty-eight for shift workers as well as the conditions of termination of employment—a week's notice of pay; they also incorporated the provisions of the 1919 award regarding women and youths.[4]

Secondary substantive agreements

These included an annual seven days' holiday-with-pay negotiated in 1921. The Council acted also as a clearing house for information on

[1] Figures supplied by the C.M.F.
[2] M. of L. *Memorandum*, Lab. 2/811/327, dated 23rd February 1925.
[3] Remarked on in a Memo of the same, January 1921. Lab. 2/811/532/2.
[4] 'Approved working rules' as agreed on in the N.J.I.C. *Minutes*, 6th January 1921.

safety and welfare,[1] though it was the A.P.C.M.–B.P.C.M. which set the pace here, not the Council.

Procedures

There was no formal, written agreement on disputes procedures comparable to the approved working rules though the Council had, from its constitution, a role as conciliator and arbitrator which it exercised in practice through agreed stages. Any question could be raised at works committee level and proceed through the District and National Council; major issues of variation and extension of the working rules could only be resolved nationally.[2] There was no provision for reference to arbitration by outside organisations and there is no evidence such was ever needed.[3]

(ii) FLOURMILLING

Primary substantive agreements

In a comprehensive national wages agreement signed in 1919, three grades of payment were established with a maximum and a minimum within each grade. Variations within the set limits could be negotiated in the different areas.[4] A sliding scale was in operation from 1921 to 1924 but after that it lapsed and there was no change in money wages for fourteen years until 1938 when the unions obtained the increase they had been pressing for since 1936.[5] A forty-four-hour week for shift workers and a forty-eight-hour one for day workers was negotiated in 1919 and by 1935 many firms were in fact on a forty-two-hour week. In 1937 the forty-two-hour week was standard and guaranteed.[6]

[1] *Minutes* of the Cement industry, N.J.I.C., 6th January 1921.
[2] As for example in South Wales in 1925 when a wage demand was made at works level as a result of an inter-union dispute and 'bidding up' to attract membership. The matter was decided by the National Council. *Memo* of M. of L. dated 5th February 1925, Lab. 2/811/327.
[3] Questions like the application of cement industry rates to transport workers in the industry and the modification of agreements relating to shift workers were submitted for discussion by sub-committees and ultimately for decision by the Council. *Minutes* 2nd March 1927 and 10th December 1931.
[4] N.J.I.C. *Annual Report*, 1920.
[5] Ibid., 1937 and 1939.
[6] Ibid., 1920 and 1937, and *Unity*, March 1937.

Secondary substantive agreements

The Council negotiated an annual holiday-with-pay in 1919, being one of the first to do so. It was also one of the most effective in organising technical training for its operatives. At the suggestion of the Board of Trade, the functions of the employers' association in this regard were transferred to the Council and a technical education subcommittee was set up in June 1924.[1] District Committees were asked to organise the establishment of suitable programmes in their areas and by 1927 the syllabuses had been revised and the scope of the scheme steadily extended—a four-year course replacing the previous one of two years and leading to a City and Guilds qualification. From 1931 to 1932 facilities for correspondence courses were also offered.[2] But it was the initiative shown by the Council in handling the question of redundancy which marked it out from the rest. It was gradually realised that the questions of pensions, redundancy payments or provisions and the possibility of a guaranteed week for those in work were all bound up with the human problem of security at work and the technical and economic problem of reorganisation with which the industry was very much concerned in this period.[3] In response to a suggestion by Bevin that special provision should be made about redundancy, the Millers' Mutual Association provided a fund to supply annuities for the older men as well as relief payments and resettlement allowances for the younger. The numbers in the end affected and the sums involved were small enough but the significance of the achievement remains. Five hundred and fifty were redundant during the peiod in which the scheme operated, 1929–31, and of these 380 were helped to resettle at a total cost of £20,000.[4] Later, in 1935–6, Spillers of Cardiff put a further £25,000 at the disposal of the Council for the needs of redundancy.[5] The attitude of Humphries, the Chairman of the Council, who shared that office in alternate years with Bevin, made the approach practical. It was Humphries too who realised that pensions for the older men affected by redundancy were desirable. The

[1] N.J.I.C. *Annual Report*, 1923 and 1924. [2] N.J.I.C. *Annual Report*, 1927 and 1932.

[3] There were 1,250 mills in 1907; by a process of consolidation which accelerated after the war there were only 550 in the 1930's. In 1920–7 there was a large number of amalgamations and a further round took place in 1929–30. The 30,000 employed in the industry in 1919 were reduced to 15,000 by 1939. Mrs. Edwards' article on 'Flourmilling' in *Further Studies in Industrial Organisation*, London 1947 (edited Fogarty), pp. 39 ff.

[4] N.J.I.C. *Annual Reports*, 1931 and 1932. [5] Ibid., 1936.

strict actuarial principles on which the scheme was run made its benefits small and its progress slow but by 1935 something like 120 men were drawing an average of 5s. weekly.[1] The J.I.C. also concerned itself with Health Improvement, working with the Health Authorities in exploring the causes of dermatitis and helping to combat it.[2]

Procedures

The difficulties of applying the national wages agreement of 1919 proved very great and to settle the many matters of interpretation which arose a regular court of appeal was established consisting of two members from each side of the Council under an independent chairman. The latter had a casting vote and the decisions of the court —published in a handbook in 1922—were binding.[3] They formed a case law for the industry. Questions of interpretation of the 1937 agreement were referred to the Council itself. Matters arising were dealt with on the spot if possible, failing which they were subject to conciliation by the unions and employers' association at mill, district and national level with the executive having power to make binding decisions. Questions affecting the variation of the main substantive agreements were introduced at national level.

(iii) ELECTRICITY SUPPLY

Primary substantive agreements

Because of the existing situation and the difficulties of deciding on and applying any national wages agreements, the Electricity J.I.C. delegated the working out of an agreed wage structure to each of the districts, subject to their ratification at national level. A cost-of-living sliding scale was introduced in 1921 but after 1927 was inoperative.[4] As a result of the comprehensiveness and completeness of the agreements 'every one of the 55,000 employees knows exactly the wages and the scale to which he is entitled'.[5] The District Councils also negotiated the standard working week and the other conditions of service.

[1] Ibid., 1930, 1931, 1935. [2] Ibid., 1928. [3] N.J.I.C. *Annual Report*, 1922.

[4] The custom developed of agreeing at each annual meeting that the rates should be stabilised for the year although the agreement on a sliding scale remained technically in force.

[5] N.J.I.C. *Minutes* of special meeting at Manchester, 20th October 1933.

Secondary substantive agreements

An annual holiday-with-pay was left to the District Councils to negotiate. The National Council took responsibility for the improvement of apprenticeship training initially[1] but after 1922 the matter is not mentioned in the minutes of the Council. Redundancy payments were made by the industry through the J.I.C. though the inspiration here was statutory.[2]

Procedures

These were not formalised until 1931. From the first they were district orientated. Questions of interpretation, application and matters arising were to be settled if possible at Works and District level and though there were cases when failure to reach agreement led to submission of the case to the negotiating committee of the N.J.I.C., there were cases too when they were referred directly to the Industrial Court.[3] In the difficult times following 1929, disputes became acute as some employers pressed for a reduction according to the sliding scale principle and the unions resisted. It was declared that in the case of failure to agree at district level the issue should be referred to the N.J.I.C. Failing settlement here, the terms of reference of the dispute were to be agreed by the N.J.I.C. before the matter was passed to the Industrial Court.[4] Since 1923 the codification and publication of all wage and other agreements had been the standard practice.[5]

(iv) GAS SUPPLY

Primary substantive agreements

The pay structure of the industry took two difficult years to evolve. There was some impatience on the union side with the activities of

[1] N.J.I.C. *Minutes*, 27th February 1922.

[2] Under the Electricity Supply Acts of 1919–22 and 1926 such payments were provided for. The J.I.C. for No. 10 area notes on 18th July 1928 payments were made up to a group of men at Erith. Lab. 2/797/827.

[3] As, for example, the Yorkshire district did in 1923 when it received an award (767) from the court; N.J.I.C. *Minutes*, February 1923.

[4] N.J.I.C. *Minutes*, 23rd October 1931. It proved impossible, even so, to agree on these terms and the Ministry of Labour was called in to help on occasion.

[5] N.J.I.C. *Minutes*, 21st December 1923 and 21st September 1928, etc.

the Council and on at least one occasion during the early days they were open in expressing their disenchantment.[1] In late 1921 a system of regional gradings of wages was agreed on with several categories of pay in each region. On the basis of these regional agreements, further adjustments could only be made nationally in accordance with a cost-of-living sliding scale.[2] National agreements on the standard week, payment for overtime and shift time had been concluded in 1919.[3]

Secondary substantive agreements

An annual six-day holiday-with-pay was accepted in 1920,[4] but later on there was some dispute over whether the industry should follow the example of the Local Authorities who gave their men more. In practice the six-day agreed nationally was only a minimum, exceeded in some areas. Where education was concerned, there was some brief interest in the matter under Board of Trade prompting in the early days[5] but nothing more was heard of it.

Procedures

Once the difficulties of getting the Council working smoothly had been overcome in the first few years, and the regional gradings were agreed, the level of conflict in the industry was reduced and wages were only readjusted nationally in accordance with the sliding scale. In any question concerning the interpretation of regional agreements the regions showed themselves ready to accept the decisions of the N.J.I.C. as authoritative and binding. Very few such questions came its way; conciliation at local and district level through the unions and the employers' association was very effective.[6]

[1] N.J.I.C. *Minutes*, 9th June 1920. O'Grady of the Gasworkers wanted the J.I.C. to abandon its attempts to sort out the wage structure and recommended that wage negotiations be conducted outside the scope of the Council.

[2] 'Zoning, grading agreement of the Regional Councils', *Gas World*, 27th September 1921. Ministry of Labour *Notes*, January 1925: Lab. 2/458/173. These agreements did not represent a consolidation of rates but basic rates plus bonus.

[3] Ministry *Memo*, 8th April 1921.

[4] Ibid.

[5] *Report on the Establishment and Progress of J.I.C.s*, p. 117: N.J.I.C. *Minutes*, 26th February 1919.

[6] The *Annual Report* of the period contained details of the Council's role as conciliator-arbitrator. For example a dispute over the refusal of one man to trim coke was taken up to the national level and the N.J.I.C. decisions were accepted. The South Wales unofficial strike in 1934 was settled by it too. Loc. cit., 1925, p. 21, and 1935, p. 18.

(V) WATER SUPPLY

Primary substantive agreements

The District Councils were left to work out the details of their pay structure in the various areas and the agreements were then ratified by the National Council. The cost-of-living sliding scale agreed on in 1921 was abandoned in 1928.[1] On hours the Council could only make recommendations to the Districts but the average normal week was forty-seven to forty-eight hours. A typical early agreement covering a district[2] graded pay into four zones with minima and maxima in each grade—78s. the maximum for the highest and 55s. the minimum for the lowest-paid adult male worker. Overtime, shiftwork and meal-times were set out also.

Secondary substantive agreements

The question of vocational training was not tackled by the Council though at least on one occasion a member suggested that it should do something in this direction.[3] Holidays-with-pay—a normal of twelve days—were only in the recommendation of the Council though in practice they were given in most districts; fourteen days annually were allowed in the agreement quoted. Some Councils provided sick pay; superannuation was the custom.[4]

Procedures

The principle of reference to the N.J.I.C. of disputes that the District Councils could not settle was accepted from the first. The latter could appoint a panel of arbitrators to visit the area if they wished. In the last resort reference to the Industrial Court was made.[5] The degree of autonomy possessed by the Councils in the districts posed problems

[1] N.J.I.C. *Report of the Annual Meeting*, 1st July 1921, and *Minutes* of N.J.I.C., 17th May 1928.

[2] The South Midlands District agreement of 1921.

[3] *Report of the Annual Meeting* of the N.J.I.C., 29th May 1925.

[4] The basis on which it was computed was given in the N.J.I.C. *Minutes*, 23rd July 1920.

[5] N.J.I.C. *Minutes*, 21st March 1921, and *Report* of the Annual Meeting, 1st July 1921.

in cases where reactionary industrial relations policies were pursued. In 1923, for example, there were complaints that the standard imposed by the Metropolitan Board represented a reversion to pre-war.[1] There were complaints also in the 1930's that the Council's recommendations in regard to holidays were not being put into practice.[2]

(vi) TRAMWAYS

Primary substantive agreements

It took four years of conflict and effort to revise the wage system in the industry. Four areas, with different gradings of rates, had been agreed in 1920. In 1924, these were overhauled and codified with a maximum and minimum in each grade.[3] Variations in accordance with a cost-of-living sliding scale were thereafter to be made nationally though District Councils were empowered to grant independent rises. A standard working week of forty-eight hours had been agreed in 1919 and on 18th February 1932 a new and comprehensive agreement covering hours of work, duty schedules, notices of permanent change and spread-over times, overtime, and other working conditions was signed.[4]

Secondary substantive agreements

An eight days' holiday-with-pay had been in force since 1919 and was confirmed in the 1932 agreement referred to. The same agreement included a clause guaranteeing a forty-eight-hour week. The J.I.C. also was concerned to link tram design, working standards and efficiency with safety precautions so that each could assist the other.[5]

Procedures

Because of the difficulties over the adjustment norm before 1924, disputes were on major issues of principle not covered by agreements or unsatisfactorily so covered. The N.J.I.C. appointed arbitrators in

[1] *Daily Herald*, 10th May 1923. [2] N.J.I.C. *Minutes*, 20th February 1931.
[3] Court of Enquiry *Report*, 3rd April 1924, S.P. 1924, XI, and *Report of the N.J.I.C.*, 13th November 1924.
[4] Lab. 2/887/132. [5] N.J.I.C. *Minutes*, 11th October 1923, etc.

cases referred to it, or interpreted the existing agreements when requested,[1] but two major courts of enquiry in the period 1921–4 indicate how great the problems were. The 1924 *Report* pointed out that there was no attempt at arbitration on the points at issue leading up to the strike; the conflict was too fundamental. After 1924 major substantive disputes were to be formally referred to the Council in the case of inability to reach agreement in the Districts. Unless the matter was decided within two hours of discussion by the Council they were to be left to the standing wages Council for decisions to be submitted to the Council within twenty-eight days. Failing agreement by the wages council in this period the matter was again in the hands of the full Council which had to reach a decision in twenty-one days. If they did not a Tribunal of two independents appointed by each side, two members from each side and an independent chairman were to decide—the Chairman not having a casting vote.[2] There was no provision for arbitration beyond this, it being reckoned that difficulties not soluble by such exhaustive arbitration were simply not soluble. Local disputes on matters arising were referred to the standing Council if not settled in twenty-eight days. In fact, the more effective substantive agreements reached as a result of the 1924 Court of Enquiry removed most of the major causes of conflict. Codification of agreements, for example that of 1932, was also thorough.

[1] e.g. N.J.I.C. *Minutes* of 10th January 1923, 11th October 1923.

[2] N.J.I.C. *Minutes*, 10th July 1924–18th February 1926. The attempt of the Council to find an area of common agreement on wages led to the use of comparative statistics: see below, p. 197.

10

The J.I.C.s as full but less efficient collective bargaining agents: agreements and procedures

(i) SOAP AND CANDLE MANUFACTURE

Primary substantive agreements

An informal wage agreement was signed before the J.I.C. was set up in 1919 but in 1925 this and subsequent modifications were consolidated into one comprehensive national agreement,[1] which provided for two grades of pay according to area. A minimum of 54s. a week for adult males on a standard week of forty-eight hours had been established in 1919. In the latter part of the 1930's the union pressed for the J.I.C. to enter into a further agreement giving them the better hours and rates already paid by Lever's and Hedleys. The result was a triple grading of firms with two levels of payment in each; this did not extend the better rates to all but allowed a reasonable improvement which the unions accepted.[2]

Secondary substantive agreements

Though in the fundamentals the agreements reached by the Council were sound and comprehensive, there was little progress beyond these. This was partly the result of the cautious attitude to trade unionism which was a legacy of Lord Leverhulme. He had no objection to 'enlightened' labour policies; he was a leader in them in some respects. But his approach was paternalistic and designed at least in part to counter the unions. Though persuaded with difficulty[3] to accept the

[1] 'Consolidated wages and conditions agreement', N.J.I.C., 4th March 1925.
[2] N.J.I.C. *Minutes*, 29th April 1937 and 2nd March, 10th May 1938.
[3] S. E. Musson, *Enterprise in Soap and Chemicals* (Manchester 1966), p. 318, shows that

fact of union representation on the Council, his attitude had the effect of keeping it on as tight a rein as possible. Armstrong of Crosfields, no less anti-union than he, had persuaded him to accept the Council itself initially. Armstrong himself was soon to regret it and its futility, hoping for a long and unsuccessful strike to put the unions in their place.[1] It is therefore not surprising that the range of interest of the Council was limited. In 1929, a union member commenting on the fact emphasised the achievements of the Flourmilling J.I.C.[2]—but the employers were not impressed. The only achievement of the Council beyond the primary issues was the securing of holidays with pay.[3]

Procedures

Because of the comparatively simple structure and organisation of the industry and of the comprehensive and yet simple agreements on the primary substantive issues, disputes were almost entirely concerning the interpretation or the application of agreements or general requests for readjustment. 'Matters arising' were few. By an agreement of 1920 requests for general changes in substantive agreements were subject to three weeks' notice, and failing agreement within the Council, to reference to the Industrial Court.[4] In this early period antagonism towards the unions produced a high level of conflict. It was not until after the conclusion of the 1925 agreement, which reasserted the procedures,[5] and after the effects of the 1926 strike had worked themselves out, that the level of that conflict was reduced. Codification of agreements in the industry was very complete. On matters of interpretation or application of agreements the Council decided either directly or through the recommendations of subcommittees.[6]

in March 1921 Leverhulme wished to break up the J.I.C. but Armstrong considered that 'if we render it innocuous it would be better tactics to keep it alive'; N.J.I.C. *Minutes* for 1921 are full of employers' threats to withdraw. Lever Bros. *Annual Report*, April 1921, comments on the difficulties with the Council. The Crosfield files contain *Memos* from the Ministry of Labour urging the Employers not to abandon the Council.

[1] Musson, loc. cit. [2] N.J.I.C. *Minutes*, 20th March 1929.

[3] Payment for six statutory holidays a year was agreed in December 1919 (*Minutes*, 1st December) and one week's annual holiday (*Minutes*, 9th November 1920).

[4] *Memorandum* dated 25th March 1920, Lab. 2/968/196/4.

[5] As before, the agreement insisted that there should be no stoppage in dispute until the conciliation and arbitration procedure was exhausted.

[6] The evidence of the Soap, Candle and Edible Fat Trades Employers' Federation to the Donovan Commission (February 1966) asserted that only twice since 1920 has there been reference to arbitration; joint recommendations on application or interpretation in response to differences at company or district level have been accepted by those concerned.

(ii) ELECTRICAL CABLEMAKING

Primary substantive agreements

Agreements on wages and hours had existed before the J.I.C., but the process of organising the wage structure and increasing the coverage of agreements was undertaken by it and in 1926 a codification was completed.[1] The firms and the unions party to it were listed and four grades of employment and pay for the time workers in the industry were established with the various skills grouped under one or the other. Hours of work, overtime, shift arrangements, etc., were also covered by the agreement. A cost-of-living sliding scale of wage adjustment was in operation from 1921.

Secondary substantive agreements

Though frequently pressed on the matter the employers refused to consider holidays-with-pay.[2] Their attitude was typical of their response to anything that the union tried to obtain beyond the bare primary substantive agreements. None of the other items in this secondary category had a serious chance of consideration by the employers.

Procedures

Within the limits of the 1926 agreement there was some flexibility by the employers. Major reclassifications took place, regrading of machines being undertaken as the processes and techniques developed. But there was no provision for changing any of the other norms—the operation of the sliding scale for example. The unions were increasingly restive under its operation but all their efforts to get the matter discussed or referred to some third party were fruitless. The most they could get was a juggling of the classifications and a manipulation of the scale and with this they had to be content. There was no formal disputes procedure on the interpretation of agreements or on other matters arising. Hence thorough codification of agreements which were incomplete pro-

[1] *Memorandum* of Agreement, 18th March 1926.

[2] The first request came in 1920 and it remained a hardy annual until 1937 when the employers conceded the principle.

cedurally was of no advantage overall. The District Councils were empowered to act as conciliators in local disputes and the National Council asked them on occasion to exercise this function, but their advances were likely to be rebuffed and *ad hoc* arrangements had to be resorted to;[1] it was not until 1941 that a full disputes procedure was worked out.

(iii) PAINT AND VARNISH MANUFACTURE

Primary substantive agreements

In 1919, the J.I.C. made the rates of pay throughout the country equivalent to the London rates which traditionally had been higher than in other parts of an industry which had been very region-conscious. The employers considered that they had been tricked into this and their resentment impeded any further attempts at improving the wage structure.[2] The industry was one which did not use a cost-of-living sliding scale adjustment of wages and the attempts of the unions to get a comprehensive agreement covering all grades was not accepted, nor was the attempt to get a minimum wage. The wages subcommittee of the Council actually agreed on a scheme which the employers rejected.[3] An agreement on the standard working week of forty-seven hours had been reached in 1919.[4]

Secondary substantive agreements

A holiday-with-pay—six days—was negotiated in 1920.[5] The J.I.C. was approached by the Home Office on safety problems but nothing

[1] As, for example, in a dispute at Johnson Philips reported in the N.J.I.C. *Minutes* for 25th February–21st April 1937; the management seemed to have objected to union participation in the D.C.'s efforts; eventually the C.M.A. mediated and brought about a settlement. There is much evidence in the minutes of the Council's meetings that problems of principle, in so far as they were real, were heightened by clashes of personality.

[2] The matter was mentioned when in 1930 the unions were making one of their repeated attempts to improve the wage structure and increase wage rates. N.J.I.C. *Minutes*, 13th June 1930.

[3] A subcommittee on grading was appointed in 1928; its report was made in February 1929 and rejected the next month by the employers. N.J.I.C. *Minutes*, 6th March 1929. Like the Pottery and the Tramways industry, the Paint and Varnish J.I.C. developed an interest in comparative statistics to bolster the case for or against pay increase. See below, p. 197.

[4] N.J.I.C. *Minutes*, 30th April 1919.

[5] Ibid., 14th October 1920.

came of it.[1] An approach by the Ministry of Health on the industry's health problems was as abortive.[2]

Procedures

The main problem leading to dispute was the failure to find a basis of agreement for the establishment of a wage structure satisfactory to the two sides. This raised major questions of principle rather than those of interpretation application or adjustment of comprehensive agreements. The employers' side constantly insisted throughout the 1920's and 1930's that their constituents thought they were being too soft with the unions and that consequently there was a danger of the Council being disbanded. The events of 1919 over the extension of the London minimum throughout the country still rankled. There was very little 'mutual trust'. In 1937 the allegation by the unions that agreements were not being kept led to an investigation of cases instanced. Of the seventy firms supposed to have been ignoring agreements this was proved of only two,[3] but the incident indicates quite clearly that lack of mutual confidence upon which the Council should have been based. In 1925 a crisis in pay negotiations led to the threat of its break up and only a reference to the Industrial Court saved it. In 1931 a further crisis resulted in the setting up of a subcommittee on the Constitution of the Council. Its recommendation[4]—that a Conciliation Committee under an independent Chairman should have power, in the last resort, to make binding decisions—was accepted by the Council, but though this did exercise its powers on rare occasions, in 1938 a further reference to the Industrial Court was needed.[5] The existence of the Council—with all its weaknesses and all the distrust—clearly then prevented serious disputes on these occasions in an industry in which employers and employees were prosperous by the standards of the time. The basic failure to organise the wage structure properly kept industrial relations in a state of tension and prevented the establishment of a satisfactory process for resolving these and similar disagreements. In its turn that failure to reach agreement on substantive issues was the result of inability to accept the co-operation norm.

[1] Ibid., 12th February 1919. [2] Ibid., 15th August 1919.
[3] *A.G.M. Report*, 26th November 1937.
[4] N.J.I.C. *Minutes*, 26th February to 19th November 1931.
[5] *Annual Report* of the Employers' Federation 1938.

(iv) HEAVY CHEMICALS

Primary substantive agreements

The principle of district agreements subject to variation on a national basis was accepted at the start but there was continual friction on every major substantive issue because the district agreements were ambiguous. The unions refused to accept the principle of cost-of-living sliding scale reductions in 1921,[1] and there was failure to agree on the norms governing shift working until 1935.[2] The forty-seven-hour week for day workers, however, was introduced in 1919. Wage reductions were imposed unilaterally by the employers after 1921 and references to the Industrial Court on wage issues in 1919 and in 1923 which were resolved more or less in favour of the men led to threats on the employers' side to abandon the Council. For the next six years the employers had but one thought—to cut wages to nullify these decisions.[3]

The increasingly progressive labour policies of Imperial Chemical Industries after 1926 imposed strains on the Council since the firm employed over half the wage-earners in the industry. In 1931, I.C.I. decided not to reduce shiftmen's rates, in 1932 it introduced a shorter working week and in 1933 it gave an increase in wages spontaneously. The decision of the I.C.I. to give a common basic rate for all workers whatever the district in 1936 produced the break which was inevitable. I.C.I. left the Council which temporarily disbanded. It was revived in 1937 and when it did, without I.C.I. on it, it soon began to level up the district rates and to grant wages and conditions which left it not far behind I.C.I.[4]

Secondary substantive agreements

Though I.C.I. was increasingly to the forefront in enlightened labour policies covering education, security and the rest, the only contribution of the Council was to encourage the granting of a holiday with pay.

[1] Chemical Employers' Federation *Minutes,* 15th March 1921.

[2] Ibid., 27th June 1935.

[3] Bottomley's paper cited above. *Report on Conciliation and Arbitration under the 1896 Act,* 1920, S.P. XIX, pp. 167 and 173. *Industrial Court Decisions,* Vol. VI, 1924.

[4] C.E.F. *Minutes,* 24th July 1931, 8th February and 24th February 1933 and 11th February 1936. Also Bottomley, loc. cit.

Procedures

The failure to produce satisfactory district agreements and relate them to the national Council made the industry prey to major conflict on basic points of principle concerning primary substantive norms throughout the period. The readiness to refer to the Industrial Court and the refusal of the employers to carry out their numerous threats to withdraw from the Council when its decisions were unfavourable, or the unions to withdraw when wage cuts were made unilaterally, indicate that on the most fundamental level an effective disputes procedure did exist and was based on a sufficient trust to prevent total breakdown of the Council. From time to time it was called upon to exercise a conciliation function in the districts[1] but no formal procedure was automatically applied. In brief, failure to agree on basic substantive norms and embody them in effective agreements vitiated any possibility of evolving a thorough disputes procedure. The failure on the substantive issues was in its turn traceable to an inability to move towards fuller acceptance of the co-operation norm.

(V) TINPLATE

Primary substantive agreements

The wage structure of the industry and the fully detailed working rules which it had inherited from the old conciliation board did not require major revision under the Council. A forty-seven-hour standard working week was agreed in 1919.

Secondary substantive agreements

It was the failure of the employers to make positive concessions here which indicated that the spirit in which they approached the Council was more that of the old conciliation board than Whitleyism. They consistently refused to accede to the union's request for a holiday-with-pay which they asked for first in 1923 and which they continued to press for until 1937 when it was conceded—as a privilege in view of the fact that Richard Thomas had already allowed it, rather than as a

[1] C.E.F. *Minutes*, 12th April 1922, refer to a successful mediation of the Council in a South Wales dispute.

right.[1] Bevin, who was a member of the Board, was aware of the advances being made in Flourmilling in the matter of pensions and redundancy. In 1927 the unions put forward a request for consideration of a pension scheme. The issue was passed back and forth until 1935 when Sir William Firth made a personal contribution of £25,000 to set the fund off. This was matched by the employers' association. In return Bevin pledged the unions to a 2½ per cent levy on wages; they objected and the scheme came to nothing.[2] The J.I.C. also showed some interest at one time in one aspect of safety needs—the provision of an adequate ratio of ambulance men to workers in each works.[3] In an industry where accidents were comparatively frequent this was a point of some importance.

Procedures

Until 1924, the J.I.C. was, in effect, the Conciliation Board under another name. But the unions, dissatisfied with this state of affairs, compelled a revision of the constitution.[4] Under it the J.I.C. had two functions—settling disputes and considering and advising on other matters affecting the interests of the two sides. It was to meet annually, day-to-day business being the responsibility of a Joint Standing Committee which was to handle disputes that reached national level and to appoint subcommittees to investigate and decide on specific issues. But all its decisions, and those of its satellites, were to be subject to the overall jurisdiction of the National Council. The Council alone could decide on questions of a general nature such as wage claims—of which three weeks' notice had to be given; matters arising were processed through discussion at local level between union and management, failing settlement locally a J.I.C. standing committee had to settle them within twenty-eight days; failing this there was provision for arbitration at the hands of an independent assessor.[5] The whole system worked well provided there was agreement on the primary substantive norms, but one was increasingly under fire and this was the most basic, the previously accepted norm governing the rate of general labourers which was one based on the price of steel and tin

[1] N.J.I.C. *Transcript*, 13th July 1923 and 29th July 1937.
[2] Ibid., 11th July 1935, 29th May 1936 and 29th July 1937.
[3] Ibid., 30th May 1930.
[4] Ibid., 6th June 1922 and 5th June 1925. The new constitution was signed on 12th August 1924.
[5] As, for example, before Sir Harold Morris in 1929. Ibid., 1st July 1929.

bars.[1] The basis of computation was complex but in 1934 the result was a wage of 41s.–42s. for an adult male general labourer at a time when minimum wages, in the trades which decided them by negotiation, were well over 50s. In 1929 the unions forced a revision of the scale because they were in a position of strength; in 1932 the employers did likewise from their position of strength and they did it, according to Bevin, in a spirit which was reminiscent of the nineteenth century.[2] Basic disagreements on matters such as these took much of the value out of the otherwise complete substantive agreements, well designed disputes procedures and the practice of codification of both. Again, the failure was in the inability to accept the co-operation norm more fully.

(vi) HOSIERY

Primary substantive agreements

The constitution of the Hosiery Council did not bind it to deal with wages though it was empowered to do so and in so far as there was any centralised negotiation on wages in the industry this took place through the Council. The district piece lists which were the standard method of wage determination were from the union's point of view unsatisfactory and they tried to get new ones negotiated and approved by the Council. They had some success[3] but the industry was expanding and processes were developing rapidly; the unions never caught up with either. A forty-eight-hour week was agreed in 1919 but the general slackness of union organisation in the trade meant that the agreement, and the payment of overtime based on it, was often not observed.[4]

Secondary substantive agreements

The employers persistently refused to consider the question of holidays-with-pay despite the unions attempt to secure it. There is no mention

[1] The process workers were paid by output. [2] Ibid., 11th July 1932.

[3] Noted in the N.J.I.C.'s *Minutes* from time to time, e.g. 13th January and 14th July 1921, 13th July 1922, 12th July 1923, etc.

[4] In fact more often than not; an enquiry revealed that only 58 out of 291 firms supposed to be observing J.I.C. agreements were paying overtime in 1938. Ibid., 21st July 1938. On the other hand wages in the industry were by the standards of the time good—averaging 80s. for men and 50s. for women according to N.J.I.C. figures not challenged by the unions. Ibid., 12th July 1932. In 1937 it was pointed out that they were from 10s. to 15s. more than paid for similar work in Lancashire. Ibid., 21st January 1937.

in the *Minutes* of the meetings of the Council of any attempt to extend the interests of the Council beyond the primary collective negotiating issues.

Procedures

Given the weakness of the industry's industrial relations structure, evidenced in the failure to get substantive agreements made and enforced, it is not surprising that disputes procedures were inadequate in principle and ineffective in practice. Any dispute referred to it could be handled by the Council but the inadequacy of agreements and the differences of approach in interpreting them or applying them, the lack of any automatic machinery of reference and the absence of any time limit set to cases referred made this meaningless. In 1931 an attempt was made to establish effective procedures and a small conciliation committee was set up to speed it but as late as 1936 it proved impossible even to get agreement on the basic works-to-district-to-national stages of settlement with the Council as the ultimate arbitrator. The reasons for the refusal to accept such a basic procedure were obscure, but they seem to have been compounded of the reluctance of firms to admit that the unions should be officially involved, the weakness of the employers' associations and the preference of firms for going their own way, the ineffectiveness of the unions and finally the absence of adequate agreements on price lists and their application.[1] The survival of the Council through all this and the fact that it established at least a framework of bargaining and procedures remains a remarkable, though limited, achievement.

(vii) WOOL AND ALLIED TEXTILES

Primary substantive agreements

'Award 249 of February 1919 fixed the basic minimum rates for all adult male and female timeworkers in the woollen and worsted manufacture and these rates remained the basis for 25 years.'[2] In 1922, the J.I.C. consolidated the various additions to these basic rates which

[1] Ibid., 21st January and 12th May 1936.

[2] 'Woollen and worsted industry; an historical survey of the building up of the existing wage structures.' Typescript in the Wool and Allied Textiles Employers Council files.

were the standard on which the rates of pieceworkers were calculated, into 75 per cent on the basic.[1] But disagreement on the norms for wage adjustment, indeed on the need for any further wage adjustment, led to the breakdown of the Council and the imposition of the terms employers considered suitable. The forty-eight-hour week had been agreed on in 1919 though exceptions were allowed officially, and unofficially became much more common as the Council weakened.

Secondary substantive agreements

The question of holidays-with-pay was introduced from time to time by the unions but nothing was done to give the idea effect. An attempt was made by the union in 1927 to get action on training and redundancy but nothing came of it either. The employers wanted a wage reduction accepted before they would consider setting up the requested subcommittee.[2] The apprenticeship scheme prepared by the Council in 1919 had not met with the approval of the Ministry of Labour[3] and the subject does not occur again in Council minutes.

Procedures

Failure to agree on norms governing the adjustment of wages was the main stumbling block. The District agreements were somewhat informal and it lay with them, not with the Council, to decide on adjustments. Year by year the unions asked for an increase, the employers for a reduction, and no agreement could be reached concerning relevant norms. The main trouble occurred in the Northern District Council which covered 75 per cent of the employment of the industry. In 1925 the employees' request for an increase led to the appointment of a Court of Investigation under Harold Morris, K.C., and in 1929 a Full Court of Enquiry under Macmillan.[4] The first was somewhat neutral in that it recommended neither reduction nor increase; the second recommended a reduction which the unions, after a ballot

[1] *Report on Establishment and Progress of J.I.C.s*, p. 89.

[2] The request was made by the Northern District: N.J.I.C. *Minutes*, 10th October 1927.

[3] Ibid., 15th April 1919. An education subcommittee of the Council merged with the Research Association in 1921. Ibid., 11th November 1921.

[4] *Report of a Court of Enquiry concerning matters in dispute*, etc., S.P. 1929–30, XV, which summarises the 1925 findings.

of their members, rejected completely. As a result the Northern Council, the effective strength of the J.I.C., broke up and soon after so too did the National Council. Only the Council in the Western District survived.[1] On matters arising the Council had power to set up a Court of Arbitration from a panel appointed. The *Annual Report* for 1922 for example spoke of four or five disputes being referred to it for settlement and being settled. Again it was the difference in principle on the norms governing wage adjustments which led to the breakdown; there were irreconcilable conflicts of attitude between employers and employees. The former still regarded wages as adjustable to meet the demands of trade, the latter thought only in terms of at least maintaining, preferably increasing, money wages and would not accept any reduction.

(viii) PORT TRANSPORT

Primary substantive agreements

The basic substantive agreement in the Port Transport industry was that which resulted from the Shaw enquiry of 1920; rates for some time workers were set out and allowances for regional differentials made. The agreement of 1924 which followed the strike of that year clarified time rates, piecework and overtime and the treatment of permanent men.[2] The superabundance of casual labour and the depression from which the industry suffered more than most made the maintenance of basic standards very difficult.

Secondary substantive agreements

The question of security of employment in the Port Transport industry was the most fundamental one it faced in the effort to improve industrial relations.[3] The effect that casualism had both on the attitude of the docker and the attempt to give him strong unions made it more than ordinarily difficult to establish a suitable pattern or substantive agreements. The 1924 dock strike led to the setting up of the Maclean

[1] West of England District Council *Minutes*, 29th October 1929, noted that the West of England had not suffered to the same extent as the North; it would appear that the J.I.C. here lapsed 1937–9 but was re-established, *Unity*, January 1939.

[2] Agreement of 26th February 1924. Lab. 2/1039/*Port Labour Enquiry*, 1931, M. of L. 331·761.

[3] Above, p. 44.

Committee on Registration and the Guaranteed Week; its efforts in this direction were earnest but limited because of the voluntary nature of the scheme. The 1930 Committee[1] added its efforts in this direction but was again hampered by the fact that it relied on voluntary support.

Procedures

Within the limits imposed by the situation of the industry the N.J.I.C. had the task of establishing national principles on wages and hours and acting as the last stage of the disputes procedure. By the 1924 Agreement a procedure was established for settlement at the local level through the Port or area committees, failing that disputes were referred to the N.J.I.C. which appointed a tribunal or panel, or itself made a binding decision.[2]

(ix) LOCAL AUTHORITIES

Primary substantive agreements

The industry was one of those which laid emphasis rather on the District than the National Council. To the District, or Provincial, Councils the rationalisation of the wage structure and the establishment of basic rates and differentials was entrusted. Their success was incomplete. Generally speaking it was in the urban areas or those in which the tradition of collective bargaining had been established that they were most effective. Theoretically, in each area zones of pay were established and in each zone grades for the various occupations were decided with a minimum in each grade. On this basic rate a bonus variable with the cost of living was added.[3] Attempts to ensure that this variation was decided nationally failed.[4] The National Council could only make recommendations on the standard working week and payment for overtime but by 1925 the working week was generally of forty-seven hours; extra payment for overtime was less usual.[5]

[1] *Port Labour Enquiry Report*, loc. cit.
[2] *Report of the Ministry of Labour 1923–1924*, S.P. 1924–5, XIV, pp. 54–7. *Industrial Relations Handbook*, 1944.
[3] Details from a Ministry of Labour Memo, 7th December 1921, Lab. 2/278/112/43.
[4] N.J.I.C. *Minutes*, 6th May 1921.
[5] N.J.I.C. *Report of Functions Committee*, 8th January 1925.

Secondary substantive agreements

Holidays-with-pay were the subject of recommendation only by the N.J.I.C. but by 1925 it was granted by most authorities; sick pay—also in its recommendation—was more rare. Superannuation became increasingly the practice and by 1937 most local authorities gave it.[1]

Procedures

Questions of interpretation of the district agreements were referred to the Council from the first[2] but the comparative weakness of organisation at all levels challenged the effectiveness of the procedures. At times the Industrial Court was appealed to without reference to the N.J.I.C.[3] and there were cases of Councils refusing arbitration in any form.[4] In 1933 the disputes procedures were clarified[5] but no provision for final arbitration was made.

(x) QUARRYING

Primary substantive agreements

In Quarrying too the emphasis was on the District Councils which, theoretically,[6] settled minimum rates and registered their agreements with the National Council. The latter had no power to make recommendations however or to co-ordinate the activities of its District Councils. There was no standard week recommended or enforced by the N.J.I.C.

[1] Clegg, *General Union*, p. 197.
[2] e.g. in the N.J.I.C. *Minutes*, 4th April 1924, details are given of the settlement of a case regarding the interpretation of the East Midlands sliding-scale agreement.
[3] As did the West Riding Council in 1923: ibid., 6th April 1923.
[4] A Ministry *Memorandum* for 15th September 1924 notes that the Lancashire employers had done so. Lab. 2/280/128.
[5] N.J.I.C. *Minutes*, 6th April 1933. Lab. 2/279/121.
[6] *Report on collective agreements*, etc., 1934, Vol. 1, pp. 87 ff., is sceptical about the practical extent of this power though the details it gives suggest that it was not negligible; it is clear that some sections, e.g. slate and road stone, were in greater difficulties than others.

Secondary substantive agreements

The National Council did not make recommendations on holidays with pay though it was in the power of the District Councils to give them—as did the Chalk section.[1] The close alliance between the latter and the cement industry no doubt influenced it in this respect. The industry had been traditionally concerned with safety problems due to the nature of much of its work. The N.J.I.C. co-operated with the Mines Department in drafting proposals on first aid and safety orders, the relevant parts of the Workmen's Compensation Act and the formation of a New Model Code of Rules for quarrying. There was considerable difference between the Council and the government departments concerned on many matters. The main problem, however, was not the measures to be taken and the incidence of responsibility but the difficulty of getting those concerned to observe such regulations as were made; the Council carried out a vigorous campaign on the matter.[2] It also worked with government departments in attempting to combat silicosis. A *Report* of the Safety and Welfare Committee of the Council on the matter was sent to the Ministry of Mines and the Council worked with the government on the 1929 Act and the subsequent investigations.[3]

Procedures

The Council asked the Ministry of Labour representative to draw up a scheme of conciliation and arbitration for the industry. According to it either party in a dispute could refer the matter to the N.J.I.C. which, within three days, was to set up a panel of four members under an independent Chairman to make a decision, if possible within three weeks of first reference. The Council was also empowered to propose conciliation where it seemed to it preferable.[4] There were few annual Reports of the Council which did not refer to some success or other in this field although the voluntary nature of the process and the loose organisation of the industry meant that by no means all disputes came its way.

[1] From 1921; *Unity*, March 1939.
[2] N.J.I.C. *Annual Reports*, 1924, 1925 and 1935.
[3] Home Office *Memo* in the N.J.I.C./Q Archives. N.J.I.C. *Reports*, 1925, 1929, 1930 and 1935.
[4] N.J.I.C. *Minutes*, 1st June 1920.

11

The J.I.C.s as partial collective bargaining agents

The *Whitley Report* was vague, if not confused, concerning the relationship of the J.I.C.s to the existing structures of collective bargaining. It is not surprising then that many industries assumed that the two could run parallel, the Councils being given tasks allied to the traditional bargaining functions through the secondary norms. The reasons for the decision varied with the situation of the Councils. The Railways industry in effect used Whitleyism as a background of inspiration and as a supplement to the procedural system agreed under the 1921 Railways Act rather than as an independent system of Councils. The Heating and Domestic Engineering industry seems never to have considered giving the Council a major role in wage negotiation. The J.I.C. in Building was more guild socialist than collective bargaining orientated from the start. Pottery, presumably because of its misguided tendency to stress a unitary concept of the industrial relationship, never invoked the powers of bargaining which were in the first instance conceded to it. Printing was too jealous of its existing traditions and the attitudes they embodied to countenance the possibility of change though the J.I.C. had originally a minor procedural role. The Boot and Shoe industry already possessed a collective bargaining structure and scope, and an appreciation of the co-operation norm, which made Whitleyism superfluous. The Silk industry J.I.C. was never strong enough to have the bargaining functions it should have had and the Papermaking industry did not possess the basic attitudes which would have made Whitleyism workable, with or without a collective bargaining function.

(i) RAILWAYS

The singular circumstances in which the railway industry was introduced to Whitleyism have already been mentioned.[1] The main

[1] Above, p. 175.

contribution of the Whitley scheme to the improvement of industrial relations was not so much in the more sophisticated machinery that it brought to bear, but the new spirit in which it wished to see machinery worked, a spirit at one with the co-operation norm. That the railways were able to come through the period of turmoil of the immediate post-war years with an improved system of industrial relations to their credit rather than a worsened one, as in mines and engineering, was mainly due to the desire for co-operation.[1] That, at the crucial time the Prime Minister, Thomas and the Directors were able to see in the Whitley scheme the answer to their problems, the means by which the rights of each could be reconciled, is an indication of the aptness of its philosophy.

The structure of collective bargaining and the main agreements had been determined before the Railways Act was passed. Failing agreement between the unions and management on any major issue, a Central Wages Board negotiated for all the regions with a National Wages Board exercising an arbitrative function.[2] The system worked reasonably well but the economic difficulties of the early 1930's led the Companies to request its revision. The result was that wages were negotiated through a Railways Staff National Council with a National Tribunal to act, not as an arbitrator but as an interpreter of agreements.[3]

The particular contributions of Whitleyism to the industrial relations system in itself[4] were the Local Departmental Councils (comparable with the Works Councils), the Sectional Councils (for which there was no strict equivalent in the Whitley scheme) and the Railways Councils (one for each region, comparable with the District Councils). The Railway Councils had no real function and eventually in 1935 disappeared; the other Councils had been given consultative functions according to the Whitley scheme but they became what the men concerned wanted them to be, namely adjuncts of the collective bargaining system, acting as interpreters of substantive agreements. Questions of working hours and meal times, holiday arrangements, transfers, redundancy—these were the issues that found their way into the deliberations of the Councils.[5] As such they did a useful job. There was no

[1] On industrial relations in the railways industry between the wars Bagwell, pp. 413 and 416, and Frank Pickstock, *British Railways: The Human Problem*, Fabian Research Pamphlet 142, pp. 17 ff.

[2] Bagwell, op. cit., pp. 409, 412, 417–18.

[3] Bagwell, op. cit., pp. 540 ff. *Report of the Special Joint Committee on the Machinery of Negotiation for Railway Staff*, 8th February 1934.

[4] J. H. Richardson, *Industrial Relations in Great Britain* (London 1938), p. 118.

[5] Pickstock, op. cit., pp. 19 ff.

demand for the more elevated role that they had been given; the Railway Councils died from inanition and under the 1935 scheme were not revived.

(ii) HEATING AND DOMESTIC ENGINEERING

The success of the Council here was based upon its work on a substantive issue—craft training. The problem of standards of craftsmanship in the industry was greater than in most because it had developed from the older craft trades—plumbing, ironworking, blacksmithing and pipe-fitting[1]—and its skills were to some extent an amalgam of these older trades while the techniques it was developing and the work it was doing was introducing new problems. In the 1920's a 'Schedule of operative heating and domestic engineers' work'[2] covered twelve types of installation which the craftsman was expected to master. The Council realised that it could serve a very useful purpose in the area of craft training. An agreement of service for the apprentices was approved in March 1920, the Education Committee of the Council took up the question of classes and technical education in the various centres throughout the country and in April 1921 the Council began to co-operate with the City and Guilds institute, then in process of revising its examination schedules and syllabuses, in working out details for courses in Heating and Domestic Engineering.[3] 'Advice to students' was published by the Council in 1923 and later the principle of day release was accepted by the employers. By the end of the 1920's the City and Guilds examinations were operative, there were formal classes in operation in six main centres and in 1936 and 1937 a National Apprenticeship Council with its area committees was established and a new agreement of service was in force. Progress was not easy in these years; the unfavourable economic conditions and the difficulty of

[1] Company histories, for example *Hadens—150 years* (London 1966) and *The story of the Association of Heating, Ventilating and Domestic Engineering Employees* (London 1954), give clues to the development of the industry from warm air stove installation in the nineteenth century to the complicated refrigeration and air conditioning of today. The development of the union from the 'Amalgamated Society of Kitchen Range, Stove grate, Gas stove, Hot water, Art metal and other Smiths' through the various Fitters' unions and White and Blacksmiths shows the many streams that joined in the industry.

[2] Published by the N.J.I.C. in 1929 and listing hot air and steam heating in buildings, ships and rolling stock, pumps, accelerators, storage tanks, ventilating, air conditioning, drying, dust extraction, cooking apparatus, hot water systems, pipe fitting, hydrants and sprinklers, air compressors and refrigeration plants.

[3] N.J.I.C. *Minutes*, 5th April and 12th July 1921.

controlling the practices of all the firms in the industry made for many difficulties. Properly indentured apprentices were numbered in the tens rather than in the hundreds;[1] but the foundations were firm and the progress sure if it was slow.

(iii) BUILDING

Though the activities of the Building J.I.C. were increasingly centred on bringing about changes in the whole system of ownership and management, which not unnaturally angered the employers and brought about the Council's demise,[2] the First Report of its Management and Costs Committee[3] contained more moderate suggestions—for example a scheme for unemployment pay provided for from a percentage on wages bills plus a state subsidy, and superannuation provided for in the same way. The details of the scheme were never worked out, however, and the whole issue soon was overshadowed by controversy over the *Second Report* of the Committee. The Training and Apprenticeship Committee's *Report* was more practical. On the mundane issues of improvement of craft training it carried out an effective and energetic propaganda campaign. Local Building Trades Apprenticeship committees were set up throughout the country with the co-operation of the Training Department of the Ministry of Labour and attempts made to procure compulsory attendance at day continuation schools.[4] The Builders' historian pays tribute to the effectiveness of the Council's work in these matters in the short period of its existence.[5] Unfortunately one of the decisions taken by the N.F.B.T.E. upon the collapse of the Council was that the work of the Apprenticeship and Training Council should cease. The J.I.C. also drew up reports on standards for scaffolding and building generally as well as for safeguards for wood-cutting machinists which were put before the Home Office but not acted on.[6]

(iv) POTTERY

The Pottery J.I.C. started off with high hopes but its career proved that without initial attention to fundamental substantive agreements

[1] *Story of the association*, etc.

[2] See below, pp. 198–9 ff.

[3] Published in 1920.

[4] *Report on the Establishment*, etc., p. 115.

[5] Postgate, op. cit., p. 442.

[6] *Report on the Establishment*, etc., p. 129.

and procedures, within or without the Council, success elsewhere was of little significance. Though empowered to deal with wages the J.I.C. never did so. Since there was no really effective system of collective negotiation in operation in the industry apart from the Council it tended to operate in a vacuum. It had some powers procedurally, responsibility for conciliation and arbitration in the industry and it used these on two famous occasions—in 1924 and in 1931. In 1924 the unions were faced with a proposed wage reduction of 10 per cent. This they refused to accept and invoked the constitution of the Council to call a special meeting. As a result the Council set up a Committee of six members from either side with Mr. Wethered, K.C., as Chairman, and Messrs. Rowntree and Clay as the independent members, the three independents having power to arbitrate in the last resort. One thing the enquiry revealed was the hopeless tangle of the wage structure which was a reproach to both sides and the cause inevitably of much dispute.[1] The decision of the Committee was in favour of the unions; instead of a 10 per cent cut they received a 2½ per cent increase in their rates.[2] Officially this was the last adjustment in rates until 1931 though the unions often complained that unofficial reductions took place. In 1931, with the depression at its height, the unions again appealed to the Council for a similar committee. It was set up on the same lines as before with the same three independents sitting. This time the decision went against the unions. That cured them of any further desire for conciliation or arbitration through the Council. When in 1935 the union negotiated increases of from 3 to 5 per cent Hollins, the General Secretary, made a point of remarking the contrast with the 1931 proceedings. In regard to craft training the Council made several attempts[3] to organise a scheme but these came to nothing. It responded to the Balfour Committee's criticisms of its selling and costing methods to the extent of recommending the establishment of a sales technique and costing course at the North Staffordshire Technical College.[4]

The J.I.C. had a most creditable record in attempting to improve industrial health. The problem was greater in the industry than in

[1] Clay's appendix to the Pottery Wages Award (*Pottery Gazette*, 1st August 1924), an award which took months rather than weeks to make because of the complexity of the situation, remarks on and reveals clearly the hopeless jungle of rates and differentials. As part of its attempt to find grounds for agreement for negotiating wage adjustments, the Council also took to collecting comparative statistics.

[2] Warburton, op. cit., p. 230. Report of the Special meeting in *Pottery Gazette*, 1st May 1924, and the *Award*, loc. cit.

[3] *Reports* of Annual Meetings, 1923, 1929 and 1933, etc.

[4] *Report* of Meeting of 15th October 1930.

most.[1] Processes, equipment and materials all required improvement in order to reduce the threat of silicosis and lead poisoning to which the pottery worker was exposed. Improvements in the glazing process, in the design of the ovens and kilns and workshops generally and the insistence of the most rigid standards of personal and workplace cleanliness were the answers and to them all the Council applied itself with commendable vigour. Its subcommittees worked with the Industrial Health Research Board,[2] it registered the complaints of the Inspectors of Factories concerning the neglect of regulations and the failure to appoint officials to see that they were observed,[3] and from 1929 onwards, as a result of its success in these matters, was highly commended by the Inspectorate.[4] There was little it could do to compel the rebuilding of workshops and kilns and the introduction of the safer processes but it did as much as it could by propaganda and exhortation. Opportunities were provided for the publication of the best methods and designs and after each meeting papers were read on the subject of improving health and efficiency in the industry.

(v) PRINTING

Here the Joint Industrial Council found a place in disputes procedures. From the first it had the obligation of considering all disputes placed before it by the District Councils, but the implications of this in an industry in which all basic issues were handled by the separate collective negotiation machinery soon became clear. It was decided that there was still a place for the Council, provided that written applications on disputed points were submitted and that failing settlement, the full Council was to consider the issue. It did so as a conciliator not an arbitrator, it being made plain in the *N.J.I.C. Report* for 1937 that the J.I.C. exists 'Not to settle differences but assist the parties to settle them'. In this capacity the Council had a useful if limited and unspectacular role to play.[5] Its only other contribution was to attempt, unsuccessfully, to improve apprenticeship training and methods; but

[1] It had the highest death rate in the 24–45 age group of any industry in 1922; *Report* of the Registrar General quoted in the *Gazette*, 1st September 1923.

[2] *Report on the Establishment and Progress of J.I.C.s*, p. 132.

[3] It called conferences of the officials responsible for the observance of regulations and gradually increased the number, importance and effectiveness of those appointed.

[4] *Pottery Gazette*, 2nd September 1929 and 2nd September 1935. In 1939 a pamphlet was issued bringing together all the regulations on health and safety affecting the industry.

[5] This was the opinion of the men concerned as recorded by Child, op. cit., p. 265.

both sides had too much to lose in handing over this matter to the Council and as late as 1938 the J.I.C. could not even accede to the request of the British Federation of Master Printers to draw up a syllabus; nor could it co-operate with the Printing Industry Technical Board in the matter of craft training.[1] In so far as there was a limited improvement in craft training standards and facilities in the period the few idealists on the Apprenticeship Committee deserve full credit[2] but it was never in a position to encourage or support any comprehensive scheme. The J.I.C.'s Health Committee had more success in dealing with the problems of the industry in its sphere.[3]

(vi) BOOT AND SHOE MANUFACTURE

The collective negotiation system in the industry was highly developed at the time that the J.I.C. was introduced and on all major substantive issues and norms, and the procedures for reaching, interpreting and applying agreements (and settling matters arising) the machinery was very nearly complete. The only substantive issues in which the Council attempted to involve itself were efforts to provide unemployment insurance under the 1920 Act and to formulate a voluntary sickness benefit scheme. The first came to nothing by the cancellation of the 1920 Act and the second was overtaken by the onset of the depression in 1921.[4]

(vii) SILK MANUFACTURE

The decision of the Silk J.I.C. to exclude wages and conditions from its scope when it was empowered to deal with them so disgusted the union members that they were thereafter moved from time to time to express their preference for a Trade Board.[5] Attempts to get a 30s. minimum for women established as a norm were not successful. The only achievement of the Council was a recommendation of the forty-eight-hour week, a recommendation frequently ignored.[6] Procedures were correspondingly ill organised. Not until 1933 was an attempt made

[1] N.J.I.C. *Reports*, 1937 and 1938. [2] Child, op. cit., p. 262.

[3] Ibid., p. 258. [4] Fox, op. cit., p. 404.

[5] E.g. at the N.J.I.C. Meeting of 19th October 1927 Birch, of the Textile Workers, did so.

[6] The National Silk Workers briefly seceded from the Council in 1932 because of its ineffectiveness in this and other matters. *Minutes*, 18th October 1932, and *Annual Report*, 1934.

to formalise them and it was agreed, at the suggestion of a Ministry of Labour official called in to advise on the matter, that mediation by trade unions and employers at local, district and national level should take place with the Council acting as ultimate conciliator but not arbitrator.[1] It was emphasised at this time that the Council did not have any powers to deal with wages. Given the weakness of the Council on the basic issues and the failure of the industry to provide an adequate collective negotiation system independent of it, it is surprising to find that the Council worked out one of the most elaborate education schemes formed by any J.I.C.[2] It is less surprising that it came to nothing.

(viii) PAPERMAKING

The Council was deprived of all responsibility for wage negotiations but it was given some procedural responsibility—there was to be no strike on any issue without its being asked to mediate.[3] The one reference made under this was in 1921 when the new agreement the employers were seeking was feared by the union would lead to a return to pre-war standards. Discussion in the Council assured them that this was not so and they accepted the agreement.[4] But there had been from the start of the Council, and from the establishment of formal collective bargaining after the war, a deep antagonism between certain sections of the unions and certain firms as well as between the unions too. The dispute at Cowans, Valleyfield,[5] in 1924 finally so split the Council that it ceased to function effectively thereafter. During its short life it had established a safety subcommittee which died with the Council. That the Employers' Federation were later convinced that hasty action had to be taken to improve standards indicates that a gap had been filled by the forgotten subcommittee.[6] The only other contribution made by the Council was to obtain the co-operation of the unions with the technical section of the Papermakers Association at the latter's request.[7]

[1] N.J.I.C. *Minutes*, 25th April 1933.
[2] Ibid., 29th October to 20th December 1923.
[3] *Constitution* of the Papermaking Industry J.I.C., February 1921.
[4] N.J.I.C. *Minutes*, 1st July 1921.
[5] N.J.I.C. *Minutes*, 11th January 1923, etc., and E.F.P.M. *Minutes*, 1922 and 1923, *passim*. In 1925 the disputes procedure still named the Council as the court of last appeal but thereafter it is dropped.
[6] N.J.I.C. *Minutes*, 12th October 1922, and the *Annual Report of the E.F.P.M.*, 1933.
[7] N.J.I.C. *Minutes*, 20th July 1922.

12

Other activities of the Councils

The activities of the Councils in other spheres can be subdivided into three main areas; the first concerns the collection and the dissemination of statistics, the second the interest in and the encouragement of improvement in industrial organisation and techniques, the third the representation of the industry's interests to the government especially and, in particular, in the matter of obtaining protection in trade difficulties.

(i) THE COLLECTION AND DISSEMINATION OF STATISTICS

It is an assumption not without justification that an organisation which has a better idea of what its performance and potentialities are in statistical terms is better able to organise its activities economically and rationally. To be fully justified, of course, the information concerned has to be accurate and as relevant as possible. Further the industry and the individual managers within it have to be in a position—through their ability and the basic strength of their organisations—to use it. The *Whitley Report* and the constitutions of the Councils based upon it had great faith in the power of information and statistics to help the industries to face their difficulties but few of the Councils seriously applied themselves to the task of collecting them at all, let alone to collecting them properly. Where they did they were mainly concerned with wage adjustment. The industry which exercised most effort in this matter was again the Pottery industry. The statistics it collected were designed to yield a generally acceptable idea of what fair wages and fair profits were. But since those relating to profit relied largely on information provided by the employers' associations they were open to challenge and challenged they were, especially on the matter of average returns on capital over the years.[1] The unions thought these were vastly underestimated but the employers refused to revise

[1] N.J.I.C. *Minutes*, 16th December 1927, etc.

them or divulge any more information. The value of the Council's efforts in collecting statistics may be doubted. Apart from the external difficulties of the industry, its structure did not encourage sufficiently the needed modernisation.[1] As for the wage structure, the superficial statistics on wages which the Council collected were no substitute for its overhaul, the need for which had been revealed conclusively by Clay's study.[2]

The interest of the Tramways industry in statistics was purely in relation to wage determination. Because the industry was in decline and because the contrast between the rates for busmen and for tramwaymen was a constant source of irritation to the latter,[3] comparative figures were of great interest to them in their negotiations. In 1920, two successive subcommittees were established to calculate the cost of living, the bonuses paid in comparable industries and the general financial structure of the industry. Their findings did not lead to settlement in the first instance but did provide the basic information on which a settlement was eventually agreed.[4] Later on several Councils, the Paint and Varnish J.I.C. in particular, collected comparative statistics to help them in their wage negotiations.[5] Other Councils republished in their annual reports official statistics in unemployment, accidents and so forth but this involved no action or effort by the Council beyond their printing.

(ii) INDUSTRIAL ORGANISATION AND TECHNIQUES

The basic organisational pattern of an industry—the size of firms, the optimum unit of production—may be well set while allowing for limited improvement in machinery and technique within the framework. On the other hand improvement in techniques may be so radical that the whole organisational structure of the industry may have to be changed. Organisational changes are in some cases brought about by economies of scale although there has been no fundamental improvement in techniques or equipment. The J.I.C. industries covered all three types.

[1] Pollard, op. cit., p. 124. [2] Above, p. 192.

[3] A Ministry of Labour *Memorandum*, Lab. 2/885, 5th November 1923, shows that the maximum rates for busmen were £4 5s. 6d., those for tramwaymen £3 6s.—and the working conditions of the former were better.

[4] *Report on Establishment and Progress of J.I.C.s*, p. 111.

[5] N.J.I.C. *Minutes*, 26th April 1938; a survey of eighty-four industries was made in order to settle disputes on comparability.

The Pottery industry was in the first category; though there were good examples of radical reorganisation in some sections, as a whole the structure of the industry remained what it had been. But even within it there was much more room for improvement in design of plant and layout of factories and the Council members were aware of and intent upon encouraging both. Papers were read after each meeting on the various technical and design problems of the industry,[1] and reports on the latest developments at home and abroad were made by members.[2] At one time the printing unions suggested that the employers might pay more attention to the improvement of machinery but this was in the context of a dispute over who should be doing what rather than a direct contribution to the improvement of efficiency.[3] On advertising methods and quality control, Bevin had some useful proposals to make to the ailing tinplate industry. Among these was his suggestion for the establishment of a canning factory in South Wales to bring home to the trade the importance of accuracy and evenness of quality in the product if the British industry was to get a decent share of this new market.[4]

Industries in which radical technological improvement was combined with structural and organisational change included Chemicals, Cement, Flour and Tinplate. Only in the last was any serious attempt made by the Council to take part in decisions concerning the future pattern of the trade. Here the trade union side of the Council led by Bevin, was very indignant that the decision on the resiting of the new rolling mills was taken without their knowledge but a subcommittee subsequently established on the matter achieved nothing.[5]

Soap and Candles and Electricity Supply were undergoing a degree of rationalisation during the period as the economic logic of larger units and consolidation asserted itself, though basic technology was little changed. Because of the effects of growing obsolescence, the Tramways J.I.C. was interested in the co-ordination of transport services.[6] The interest of the Councils in the other industries did not extend to this sphere—with one exception, building, and here the concern was very radical indeed.

There were from the first vested interests at work in the Council

[1] In January 1924, for example, the Council heard a paper read by a representative of Pilkingtons on stove design. *Pottery Gazette*, 1st February 1929.

[2] Colonel Kent reported on his visit to America and the inspection of the methods in use in the twenty factories he examined. Ibid., 2nd August 1926.

[3] Child, op. cit., p. 266.

[4] N.J.I.C., *Transcript*, 1st July 1929.

[5] Ibid., 11th July 1935.

[6] For example a paper on the subject was read by a trade union member at a meeting on 13th July 1927.

which owed their inspiration rather to socialist and allied ideas rather than to Whitleyism, but the advent of the Whitley scheme gave such interests a plausibility and an entrance to the affairs of the industry they would have otherwise lacked. The scheme for reorganisation was produced by the Management and Costs Committee of the Council of which an employer, Thomas Foster, was Chairman. The first report of this Committee was a pedestrian affair, compared at least with that of its successor which 'glimpsed the possibility of the whole of the building industry being welded together into one great self-governing democracy of organised public service. We believe,' the Committee reported, 'that the greatest task of the industrial council is to develop an entirely new system of industrial control by the members of the industry itself, whether by hand or brain, and to bring them into co-operation with the state as the central representative of the community they are organised to serve. Nothing short of this will produce the full development of the team spirit in industry, which is the Key to the whole problem of industrial production. Nothing short of this is worthy of the high ideal for which our industrial council stands.'[1] Management must be salaried and capital hired at the going rate with the surplus earnings being divided between producers and consumers. Not surprisingly the minority report disagreeing with all this was signed by five out of the seven employers on the committee who noted that 'we have not found among the members of the Employers' Federation anyone who agrees with the proposals'.[2]

The proposals of course went far beyond the logic of Whitleyism. The scheme for the National Guilds from which it took its inspiration was in fact published by the Council together with the Foster Report.[3] The employers followed up the objections of the five members of the committee by refusing to have anything to do with it although they accepted the need for the Council and continued their support for it.[4] R. B. Chessum led the attack on the *Report* in the Council. After a long and acrimonious dispute which led to the danger of a disorderly end to the proceedings, according to one reporter,[5] the report was referred back. In the meantime Chessum and those who thought like him continued to keep up the pressure within the Employers' Federation which eventually withdrew from the Council in 1922.[6]

[1] Revised draft of the *Interim Report* of the Management and Costs Committee of the Industrial Council for the Building industry, 1920, Part II, Appendix 1, para. 1.
[2] Ibid., Appendix III. [3] Appendix II. [4] *Annual Report of the N.F.B.T.E.*, 1920.
[5] In *The Master Builders' Association Journal*, 1st September 1920; the meeting took place on 12–13th August 1920.
[6] *N.F.B.T.E. Report* of meeting 3rd November 1920. *Annual Report*, 1921: *N.J.I.C. Report* of the meeting of 18th May 1922 when the N.F.B.T.E. resigned from the Council.

(iii) THE REPRESENTATION OF INDUSTRY'S NEEDS

In industries which suffered from overseas competition the trade unions and employers possessed a ready-made community of interest to which many of them gave effect in practice. Events were to provide the pressure for protection; the Councils were simply one of the interested groups ready to see that the lesson of the situation was learned and that they received whatever benefit could be gained.

The Boot and Shoe industry J.I.C. was concerned to get the industry included under the limited protection of the Merchandising Marks Act,[1] the Quarrying J.I.C. to ensure that British materials were used in preference to foreign ones on public works though the response to its efforts was to emphasise that better marketing methods and better delivery dates were its need rather than preferential treatment.[2] The Hosiery industry J.I.C. was earnest in pursuit of the protection of the Merchandising Marks Act and later protective legislation;[3] so too was the Silk industry—this being the one aim which it pursued consistently.[4] Not all the J.I.C.s which could have pursued the same line did so. The trade unionists on the Tinplate J.I.C. told the employers that the best assurance of prosperity was efficiency and adaptability not preferential treatment.[5]

On other matters in which the Councils acted for the industry no identifiable pattern emerges. The Electrical Cables J.I.C. was on one occasion referred to by the Board of Trade concerning enquiries made to it about the supply of British cables to foreign countries; the Council passed the matter on to the Manufacturers' Federation.[6] On the other hand the unions did work very closely with the employers in this industry, through the J.I.C., in urging railway electrification and telephone developments, which would increase the demand for cables.[7] The Electricity J.I.C. pressed the right of the Council to be represented on the Joint Board for the industry[8] and made known its support for the Electricity Supply Act of 1933.[9] The Heating and Domestic Engineer-

[1] Fox, op. cit., p. 451.

[2] *Report* of deputation to Herbert Morrison, 17th December 1929, and *N.J.I.C. Annual Report*, 1930 and 1933.

[3] From 9th January 1919 onwards there were few reports which did not contain some reference to protection—the obtaining or the working of it.

[4] N.J.I.C. *Minutes*, 24th July 1919, etc., and *Annual Reports*, 1934 to 1936.

[5] N.J.I.C. *Transcript*, 6th March 1924.

[6] N.J.I.C. *Minutes*, 22nd September 1920.

[7] N.J.I.C. *Minutes*, 21st January 1931, etc.

[8] N.J.I.C. *Minutes*, 16th February 1923.

[9] Ibid., 15th September 1933.

ing industry J.I.C. tried on several occasions to get a settlement to the vexed question of demarcation between plumbers' work and that of its operatives, and several of the Councils were approached to give evidence to official enquiries or Royal Commissions.[1] The Tramways J.I.C. sought revision of the procedures regarding police summonses[2] and the Water Supply J.I.C. received an extraordinary request from the Association of British Chambers of Commerce in 1926. It asked that the sheltered industries should remember that they possessed advantages in the setting of wages which others did not and requested them to keep their wages in line with those in the export trades.[3] Many of the Councils were represented at gatherings such as the League of Nations Union Conference in 1927 and several were active in the Association of J.I.C.s, which will be discussed in more detail later.

[1] So the Pottery J.I.C. to the Balfour Committee, the Local Authorities J.I.C. to the Royal Commission on Unemployment Pay and the Quarrying J.I.C. to the Fair Wages Committee.

[2] N.J.I.C. *Minutes*, 12th May 1927, etc.

[3] The letter is in Lab. 2/920/390/1.

13

The Whitley Councils and government policy on industrial relations

(i) THE QUESTION OF STATUS

The Whitley scheme was presented to the British people and British industry, after much hesitation and sounding of opinion, as having official approval.[1] The extreme caution of the *Report* itself in avoiding any suggestion of compulsion in the application of its remedies was reflected by a government which was quickly to show more liking for a return to 'normalcy' in social and economic policy than its Coalition mandate justified. Caution was generally made necessary by the inevitable reaction against government interference once the war was over and by the tradition of voluntarism in British industrial relations. Yet the refusal of the government to accept Montagu's recommendations on procedure regarding the *Report* suggests that the caution was overplayed. To have called together small formal Conferences between the Prime Minister and the leaders of each industry to recommend to them in the warmest terms possible the implementation of the *Report* was not more in principle than the government was to do on a much more grandiose scale in the National Industrial Conference of 1919 for much more dubious purposes. It is not that such a procedure would have guaranteed the wider application of the scheme although Lloyd George and J. H. Thomas negotiated for Whitleyism on the railways. It is failure to use it that indicates the lukewarmness towards the *Report*. The leaving of the task to the Ministry of Labour and Reconstruction, together with the reluctance of the government to implement the recommendations of the *Report* among its own employees until forced, confirm the suspicion that there was no real conviction behind its acceptance.

The Ministry of Labour for its part showed very considerable

[1] See above, pp. 113 ff., especially Roberts, 'Question for decision' in the *Report*, there cited: 'The establishment of the J.I.C.s on the government's suggestion . . . implies a degree of Government recognition hitherto conceded to no industrial association and will be regarded as entitling the new organisation to a special position in relation to the government.'

energy in the first stages. As already noted[1] few of the J.I.C.s were established spontaneously. With the exception of the two or three industries which were developing towards J.I.C.s independently of Whitley, even industries well disposed towards and able to form Councils needed the encouragement of official intervention and direction. Many—Quarrying, Cement, Electricity, Gas, Water Supply, Tramways, Papermaking, Cable Manufacture, Hosiery and Silk (to say nothing of Railways and Docks)—were actually pressured into the formation of Councils. The Local Authority J.I.C. was later to claim that it had been practically forced on the industry[2] and a similar recollection lingered on in others too, for example Hosiery[3] and Electricity supply.[4] There was in the first stages Ministerial support for the drive. At a Conference of I.I.R.C.s in February 1919[5] Shackleton of the Ministry of Labour, speaking in the presence of Auckland Geddes, pointed out the Trade Board alternative to I.I.R.C./J.I.C.s and went so far as to say that the cotton and the coalmining industries would do well to adopt the Whitley scheme which had many advantages for them despite their pride in the effectiveness of their own collective negotiation arrangements.

But the Coal Controller had informed the Ministry of Labour that it would be as well if for the moment the government left the industry alone to sort out its own industrial relations, and that he was confident of the ability of its leaders to overcome difficulties.[6] By 1919 it was plain that more than this was needed and the Ministry began to explore the possibilities of a Council being set up. The North Staffordshire and the Lancashire area, with some considerable support in Yorkshire, were, it considered, ready to set up pit and district committees on the Whitley model but powerful forces in the unions—Smillie and Smith leading them—were holding out for nationalisation.[7] By the end of the year the Ministry officials concluded that nothing could be done. There was no common ground between the parties. 'The primary condition for the success of Whitleyism', said a Ministry of Labour official,[8] 'is the

[1] Above, pp. 141 ff. [2] Above, p. 143. [3] Above, p. 142.

[4] A trade union member made the added point that the Councils had been accepted under protest at a time when the unions were strong and that in their time of weakness the Councils had a right to expect government support for their decisions. Ministry of Labour *Memorandum*, 17th March 1922, Lab. 2/673/143/19.

[5] *Report of the Proceedings of the Conference of Chairmen, Vice-Chairmen and Secretaries of the I.I.R.C.s at Caxton Hall*, 18th February 1919, N.J.I.C./Q Archives.

[6] 'History of the negotiations with the Ministry of Labour re the appointment of a J.I.C. in the Coal Industry', Lab. 2/387/12082/3. [7] Ibid.

[8] Ibid., *Memorandum* on the proposed appointment of a J.I.C. in Mining by J. L. Ramsbottom, 24th October 1919.

attitude of the parties.' In mining the attitude was not favourable.

The Ministry had no more success with the Engineering industry. Here it was the Ministry of Reconstruction's Advisory Council on Labour and Industrial Organisation which attempted to persuade the industry, but having met some of the chief employers and trade unionists this body reported that 'it does not appear to us to be advantageous for us to continue our investigation any further in the matter'.[1] As Clay[2] points out, the engineers were too concerned with the restoration of pre-war practices and the possibility of workers' control to notice Whitleyism.

Industries which on the other hand had succumbed to the blandishments of the Ministry had every right to think that they were part of the official organisation of industrial relations as laid down in the *Whitley Report* and adopted by the government. The J.I.C.s were official in the sense that the government said it wanted to see them and had, through the Ministry of Labour, pressured those who could be pressured into accepting them. Industries whose organisation was weak, whose leaders openly or covertly questioned the acceptance of trade unionism or the necessity of collective agreements, should hardly have been allowed to act as a basis for government industrial policy after the events of 1917–19. But from 1920 onwards the plea that nothing could be done to force the pace of Whitleyism was made time and again, and no initiative could effectively be taken against the industries whose attitudes were contrary to it. Rather they must handle their own affairs. The Geddes Report on public expenditure in 1921–2 even considered the possibility of abolishing the Ministry of Labour and returning its necessary functions to the Board of Trade. As it was its expenditure was nearly halved and the Industrial Relations Division, whose special section devoted to Industrial Councils was the heart of the drive, was reduced in staff from 115 to 20.[3] In such an atmosphere, which grew less and less favourable over the years, the anomalies in the position of the Ministry regarding the Council were gradually revealed. The pressures it had been able to exert in the first years were, of course, the result of circumstances rather than any specific powers committed to it. In fact it possessed no powers at all except those which the Councils individually conceded. It had no right of representation

[1] *Report of the Council*, 1918, Lab. 2/491/580. [2] Op. cit., p. 159.

[3] *First Interim Report of the Committee*, S.P. 1922, IX, pp. 141 and 143. *Ministry of Labour Report* (1923–4), S.P. 1924, XIV, Appx. II, p. 228. In reply given on 17th March 1922 to a protestation from the Electricity J.I.C. on the lack of government interest in the J.I.C.s, Shackleton referred to the Geddes Report as 'having bearing on this subject and could not be ignored', Lab. 2/673/143/19.

at their meetings, to receive minutes or other data or to be consulted on any matter. One result was that it had no complete idea of what was going on and its records of the Councils throughout the period are incomplete. After 1933 they ceased to be kept, though Liaison Officers continued to attend a number of their meetings.

(ii) THE DEMAND FOR STATUTORY SUPPORT OF J.I.C. AGREEMENTS

The main pressure on the government to make good the promise of Whitleyism came through repeated requests for statutory enforcement of agreements. The *Whitley Report* had suggested that such powers might be given provided the Councils wanted them[1] and it was soon clear that they were wanted. The main pressure came through the Association of Joint Industrial Councils, an organisation formed at the instigation of Mr. T. B. Johnston of the Pottery J.I.C. whose connection with the sort of ideas the Whitley Councils embodied went back to the 1890's.[2] The Pottery J.I.C., and its secretary, Mr. P. H. Hand, who was also the secretary of the Association, remained throughout the strongest supporters and the organisational mainstay of the Association. Despite its official-sounding title and its earnestness in the pursuit of its object (its purpose was, 'reflecting the collective views of the J.I.C.s on legislation affecting them'), the Association seems not to have gained the confidence of the J.I.C.s as a whole. Perhaps the difficulty was that the J.I.C.s were not 'a whole' but a widely disparate group of organisations with different antecedents, objects and problems. They certainly shared no collective enthusiasm for Hand's conception of the Whitley ideal. Many of the records of the various Councils bear evidence of approaches made by the Association—for information, for opinion, support or contributions to expenses. They show how tenuous was the Association's hold on the industries which had J.I.C.s. Contributions were few and given grudgingly; the Tinplate Industry was but one which brushed off its request for support of its plea for statutory powers. The J.I.C. pointed out that it and its predecessor had had a long and successful history and did not need to be told how to run its affairs.[3] The crusading attitudes of Johnston and Hand were no doubt annoying to the less dedicated. A Ministry officer referred disparagingly

[1] 'It appears to us that it may be desirable at some later stage for the state to give sanction of law to agreements made by the Councils, but the initiative should come from the Councils themselves' (para. 21).

[2] Above, p. 38 and below, p. 240.

[3] Letter of 28th July 1928, Lab. 2/713/1298.

to 'Johnston's pet scheme for a charter for J.I.C.s'.[1] Hand's insistence over the years can hardly have endeared him to those who were time and again reminded of the cause.

The Association was not the first to suggest that statutory powers be given to the Councils; several individual J.I.C.s had already requested them. Nor was the idea of such statutory support an innovation by the Whitley Committee. It had been recommended by the Industrial Council in 1913 and of course the Munitions of War Act, 1915, and the Wages (Temporary Regulation) Act of 1918 had given the relevant Ministries power to apply agreed rates throughout a trade or an area. Neither in theory nor in practice, therefore, would there seem to have been any objection to such legislation for the Councils provided it was purely permissive—and this it was always intended to be by those who supported the idea. But apart from a brief period in 1924 when, but for the accident of dissolution, a Bill which gave the powers asked for would have been passed, all attempts to secure it were of no avail.

The first serious and sustained efforts were made in 1920. Replying to a question in the House,[2] Sir Robert Horne, the Minister of Labour, said that he could not give an undertaking on the matter since he had been unable to obtain an expression of opinion from the T.U.C. and there was by no means a majority of the Joint Industrial Councils in favour. The reply missed the point that was to be missed so often in the future here and elsewhere, that what was being asked for was not a law *compelling* the observation of agreements made by all J.I.C.s but a law *permitting* compulsion to be applied when the J.I.C. concerned and hence both employers and employed wished to possess such powers. There were crucial questions to be faced even if this point was taken, questions about what proportion of employers and employees should be represented before the powers were given, what was to happen in doubtful cases and so on. But Sir Robert launched into a disquisition on the impossibility of making observance of collective agreements in general legally binding, though this also was beside the point. Since he had laid such stress on the question of T.U.C. approval, however, there were attempts made to get a decision from Congress. In 1923 it duly came up and Stephen Walsh, a miners' M.P., attacked the idea which, he said, amounted to compulsory arbitration.[3] Sherwood of the General Workers' Union insisted that it was not a question of compulsory arbitration but of enabling industries whose J.I.C.s were weak to bring reluctant firms into line. Defeated in 1923 the motion

[1] *Memorandum* of Ministry of Labour official, 26th January 1920, Lab. 2/715/1920.

[2] The reply is given in full in the *Report on the Establishment and Progress of J.I.C.s*, p. 167.

[3] *Report of the T.U.C. Congress, 1923*, p. 279.

reappeared at the next Congress, moved by Poulton of the Boot and Shoe industry J.I.C.[1] To him the matter was one of getting the 10 per cent of employees who undermined the efforts of the other 90 per cent to be brought under control. As so often happens, the methods of organising Congress debates encouraged confusion. One speaker said that the J.I.C.s had failed and that only organisation of the workers would help. Another, Pollitt, countered by moving a motion opposing compulsory arbitration though this had nothing to do with the case. The supporters of the idea had better luck the next year when a resolution was moved urging on the government the desirability of giving to national agreements freely entered into by J.I.C.s or similar bodies, the same validity as trade board agreements when the parties involved requested it.[2] They had already been beaten to it for in 1924 the Industrial Councils Bill had passed its second reading.

The Bill, which had the Association's support, was introduced by Mr. Frank Murrell, a master printer and an advocate of the Council in that industry. It envisaged the Minister of Labour responding to a request from any organisation which had no J.I.C. by calling a conference for the establishment of one. If convinced it was wanted then the Minister could approve of its establishment according to rules drawn up by the organisations involved and approved by the Minister. Once established the Council, and any already established Council, could apply to the Minister for an order enforcing any decision made on any item of the schedule included in the Bill. Since that schedule was taken verbatim from the *Whitley Report*, paragraph 16,[3] there was many a potential headache for a Minister if a Council's enthusiasm exceeded its prudence. Time for appeal was allowed and the Order in question had to be laid before the House for fourteen days. If it went through, the Minister, the J.I.C., the trade unions, the employers' associations or any aggrieved individual or group could see that it was enforced and the offenders were open to a £50 fine or imprisonment if they wilfully continued to evade its provisions.[4] In the debate on the second reading[5] there were many testimonies from the members on the virtues of the Councils, although there were doubters too. Isaacs of the Printers, Oakes of the General Workers and Poulton of the Boot and Shoe operatives emphasised the value of

[1] *Report of 1924 Congress*, p. 485. He was supported by Richards (also of the Boot and Shoe operatives) who attacked the militants' views saying that they had a 60s. minimum, 75s. piecework and owned seventeen factories; 'knowing our employers' difficulties we can see something of their point of view and do not wish to be always in opposition to them'.

[2] *Report of the T.U.C. Congress, 1925*, p. 540.

[3] Above, p. 104.

[4] *Bills Public* (ii), 1924, p. 653.

[5] 174 H.C. Deb. 5S, col. 759 ff.

the new approach. Dukes in particular pointed to the contrast between his experience on J.I.C.s and the other non-J.I.C. negotiation bodies to the very great credit of the former. The Bill passed by 236 votes to 16 and it was only the accident of dissolution which prevented it becoming law.

1925 and 1926 brought the threat and the reality of the national strike and there was no Labour Government or sympathetic House to encourage legislation. 1927 was even less propitious; legislation in industrial relations in that year was not a happy subject for the trade unions. Early in 1927, however, the Association sent a deputation to the Ministry of Labour seeking its support in getting legislation through and on the basis of a survey it carried out among all the Councils, the Ministry decided that there was no general demand for it.[1] In the meanwhile the A.J.I.C. had been working with the T.U.C. in trying to agree on a formula they could present to the government. But before they could get out a draft Mr. Geoffrey Le Mander, whose interest in the legislation seems to have stemmed from representations made to him by one of the smaller J.I.C.s (in the lock-making industry) which was centred in his constituency, presented an Industrial Council Bill as a private measure in June 1930.[2] Le Mander had previously sounded out the new Labour Government on the question of following up the C.I.R.I.R. suggestion of a National Industrial Councils and of enquiring into the affairs of the J.I.C.s. Bondfield, as Minister of Labour, rattled out the sort of statistics[3] which might have appeared impressive at the time but which the Ministry records indicate were of dubious significance. By the time the Le Mander Bill came up for second reading the T.U.C., through Hayday, and acting in concert with the A.J.I.C.s, requested its withdrawal in view of the Rates of Wages Bill which was going to be introduced and which secured the essential powers requested concerning agreements.[4] The agreed measure was presented in 1931, but at that time the government had other things on its mind and

[1] Lab. 2/713/327/1930.

[2] 240 H.C. Deb. 5S, col. 973. *Bills Public*, 1929–30, II, p. 363.

[3] 23rd January 1930, 234 H.C. Deb. 5S, cols. 313 and 494. Ramsay MacDonald had answered the questions about the C.I.R.I.R. but had shown no enthusiasm. Ibid., 230, col. 420, 17th July 1929.

[4] Ibid., 252, cols. 781 ff. Le Mander refused but the House was counted out and the Bill was not passed. The agreed Bill and the Le Mander Bill differed mainly in that the latter empowered the Minister of Labour to set up Councils on the request of a majority of trade unionists and employers. It would then have full responsibilities under Clause 16 of the *Whitley Report*, with statutory backing for decisions on them. The Rates of Wages Bill was concerned with all agreements on wages and with them only.

by November the National Government was in power and hopes of the required legislation were doomed again. Le Mander did not give up. Further Bills were presented in 1932 and 1933, and as late as 1935 Hand was still leading deputations to the Ministry, but under the governments of the 1930's there was never any real prospect of success. The passing of the Cotton Manufacturing (Temporary Provisions) Act of 1934, however, provides evidence that statutory support for agreements would work in peacetime, given the right conditions.

The purpose of the Act was to 'make temporary provision for enabling statutory effect to be given to wages agreed between representative organisations and cotton manufacturers'[1] and it was introduced in the light of the problems of the cotton industry and above all in response to a whole series of petitions to the Minister and the Prime Minister and the Board of Trade for action to prevent undercutting in an industry which had long been noted for the thoroughness of its trade unionism and the comprehensiveness of its collective negotiations.[2] Under the Act the Minister could appoint a Board to investigate the question of collective agreements and their observation provided that he was convinced that those who applied for one from the industry did in fact represent a majority of the employees and the trade unionists therein. The Board itself had power, once set up, to decide whether that majority was interested in the matter; if its decision was that it was not so interested then it could cease its activities. If it decided to proceeed it could, after proper investigation and consideration of all points of view and objections, decide rates, how they were to be earned and who they covered. Consequent decisions were to be posted in all the workplaces affected. The penalty for disobeying such an order was to be a £10 fine. Either organisation which entered into agreements of this kind could apply for its revocation under three months' notice. The Minister also had power to set up an independent enquiry concerning the possibility of abolishing the Board if he thought fit.

The first application under the Act was made by the Cotton Spinners and Manufacturers Association and the Amalgamated Weavers Association who between them controlled 57 per cent of the looms and 77 per cent of the weavers respectively in a section of the industry in which the 1931 Census showed over 190,000 were employed. After six months of negotiation through the Board, whose proceedings were held in public, and after dealing with eighteen objections to the Orders,

[1] *Public and General Acts 1933–4*, Ch. 30, 28th June 1934.

[2] *Correspondence on the Cotton Manufacturing Act*, Lab. 2/2033/1525, includes petitions from fourteen borough, twenty-one urban and two parish councils in the cotton-manufacturing areas sent in late in 1933.

a uniform list of rates agreed by the two sides was fixed.[1] In 1937 the two organisations made a further joint application, expressing their satisfaction with the working of the previous Order. They claimed that the 1935 measure had not driven firms out of the area or retarded development in efficiency. The new order was granted. Though no two industries are alike and the application of the same procedures to the need of other industries through an enabling act would not necessarily have produced results which were as satisfactory to both sides as the Cotton Act, it was not possible in the light of the Cotton Act and its effects to claim that what had been proposed by the Association was basically unworkable in practice. Not surprisingly Hand was soon to seek to have it extended to all industries through a general enabling act.[2] The Ministry's response was a *Memorandum* showing that not all J.I.C.s supported the Association and that some J.I.C.s were positively opposed to legislation on this matter. It is not easy to see what relevance this had to the proposals of the Association, permissive as they were, fully covered by the Whitley proposals and justified by recent events.

(iii) THE LATER ATTITUDES OF THE MINISTRY OF LABOUR

One thing that is clear from all these dealings with the Association and the question of statutory support for agreements: the officials of the Ministry gave them no encouragement. The role of the Ministry of Labour was an enigmatic one. The Ministry had been set up during the war and in the reconstruction period had had its share, perhaps more than its share, of those who were determined to seek fulfilment of reconstruction promises. Some of the publications of the Ministry's Industrial Councils division and the energy shown by the officials in setting up Councils testifies to a driving conviction rather than a bureaucratic sense of duty. Once the situation returned to an unimaginative and economy-minded normality, and Ministers of Labour were no longer former trade unionists or labour sympathisers but representatives of a party which increasingly in this period gave credence to the conspiracy theory of trade unionism and the labour movement generally, its schizophrenia was bound to increase. In so far as there was a national policy on industrial relations, this was represented in

[1] Details from Lab. 10/9/709/1935. The order came into force in July 1935.

[2] Letter in Lab. 10/13/1147. He was asking the Ministry to receive another deputation; the date was 25th July 1935, ten days after the first order under the Cotton Act had been made.

Whitleyism. The difficulty was that support of Whitleyism could not be separated from encouragement of trade unionism and trade unionism had political implications which were certainly anathema to perhaps most active Conservatives in politics and many Conservative supporters in industry. The Ministry of Labour and its officers were, therefore, in the impossible position of acting in theory to support trade unionism while serving a government, and co-operating with industrial interests which, except during the two brief periods of Labour Government, were at best doubtful about the value of that institution. In practice, whether from personal bias or otherwise, officials tended to accept the *status quo* whatever it was, and this was usually anti-union or unsympathetic to it. By 1924 it was 'strongly held by the Ministry of Labour that the time was not yet ripe for the imposition of compulsory powers'.[1] The Ministry throughout persisted in seeing the request for *permissive* legislation as one for 'imposition of compulsory powers'. Successive Ministers of Labour, of course, being in the main Conservative, took a similar view.

The official policy of the Ministry as expressed in several places[2] was that it was no longer concerned with propaganda for Whitleyism but was 'quite prepared to give assistance in setting up any form of approved machinery' which included Whitley J.I.C.s. Le Mander's attempts to get the Minister of Labour in the 1929 Labour Government, Margaret Bondfield, to commit herself on the matter got nowhere. It would seem that, to the scepticism of her officials, she added a certain socialist disdain for Whitleyism. She gave chapter and verse for the number of Councils still in existence and noted that some 33 were attended by Ministry officers and that from these and others accounts of their work were received. But she would have nothing to do with enquiries into their effectiveness. To her there was no halfway between setting up a Trade Board and a completely voluntary system of negotiation.[3] To a request from Hallam of the Local Authorities J.I.C. in 1921 for an enquiry under the Industrial Courts Act into the working of the Councils, Sir David Shackleton had returned a non-committal reply.[4] The *Report on the Establishment and Progress of the J.I.C.s*, which was published by the Ministry in 1923, while being a useful work of reference, did nothing to explore the real causes of the slow-down of effort or the means of overcoming the difficulties in the way of the Councils. Legget expressed the view that the T.U.C.'s acceptance of

[1] 174 H.C. Deb. 5S, col. 811.

[2] E.g. Ministry *Memorandum* of 27th March 1929 in Lab. 2/1309/671, Part 1.

[3] 234 H.C. Deb. 5S, cols. 313, 494, 2056.

[4] Report of a J.I.C. Deputation to the Ministry in Lab. 2/278/112/43.

the principle of statutory support for agreements could be ignored as not serious[1] and in general the official reply to the representations of the A.J.I.C. tended to be a survey to show that not all the J.I.C.s agreed with its proposals or[2] that it was in itself not representative; neither of the objections having any real bearing on the issue. When the Scottish T.U.C. produced a plan of its own for establishing collective negotiation machinery where none existed and for repairing it where it had broken down, the Ministry's Chief Conciliation Officer in the Northwest area objected that under it, Conciliation Officers would have to restore or set up such machinery. This, he said, was tantamount to the Ministry doing the trade unionists' job. It was understandable, he continued, that the unions should make this request. They had felt the draught of recent events very badly and had found no remedy in trade union action or political activity. But it was not for the government to do the work of the unions whose intent and methods were political in their implications.[3] Such an attitude does not well accord with the official contention that the job of the Ministry was to assist in the setting up of any form of approved machinery. Nor does the attempt of the Manchester C.C.O. to persuade the Electricity J.I.C.'s representative not to support the Le Mander Bill on Industrial Councils; it would be time to take action 'when the Bill had got to the second reading and our department felt that it was necessary to take an interest in it'.[4] It is not surprising that the various deputations from the J.I.C.s, especially those which pointed out to the Ministry that they had come into being at its behest, should accuse it of losing interest. In the matter of statutory support for agreements it was emphasised by the Local Authorities J.I.C. that in its case the government did not even have the excuse that the industry involved private employers.[5] It was all a far cry from the first letter signed by George Barnes requesting the adoption of the *Report*. The government and the Ministry had clearly lost interest.[6] The new Minister of Labour under the National Government in 1932 was optimistic enough to suggest[7] that the new legislation might be introduced when the N.C.E.O. gave its support as the T.U.C. had done. A cynic might have been forgiven for regarding the answer as a joke in poor taste. The N.C.E.O. was the last organisation to encourage Whitleyism.[8]

[1] Lab. 2/713/1928. [2] As in 1928 Lab. 2/713/327.
[3] Lab. 2/1467/668/733, 10th February 1933.
[4] Lab. 2/2012/683. *Memorandum* dated 14th June 1932.
[5] Lab. 2/851/805/3. *Report* of deputation 8th January 1926.
[6] Lab. 2/280/129/3. *Memorandum* to the Ministry on 6th May 1927.
[7] Lab. 2/2012/683. Deputation led by Hand to discuss the question of legislation to support agreements. [8] Below, pp. 252–3, for a consideration of N.C.E.O. policies.

That the legislation giving the permissive powers requested by the A.J.I.C.s would have been acceptable to the trade unions, that it would not have disturbed the pattern of industrial relations and the principle of voluntarism and that it was capable of producing just such effects as were claimed it would seem to be beyond dispute. The experience of the Cotton industry and the facts of 1925–31, when the T.U.C. showed itself clearly in favour, support the view. What is less clear is that the provision of such legislation would have solved the problems of the Joint Industrial Councils themselves. Those whose case nearly approximated to that of the Cotton industry, in which membership of organisations and traditions of effective bargaining were strong, could clearly have benefited; the Boot and Shoe J.I.C., for example, whose advocates in the 1924 T.U.C. debate quoted spoke of their concern to counter the 10 per cent of employers not observing agreements. But most of the Councils which looked to the legislation for help in their difficulties would hardly have been in a position to benefit. It is highly doubtful, for example, whether Pottery, Hosiery and Quarrying could have approached the Minister with a group of employers and wage-earners who genuinely represented even a bare majority of the trade. The various Bills only mentioned that a majority was needed for the Minister to act. The important question of what constituted a majority and how it was to be judged was left open, but it is unlikely the weaker trades would have qualified however it had been defined. In the debate on the Bill introduced in the 1933–4 session, Le Mander was brought to agree that it must be something over two-thirds, perhaps even four-fifths in favour before the required machinery could be put into action.[1] The care taken in the Cotton legislation, the power given to the Board to discontinue its work if the proceedings were unacceptable to the majority, was an indication of the care needed to make sure that the majority was not being railroaded. How many of the J.I.C. industries would have withstood this scrutiny even had they got as far as convincing the Minister that the preliminary steps could be taken, it is hard to say. It would have been very few. It would have been very few throughout industry as a whole.

In any case, legislation to encourage and maintain agreements implied the positive acceptance of collective bargaining and the strong trade unionism which made it possible. As has been noted, the fact that most of the governments of the period were Conservative meant that this acceptance could not be taken for granted.

Hoping for such legislation was then, on the whole, unrealistic. It was also largely irrelevant to the needs of the J.I.C.'s. What was needed to

[1] 286 H.C. Deb. 5S, col. 682.

strengthen the Councils was a more complete acceptance of the co-operation norm in each industry. Where the norm was accepted, what collective bargaining potential existed could be developed as effectively as circumstances allowed. Effective Whitleyism got the best out of the collective bargaining possibilities because acceptance of the co-operation norm meant that collective bargaining was built on a sound basis. It was ideology and attitude, the rejection of the co-operation norm, not lack of legislative support, economic conditions or organisational weakness which challenged the Whitley scheme and set such narrow limits upon it.

14

The Whitley scheme assessed

(i) AS AN ANSWER TO THE PROBLEMS OF INDUSTRIAL RELATIONS AFTER THE WAR

The *Whitley Report* identified three main problems—deficiencies of the existing bargaining system and disputes procedures, the demand of wage-earners for a higher standard of living, and the demand for workers' control. The first two were correctly identified and continued to be a source of difficulty in industrial relations throughout the inter-war years. The third figured in immediate post-war demands, but interest proved to be ephemeral. There was a strong case, and it became stronger as the years went by, for the national ownership of some key industries in view of the need for a reorganisation that only national ownership could achieve. This awareness made its way into the national consensus and had its effect in the Nationalisation Acts of the 1945 Labour administration. The urge behind the demand for nationalisation, which had been part of the railwaymen's and miners' programme long before syndicalism and workers' control, was that through it they would more easily get recognition and better wages, hours and conditions. This too was in itself a reasonable plea. On the other hand, the ideologically motivated demand for workers' control, or for nationalisation and public ownership, was largely artificial, how ever it may have appeared in 1916–17.

The remedies of the *Report* for these three problems were the improvement of the machinery of collective bargaining and disputes procedures in the spirit of wartime co-operation and the encouragement of workers' participation both to meet the popular demand and to improve the productivity which was to provide the means of raising living standards. These aims were combined in the suggestion for industrial councils at national, district and works level. Councils were to overhaul existing structures of bargaining and disputes settlement, encourage a wider range of topics in negotiation and increase efficiency. The assumption, therefore, was that the complete answer to the problem of industrial relations was to be found in co-operative improvement of structures and procedures, and the exhortation to develop them generally. The assumption was hardly justified. Expecting the unions to devote themselves wholeheartedly to the task of production while giving them no assurance on security or increased standards of living was at best over optimistic. The *Report* cannot be faulted for failing to find a *solution* to this problem; it can be faulted for failing to *identify* the factor which posed a major challenge to that improvement in industrial relations it was hoping to bring about. It was this which was the essential weakness in the *Report*—not the supposedly essential differences on ultimate social ideals as the *Fifth Report* suggested.[1] Trade unionists, it turned out, were not opposed to a system based on the profit motive provided their rights and the rights of their members were safeguarded. The backing of the movement in the 1920's was to be for improvement in wages and conditions within the existing system.

Despite this weakness in the *Report*, it had much to offer industry for the improvement in industrial relations. It had much to offer, not because it was wildly innovatory, but because it built soundly on the already existing foundations of the British industrial relations system. It detected above all the most important thing; that the immediate need was a shift in attitudes which would make the right sort of organisational changes possible. The improvement in conciliation methods which it recommended, the better arrangements for collective negotiation, assumed a readiness on the part of the unions and employers to continue to accept the wartime assumption of co-operation. The most commonly held view has been the one advanced by Clay[2] that, 'stripped of its verbiage', the *Report* amounted simply to a recommendation of improved conciliation methods, trade union recognition and extension of the scope of collective bargaining. Clay recognised[3] the value of the organisational changes recommended by the Report but doubted that it said anything beyond this. He thought that if the Ministry of Labour had been content to put on hand an informal series of meetings aimed at improving the organisation of industrial relations, more would have been achieved.[4] But the mining and engineering unions whose rejection of the scheme was to prove most significant because of the course of events in the 1920's and 1930's, were intent on something more than improvement of the existing system; they had convinced themselves they wanted to replace it.[5] Some of

[1] Above, p. 101, and Clay, op. cit., p. 153.
[2] Op. cit., pp. 153 and 157.
[3] Ibid., pp. 155–78.
[4] Ibid., p. 157.
[5] See above, pp. 83 and 203–4.

the phraseology of the *Report* did not, it is true, help its cause[1] but the engineers were totally against it in any case, and so were the miners. The identification of the former with workers' control seemed complete with the election of Tom Mann to the Secretaryship of the A.S.E. in 1919. His articles in the union magazine after this proved a godsend for the belligerent employers. In the strike of 1922 the employers claimed they were defending the existing system of ownership against those who were bent on its destruction. What they really wanted to do was to hang on to the 'managerial prerogatives' of the 1890's and even the 1850's.[2] All in all the industrial relations system in engineering continued to manifest that bitterness and suspicion which crippled any hope of a more positive reform of collective bargaining. We are still paying for this today.

The miners lost Robert Smillie, 'their most sage and farsighted leader',[3] because they would not consider compromise in 1921. At the 1928 T.U.C.[4] Smith, his successor, regretted the sensationalist speeches which led to the rejection of the second part of the Mining Act of that year. There were signs that the owners were a little more amenable to reason at the end of the war[5] but they found it easy enough to return to their traditional belligerence when the unions challenged them.[6] Industries like this then would have treated the invitation with the same scorn as they treated the *Report.* They did not want to help anyone to improve the system; they thought they wanted to replace it. In the meantime they were content with the conflict theory of bargaining and its practice accordingly. The employers remained content with it too. In 1927 they were boasting that they had the best of conciliation schemes in operation in their respective industries[7] and wondered how anyone could suggest that things were not as they should be. The improvements in collective bargaining and conciliation which were achieved by the Councils were real enough. But it was precisely because they adopted a new essentially co-operative approach to the whole situation that they were able to make progress. They assumed that there was a possibility of positive co-operation between the

[1] See above, p. 107.
[2] Pribićević, op. cit., pp. 49 ff. Jeffreys, op. cit., pp. 222 ff.
[3] Arnot, op. cit., Vol. 2, p. 296. [4] *Report*, p. 437. [5] Above, p. 203.
[6] J. R. Raynes, *Coal and its Conflicts* (London 1928), pp. 292 ff. *Sankey Report* (Second stage), S.P. 1919, XI, p. 333. *Report* signed by mineowners and their allies. The *Samuel Report*, S.P. 1926, XIV, p. 228. W. A. Lee, *Thirty Years in Coal* (London 1954), pp. 13 ff.
[7] 'Thirty years of Industrial Conciliation' published by the E.E.F. in 1927 and Sir Adam Nimmo (quoted Raynes, op. cit., p. 292) in the *Iron and Coal Trades Review*, 1927.

two sides on the basis of mutual acceptance of rights and collective agreements reached and applied in this spirit. The Ministry of Labour emphasised, as we have seen,[1] that the primary condition of success of the Whitley scheme was the attitude of the parties; given the readiness to co-operate, it could work. Without such readiness it could not. Simply urging on industry better collective bargaining *machinery* was not enough. What gave the Whitley Councils the edge in reducing unrest and improving collective bargaining was not the machinery itself but the spirit in which the industrial relationship was approached and the consequent readiness to attack the problems of rebuilding wages and other structures positively and co-operatively. The observation of Clay[2] that the difference in the strike incidence in the J.I.C. and the non-J.I.C. industries was too great to be accidental is interesting but of itself said nothing. It is only when we appreciate that it was attitudes affecting organisation which provided the means to reduce strikes that it falls into place. In so far as the *Report* stressed the importance of attitudes it was not guilty of adding to the flood of verbiage. It was making a profound and lasting contribution to the improvement of collective bargaining as the experience of the more successful Councils shows.

On the basis of the pattern of experience of the Councils it is possible to trace the evolution of the norms and the institutions of collective bargaining through the scheme as a whole; by using the pattern of norms laid down in the Introduction we see this development as well as understanding precisely why the scheme was relevant to the inter-war problems of industry.

(ii) AS A CONTRIBUTION TO THE EVOLUTION OF THE NORMS AND INSTITUTIONS OF COLLECTIVE BARGAINING

The contractual co-operation norm

The pattern of norms which governs collective bargaining must be seen as stemming from the first of them, *the co-operation norm.* On the basis of mutual acceptance and the recognition of equal rights to exist in industry and negotiate on all matters of interest, employers and the unions enter into agreements which bind them morally, provided of course that the agreements in question truly represent the needs of those

[1] Above, pp. 203–4. [2] Op. cit., p. 169.

subject to them. The logic of these agreements is that on the basis of self-interest the two sides will co-operate to make them effective in order to improve all aspects of industrial performance, including productivity where possible. This of course can only be fully realised within a full employment welfare state.

One obstacle to the full acceptance and implementation of the co-operation norms through the Councils was clearly the lack of a full employment welfare state. But even without it it was possible to lay the foundations of a more co-operative collective bargaining system provided the will to do so was there. Too often it was not because the old suspicions and fears predominated. One mark of this was the refusal of the employers on most Councils to commit themselves to the full support of trade unionism. A few did, for example Cement and Electricity Supply,[1] others limited themselves to pointing out that the J.I.C.s settled wages and conditions and that the unions were parties to the Councils, for instance the Electrical Cablemaking J.I.C. and that in Wool and Allied Textiles. That serious-minded men concerned with the day-to-day conduct of industrial relations should think it important to make such a distinction speaks volumes for the state of industrial relations. There was a strong note of personal animosity in some of the conflicts between unions and employers that are traceable from the records—as in Cablemaking.[2] But the ideological antipathy was more evident among the employers. Industries with a militant tradition, such as the Gasworkers and to some extent the Tramwaymen, found it possible to adapt to the more co-operative Whitley approach. The main objection on the unions' side was practical—the poverty of gain through the Councils. The Silk workers and the Pottery workers found ground for complaint in this.[3]

Overall, then, the co-operation norm had effect not so much in precept, as in practice. From the experience of the Councils it is clear that in some of them the dominant figures or groups were prepared to

[1] Though the Electricity Supply originally contained private companies 'very hostile to the unions', M. of L. Memo in Lab. 2/912/108, 16th November 1927. Similar elements were present among the Papermakers: E.F.P.M. Executive *Minutes* of meetings 4th June 1926 and 26th November 1926; their President pointed out to them the futility of their attitude. Lever's antipathy to the unions was notorious and has already been commented on. The employers on the Paint and Varnish J.I.C. were always complaining that they were considered too soft by other employers in the industry.

[2] In 1923–6 more than a dozen Council meetings were dominated by a personal wrangle between one union official and one firm; in 1924 the firm withdrew from Council meetings until certain remarks were retracted.

[3] *Pottery Gazette*, 1st May 1923, and 2nd May 1927. Silk Industry N.J.I.C. *Minutes*, 19th October 1927 and 17th January 1933.

accept in practice that with a sufficient effort, it was possible to work out agreements and procedures which would satisfy the legitimate needs of both sides while producing a greater smoothness in industrial relations. There was a desire to co-operate on terms realistic to both sides. The way, for example, that those industries detailed in Chapter 9 set out to organise their wages structures and disputes procedures and did so, despite all difficulties, shows that there was a different spirit at work here than in the industries in Chapter 10 which were less successful precisely because of their inability to generate enough mutual trust. The success of the Councils in Chapter 9 in overcoming the main substantive disputes by reference to the sliding scale of wages according to the cost of living is indicative of the desire to find a mutually acceptable compromise rather than to impose a solution by force. In fact most of the employers did not demand adjustment downwards when they could have done—which marks a great change from the narrow attitudes elsewhere prevalent even in some Councils. The ability of the Councils in Chapter 9 to agree on such comparative 'concessions' as holidays-with-pay is a further mark of the readiness of the employers to try to gain co-operation through a more open positive approach than through the older narrow and combative attitude which can be summed up as a rejection of the co-operation norm.

By contrast the Councils in Chapter 10 kept too much of that old attitude. In Soap and Candle manufacture there was the heritage of Lever's antipathy to the unions which did much to make otherwise good progress slower than it might have been. The long haggling because of the unwillingness of the employers to raise wages to meet those of the better firms in the 1930's pinpointed the sort of problem which the fuller acceptance of the co-operation norm would have avoided. In Electrical Cablemaking the failure to evolve procedures for adjusting the terms of agreements or applying and interpreting them, and the repeated rejection by the employers of the request for holidays-with-pay in many instances revealed a guardedness which was alien to co-operation. Paint and Varnish and the Heavy Chemicals J.I.C. were haunted by the suspicions of the employers that they had been taken for a ride in earlier years; there was little mutual trust here. Tinplate had problems connected again with the refusal of the employers to consider changing the basis of the computation of wages for certain grades; the Hosiery Council was paralysed by the refusal of the employers to consider a revised wage structure under the Council's supervision and the Wool and Allied Textiles J.I.C. collapsed finally because there was no way of compromise between the unshakeable principles of the two sides. Other Councils in Chapter 10 had little success because their organisation was not strong enough for effective bargaining but the overwhelming cause of failure was not in organisation but in attitude. All in all, the scheme provided those who were more inclined to accept the co-operation norm with the opportunity and the means to give it practical effect. Where the inclination to reject it or to have reservations about it was dominant, little could be achieved.

Organisation

The contribution made by the Councils scheme to the organisation of industrial relations stemmed from its insistence that the organisation should be properly interlinked between local, regional and national level and that it should be based on permanent organisations, Councils which were formally constituted and met regularly. For reasons already discussed[1] local works organisation did not develop, but the degree of success attained in establishing regular meetings at national and regional levels according to the needs of the industry was considerable.

The realisation that the requirement was for the organisation of bargaining at the level which best suited the needs of the industry was a by-product of the scheme. Initially it was imagined that the national organisation would be the natural focus; but this was not the case in all industries.[2] On the basis of the accepted need to reorganise the industrial relations of the industry, however, it proved possible to make adjustments accordingly.

More fundamentally, the existence of the scheme and the commitment of the Ministry to forwarding it, enabled many industries which did not have effective collective negotiation machinery to acquire it. They also had the advantage of building up that machinery more in accordance with the co-operation norm, hence avoiding many of the weaknesses of the older established systems.

A logical implication of the organisation norm is the need for some kind of provision for arbitration at national level and for the general regulation of the whole collective bargaining system by some nationally representative body. The logic of this was, and is, apparent, but before it can be successfully implemented it requires that the industrial relations system at lower levels is complete and efficient and that the national economic policy is synchronised with it. In its time the Whitley Committee, like the Industrial Council, tried to provide for this despite the difficulties. The *Fourth Report* of the Committee suggested

[1] Above, p. 155. [2] Above, pp. 154–5.

that, without prejudice to the voluntary system of collective bargaining, an arbitration court should be set up to judge on cases submitted to it and means should be provided so that an independent enquiry could be made into the facts of any dispute at the discretion of the government department concerned. The upshot of this recommendation was the Industrial Courts Act of 1919 under which a system of such courts was set up, together with provision for the Courts of Enquiry.[1]

Interpretation and application

The need for agreements to provide adequate means of applying and interpreting them is absolute and essential. Where these provisions are complete there is a chance of substantive case law developing with a resulting improvement in industrial relations. The best example of this happening was in the Flourmilling industry. Here the Council set up a regular court of appeal to hear cases arising out of the 1919 agreement and, because the co-operation and organisational norms were also effectively accepted and implemented, and because the primary substantive norms were well handled, the system developed coherently. Just as the proper use and application of this norm was one of the reasons for the success of the Flourmilling industry J.I.C., the failure to develop and apply it was one of the reasons for the difficulties of other Councils. The Cablemaking J.I.C. provided no proper procedure for handling questions of interpretation and application and so added to its difficulties. In general a clear understanding on the needfulness of this norm was lacking because the primary substantive norms were in dispute.

Codification

Where the other procedural norms are accepted and given practical effect and when there is agreement on the norms governing minimum wages and conditions and the manner of their adjustment, the next step in the development of adequate collective bargaining is to codify all the agreements and the procedures. Where this is done every man in the industry knows what his rights and obligations are in all matters subject to collective bargaining and its rules, and in consequence need-

[1] S.P. 1918 VII: Public and General Acts 1919. 9. 10. Geo. V Ch. 69: Report of the Ministry of Labour 1923–4. S.P. 1924–5 XIV, pp. 34 ff.

less misunderstandings are avoided. Some of the Councils did reach such a stage of development that this codification was possible. The Flourmilling industry and Electricity Supply provide two examples. But in general the degree of procedural and organisational sophistication required before this codification became practicable or relevant was lacking. For example, the Soap and Candle trades had a comprehensive national agreement and the Electrical Cablemaking industry codified its previous agreements in 1926, but other factors prevented industrial relations and collective bargaining in these industries developing as satisfactorily as in Flourmilling and Electricity Supply.

Minimum wages and conditions

The insistence that whatever else the economic system did it must provide the average worker with decent work at wages and in conditions which suited his human needs was a mark of union policy over the years. This was specified as one of Labour's expectations after the war by the T.U.C. in 1916, when other organisations like the Garton Foundation were concentrating on the less tangible benefits.[1] The deficiency of the *Whitley Report* in respect of wages and security has been noted. Satisfactory overall settlement of disputes over this issue, or these issues, could not begin until there was national agreement on the context in which industrial relations were carried on, i.e. full employment and social security. As we know to our cost, even when this is agreed much remains to be done, but today no active politician who denies the ideal would get a hearing. But in the period we are dealing with the notion that somehow wages and conditions were at the mercy of economic laws beyond the power of man to control was still too prevalent and those who rejected it could not at the time give a satisfactory theoretical alternative. Given this gulf of disagreement, the best that could be hoped for was a working compromise and some industries, the most successful in fact, found this in the cost-of-living sliding scale which at least established, by agreement, a minimum wage equal to that prevailing when the scale was introduced. One industry, Soap and Candles, agreed on a minimum wage but this proved to be lower than the lowest rates in the bigger firms and so provided no cause for union satisfaction. The point about the sliding scale was that it was one which, when combined with an adequate and agreed wage structure on a district or national basis, could be accepted by both sides.

[1] See above, pp. 88–9 and 96.

Adjustment

The sliding scale according to the cost of living also provided the most effective and least controversial means of handling thorny matters of wage adjustment. When combined with the more positive approach to the questions of collective bargaining detectable in the industries which accepted the co-operation norm more fully the resulting improvement in industrial relations was considerable. In most of these it became the practice that the scale was not invoked when the cost-of-living trend was downwards. Where it was insisted on in the hard times of the 1930's—as it was in Electricity and in the Railways—there were problems. There were problems too in some industries where the unions were restive because the operation of the scale did not allow them positive improvements when the cost of living remained reasonably stable. The Cablemaking industry and the Flourmilling unions felt this constraint.

It is the contrast with the industries which did not reach such a compromise that the advantages of the sliding scale were, for all that, apparent. The Wool and Allied J.I.C. broke up because it could not reach agreement on the norms governing wage adjustment. The Chemical and the Paint and Varnish J.I.C.s were likewise prevented from making any real progress because of the same difficulty while the attempt of Tinplate employers to maintain the selling price sliding scale for some of their workers had an unfortunate effect on industrial relations in that industry. The sliding scale according to the cost of living, whatever its defects, at least secured a working agreement and one which marked a step away from that sort of nagging conflict which prevented positive improvement in other aspects of industrial relations.

Redundancy and pensions

The importance of this aspect of security, the provision of compensation for redundancies, was little realised. At the time the Flourmilling industry was the only one which made a real effort to handle it and this effort was, in terms of the scale of the problem even in one small industry like Flourmilling, not very extensive. In Electricity Supply the initiative came from statutory provisions rather than the Council. The Water Supply industry had a superannuation scheme. The effort of Ernest Bevin to get the Tinplate industry to provide pensions and redundancy payments foundered on jealousies and ignorance within the union ranks. The Dock Labour Board was concerned more to stabilise employment by the reduction of casualism than to provide for the redundant. The Local Authorities operated a superannuation scheme.

Holidays-with-pay

The contribution of the Whitley scheme to growth of holidays-with-pay was decisive and well recognised, as the *Report* of the Committee on the matter made plain.[1] Far more J.I.C. industries granted holidays-with-pay *pro rata* than any other group. Cement, Flourmilling, Soap and Candles, Electricity, Water and Gas Supply, Tramways, Paint and Varnish, Chemicals, and Local Authorities made recommendations or provided for them; Electrical Cable Manufacturers, Tinplate, Wool and Allied and Hosiery employers all refused to give them despite the repeated request of the unions through the Councils. In Quarrying the opposition seemed less strong, but in the event no recommendation was made.

Safety, health, welfare

The Cement J.I.C. co-operated with the main employers' association on matters of safety and welfare though the initiative was with the latter. The Flourmilling Council was active in improving industrial health. The Tramways Council took an interest in industrial safety and in Quarrying, an industry in which problems of safety and health had always been very real, the Council was especially active. The achievements of the Pottery J.I.C. in improving health standards were admitted to be considerable; the Printing Council also made a contribution in this matter.

Training and education

Flourmilling was one of the leaders in the improvement of trade education through the Councils, but the most impressive effort in this regard was made by the Heating and Domestic Engineering industry

[1] S.P. 1937–8, XII, p. 8.

J.I.C. The Building Council in its short existence promised much in this regard too, but the effort died with the Council. The J.I.C. in Printing provided a focal point for those who wished to improve craft training standards and methods there but vested interests of unions and employers defeated it. The Silk industry J.I.C. surprisingly, considering its general weakness, evolved one of the most elaborate schemes for general, as well as craft, education of its workforce; not surprisingly, however, it came to nothing.

Organisation and efficiency

The Councils were here interested in three distinct problems, the collection and dissemination of statistics, the improvement of organisation and efficiency and the representation of the industry's needs.

Interest in the first was mainly the result of the need to find ammunition in wage negotiations. The Councils had a considerable effect on the use of statistics for comparability tables; the Pottery, Tramways and Paint and Varnish industries were among those which made use of statistics in this way. In the improvement of industrial organisation, Pottery again was a leader but the most spectacular attempts in this field were made by the Building industry which wanted to do no less than replace the existing system of organisation and control. Representation of industry's needs was mainly effected through pressure on the government, though there is little evidence to show that this had much effect.

PART THREE

The National Industrial Conference 1919-21

15

The National Industrial Conference 1919-21: Origins

(i) CIRCUMSTANCES OF ITS CALLING

Post-war industrial unrest

On 18th February 1919, *The Times* announced that the government was to call a Conference of the industries threatened with strikes in order that the general situation might be discussed and the views of those concerned obtained. It met for the first time on 27th February and for the second and last on 4th April 1919. It was a response to a situation of crisis in industrial relations, caused mainly by the immediate threat of the miners but with the discontent of the railwaymen also in the background and the likelihood of action by the Triple Alliance. The threat was not, however, one that portended violent social upheaval as some feared. It was an expression, in the most direct and effective way, of the determination of the wage-earners that wartime promises should be redeemed and in directly tangible forms—better working conditions, more wages and solid evidence of social reconstruction.

The threat of renewed industrial unrest after the war had been one of the reasons the Whitley Committee had been set to work but neither the attitude of the government nor that of the major trade unions had given the *Report* hope of serious application throughout industry. The immediate post-war months[1] showed the fears well founded. There was a major dispute in cotton during the election campaign. In

[1] *The Times,* November 1918–February 1919. *Report on Conciliation and Arbitration under the 1896 Act,* 1919, S.P. 1920, XIX. *Annual Register,* 1919. C. Mowat, *Britain Between the Wars* (London 1962), pp. 38 ff. A. Marwick, *Britain in the Century of Total War* (London 1968), p. 147. G. D. H. Cole, *A Short History of the British Working Class Movement,* Vol. 3, pp. 165 ff. A. Taylor, op. cit., pp. 138 ff. P. S. Bagwell, op. cit., pp. 375 ff. G. Blaxland, op. cit., pp. 118 ff. R. Page Arnot, op. cit., Vol. 2, pp. 183 ff. B. Pribićević, op. cit., pp. 37 ff. A. Bullock, op. cit., pp. 99 ff. Jefferys, op. cit., pp. 187 ff.

January troops and tanks were deployed against the engineering workers in Glasgow and during the same dispute there was rioting and street fighting in Belfast. In January the miners were also out in some areas but it was the threat that they would strike on 19th March unless they saw the industry nationalised, their pay increased by 30 per cent and the working day cut to six hours which was more significant. The action of the South Wales section during the war had shown the mood of the miners. Their strength was so great that they had then forced the government to back down and grant their demands and the Federation was supremely confident now that they could get what they wanted. The railwaymen had an axe to grind too, but since they already had, as it seemed, nationalisation of their industry assured, they had less incentive to introduce a 'socialist' flavour into their demands. Demands there were, however, and they were under negotiation in February. Nor were the engineers entirely satisfied with their recent hours settlement. The close interlinking of this turmoil in industrial relations with the calling of the Conference is reflected in a consideration of the events of February.

On the 17th, the day the government announced it, the miners' demands and threats stood unanswered and the country was only a month away from what it feared would be a disastrous struggle. On Monday the 24th a Bill setting up the Sankey Commission was passed,[1] but the miners had not said whether they would participate. On the next day, 25th February, the Triple Alliance met to decide what action it would take in support of the miners. The threat from them and from the railwaymen remained as the Conference assembled.[2] As it turned out, however, 27th February was the crucial date; after this whatever initiative had been in the hands of the industrial labour movement began to slip from its grasp.

Current ideas on the nature of the unrest that the country was facing were varied.[3] There was a strongly expressed conviction in some quarters that the demands of labour were an English equivalent, milder and less outrageous, but basically as pernicious and destructive as the Russian social revolution. It was a conviction that Lloyd George had

[1] 112 H.C. Deb. 5S, col. 1383, 24th February, cols. 1441 ff., 24th February.

[2] Beatrice Webb's *Diaries*, 1912–24, p. 151, gives a graphic account of how, after his speech to the Conference on the 28th, Lloyd George was 'blackmailed' by the miners' representative into accepting the Labour Members on the Sankey Commission.

[3] A. Gleason, *What the Workers Want* (London 1920), pp. 26 ff., 250 ff. and *passim*. R. A. S. Redmayne, *Men, Mines and Memories* (London 1942), pp. 211 ff. The official-sounding *Memorandum on the Causes and Remedies of Industrial Unrest,* drawn up by G. D. H. Cole (S.P. 1919, XXIV), was more hopeful than factual in its assertion that the unions were seeking the replacement of the capitalist system.

seen fit to foster[1] during the election campaign and which the heavier papers, encouraged by the further happenings on the Continent throughout the winter, kept on emphasising. The Leeds Convention of June 1917, the occasional outbreaks of violence during the strikes of January and February, even the isolated mutinies among troops demanding demobilisation, were readily enough seen as justification of these fears. The excesses of some labour propagandists added to them. Now, as later, one of the worst enemies of the real reforms that were needed was the exaggerated demands and claims made by this minority. It was all too easy for opponents of reform to quote them as a justification for holding the line wherever it happened to be. The mineowners were as adept at the tactics as the engineering employers; both found the words and actions of a few extremists useful in justifying their opposition to all claims for change.[2]

The causes of strife were complex; war weariness, the frustration of labour's political hopes in the 1918 election, the Bolshevik taunt, the evidence of profiteering, the awareness that little had changed and that hopes of a new social order were being thwarted, the general unease that came with the mass demobilisation of men brutalised and disorientated by war—all these mingled together to provide ample cause for general discontent. But it was never revolutionary in its ends or its means. What the people wanted was a revolution 'in public outlook and thought rather than a revolution of force'.[3]

The present discontents, said Thomas to the National Industrial Conference, 'are not the work of agitators but the products of age-long expectations accelerated by the developments of war',[4] and with this view the Prime Minister agreed. Even the formidable Smillie,[5] at the

[1] Reported in *The Times*, 14th December 1918: 'Suppose Labour got in. That is exactly what happened in Russia. The same would happen here.' On Lloyd George's obsession with Bolshevism see Marwick, pp. 146 ff. The only real signs that there was a possibility of extra-constitutional action by the Labour movement came in 1920 with the Jolly George incident and the later Councils of Action. Bullock, op. cit., pp. 133 ff. Taylor, op. cit., pp. 143. Mowat, op. cit., p. 41.

[2] E.g. Raynes, op. cit., p. 156. The *Samuel Report*, loc. cit., p. 228, called on the owners to stop accusing the unions of aiming to destroy the industry. The engineering employers in 1922 presented their opposition to the demands of the unions as a defence of the principle of private enterprise. Above, p. 217.

[3] Henderson's words at a meeting of the Provisional Joint Committee of the N.I.C., 26th March 1919. Gleason, an American, asserted that the British 'like to be energised by loud explosions into a dignified sure-footed motion', op. cit., p. 151.

[4] *Full Report of the Speeches at the Meeting of the N.I.C.*, 27th February 1919, H.M.S.O. 1919, p. 25.

[5] Quoted in J. E. Williams, *The Derbyshire Miners* (London 1962), p. 612. See also Arnot, op. cit., p. 187.

head of the Miners' Federation, had introduced their demands in terms which were perfectly reconcilable with accepted trade union aims. It was not nationalisation for its own or ideologies' sake that was wanted, it was a way to make sure that in future the appeal to economic necessity should not override the human needs of the miner and his family. He was to resign when the extremists showed they were unwilling to show moderation in their demands and later Smith was to regret the effect of sensational speeches.[1] It was the deep-felt determination of the wage earners that they deserved some immediate alleviation of their lot which caused the upsurge of unrest but it was precisely because it was not intended to be revolutionary in ends or means that it could so easily be diverted by a National Industrial Conference and a Sankey Commission. The euphoria in which the first and the second conferences met was the result of a genuine relief and spirit of goodwill. This spirit was exploited by a government in a tight corner and the words of Lloyd George to the Conference and to its Provisional Joint Committee kept the hopes burning during the crucial period. It was the completeness of the exploitation and the gullibility of the delegates which indicates so conclusively that the desire above all was for co-operation and reconciliation rather than conflict. The miners were soon to lose the support of their allies when they insisted on sticking to their total demands rather than making an honourable compromise.

(ii) INFLUENCES ON THE CONFERENCE AND ITS WORK

Industrial parliaments and peacemaking

The idea of some form of Industrial Council, Conference or Parliament, however unclear the advocates of the idea were on its function, had not died after the failure of the 1911 experiment. The British Association's Report on Industrial Harmony had made a revived Industrial Council part of its plan[2] and though the presence of Macara at its meetings partly accounted for this, the Council did have a real function as a final court of appeal in its overall scheme. The Federation of British Industries, in its reply to the *Whitley Report*,[3] had stressed the necessity for some central national body, the National Industrial

[1] Above, p. 217. [2] Kirkaldy, op. cit., p. 44.
[3] *Memorandum on the Whitley Council's Scheme*, 3rd August 1917.

Alliance of Employers and Employed had called for a national round-table Conference in October 1918[1] and claimed to have aroused considerable support for the idea. A Conference of Representatives of Employers and Employed had in fact been called on 13th November 1918 by the government itself with the particular intention of getting the advice of industry on the restoration of pre-war practices[2] and at this Conference Lloyd George had spoken in terms suggesting that the development of common interests between employers and employed required concrete expression. The idea acquired more and more appeal as the threats of January and February 1919 took shape. A Congress of Labour was suggested in *The Times* on 20th January, and J. R. Clynes appealed for a Parliament of Labour on the 25th.

It was a time when the Peace Conferences were being prepared and discussed and a conference to settle industrial warfare seemed an equal necessity. The 'comradeship of the trenches' still had its appeal and the government still was, formally at least, a coalition of all classes. The idea took shape with the most authoritative backing that industry could provide. On 13th February the Federation of British Industries resolved that 'the Federation should take . . . immediate action in conjunction if possible with the Engineering Employers' Federation and the National Organisations representing labour with a view to summoning a joint Conference of employers and employed for the formation of proposals for dealing with the present grave conditions of industrial unrest'.[3] On the same day Lord Henry Cavendish Bentinck was being told in the House that the government did not see its way to setting up a Conference of this sort,[4] but by some process it had by 17th February changed its mind and Lloyd George announced that such a Conference, with the specific purpose of enabling it to have a general discussion with the representatives of industry on the current difficulties, was to be called.

The attitude of industry and the immediate needs of government policy

That the Federation of British Industries should have been so wholeheartedly identified with a move to discuss industrial relations and related problems is significant both in itself, because its support no doubt played a large part in the calling of the Conference, and in the contrast it provided with later attitudes. It was later to be said that

[1] *Industrial Unity*, October 1918. [2] *Minutes* of the Proceedings, M. of L. 331.1.
[3] Report in *The Times*, 14th February 1919. [4] 112 H.C. Deb. 5S, col. 261.

the F.B.I. had no part to play in such matters, being only concerned with the trade and commerce. Whether the E.E.F. fully approved of the F.B.I. approach is doubtful. Its own policy regarding industrial relations in its own industry had been to confine collective dealings with the unions to the minimum.[1] The F.B.I. during the war and up to this time had been much more co-operative. In the first instance it had been concerned with the general industrial relations problem; only later, and under the ungenerous influence of the N.C.E.O., discussed in more detail below, did it become customary to claim the distinction of function between the two organisations on hard ideological lines. An undated pamphlet on the Federation,[2] obviously published sometime in 1916–17, speaks of its role in 'organising and developing industry after the war in co-operation with labour and in conjunction with the government and government departments'—an idea which would have moved later spokesmen of the employers to apoplexy. It was the F.B.I. which spoke for the employers in approving the Whitley Report[3] and the *Annual Reports* of the organisation in the immediate post-war period[4] give accounts of the Ministry of Labour section concerned with J.I.C.s and of the work of the National Association of Employers and Employed. In its *Report on the Control of Industry*[5] it quotes with approval Gosling's address to the T.U.C.[6] in which he indicated the real nature of labour's ambitions—a right to participate in all decision-making affecting the working lives of wage-earners. The F.B.I. attitude, however, turned out not to be the one that wielded most influence in the employers' Councils but it was the F.B.I. attitude, that of wartime co-operation, which was evident among the employers who attended and supported the Conference. On the labour side, the man most convinced that the Conference was worth while was Henderson,[7] Secretary of the Labour Party and a man who had good reason to distrust Lloyd George. He found himself opposed within the trade union movement by men like Bevin and Thomas, who, as Taylor remarked,[8] were at once aggressively working class in character while

[1] On the formation of the E.E.F. see above, pp. 40 ff. The National Employers' Federation was formed in 1913 after the Midlands engineering strike of that time and consisted of engineering and metal-working interests. In September 1918 the two amalgamated to form the Engineering and Allied Employers' National Federation (E.A.N.E.F.). The old initials, E.E.F., are used for convenience. *Employers' Year Book*, 1920, pp. 59 ff.

[2] Entitled *The Federation of British Industries.*

[3] Above, p. 119.

[4] E.g. for 1919.

[5] Published under that title in July 1919. That is at the time of the Sankey Commission and its reports.

[6] Above, p. 90.

[7] A. Hamilton, *Arthur Henderson* (London 1938), p. 211. Above, page 59.

[8] Op. cit., p. 141.

not being concerned merely to resist. They negotiated with the employers as equals in their effort to get the best bargain for their men, having little patience with those who hoped for the socialist new dawn. They embodied the spirit of collective bargaining based on the co-operation norm, that is—insistence on autonomy and getting the best bargain but readiness to co-operate in a spirit of mutual trust unhampered by ideological objections to capital. They had, however, less trust in the good faith of the government with which they were dealing than Henderson.[1] Events confirmed their suspicions but they also confirmed the soundness of Henderson's instinct. He took what he thought was a chance to get government policy working in favour of establishing minimum standards in wages and hours knowing that until there was a national policy on these matters the efforts of the unions would be undermined. The right sort of policy was above all, the policy of full employment and high wages, and it was to take the depression, another war and a revolution in economics and politics before this could be achieved. But, however far in the future and however different the means to the end, it was the right end that he sought.

Whatever the hopes and fears of labour and whatever the motives that moved the employers, it was not they but the government, and Lloyd George in particular, who were pulling the strings, and who made the Conference possible. With his sound politician's instinct and his understanding of the sort of people he was dealing with in a situation which many said was basically revolutionary—an illusion he had chosen to foster—he set on hand the Conference to which came over 800 delegates[2] from trade unions, Trade Boards, the J.I.C.s and the I.I.R.C.s, the T.U.C., the Scottish T.U.C., the National Alliance and the Employers' Associations. It was for a brief period the wonder of the world and the subject of much favourable comment at home and abroad.[3] But the Triple Alliance industries representatives only attended to protest and the shrewder observers noted that the whole thing depended upon the policy of a government which did not encourage much optimism in these matters. The passing weeks and months proved their fears only too well grounded.

[1] *Full Report of Speeches*, etc., pp. 23 and 61. Bullock, op. cit., p. 96.
[2] *Report on Conciliation and Arbitration under the 1896 Act*, 1919, S.P. 1920, XIX, Appx., pp. 39 ff. Gleason, op. cit., pp. 70 ff.
[3] Below, pp. 245–6 and 249. *The Times*, 5th April 1919, and Huth Jackson in *The Employers' Year Book*, 1920, p. 118, who went so far as to say 'it will never be known how much that meeting and discussion did to help the equilibrium of the country'.

16

The Conference and its Provisional Joint Committee

(i) THE FIRST CONFERENCE, 27TH FEBRUARY 1919

The proceedings and the appointment of the P.J.C.[1]

The Prime Minister and the Minister of Labour, Sir Robert Horne, attended the meeting on the 27th. Horne gave as the government's reasons for calling it the wish to discuss with the men involved the problems of the moment and the government's plans for tackling them. On unemployment—the donation was coming to an end and the government would reduce it but extend the period of its availability.[2] Ministry of Supply contracts would be hurried up and the housing schemes would go ahead quickly. The government further had no objection to the reduction of hours or the establishment of minimum wages by law provided that production costs did not suffer. The Whitley scheme was the great hope for industrial relations, the 'great positive reform to which one looked with the greatest hope for the prevention of industrial disputes in the future'. All in all the government had every intention of acting to meet the demands of those 'Fresh aspirations kindled in men's breasts by the power of war and the sense of the value of the human spirit which demands for the toiler better conditions of life and more adequate opportunities of leisure.'

It was a speech which had something for everyone and exactly caught the mood of generous optimism which pervaded the whole

[1] *Full Report of Speeches*, etc. *Report on Conciliation and Arbitration under the 1896 Act*, 1919, loc. cit. *The Times*, 28th February 1919.

[2] The donation was provided in November 1918 to reduce the difficulties that might follow if massive unemployment followed demobilisation. The scheme included civilians too and the scale of payments was by later standards generous. Pollard, op. cit., p. 248.

Conference. The moderate labour leaders who wanted the improvements which were promised but who did not want to face the country with revolutionary change in getting them were catered for because they were assured that they could get these things peaceably. At the same time Sir Robert sounded a note of warning about the futility of industrial unrest and of reducing production which would soothe the employers present. And if the unions were annoyed that the demobilisation of state factories was going to move along as fast as possible they were encouraged by the fact that minimum wages and a standard working week were within their grasp.

Though from the reception they received and from the good temper of the Conference generally it was clear that those who asked awkward questions about all this were not very popular, awkward questions were asked.[1] Brownlie, for the engineers, wanted to know why unemployment pay should be cut since clearly every man, woman and child had a right to maintenance. Ammon stated that the fatal flaw in all this was the absence of any firm commitment from the government to do anything. He was not impressed by the Minister's hopes of reducing hours consistent with the needs of private industry; there were too many escape clauses. Allan Smith soon emerged as the chief spokesman of the employers' side. This was a strange enough circumstance given the fact that at the moment his Federation only represented one section of the employers and the Federation of British Industries, much more generally representative and at this time interested in the problems of industrial relations, had its representatives there.

Smith was cynical of the action of the Prime Minister who 'conceived in his wisdom, this Conference'. Industry, while willing to fall in with whatever was proposed, was better advised to sort out its own problems, the trade unions with the employers: the problems were after all only temporary. Thomas, speaking for the Triple Alliance industries, strongly disagreed that the trouble was temporary and that the government should not interfere. The Alliance stood for national ownership of mines and transport and those who could read the signs of the times saw that the present troubles were the result of labour's determination to get a better life, to fulfil now their age-long expectations. Henderson also took exception to Smith's assertion that the trouble was temporary and he did not accept that the sort of Industrial Committee that Smith suggested would be enough to carry on the Conferences' work. It was not enough to accept the reports of government departments and keep an eye on the situation as it developed. The functions that Henderson thought such a committee should have

[1] *Report of Speeches*, pp. 14 ff.

were much more positive and to the point—it should look to questions of wages, hours, unemployment and the problems of trade union and employer co-operation and it should make reports according to a definite and tight schedule. Lloyd George, showing a high good humour matched by that of the Conference, and accepting Henderson's contention that the trouble was not temporary, moved the motion Henderson had proposed after slightly amending it. The Conference accepted it overwhelmingly.[1] It said that the Conference was

> of the opinion that any preventable dislocation of industry is always to be deplored and in the present critical period of reconstruction might be disastrous to the interests of the nation, and thinking that every effort should be made to remove legitimate grievances and promote harmony and goodwill, resolves to appoint a joint Committee, consisting of equal numbers of employers and workpeople, men and women, together with a Chairman appointed by the government, to consider and report on the causes of the present unrest and the steps necessary to safeguard and promote the best interests of the employers, workpeople and the state and especially to consider
>
> 1. Questions relating to hours, wages and general conditions of employment.
> 2. Unemployment and its prevention.
> 3. The best methods of promoting co-operation between capital and labour.
>
> The Joint Committee is empowered to appoint such subcommittees as may be considered necessary consisting of equal numbers of employers and workers; the Government to be invited to nominate representatives for each. In view of the urgency of the questions, the Joint Committee is empowered to arrange with the Government for the reassembling of the National Conference not later than April 5th for the purposes of considering the Reports of the Joint Committee.

[1] *Report of the P.J.C.* presented to the meeting of the Industrial Conference, 4th April 1919, S.P. 1919, XXIV.

(ii) THE P.J.C. AND THE SECOND CONFERENCE, 4TH APRIL 1919

The membership and work of the P.J.C.

The Committee consisted of thirty members from each side, including their secretaries, plus a Secretary and a Chairman appointed by the Ministry of Labour—C. S. Hurst and Sir Thomas Munro respectively.[1] The spokesman for the employers' side was Sir Allan Smith, K.B.E. (Engineering). The other employers' representatives were: Mr. E. J. Brown (Building), Mr. E. J. Burt (Quarrying), Sir George Carter, K.B.E. (Shipbuilding), Mr. Benjamin Talbot (Iron and Steel), Mr. J. W. Madeley (other Metal Trades), Mr. J. A. Crerar (Clothing), Mr. W. Hamlin-Hamshaw (Vehicle Building), Mr. A. F. Blades (Printing), Mr. J. J. Stark (Laundries), Mr. Sydney W. Pascall (Food Manufacture), Sir W. Raeburn, M.P. (Shipping), Sir A. K. Butterworth (Railways), Mr. A. E. Tanner (Cable Manufacture), Mr. H. Padwick, C.B.E. (Agriculture), Mr. J. T. Goudie or Mr. P. H. Lockhart (Rubber Manufacture), Mr. Roscoe Brunner (Chemicals), Mr. Walter Birch (Furniture), Mr. David Milne Watson (Gas), Mr. F. J. Farrell (Silk), Mr. Owen Parker (Boots and Shoes), Mr. Thomas Robinson, M.P. (Bleaching, Dyeing and Textile Printing), Mr. C. R. Seddon (Paper), Mr. T. B. Johnston (Pottery), Mr. Randle L. Mathews (Leather), Mr. G. A. Dutfield (Transport), Mr. Fred Holroyd (Cotton), Mr. Henry S. Clough (Wool), and Sir Alfred Booth, Bart., or Colonel H. Concannon, O.B.E. (Dock and Riverside), and Mr. J. McKie Bryce, Secretary.

The spokesman for the trade unions was the Rt. Hon. Arthur Henderson (Friendly Society of Ironfounders). The other trade union representatives were: Mr. W. Bradshaw (National Federation of Building Trades Operatives), Mr. H. Parker (National Council of Mine Workers other than Miners), Mr. John Hill (United Society of Boilermakers and Iron and Steel Shipbuilders), Mr. C. Duncan (The Workers' Union), Mr. W. J. Davis (National Brassworkers and Metal Mechanics), Mr. A. Conley (United Garment Workers' Trade Union), J. Compton (United Kingdom Society of Coachmakers), Mr. A. E. Holmes (Printing and Kindred Trades Federation of the United Kingdom), Miss Margaret Bondfield (National Federation of Women Workers), Mr. W. Banfield (Amalgamated Union of Operative

[1] Ibid.

Bakers, Confectioners, etc.), Mr. W. F. Purdy (Shipconstructors and Shipwrights' Society), Mr. W. F. Dawtrey (Steam Engine Makers' Society), Mr. G. H. Stuart-Bunning (Postal Workers), Mr. R. B. Walker (National Agricultural Labourers and Rural Workers' Union), Mr. J. Turner (National Amalgamated Union of Shop Assistants, Warehousemen and Clerks), Mr. J. C. Gordon (National Amalgamated Sheet Metal Workers and Braziers), Mr. A. A. Purcell (National Amalgamated Furnishing Trades Association), the Rt. Hon. J. R. Clynes, M.P. (National Federation of General Workers), Mr. J. Cross or Mr. J. Hindle (United Textile Factory Workers' Association), Mr. E. L. Poulton (National Union of Boot and Shoe Operatives), Mr. Gilbert W. Jones (Operative Bleachers, Dyers and Finishers' Association), Miss A. H. Tynan (Society of Women Welders), Mr. W. J. Wentworth (Amalgamated Society of Woodcutting Machinists of Great Britain and Ireland), Mr. J. Marston (National Union of Police and Prison Officials), Mr. A. Logan (Central Ironmoulders' Association), Mr. J. Whitehead (West of Scotland Brass Turners, Fitters, Finishers and Instrument Makers' Trade Union), Mr. H. Stansfield (National Society of Coppersmiths, Braziers and Metal Workers), Mr. C. G. Ammon (Port of London Docks and Wharves Staff Association), Mr. J. J. Mallon (Trade Board) and Mr. G. D. H. Cole (Secretary).

There was a strong connection between the membership of the Committee, those prominent in the J.I.C.s in their industries and those who had taken some part in the 1911 Industrial Council. Some of them indeed had been connected with the schemes for co-operation which went back into the 1880's and 1890's.[1] The Committee met for the first time on 4th March 1919, and it was addressed at that time by Lloyd George who was at his most lyrical. 'You will', he said, 'get this land into such conditions of happiness and contentment as it has never seen' and their work would be a model for the whole world. But Henderson was determined that there should be no needless wasting of time; he had had prepared a scheme of subcommittees on the questions before the Committee and a schedule for the completion of their work. Three subcommittees were set up—on unemployment, wages and allied questions and trade union-employer

[1] Davis had been active in support of the Birmingham Alliances, Johnston in the Industrial Alliances of the 1880's and 1890's (Clegg, Fox and Thompson, op. cit., pp. 194 ff., Phelps Brown, pp. 137 ff. T. B. Johnston, *Industrial Councils and their Possibilities*, Manchester 1919). Johnston, Burt, Milne Watson, Seddon, Poulton and Clynes were active in support of Whitley Councils, Carter, Johnston and Henderson had been involved in the Industrial Council in 1911.

co-operation.[1] The activities of the subcommittees on unemployment brought to light once again the fact that the main stumbling block to the improvement of industrial relations through improved collective bargaining, once the will was there, was disagreement on the primary substantive norms—wages, hours and conditions and security. The employers said that with sufficient increase in productivity, costs would fall, more would be sold and more would therefore be employed. The unions proved to their own satisfaction that too many were paid too little and so purchasing power was inadequate. The draft report left the two opinions side by side and the eventual *Report* glossed the matter over.

The Report and the Second Conference

In the *Report*[2] (Clauses 2 to 5) the Committee recommended a maximum legal working week for all and that exceptions to this should only be by special agreement of the parties; where only one side wanted the variation, a Conference could be called by the Minister but agreement still had to be reached between the two sides. Reference could be made to a competent authority approved after consultation with the National Council in cases where no agreement was reached (Clause 6). On the decision of that authority the Minister could grant or reject the application provided always that proper pay for overtime was given and that systematic overtime was to be discouraged (Clause 7 and Clause 10). Night shift, Sunday and other holiday work was to be subject to special consideration by the National Industrial Council (Clause 11). The procedure envisaged by the Committee therefore was that a Central Act should be passed establishing the principle of a maximum working week of forty-eight hours but that where negotiations under Clause 6 were in operation the application of the Act could be suspended in particular cases for up to nine months.

On wages[3] the Committee recommended a legal minimum time wage of universal applicability (Clause 1). An Act for this purpose should be passed and a Commission immediately set up to decide just what the rate would be and by what methods the rates decided should be brought into effect (Clause 2). Trade Boards should be set up at once in the less well-organised trades and the Act should be reviewed to facilitate the minimum wage-fixing activities of the Boards

[1] P.J.C. *Minutes*, 4th March 1919; *Report of the Subcommittee on Unemployment*, 19th March 1919: *Report of the P.J.C.*, etc., 4th April 1919.

[2] Ibid., pp. 7–8, Clauses 1–12.

[3] Ibid., pp. 8–9, Preamble and Clauses 1–7.

(Clauses 3 to 4). The Commission was to be appointed by the Minister of Labour upon the recommendation of the N.I.C.: it was to consist of equal numbers of trade unionists and employers under a Chairman appointed by the government (Clause 5). The Committee further recommended[1] that the Wages (Temporary Regulation) Act of 1918 be extended for a further six months (Subsection: Clause (1)) and trade conferences should be held on the question of how to reconcile war advances and bonuses with standard rates (Subsection (2)). The parties should consider the desirability of establishing a procedure for the national periodical review of wages over the whole trade of the country (Subsection (3)).

On the subject of negotiation[2] between trade unions and employers these should be on the basis of full and frank recognition of the rights of the organisations on each side to represent their members (Clause (a)). On this basis, proper organisation for the avoidance of disputes should be worked out (Clause (b)). Members should accept the jurisdiction of their own representatives and the right of any wage-earner to be a member of an appropriate union was to be regarded as inviolable (Clauses (b) to (c)).

The difficulties of the subcommittee dealing with unemployment have already been alluded to. It recommended organised short time,[3] the restriction of overtime in the times of depression, government orders to be staggered to meet the demands of depression, stimulation of house building, state development of suitable industries and the use of Industrial Councils as an agency in preventing unemployment (Clauses 1 to 7). The difficulties which had been found regarding under-consumption and under-production were mentioned in Clause 6. During unemployment adequate maintenance should be paid and provision for trade and other education during unemployment were to be made (Clause 9). The limitation of child and female labour was to be considered as a means of preventing unemployment (Clauses 8 and 10–11) and better old-age pensions and sickness benefits were recommended (Clause 12).

The National Industrial Council[4] which was to be central to all this should not seek to supplant any existing organisation but to coordinate; it therefore had only an advisory function. It should be elected not appointed and it should be fully representative of all sections of industry. In its role as a promoter of industrial peace it should be

[1] Subsection (1) to (3), p. 9. [2] Ibid., p. 10, Introduction and Clauses (a) to (c).

[3] Pages 10 to 12. Introduction and (a) Prevention of unemployment (Clauses 1 to 7) and (b) Maintenance of unemployed workpeople (Clauses 8 to 12).

[4] Pages 12–14. Preamble, Objects (a) to (f): Constitution I (Clauses 1 to 8) and II Clauses 1 to 10).

given an official advisory capacity by the government and should issue statements on industrial questions when asked to do so (Preamble). General questions concerning industrial relations, measures to head off disputes and legislative proposals concerning industry should all come within its purview (Objects (a) to (f)). It was suggested that it should consist of 400 members all told[1] and should meet twice yearly with a Standing Committee to meet as often as required. The Minister of Labour should preside when possible. Voting was to be according to the two blocs with a majority on both sides required before a measure was passed. The government was to finance the operation (Constitution 1 to 8). The Standing Committee of the Council should have the power to take such action as it decided was necessary to carry out the objects of the Council, consider references to it by that Council or the government and should report to the former its conclusions (Constitution II (1)). This Standing Committee was to meet once a month (II(6)).

The Committee's report was rounded off by remarking on the spirit of amity that existed between the sides during the meetings and expressed the hope that the problems to be tackled would be tackled in the same spirit.[2]

When the full Conference reassembled on 4th April to approve the *Report* the general atmosphere of good humour and goodwill was remarked upon as singular[3] given the predictions of revolution and disaster. Henderson had already discussed the *Report* with the Prime Minister, who, according to one report, was delighted with the work done in such a short time.[4]

The Prime Minister himself could not be present at the meeting on 4th April because of the needs of the Peace Conference, but the Minister of Labour, Sir Robert Horne, read a letter from him saying that the *Report* would receive immediate and sympathetic consideration from the government if approved by the Conference. Horne himself remarked that he would not be there if he did not think that the principles of the *Report* would receive the approval of the government. *The Times* observed that the onus was on the latter to show its good faith. There was already a note of anxiety at the Conference concerning the government's intentions and both Henderson and Smith indicated that legislation should be on the books as soon as possible. But the

[1] The rules according to which the Labour side was to be elected were given in an Appendix to the *Report*. They were drawn up by Cole on the basis of twenty industrial groups and the scheme provided the basis of representation at the T.U.C. under the reorganisation of 1920.

[2] *Report*, p. 15. [3] *The Times*, 5th April 1919. [4] Ibid.

general air was one of euphoria and goodwill. Thomas had a good word to say for the *Report*, though he still wanted to know what it was going to do about workers' control. It was accepted by the Conference in an overwhelming vote of confidence and anticipation. The members then dispersed to await the decision of a government whose leader had already expressed his delight at the report and whose Minister of Labour had said he would not have attended the second meeting of the Conference had he not been prepared to see the government accept its main recommendations. The Conference members had every reason for assuming that there were only matters of detail to sort out.

(iii) THE GOVERNMENT HEDGES: APRIL–AUGUST 1919

The refusal to appoint the National Council

It was 29th April before the government showed what response there was going to be to the events of 4th April. On that day Horne told the House[1] that the government would meet representatives of the Conference, the P.J.C. to be precise, on 1st May. This in itself was strange. It had been assumed that acceptance of the proposals of the Conference would have been more or less automatic. This would have meant that the arrangements for the National Industrial Council be published and the government's intention on the legislation on wages and hours be made known. The Provisional Joint Committee had only existed to draw up the *Report* and with its acceptance there was no further need for its services except in so far as the Conference wished to give it further work; and the Conference was not being recalled. The real representative of the Conference should have been the Industrial Council it had proposed; this was designed to have its own methods of continuous action and of liaison with the government. Someone should have noticed at this point that the government's proposal was out of order and that the reasons for it could hardly be good ones. If there had been any doubts on that score the events of 1st May should have cleared them up.

The proposals then made[2] contradicted in principle two of the main points of the *Report*; the government intended in any legislation

[1] 115 H.C. Deb. 5S, 1919, col. 55.

[2] *Minutes* of the meeting of the P.J.C., 1st May 1919.

on hours that the agricultural workers should be excluded from the start and that there was not to be *legislation* on minimum wages but an *enquiry* into what the minimum should be.

Further the onus of setting up the Council was placed upon the Committee rather than on the government or the Ministry. Against all this the words of praise that Horne had for the work of the Conference[1] were of little value. Not unnaturally the Committee was in some confusion. Smith said they could not wait for the Commission, they wanted legislation at once. Bramley supported him. No, the Minister would not commit himself to saying that in any legislation to be considered payment for hours over forty-eight would be guaranteed overtime rates. The government had decided to extend the Wages (Temporary Regulation) Act for six months, but that was the only concession at this stage that the Conference's work had gained. Smith was insisting that the whole matter required a reference to the constituents of the two parties. From them they could get the power to set up the Council. An adjournment was agreed so that the reference could be made. From this meeting it emerged that the government and the employers' side, led by Smith, had reasonably clear ideas about what they wanted to do in the circumstances. The government was not willing to introduce the legislation. It was only willing to set up a commission to enquire into minimum wages and to draft bills which excluded the two classes of wage-earners indicated. The employers' side would, ostensibly, have liked to have seen the government legislate. Failing that they wanted to refer to their constituents. The logic of this is not clear. They did not need to refer to their constituents. The constituents of the Committee were in fact the members of the Conference and not the individual trade associations and unions and that Conference had already approved the setting up of the Council. In this confusion the only party without a clear policy was labour. It let the government block it with promises and the employers mislead it with false issues and between the two lost what little control it had of the situation. It could and should have called the bluff of the government and the employers at this time; instead it allowed another month to go by before the P.J.C. met again and at this meeting it became clear that not only had the labour side lost control of the situation, but the Committee had too.

[1] The spirit which had emanated from the Conference 'had had a most beneficial effect' and was being followed with interest in America and on the Continent. Ibid., p. 5.

Government proposals, May 1919–August 1919

At this next meeting in May,[1] Horne observed that the adjournment had cleared up nothing. He and Smith then continued their argument about who moved next. Horne wanted the Industrial Council to be set up because the *Report* recommended it; Smith urged the government to introduce legislation. The ambivalence of Smith's position at this point becomes remarkable. As the representative of the Engineering Employers and speaking for the N.C.E.O. it is almost unbelievable that he should be demanding legislation on these issues; the E.E.F. and the N.C.E.O. would not have approved either for one moment. Yet his opposition to the establishment of the Industrial Council was as persistent as his demand that the government should legislate. This caused the government maximum embarrassment, exerted pressure for what he well knew could not be conceded but gave the appearance of being in full support of the Committee Report. At the same time it prevented the establishment of a National Industrial Council which might still bring the co-operative hopes of the Conference, and the country that supported them, to the forefront again. Whether accidentally constructed or not that position suited the interests of the N.C.E.O. admirably. Meanwhile the Committee's meeting resolved nothing on either issue. The most the government would concede on wages was a Commission of Enquiry but it was reluctant to include all employments in any proposed legislation; new exceptions were in fact suggested on 29th May—the Minister doubting whether clerks and post office workers were engaged in 'industry'. Yet he was still full of praise for the Conference and its work.[2]

On 13th June the Committee met again[3] and this time it had draft Bills on wages and hours to consider. It found neither acceptable for the reasons that it had found government proposals unacceptable all along—that whereas the *Report* was prepared to accept the idea of exemptions from the general rulings on minima and the standard week, these were to be negotiated as exemptions after the legislation was in force and they would only be allowed on the conditions laid

[1] *Minutes* of the meeting of the P.J.C., 29th May 1919.

[2] He could not 'sufficiently express in words' his appreciation of what the Conference had done. 'I am speaking absolutely from my heart . . . I expect you to believe that the government in this matter is determined to carry out your wishes and make fruitful and put into legislative enactment the principles you have enunciated.' Again he remarked on the impression made abroad. Ibid., p. 2.

[3] *Minutes* of the meeting of the P.J.C., 13th June 1919.

down by the *Report*. The Committee adjourned *sine die*. In August, legislation was introduced into the House,[1] but regarding wages it was only concerned with the establishment of a Commission of Enquiry and on hours certain classes of employee were specifically exempted from its provisions. The Bills were left with the House over the vacation in the hope, said the Prime Minister, that members would think on them. In the meantime the last legislative support for wages went with the lapsing of the extended Wages (Temporary Regulation) Act of 1918.[2]

(iv) THE GOVERNMENT AND THE EMPLOYERS LOSE INTEREST

The attitude of the parties to the P.J.C.

From now on the efforts to make the Conference and its *Report* come to something were all on the labour side. A meeting of the P.J.C. was called at its insistence in November 1919.[3] According to Henderson there had been an understanding between the government, the employers and the unions in negotiations after the last meeting of the Committee as a result of which the previous difficulties had been in principle resolved. This both the employers and the government representative denied and the meeting became a lengthy wrangle on the point. Again no conclusion was reached. The Committee adjourned with Henderson's insistence that they must know where they were being countered by Munro's inability to promise when the next meeting of the Conference would be held. As the official representative of the Ministry of Labour he could hardly say otherwise. It had been made clear to the deputation of the T.U. side of the P.J.C. on 21st October 1919, that the government had no intention of handing over to the N.I.C. its responsibilities in the matter of legislation.[4] In itself this was fair comment. It ignored, however, the events of the previous months. Moderate labour leaders had put their trust in government promises that the N.I.C. would decide policy. On the testimony of the government itself their participation in the Conference had helped immeasurably to calm the situation. To be told to mind their own

[1] 119 H.C. Deb. 5S, col. 1996, 18th August 1919.
[2] 120 H.C. Deb. 5S., col. 1709, 6th November 1919. 121 H.C. Deb. 5S., col. 670, 17th November 1919.
[3] *Minutes* of the meeting of the P.J.C., 5th November 1919.
[4] Lab. 2/556/7809.

business was in effect an admission on the government's part that it no longer had use for them now they had served their purpose.

The Washington Convention of the I.L.O. further confused the issue. The Convention agreed on in October–November 1919 established the principle of minimum wages and standard working week to be legally enforced and in so far as it did it made sense to merge British policy with their proposals. In fact the Convention was never ratified[1] and the Bill which the Ministry suddenly presented to the P.J.C. in June 1920, with the assertion that it was in accordance with the Convention, accorded neither with it nor with the *Report* of the Conference.[2] In any case both sides were strongly to assert that to be thus presented with a *fait accompli* was not good enough. From here on their attitudes diverged. Smith was for abandoning any further attempts through the P.J.C.; his point was that the mandate of the Conference had been revoked by the fact that Britain was a member of the I.L.O.[3] and bound by its decisions. The position was, to say the least, a surprising one in the light of the views of the E.E.F. and the N.C.E.O. on the matter of legislative, or any other government interference in industrial relations.[4] The union members were not convinced that the logic of Smith's conclusion bore examination. They certainly did not want to accept the Bill as it stood but they did not see why they should reject it entirely and disband. They waited to examine and adjust it if they could and they said so quite pointedly. So it was that the P.J.C. led another year of doubtful existence as it adjourned so that the members could 'consult their constituents'.

The N.I.C., government policy, and the N.C.E.O.

The last meeting of the P.J.C. took place on 19th July 1921; it had been called at the insistence of the trade union side, now convinced that there was no further hope of achieving anything and anxious that

[1] 136 H.C. Deb. 5S., col. 2182, 23rd December 1920; 142 cols. 479 ff., 27th May 1921; see below, p. 252.

[2] *Minutes* of the meeting of the P.J.C., 17th and 28th June 1920. A *Memo* by H. Wolfe in Lab. 2/821/615/2 states that the reason why the Cabinet would not ratify the Convention was that it had the appearance of being in restraint of trade.

[3] Ibid., 28th June 1920.

[4] When it became clear that the government was not going to ratify the Washington Convention Smith did say it would raise problems; the Ministry official considered he might join forces with Henderson on the minimum wage issue, Lab. 2/821/615/2. If the official was right, this only adds another dimension to the mystery of Smith's attitude.

the government should not be allowed to quietly forget the whole matter; if it was to be allowed to expire it might make a final protest. Henderson, Smith and Munro all took the opportunity to protest at the way the government had treated its creation, expressing their disappointment that it had refused to carry out obligations 'which it had undertaken with practically no restraint'[1] when the troubles of 1919 were at their height. That the Prime Minister and the Minister of Labour were conscious of the value of the Conference in the difficult circumstances of that time their own words testify—even at the point of the resignation of the Committee.[2] That, for reasons examined in more detail below, the proposals made by the Conference would not have achieved their aim even if applied wholeheartedly is beside the point. The part played by the Conference in quelling the unrest in the February–April of 1919 was crucial and, whether planned or not, combined with the manipulation of the Sankey Commission in what appears to be a very subtle strategy. The Commission and the Conference began work together; throughout March the Provisional Joint Committee was at work, convinced that its recommendations, if approved by the Conference, would become law.[3] The first stage of the Sankey Commission's work was finished by March 20th[4] and kept alive the miners' illusions that nationalisation was just around the corner. While the second stage got under way the National Industrial Conference met again with great pomp and circumstance on 4th April and produced more false optimism. In the meanwhile the railwaymen were being persuaded not to persist with their claim for nationalisation or workers'control.[5] As the government stalled on the N.I.C. Report and the second stage of the Sankey Commission hedged on nationalisation more and more of the initiative passed to it.[6] While the miners hung on to their hopes of nationalisation despite the apathy

[1] *Minutes*, 19th July 1921.

[2] In replying to the letter containing the resignation of the Committee the Prime Minister spoke of the good work it had done to inculcate a spirit of co-operation in industrial relations between employers and employed at a crucial time, Lab. 2/775/1730. His and Horne's appreciative words at the various meetings of the P.J.C. have been quoted already, pp. 240, 243, and 245–6. Both were aware of the work of the Conference in 'creating a steadying influence' during reconstruction; a steadiness for which Lloyd George had appealed in his preface to the booklet dated 8th March 1919, containing the full speeches of the first meeting of the Conference.

[3] At the meeting of the P.J.C. on 26th March, just before the *Report* was presented to the Conference for approval, Henderson referred to the time 'when the Report becomes an Act of Parliament'.

[4] S.P. 1919, XI.

[5] Bagwell, p. 406. Above, p. 145.

[6] The second stage of the Sankey Commission reported on 20th June without a majority for nationalisation. S.P. 1919, XI, pp. 305 ff.

of the rest of the trade unions, there was a further delay on the promised legislation on hours and minimum wages until in the last three months of the year the first attacks on the advances of wartime were made, in the attempt to force the definitive offer on the unions.[1] From now on, instead of trying to make advances in reconstruction, labour's efforts would be needed to hold what they had gained.

The truth is that the hopes of labour were doomed from the moment the results of that election were announced. The House of Commons and the government were not the sort that would make it possible for the hopes of wartime reconstruction to be realised. In industrial relations it was to become increasingly apparent that it was not the hope of an improved standard of life, Whitleyism and wartime co-operation that was to prevail but the free play of economic forces and the spirit of the N.C.E.O. These facts of political and industrial life were to make the N.I.C. an irrelevance from the start.

The Cabinet and the Coalition Parliamentary majority were the key to the situation.[2] It was a Cabinet based on a Conservative majority which was more representative of the business interests than that political grouping had been before the war. Moreover there seems to have been a general hardening in Conservative attitudes irrespective of social background or avocation. The Coalition had come to power with a considerable record of wartime social reform behind it. This proved to be no accurate guide to peacetime performance though the Election Manifesto,[3] and the King's Speech at the opening of Parliament, said most of the right things as did the Prime Minister in the following debate.[4] But the readiness of the government to soften the blow of unemployment with the dole was perhaps the last sad relic of the bold hopes of that time. The irony of the matter is that the N.I.C. was called into being to enlist the help of those who, though angry at things as they were, did not wish to destroy but to build a better system out of the one existing. This it succeeded in doing because it was given a totally erroneous impression of government intentions concerning reconstruction in general and the recommendations of the Conference in particular. Earnestness in reconstruction required an economic policy that would enable it to be paid for. The Reports of

[1] Bagwell, op. cit., pp. 375 ff. Blaxland, op. cit., pp. 125 ff.

[2] Mowat, op. cit., pp. 2 ff., Marwick, op. cit., pp. 94 ff., Taylor, op. cit., pp. 128 ff.; also J. McEwan, 'The Coupon Election of 1918 and the Unionist Members of Parliament'. *Journal of Modern History*, September 1962. T. Wilson, 'The Coupon and the British General Election 1918'. Ibid., March 1964. P. Abrams, 'The Failure of Social Reform 1918–1920'. *Past and Present*, April 1963.

[3] *The Times*, 22nd November 1918.

[4] 112 H.C. Deb. 5S., col. 47 ff.

the Cunliffe Committee[1] were accepted 'in principle and in detail'[2] by the government and they were based on the idea that the return to the Gold Standard was the first requirement of national economic health. Such a policy ruled out large-scale social reform. In war the financial interests had been shown that the economy could be made to meet the nation's needs if required; they had, in 1914, 'decided that the war would be over by Christmas because there would be no more money'. When it went on they 'solemnly declared that no war ever ended for lack of money'.[3] There was no such violent spur to re-thinking in peace.

By accident or design (and it would appear that it was by accident),[4] the economy was left to swing on uncontrolled through the first year of peace. Then came retrenchment. Deflation began early in 1920 and the mood of the House became more and more sombre and gradgrind. It reached its peak of masochism in the appointment of and the work of the Geddes Committee with its infamous 'axe'.[5] One touchstone of the earnestness of government social reforming intentions was the housing question. 'Homes fit for heroes' was the battle-cry of reconstruction but it was one that was quickly forgotten. Addison would appear to have been the scapegoat for the failings of others. It is clear in any case that there was no disposition to provide housing as a social service. 'We do not have the means to carry out all the programme of amelioration and improvement which it is sought to carry out at once,'[6] said Chamberlain. In particular 'the policy is that houses should be let at true, normal economic rent'.[7]

The other touchstone of government intentions was industrial relations and especially the application of the *Whitley Reports*. We have seen what became of this hope. And though originally the N.I.C. was at least partly inspired by the F.B.I.'s more positive attitudes of co-operation with the unions, it became increasingly evident that a

[1] *Interim Report* of the Committee on Currency and Foreign Exchanges after the War (15th August 1918). *Final Report* of the same (3rd December 1919) and the Treasury *Minute* (15th December) accepting both are in S.P. 1918, VII, and 1919, XIII and XXXII.

[2] Pollard, op. cit., p. 216.

[3] McKenna, op. cit., p. 235.

[4] On economic policy in general Pollard, op. cit., pp. 214–15. In this period 'the constitution was almost suspended' according to K. B. Smellie, *One Hundred Years of British Government* (London 1937), p. 364. See also H. Daalder, *Cabinet Reform in Great Britain 1914–63* (Oxford 1964), pp. 54 ff. A. Chamberlain, *Down the Years* (London 1935), p. 139. A. Boyle, *Montagu Norman* (London 1967), pp. 124 ff.

[5] *The Committee on National Expenditure* issued three *Reports*, December to February 1921–2, and was debated in the House on 1st March 1922. S.P. 1922, IX, and 151 H.C. Deb. 5S, col. 427 ff.

[6] 116 H.C. Deb. 5S., col. 2159, 4th June 1919.

[7] 119 H.C. Deb. 5S, col. 643, 7th August 1919.

harder line had developed, or re-emerged, among the employers. That harder line was summed up in the attitudes, spokesmen and policies of the N.C.E.O. The N.C.E.O. came into being in fact as a result of the Conference[1] and circumstantial evidence, not least the fact that the E.E.F. was the backbone of the Confederation,[2] suggests that its main aim was precisely to prevent anything coming of this gathering. The N.C.E.O. was as Citrine put it 'as belligerent as any trade union'. Its essential philosophy was summed up by Allan Smith who led a delegation of the Confederation to the Ministry of Labour in October 1920. He warned the government then that it was time for them to stop interfering. Overseas competition must be met and any attempt to impose minimum standards would result in firms going out of business. 'The issue is plain. Is it desired that we should have unreasonably inflated wages or is it desired that we have employment? The answer to one of these questions will determine what the government will do.'[3] For Smith and those who supported him those wages were inflated which did not enable the employer to meet overseas competition; the notion of minimum standards was alien to him. The N.C.E.O continued to oppose with tooth and nail attempts to get the I.L.O. Conventions, which aimed at establishing minimum standards, ratified.[4] The unpleasantness of the forces which rallied to these employers' organisations needs to be emphasised. The belligerence of the unions, real or imaginary, has passed into history. That of the employers is passed over in silence. One writer of the time noted that, though the social responsibility of the trade unions was often dubious, that of the employers was even more so; 'there are activities of these latter in which the interests of the community are not merely neglected but positively jeopardised'.[5] According to Davidson, Baldwin, when at the Board of Trade in 1921–2, had a particular dislike for employers' associations and for their officials. Because they worked for a salary and had to justify it such men were not interested in improving industrial relations. Davidson singled out Smith in particular whom he personally 'detested'[6] for his hardness and for his habit of referring

[1] *Annual Report of the F.B.I.*, 1919, p. 17. *Employers' Year Book*, 1920, p. 5. And J. H. Richardson, *Industrial Relations in Great Britain* (London 1938), p. 82.

[2] Citrine, op. cit., p. 244.

[3] The account of the delegation is in Lab./2/647/WA/4781. It records that the Minister specifically asked if Smith spoke for everyone concerned. Strictly he represented only the Midlanders.

[4] Richardson, op. cit., pp. 92 ff.: above p. 248 and below p. 290: Lab. 2/992/786 records the N.C.E.O.'s unflinching opposition to ratification. [5] Orton, loc. cit., p. 262.

[6] J. C. C. Davidson, *Memoirs of a Conservative* (ed. R. R. James), (London 1969), p. 106. Also see Citrine, op. cit., p. 247.

to the workers as 'the enemy'. Though the F.B.I. increasingly began to adopt meaner attitudes as the depression deepened in the early 1930's it is clear that the real culprit was the N.C.E.O. For its part, this organisation never quite forgot the nightmare that the 1919 Conference gave it. In 1928 the Ministry of Labour[1] noted that the reason for the N.C.E.O.'s objection to the initiative taken by Mond in that year was the memory of the shock registered by the threat of legislation in 1919 on minimum wages and the standard week. Smith, the main employers' spokesman at the N.I.C., even before the N.C.E.O. was formed, outlined its basic convictions at the first meeting in February 1919. Industrial troubles were only temporary and all would be well if industry would only be left to work out its own difficulties in its time-honoured way. He was at the time contradicted by the Prime Minister as well as the unions. At the end of it all, in the late 1920's, the Minister was telling the House that nothing on the lines of the Conference suggested was needed. Trade Boards, the J.I.C.s and the existing collective bargaining machinery could handle the question of wages and hours without further legislation.[2] Of course, the determination of policy was the job of government not of the N.I.C.; the fact is that the government had misled the Conference into believing that it could determine that policy and the deception had gained time at a crucial period.

[1] Lab 2/775/204. *Memo* of 17th July 1928.

[2] 135 H.C. Deb. 5S, cols. 1229, 2156, 1st and 8th December 1920.

17

The Conference assessed

(i) AS AN ANSWER TO THE PROBLEMS OF INDUSTRIAL RELATIONS IN 1919

As those who took part in the Conference saw it, the industrial unrest with which they were faced, and which they sought to alleviate, was a symptom of general social discontent. In its turn that discontent was caused by impatience for conditions commensurate with wartime hopes and expectations which it was becoming apparent would not be fulfilled. In so far as so complex a situation can be said to have had one cause this would seem to have been it. The problem therefore was correctly diagnosed. Despite the scale of the unrest it was never revolutionary in its nature; it aimed at a more rapid evolution of the existing processes of social amelioration. This too the Conference realised and sought remedies accordingly. The main ones—the National Industrial Council and the establishment of certain primary substantive norms of collective bargaining by legislation—were however only partly correct in theory and impossible of achievement in practice. Other recommendations on which in the issue it laid stress, public works and housing schemes especially, had the same merit but they lacked the framework of economic policy which would make them effective. They were increasingly to be seen, however, by a growing body of economists and publicists as an essential component of such policy and by degrees the theories which would justify them were to be hammered out. Other specific remedies of the *Report*—better pensions, unemployment pay, retraining facilities and sickness benefits—were part of the same pattern and, within it, relevant. So also were its recommendations on restricting child and female labour. The theoretical inadequacy of the proposals of the Conference as an answer to the problems it correctly analysed lay in its inability to see that the substantive norms could not be secured simply by legislation alone. There had to be the economic policy which would secure full employment and high wages. One of the employer members of the Conference put his finger on the problem: 'our experience goes to show that the fear of unemployment has been the main objection to new equipment, increasing productivity and the consequent displacement of labour'.[1] Far from pursuing a policy to provide for the security required, the government was bent on those proposals which were suited to the recommendations of the Cunliffe Committee.

As the recommendations of the Conference concerning the substantive norms was inadequate in theory so too were those concerning the National Industrial Council. Given the pattern of events in industrial relations in the early 1920's, the failure of the government, the miners and the owners to see enough sense to accept the realities of the situation, the bitter conflict between the engineers and their employers and the events which led up to the national strike, the persistence of the unemployment problem and the lack of any means of solving it, the hopes reposed in an Industrial Parliament were slim indeed. This does not detract from the need for some overall organisation to survey the industrial relations system in any fully rational such system. It is merely to point out that the pre-conditions for the success of such an organisation must exist before it can be of use. But it was not the National Industrial Council suggestion which makes the Conference of most significance in the present context. That significance was in its insistence on the need to secure the substantive norms. The means it advocated—legislation and certain social policies—were theoretically inaccurate or incomplete but they at least underlined that a political and social responsibility existed to secure the right conditions. This in itself marks a line of thought that became more and more relevant in the coming years.

(ii) AS A CONTRIBUTION TO THE EVOLUTION OF THE NORMS AND INSTITUTIONS OF COLLECTIVE BARGAINING

The fact of the calling of the Conference and the temper of those involved in it, as that temper was reflected in the meeting and noted by the observers, was that of the overwhelming acceptance of the co-operation norm. At a time when there was talk of revolution and of the need to replace the existing system with nationalisation or workers' control, this gathering testified that the way to overcome the problems of British industrial relations was through the acceptance of the

[1] 121 H.C. Deb. 5S, col. 996, 19th November 1919.

legitimate rights of the legitimate interests of employers and unions in industry, and the building up of free agreements between them. In invoking the law in support of minimum wages and basic conditions the Conference was attempting to use the law as the tradition of voluntarism allowed it to be used—to forward the work of the voluntary system by supplying its defects.

The organisational recommendations of the Conference regarding the machinery of collective bargaining and its revision were very general; perhaps it was considered that the *Whitley Report* had said all that could be said on this. Certainly, if it were assumed in the Conference that the government was committed to the Whitley scheme, little more needed to be said. But the recommendations for a National Industrial Council reasserted the conviction of the Industrial Council that the voluntary system of industrial relations needs some kind of overall supervisory organisation, again on the basis of voluntarism, to fulfil the needs of such a system. However plausible the theory and neat the plan, the preconditions for such a Council did not exist.

In the other procedural norms, *interpretation and application* and *codification*, the Conference, of its nature, was not interested, these being aspects of the organisational norm in its application to individual industries.

The dominating feature of the Conference's work and endeavours was its emphasis on the *minimum wages and conditions* norm. In the circumstances of the time it could not have been expected to understand the economic logic that its demands implied, still less how to meet the needs of that logic, though, as we have seen, the stress on a national political and social responsibility was the right one. In bringing these needs to the fore and emphasising the idea that work should provide the worker with certain human needs and human standards regarding wages and conditions, the Conference was bringing to the evolution of the norms of collective bargaining a touch of reality which was missing from the Industrial Council's and the Whitley Committee's work. That work should bring human rewards to the human being who did it had long been an instinctive demand of the unions. In putting it now firmly among agreed norms the Conference had marked an important advance in their evolution.

Regarding the *adjustment norm*, the Conference also had an important observation to make in suggesting that the parties should consider instituting a procedure for periodically reviewing wages in the country as a whole. Agreeing on the timing of such a review is only part of the problem. The bigger one concerns the actual percentages of the adjustment.

On the secondary substantive norms the *Report* only concerned itself with those connected with the problems of public policy in providing for these needs. In this, as in everything else about the Conference, there was a down-to-earthness. It was a gathering that took place in the aftermath of war and it was one in which the trade unions were aware of their power and the necessity of influencing national policy. In their efforts they met an unusual degree of response among the employers involved. Unfortunately it was not one that the real centres of power in employers' councils reflected.

PART FOUR

The Conference on Industrial Reorganisation and Industrial Relations 1928–9

18

The origins of the Conference

(i) THE CIRCUMSTANCES OF ITS CALLING

Changing assessments of the problem of industrial relations

It was the response of Sir Alfred Mond[1] and a group of other industrialists to a passage in the Presidential address of George Hicks[2] to the 1927 Trades Union Congress which eventually resulted in the assembling of the Conference. 1927 was the year of the Trade Disputes Act and the year after the National Strike of 1926, a time not without its problems in the field of industrial relations, yet the Conference was less of a response to immediate necessities than any of the previous attempts at national consultation. The lull after the strike in 1926 and the controversy surrounding the Trade Disputes Act[3] provided the occasion for fruitful reflection in many quarters. But these events were the occasion rather than the cause of the talks. The real reasons for the calling of the conference are to be found in the awareness of both trade unions and employers of the need for some reassessment of their total relationship in industry, an awareness given edge by the development of industrial organisation and the problems that faced industry in general at home and abroad. The Conference took place because the

[1] *Alfred Mond* (1868 1930), 1st Lord Melchett. Son of Ludwig Mond who, with John Brunner, did much to develop the heavy chemical industry in this country. Educated at Cheltenham, Cambridge, Edinburgh, Inner Temple. Practised as a barrister briefly until 1897 when he joined Brunner Mond. Liberal M.P. 1906–26. Joined the Conservative Party in 1926. Created Baron 1929. Hector Bolitho, *Alfred Mond*, London 1932. D.N.B.

[2] *Report of the T.U.C. Congress, 1927*, p. 67. *George Hicks*, b. Hampshire 1879, National organiser of the Operative Bricklayers 1912–14 and G.S. 1919–21. President of N.F.B.T.O. 1919–23 and General Secretary of the A.U.B.T.W. since 1921. Very much a Russophile. Citrine, op. cit., p. 103.

[3] The 'national strike' proper lasted from 3rd May to 12th May 1926. The T.U. Disputes Act received its second reading on 2nd May 1927, and the third on 23rd June. 205 H.C. Deb. 5S, col. 1035 ff., and 207, col. 2080 ff.

unions and the employers wanted it. It owed little to the promptings of government, such as they were, for industry to secure 'peace';[1] it owed less still to the efforts of individuals and organisations to urge peace as the first priority. The participants in the Conference thought primarily in terms of securing the conditions which would enable them to rationalise their relationship; such rationalisation would produce industrial peace as a by-product, not as a condition to be sought at any price.

The awareness of the need for this reassessment had been long maturing. The immediate incentive for making it came more from the realities of the post-war economic situation, combined with the developments and needs of industrial organisation, than from any other source. In facing these problems the interests of unions and management were largely the same. Both required a healthy economy and both required to reap the fruits of rationalisation. They had much more to gain from working together to secure these things than they had in keeping each other at bay.

The scale of the post-war depression and the controversy surrounding the return to the Gold Standard raised serious doubts about the ability of free trade and a monetary and credit system based on the free movement of gold to ensure the prosperity all sought and hoped for.[2] Industrialists considered that the way the system worked benefited the bankers and financiers more than it did the trader and the manufacturer; it was the power behind this system rather than the unions which was the main enemy. For its part labour was ready to seek out an answer to the problem of unemployment where it lay and it was also becoming increasingly aware that economic and monetary factors were crucial. Socialist illusions did not help it, it is true,[3] it was the pragmatic trade unionists who sought the talks and welcomed them,

[1] R. K. Middlemass *Baldwin* (London 1969), p. 453, suggest that the Prime Minister brought pressure to bear in ensuring that Mond's letter had a sufficiently impressive list of names attached. But it was Mond's initiative and his interest in these matters which made the approach possible and plausible.

[2] The effect of Keynes' articles in the *Evening Standard* in 1925 on the minds of men like Citrine is recorded by the latter, op. cit., pp. 136 ff. See Bullock, op. cit., pp. 265 ff., and Mond, *Industry and Politics* (London 1927), pp. 55 ff.; a speech delivered in October 1925. The state of informed opinion generally is recorded in Skidelsky, op. cit., pp. xiii, 10 ff. and 51 ff.

[3] To the Socialist, unemployment was only part of the problem of poverty which could not be cured under capitalism. Though rejecting Marxism, English Socialists had no policy to span the period between present capitalism and future socialism. Skidelsky, op. cit., pp. 27 ff. The immediate needs of the trade union movement were better provided for by the policies of Keynes-type Liberals than Snowden-type Socialists.

rather than those who were convinced that the whole system was wrong and needed not modifying, but replacing.

With the abandonment of trust in the invisible hand's control of the economy went an abandonment of belief in its effectiveness in deciding the best form of business organisation. Rationalisation[1] was the key word at the time and rationalisation meant some degree of restriction on the perfect competition which had been theoretically the ideal system. The larger firm with the more complex organisation required greater sophistication in its labour relations as in all other aspects of its operation. It was easier for it to see the advantage of having labour as partner rather than as rival and for labour to be prepared to work more peaceably with a firm whose resources and whose philosophy of management could be more accommodated to its demands. These two aspects of developing thought, the need to control the economy rather than be controlled by it and the need to seek labour's co-operation in giving policy effect, were evident in the Liberal Industrial Enquiry, 1925–7.[2] They received a boost from the example of the Germans and the French, both of whom had set up National Economic Advisory Councils (on which the unions were also represented), to keep the government informed of their needs and opinions on the national economic situation.[3] This was a clear pointer to those among the trade unionists and their allies who had never given up hope of some form of a National Industrial Council. Henderson was one of those who in early 1927 was spelling out the lesson and appealing for a revived N.I.C. with added powers; Pugh also was of the same mind.[4] There were others ready to disabuse them but they made a powerful point nonetheless.

It was these fundamental issues and developments affecting the thinking of the trade union leaders and the employers which disposed

[1] Bolitho (op. cit., p. 290) claims that Mond coined the word which he defined as 'The application of scientific organisation to industry by the unification of the processes of production and distribution with the object of approximating supply and demand.' The C.I.R.I.R. itself used the description-definition of the World Economic Conference. On rationalisation in general: Pollard, op. cit., pp. 167 ff.

[2] Below, p. 273, footnote.

[3] A Ministry of Labour *Memo* on Industrial Parliaments prepared in 1928 mentions the influence of these experiments. At the 1929 Congress Ben Turner (*Report*, p. 66) referred to them in relation to the C.I.R.I.R. The German Federal Council was set up in 1920 and the French National Economic Council in 1925. Lab. 2/775/204.

[4] In *The Times*, 12th April 1922, Henderson blames the government for the failure of the N.I.C. In a speech at Falkirk on 11th January 1927 he suggested the P.M. should form a Council on the lines of the continental models. At the League of Nations Union Conference in February 1927 Pugh put the same idea forward. It would handle labour questions as well as advise on economic policy. Ministry of Labour, loc. cit.

them to calling and carrying on the Conference. They could not however fail to be affected to some extent by movement of public opinion also. The correspondence columns of *The Times* are perhaps as safe a guide as any to the more thoughtful currents over the period. The letters from industrialists and their allies are of most interest since the readjustment required of them to meet the new situation was greater, for the trade unionist involvement in a meaningful conference would be seen as an advance. To many employers, for the reasons which are discussed in the next section, it was a retreat.

The national strike: threat and impact

The movement of informed opinion, as opposed to the appeals by politicians for an industrial peace which would get them off the hook, fluctuated throughout 1925 to 1927 with the rise and fall of passions over the national strike and the Trade Disputes Act. In the later part of 1925 F. V. Willey[1] compared the American situation with ours and blamed the employers for the deficiencies revealed by his comparison. Industrial leadership was not keeping up with the evolution of events in its field; the spirit of industrial relations must change, employers must see that the ambitions of labour are reasonable and that they must be accommodated; greater productivity in return for genuinely greater rewards was the only answer. This began a flurry of letters and leaders which emphasised the Whitley scheme and the need for a new spirit. Sir H. Bowden suggested a conference between a small group of trade union leaders and employers to discuss the matter.[2] Mond supported him.[3] The gap between employer and employee must be bridged. In particular the retrogressive, the greedy and short-sighted employer, whose attitude crippled industrial relations, must become a thing of the past. Early in 1926 Ben Turner[4] appealed for a joint

[1] *The Times*, 2nd November 1925. F. V. Willey, *Report on a Visit to the U.S.A.*, London 1925. The Hon. Vernon Willey was born in Bradford in 1884. Educated Eton and Oxford. Partner in the family firm of wool merchants. Controller wool supplies, etc., 1916, after service at Gallipoli. Unionist M.P. 1918–22. Was later to be one of the inner Mond group.

[2] *The Times*, 12th November 1925. In two articles in *The Empire Review*, February 1926 and March 1927, he elaborated his ideas; like many an advocate of 'harmony' he had a unitary concept of the industrial relationship.

[3] At a meeting of the British Society of Gas Industries on 12th November. Sir Robert Hadfield, another participant in the Mond talks, was present. *The Times*, 13th November 1925.

[4] At the A.G.M. of the textile workers. *The Times*, 11th January 1926.

council of trade unions, employers and consumers to put pressure on the government to act in industry's favour. Bowden wanted an Industrial Locarno. In the aftermath of the national strike Snowden was urging industry to pull together to solve its difficulties and asserting his support of co-operation between union and employers.[1] It did not go without notice either that the shipbuilding employers and trade unions had been co-operating on a report concerning the problems of the industry which were in their way every bit as great as those of mining.[2] In October the American example was being yet again urged as a better approach to industrial relations. The British employer regarded the smallest wage possible as the ideal; anything more meant that labour got above its station. The American way was to pay good wages for good output.[3] In December 1926, Lord Weir[4] joined those publicly advocating an Industrial Council or Conference, though here, as in other aspects[5] of his activities, Weir hardly showed himself possessed of the sort of attitude which would win trade union co-operation. Lord Henry Cavendish Bentinck, whose search for some form of nationally agreed policy between unions and employers goes back to the war years, was, with greater credibility, also urging a Conference. A very significant contribution, little appreciated by the Conservative Party as a whole, came from M.P.s Jack Hills and Harold MacMillan. It attacked the proposal for anti-union legislation and said that legislation was needed to strengthen rather than weaken their position. The ideas here expressed were expanded into book form; statutory support for collective bargaining and the positive encouragement of J.I.C.s were among the recommendations.[6] Early 1927 brought the interest in the German and French Economic Councils already referred to; it also brought the initiative of Lord Weir in approaching Bevin to get some conference organised,[7] an initiative which foundered on the coming Trade Union Disputes Act. When Baldwin appealed yet again for a negotiated industrial peace later in the year, after the Act had been passed, it was not surprising that the trade unions treated him with scorn. On the eve of the 1927 Congress, Citrine made it

[1] Ibid., 23rd June 1926. [2] Ibid.

[3] Leader 21st August and letter of 15th October 1926.

[4] Weir called for the conference in a speech in the House of Lords on 14th December. See *The Times* of the 15th. [5] Below, p. 275.

[6] The letter appeared on 10th December 1926. The book *Industry and the State* in April 1927. See Macmillan, *Winds of Change* (London 1966), pp. 223 ff.

[7] Bullock, op. cit., p. 392. Weir was high in Baldwin's estimation. He had been asked to be Minister of Transport but had refused; he had, however, chaired the Committee on the Supply of Electricity which had recently reported. Middlemass, *Baldwin* (1969), p. 450, notes that the approach made by Weir to Bevin had Baldwin's approval.

plain that it was not industrial peace as such but the agreements on which it could be based which interested the unions. The Congress itself showed that, despite everything, the unions were not averse to co-operation; far from it. But like Citrine they wanted to know what the terms of that co-operation would be.[1] Given this background in public opinion it would have been surprising if Hicks' words had fallen entirely on deaf ears. That the response had to be an unofficial one, however, was inevitable given the nature of the employers' organisations and their known policy at the time. Precisely what forces were at work in disposing the T.U.C. and the Mond group to welcome this opportunity of consultation is now examined in more detail.

(ii) INFLUENCES ON THE CONFERENCE AND ITS WORK

The C.I.R.I.R. owed its existence above all to the efforts and the will of the trade unions and the employers. For reasons to be examined, the unions found it easier to organise for such an undertaking and were the more in favour of it. As Bevin put it,[2] there were only two types of employer—those for the unions and those against them. Those for the unions were ready to regard such an initiative as Mond's with some favour. Such employers, though not numerically strong, did represent the more realistic and open minded, those who were governed by the needs of the future rather than the prejudices of the past.

Rationalising industrial relations: the trade union approach

The trade unions had been trying to rationalise their position in British industry since the early nineteenth century. Before 1840 there had been an attempt to establish national and all-embracing unions. Between then and the formation of the T.U.C. in 1868 efforts had been more sectionalised and after the Congress was formed there was an occasional probing to find some way of co-ordinating and better organising the general interests of the movement. Difficulties were however, great and the conflict between the General Federation of Trade Unions, formed in 1899 as a mutual insurance agency against

[1] Report of the speech at Usher House, Edinburgh. *The Times*, 5th September 1927. Baldwin was genuinely interested in improving industrial relations but he was too much under the influence of the right to give his instincts full rein. Middlemass, op. cit., p. 449.

[2] *Report of the T.U.C. Congress, 1928*, p. 447.

the cost of long strikes, and the T.U.C. Parliamentary Committee underlined them.[1] At the outbreak of war the unions were still outsiders both in national Councils and in industry. The war did much to change that and the address by Gosling to the 1916 T.U.C. proved, in the long run, to be most percipient in its understanding of its possibilities. If it was to fulfil them, the T.U.C. had to develop its organisation and powers, as he pointed out. It was in fact almost by accident that Congress came to do this, an accident stemming from the 1919 railway strike.

In 1919 the Triple Alliance was the only central organisation for trade union action which could claim to possess, even in theory, the power to co-ordinate a significant section of trade union strength. It had, however, defects, considerable defects in both its inspiration and its organisation. Thomas refused to call on it during the 1919 strike and by 1921 it was defunct.[2] It was the Mediation Committee formed largely at the instigation of Ernest Bevin during the same strike of 1919 that paved the way to the development of the co-ordinating powers of the General Council.[3] But the road was not an easy one. The unions were jealous of their autonomy and it was only the incidental circumstances of the 1924 Congress which led to them being formally granted. The moderates had been urging since 1921[4] that such powers should be given because the moderates wanted to see them used as Bevin's mediation committee had used theirs—co-ordinating and using the strength of the movement, yes, but using it to find negotiated agreements within the existing pattern. In 1924 there was even more than the usual evidence of confusion and conflict in the mind of Congress. The efforts of the militants led to the required powers being given to the T.U.C. General Council.[5] But Congress was simply putting its seal on a *fait accompli* whether it knew it or not. These powers had already been exercised by the Council for nearly a year and there was little comfort for the militants in the way it had used them. Negotiation and conciliation, persuasion rather than threat of force had worked very

[1] On these developments see the Webbs, *History*, pp. 117 ff., 134 ff., 186 ff., 280 ff. and 554 ff. Phelps-Brown, op. cit., pp. 244 ff. Clegg, Fox and Thompson, p. 266. Lovell and Roberts, op. cit., pp. 7 ff.

[2] Bullock, op. cit., pp. 103 ff., 133 ff., 151 ff. and 172 ff. Blaxland, op. cit., pp. 123, 135 and 155. Bagwell, op. cit., pp. 378, 399 ff. and 460 ff. Arnot, Vol. 2, pp. 309 ff.

[3] Bullock, op. cit., p. 107. Blaxland, op. cit., p. 136. Lovell and Roberts, op. cit., pp. 65 ff.

[4] *Report of the T.U.C. Congress, 1921* (pp. 381 ff.), 1922 (pp. 396 ff.), 1923 (pp. 378 ff.)

[5] *Report of the T.U.C. Congress, 1924*, pp. 347 ff. At the same time the Council was also asked to make a report on trade union structure; it was to be presented in 1927 and extremely relevant to the events of that year. Citrine, op. cit., pp. 221 ff., and *Report of the T.U.C. Congress, 1927*, pp. 99 ff.

well indeed and the industries assisted had expressed gratitude.[1] It was against this background that the Congress intervened in the 1926 conflict, not as a result of any new-found belligerence, but as a result of previous success in peaceful settlement of disputes. That the support of the miners in 1926 should be cast as an attempt at a 'General Strike' was the result of the trade unions' own confusion of mind, the intransigence of the miners and of the owners and the inability of the government to face up to its responsibilities.[2] The mining industry would have had a very difficult time even had good sense prevailed; with the absence of it on all sides a collision course was inevitable. If there is anything that can be placed on the credit side of what was from every point of view a national disaster, it is that through the national strike the trade union movement could purge itself of the dangerous illusion which a minority of its members had only been too willing to foster—the illusion that progress lay through some form of violent and spectacular direct action. Such had never been the real ambition of trade unionists in general and it was beneficial to have the notion once and for all discredited. Meanwhile their real aspirations were being formulated by men like Bramley and Citrine in the first instance since it was their responsibility, at the centre of the General Council's affairs, to guide its work and particularly to respond to the request for a report on trade union structure, a report which would raise the question of the role of trade unionism in the British system. Bramley[3] had worked almost as hard as Henderson to achieve something through the N.I.C. of 1919–21 and had not abandoned hope even after its failure.[4] But it was Citrine,[5] who succeeded Bramley, who had the task of drawing up the report in question, and it led him to ask fundamental questions concerning the

[1] *Reports of the T.U.C. Congress, 1922*, pp. 106 ff., and *1924*, pp. 126 ff. The disputes had been in Boilermaking (April–November, 1924), Dock Transport (February 1924), Tramways (March 1924), Engineering and Ships (April 1924) and Building (July 1924).

[2] Such would seem to be the conclusions justified by the main authorities. Mowat, op. cit., pp. 296 ff., Marwick, pp. 162 ff., Taylor, pp. 238 ff., and Bullock, pp. 279 ff., Blaxland, pp. 186 ff., Middlemass, *Baldwin*, pp. 380 ff., R. R. James, op. cit., pp. 227 ff., Julian Symons, *The General Strike*, London 1953, pp. 228 ff., especially, and Citrine, op. cit., pp. 143 ff. The Conservative conviction that in the T.U.C. and the 'general' strike they were facing a Communist plot (R. R. James, op. cit., p. 227) is a commentary upon current ignorance and failure of communication.

[3] *Fred Bramley* (1874–1925), cabinet-maker, born Yorkshire. National organiser for the Furnishing Trades Association before becoming assistant to Bowerman at the T.U.C. 1917. General Secretary of the Congress in 1923. Citrine, op. cit., p. 75.

[4] *Current Opinion*, September 1922, carried an article by him under the title 'Consultation or Conflict' which called for an Industrial Parliament.

[5] b. Liverpool 1887. Assistant General Secretary E.T.U. 1920–3, of the T.U.C. 1923 and General Secretary of the latter 1926.

nature and the role of unionism. Function, as he put it, must determine structure,[1] and his consideration of the functions of trade unions brought him up against the problems of its adaptation to the needs of its time, problems to which Gosling had directed Congress's attention in 1916 but which events had contrived to confuse or obscure. Despite the setbacks of 1921–6, the unions were powerful and influential in national councils and they now had, in men like Citrine and Bevin,[2] leaders who could afford to take what can be called a statesmanlike view, confident, well informed, conscious of power but responsible too. It was this combination of Citrine and Bevin, one of the most brilliant in the whole history of the trade union movement, which was to make the case for the C.I.R.I.R. so irresistible. These two men would have been outstanding in any organisation at any time. That at this crucial moment the trade union movement had them at its disposal was a tribute to its maturity and strength. The power and coherence of their arguments in favour of the C.I.R.I.R. at the T.U.C. Conferences exposed the inadequacies of the case presented by their critics.

Citrine's view of the general role of the unions as given in the *Report* on trade union structure was that they were the first of all to secure improvement of wages and conditions, secondly to seek a measure of control of industry and thirdly to defend the wage-earners against the 'onslaught of capitalism'.[3] The latter phrase, he admits, was partly the result of convictions that owed something to Marxism, though there was evidence enough, before, during and after the national strike,that some of the opponents of the unions were looking forward to a crippling confrontation.[4] The intention in any case was defensive, not offensive, while the positive functions of trade unionism were precisely such as the movement had always accepted—primarily concerned with the improvement of wages, hours and conditions. 'Some measure of control' was perfectly reconcilable with those aims and the system in which they were evolved, indeed it was demanded by it in view of the developing nature of the industrial relationship.[5] Streamlining the unions

[1] Op. cit., p. 222.

[2] *Ernest Bevin*, born Somerset in 1881. S.D.F. member. 1910 joined Dockers' Union. In 1921 became the first General Secretary of the T.G.W.U. He was, in Hobsbawm's words, 'the most important trade union leader of the post 1918 period'. *Labouring Men*, p. 339.

[3] Op. cit., p. 222.

[4] Above, pp. 174, 252, 268.

[5] Since 1924 the objects of the movement had included securing 'proper provision for adequate participation of workers in the control and management of public services and industries'. But as the debates and Reports in the 1930's showed, the movement as a whole did not regard these as very important. See T.U.C. Standing Orders, also *Reports of the T.U.C. Congress, 1931*, pp. 433 ff., *1932* pp. 206 ff., and *1934*, pp. 189 ff.

according to some neat plan, his *Report* concluded, was not possible, though the problems of sectionalism were great. It was suggested that they could be reduced by encouraging adjustment to new needs, especially through a proper programme of education. With the function of trades unions seen in this light—the improvement in wages and working conditions and the attempt to obtain some measure of control—it was also suggested that the General Council had a role as a centralised body acting for the whole movement on the more general questions affecting it. This role was conceived as analogous with what Citrine thought were the powers of the N.C.E.O. in acting for the employers. He was to find that this was a rather exalted view of the employers' organisations in general and of the N.C.E.O. in particular.

What, in summary, is clear from these developments is that by 1927 the trend of thought in the trade union movement had been towards some concept of a centralised power of the General Council which would enable it to look after the interests of the movement on the wider general issues and by whatever method seemed most suitable. That one of its possible roles should be to meet with the employers to discuss common problems was entirely in accord with this conception. When at the 1928 Congress[1] Citrine spoke of the Conference as simply the next sequential step in the development of the role of the movement he was speaking the plain truth. He and many others were aware that the needs of a changing situation gave labour a new potential.[2] It was a potential that well accorded with the essential ambitions of the T.U.C. The unions did not want to 'fight' for fighting's sake, they wanted to work with the system while securing their own rights and freedoms. Any other view of the real ambitions of the British trade union movement was out of touch with reality.

Rationalising industrial relations: the employers' approach

The unions could speak through the T.U.C. when they wanted to engage in such a Conference as this. The employers were more divided among themselves and they possessed no comparable organisation at the centre anyway.

The N.C.E.O., the dominant partner in the N.C.E.O.-F.B.I. axis

[1] *Report of the T.U.C. Congress, 1928*, p. 413.

[2] Op cit., p. 243. His article in the *Manchester Guardian* supplement of 30th November 1927 (W. Milne Bailey, *Trade Union Documents*, London 1929) and his broadcast talk of 16th November 1928 (*The Labour Magazine*, December 1928) indicated the extent to which he had developed his ideas in this direction.

on matters of industrial relations, was dedicated to the *status quo*. Its members wished to keep as much as they could of pre-war attitudes and structures and even if their approach could not command the assent of the more realistic employers it was sufficiently entrenched to prevent any alternative taking its place as the 'official' employers' view. The N.C.E.O. spoke for the employers as a whole after the N.I.C. in February 1919. It was concerned to maintain that there were two totally distinct areas of employers' interests—labour matters and the rest—and that two distinct associations were therefore needed. Once the N.C.E.O. had the responsibility for the latter the hopes of a more liberal F.B.I. approach were gone.[1] The only role of the trade unions was as limited collective bargaining agents in each industry, subject to the overriding needs of the accepted economic laws. Interestingly enough the Association of British Chambers of Commerce did show much interest in labour matters despite its being primarily concerned with commercial affairs; it was no more hopeful than the N.C.E.O.[2]

Outdated attitudes and the insistence that labour problems must be seen in isolation from the total industrial problem did not aid the development of positive and coherent policies by the employers as a whole. A further weakness was the ambivalent attitude of many to any sort of association.[3] The value of collective action to the wage-earner was reasonably clear even to those who were not members of unions. The employers' case was different both in regard to association for trade and for labour matters. He did not need either so much and he tended much more than the wage-earner to look upon his equals as his rivals from whom he should keep aloof. The main incentive to the formation of associations concerned with labour problems was in fact the need to meet the challenge of unionisation.[4] Even so many big firms stayed out of them either because they felt they did not need their support or because they wanted to set their own standards for the unions as far as they could. Many small firms also reckoned they could

[1] Above, pp. 234 f. and 251–2 f.

[2] The A.G.M. of the Association 1923 resounded with the need to make economic laws understood and dominant, i.e. the 'unsheltered' trades should set the pace in wages and conditions. It even carried on a campaign to this end as noted (above, p. 201). The National Union of Manufacturers was against 'sobstuff' legislation and was contemplating an attack on the Insurance Acts and trade unions. *The Times*, 1st July 1926.

[3] The growth of associations had been constant just the same—especially encouraged by the war. Pollard (pp. 165–6) and above, p. 91.

[4] Richardson, op. cit., pp. 78 ff., and Phelps-Brown, p. 263. Most were moved by a determination as Bevin (*Report of the T.U.C. Congress, 1928*, p. 446) put it, to prevent either side breaking away from the pre-war patterns of behaviour.

do without the assistance of membership of an association. For them the motive was likely to be the freedom to ignore agreements reached between unions and employers in their areas.

With all these cross currents to be reckoned with it was more than difficult to organise a group capable of speaking for all the employers nationally; it was impossible. For the moment, as the later involvement of the F.B.I.-N.C.E.O. was to show, the old suspicions remained but the mentality of the Mond Group was more in line with future developments which were already taking clear shape. The growth of big business, the joint stock company[1] or the public corporation,[2] had increasingly separated the roles of ownership and management and placed the latter in the hands of men who saw it more as a profession than as a business.[3] The aim of the professional manager, as Lloyd[4] put it, was to combine the entrepreneural skills of the old-fashioned business man with those of the powers of organisation and administration of the civil servant.

The professional manager was more likely to see management as a science than the entrepreneur pure and simple did.[5] As a science, management sought to combine the production, accounting and personnel aspects of its job within one comprehensive philosophy which embraced planning, co-ordination and control. For purely practical business reasons alone, the professional manager realised the need to treat his employees well.[6] To regard proper treatment of the most important element in production—the worker himself—as something which could be left to the harsh realm of impersonal economic law was simply irrational. A co-operative workforce was preferable to one that was not co-operative and the way to treat the workforce in order that it might co-operate was to be prepared to respect its rights as it saw them and negotiate with its legitimate independent representatives. Some were prepared to go further and see labour as the partner of management and ownership in the running of the firm. Mond himself made the point emphatically: 'Management has a dual responsibility.

[1] Pollard, pp. 161 ff.

[2] For example, the development of electricity under State supervision led to the setting up of the C.E.B. in 1926. The B.B.C. was formed in the same year. Pollard, op. cit., pp. 99 and 159.

[3] Ibid., p. 163. This distinction between ownership and management is one of the reasons for the growth of professionalism in the latter. But professional management is also an attitude of mind which can be possessed by those who own *and* manage, as for example Sir Alfred Mond.

[4] Op. cit., p. 391.

[5] The effect of the war in developing scientific management has been pointed out above, pp. 91–2.

[6] See Urwick and Brech, op. cit., pp. 12 ff., 88 ff., 91 ff. and 181 ff.

It is in a sense a kind of arbitrator between the claims of labour and capital. It is the duty of the director of one of our great industrial concerns to have regard for the just claims of workers who are, after all, their partners in their daily work more than the shareholders.'[1] Arthur Baker, another participant in the talks, spoke of 'capital, labour and management as co-workers in the enterprise and upon that work depends the success of the enterprise'.[2] Large firms with a professional approach to management could and did develop the worst kind of paternalistic policies which had a positive anti-union content. But persistent attachment to policies of this kind required a depth of ideological objection to trade unionism which few pragmatic business men could sustain. It was, as most sensible men could see in the end, self-defeating. The trend of the times was against such paternalism. The unions were more and more a part of things and the value of getting their co-operation in the necessary reorganisation of industry was correspondingly more valuable.

Although many names had been connected with the idea of such a Conference in the period 1925–7, it was hardly surprising that the response to Hicks' offer was made by a group organised by Mond. The fact that he was only a recent addition to the Conservative ranks was a help rather than hindrance—it is perhaps significant that it was left to a man who had been bred in Liberal principles to take this step. The Liberal intellectuals who were responsible for the Industrial Enquiry[3] were to show more awareness of the real needs of the situation than any other group. Mond was linked with this sort of liberalism by a political allegiance of a lifetime. In industrial relations, he was in the tradition of Mundella, Macara and Whitley in his belief in the possibility and desirability of an industrial system which met the needs of the unions while leaving the traditional structure of industry in essentials unchanged. If Baldwin's speech at the Lord Mayor's banquet later in November was any guide it would seem that Mond's example in introducing a new scheme of industrial relations into I.C.I. was not lost on the Prime Minister whose government had recently passed the Trade Disputes Act. Baldwin dwelt upon the fact that the

[1] *Industry and Politics*, p. 38.

[2] Address to the Federation of Papermakers (*Report* of same, 1924–5).

[3] The Enquiry had been at work in 1925 and published a *Report* early in 1928 (*Britain's Industrial Future*, London 1928). Its recommendations on industrial relations strictly speaking were not as apt as those of the C.I.R.I.R.—there was no group of industrialists or trade unionists of the calibre of the C.I.R.I.R. joint subcommittee on it. It did, however, emphasise the importance of the primary substantive norms (ibid., p. 466).

I.C.I. plan relied upon full co-operation with the unions.[1] That it should have become public just at the time of the talks was conclusive evidence that Mond meant what he said. Despite the bitter comments on his character and motives made by opponents on the union side,[2] he had much more to offer the unions than most. He had long been critical of the existing organisation of industry,[3] the attitude of employers to the unions,[4] the failure to realise that the desires of the wage-earner for security and advancement should be recognised as inevitable and welcomed,[5] the callousness towards unemployment.[6] He had long supported the J.I.C.s[7] and had been consistently critical of the over-reliance in national policies on banking advice.[8]

In addition to Mond there were in all some thirty-five who identified themselves with the group or met with the unions at one of the three meetings of the full Conference.[9] Because it was so loosely structured and informal in its approach and because the active participants—those who formed the subcommittee which met with the T.U.C.'s Industrial Committee—was small and yet in itself complex in the interests represented in it, it is not easy to characterise either that group or the larger one, or to assess it in terms of industrially significant influence or strength. The T.U.C.'s research department saw it in terms of directorships—there were 189 among its membership[10]—but neither this nor the fact that it also contained a scattering of N.C.E.O., A.B.C.C. and F.B.I. office-holders from Presidents downwards tells a great deal in itself.[11] The relationship between a firm and its directors—especially on personnel matters—is very varied and where there are multiple directorships there is little likelihood that it will amount to

[1] His speech at the Guildhall is reported in *The Times*, 10th November 1927. At this time I.C.I. employed in excess of 40,000 workers. The scheme was based on a network of factory group and national level councils. Mond's son was appointed labour director of the company. J. R. Clynes of the N.U.G.M.W., the main union concerned, gave the scheme his full support. Bolitho, op. cit., p. 305. *Unity*, March 1928.

[2] Bevin's observations on them 1928 Debate *Report*, p. 477.

[3] *Industry and Politics*, pp. 48, 202 and 230.

[4] In a lecture to the Harvard Business School in October 1928 he strongly criticised the suspicion of and opposition to trade unions which characterised many British business men. Bolitho, op. cit., p. 309.

[5] *Industry and Politics*, p. 2. Bolitho, p. 312.

[6] *Industry and Politics*, pp. 55, 66 and 83. This refusal to accept unemployment as an act of God was another characteristic of the Liberal mind at the time. Skidelsky, op. cit., p. 52.

[7] *Industry and Politics*, p. 65.

[8] Op. cit., p. 58.

[9] See Special Note, pp. 278–9. Some of the names are already familiar—Johnston, Humphries, Milne Watson, Baker, Willey and Seddon. Above, pp. 136, 166, 240, 269, and 273.

[10] *Report of the T.U.C. Congress, 1928*, p. 407.

[11] Weir was a past President of the N.C.E.O., Milne Watson the current President. Vyle was a past President of the A.B.C.C. and Rylands of the F.B.I.

much in one or all the firms. Further, the office-holders or officials in employers' organisations were much more at the mercy of their members in policy-making than the General Council were of theirs. It is in educational background and outlook that the real significance of the group is to be sought rather than in detailing positions in the industrial hierarchy.

In the first place, the inner group which met with the T.U.C.'s Industrial Committee[1]—Mond, Ashfield, Londonderry, Courtauld, Hirst, Milne Watson, Weir and Willey (with Humphries as substitute member)—were overwhelmingly of the type of employer who had already made a real effort to improve personnel policies and work with the unions. Mond, Ashfield, Milne Watson, Courtauld, and Humphries were all outstanding in their conviction on the value of good labour relations and of co-operating with the unions.[2] Their involvement in the C.I.R.I.R. was a logical extension of known policy.

Willey[3] had been one of those who had been most strenuously urging a change in attitudes to the unions and industrial relations since the middle of the 1920's and though Londonderry and Weir had backgrounds in industries in which industrial relations were chronically inadequate and to some extent shared the defects of their fellows,[4] they had given evidence that they wanted at least to try to improve the situation. Londonderry had disagreed with the rest of the owners in 1926,[5] and Weir's discussions with Bevin have been noted.

The pattern of industries represented among the whole group of thirty-six is not easy to trace because of the multiple directorships among them. If we confine this identification to those clear cases in which individuals were closely allied with one industry, *Engineering and Shipbuilding* had most representatives (Aberconway, Austin, Bowden, Harrison, Manville, Parsons, Avery, Vyle and Weir), and, if we include

[1] Below, p. 366.

[2] Mond's arrangements for industrial relations in I.C.I. have been noted. Ashfield's policy had always been to work with the unions (H. Clegg, *Labour Relations in London Transport* (Blackwell 1950), pp. 13, 15, 36). Milne Watson almost single-handedly persuaded the gas companies to accept collective bargaining (Clegg, *General Union*, (Blackwell 1954), p. 151. See also Stirling Everard, *The History of the Gas Light and Coke Company*, London 1949). Courtauld saw no contradiction between his acceptance of trade unions and his attempt to introduce better labour policies, the two were complementary (S. Courtauld, *Ideals and Industry*, London 1949, p. 130). Humphries' influence on the J.I.C. in flourmilling has been mentioned above (p. 166).

[3] Above, p. 264.

[4] Weir had been involved in a dispute with Hicks over the payment of engineers working on steel houses—the issue being whether they should be paid the engineers or the building trade rate—the latter being higher. *The Times*, 28th January, 17th February and 4th March 1926.

[5] Citrine, op. cit., p. 153.

electrical engineering, Hirst too. *Iron and Steel* were represented by Bond, Dorman, Brown, Hadfield, Mills and Rylands, *Coalmining* by Londonderry and Davies; *Textiles* by Courtauld, Lee and Willey; *Chemicals* by Mond and McGowan; *Gas* by Milne Watson; *Tobacco* by Baron; *Pottery* by Johnston; *Printing* by Hazell; *Flourmilling* by Humphries; *Papermaking* by Baker; *Civil Engineering* by W. Hadfield, and finally *Petroleum* by Cadman. Although in terms of size the range of firms they represented was wide, the large firms dominated; but several, Humphries, Hazell, Johnston for example, were from those small in size when compared with giants like those controlled by Mond and Milne Watson.[1] Varied too was the nature of the industries' products, from coal to flourmilling, also their stages of development from the oldest, printing and pottery, to the newest, electrical engineering and motor vehicles. Perhaps more important was the fact that salaried management and inherited wealth and position were there in about equal proportions. If the group as a unit had the attitudes of professional management it was organisational needs rather than background and status which made it so. Twelve out of the thirty-six at least had inherited wealth (in many cases considerable) and their position in industry: they were Mond, Aberconway, Courtauld, Davies, Sir Robert Hadfield, Hazell, Lee, Londonderry, Weir, Rylands and Willey. Five more: Austin, Baron, Dorman, Hirst and Parsons had built up their own businesses either in true entrepreneural style or through the business exploitation of a personal, scientific or engineering ability, even genius. Austin and Dorman were engineers, Parsons was also an engineer but came to industry through an academically brilliant career. Hirst was a chemist by training who saw the possibilities of the electrical engineering industry and became one of its founders in this country. Most of the others would be accounted professional managers, about half of the whole group. Ashfield, Milne Watson and Stamp were outstanding men by any standards; the first two especially dominating in their particular fields.[2] Apart from the inner Mond

[1] Taking employment as a basis of comparison, I.C.I., as already noted, employed in the region of 40,000, the Gas Light Co. about half that. Pountney, the Coxes Lock Milling Co. and Hazell Watson and Viney were by this standard small family firms.

[2] Milne Watson's contribution to the building up of the gas industry over the years, and especially in its fight back against electricity, is recorded by Everard, op. cit. Lord Ashfield reorganised the London Underground and was sufficiently supple in his approach to accept Morrison's means, a public corporation, to the end of the unified control he sought, even though he would have preferred to avoid public control. H. Morrison, *Socialisation and Transport* (London 1933). Pollard, op. cit., p. 154.

group there were several other names, Hadfield, Baker, Hazell, Rylands, Seddon and Johnston, for example,[1] which were also prominent in their own industries in support of proper personnel and labour policies in co-operation with the unions.

A further characteristic of the group, criss-crossing the other factors mentioned, was a remarkable variety of experience outside either this country or the industry with which the individuals eventually became most identified. The significance of the fact cannot be exactly judged in the absence of any comparable statistics concerning men at the same level of industrial management, but it would seem certain that it is significant in understanding their approach to industrial relations. Half of them had had a university education or its equivalent. Law and the natural sciences or engineering predominated with the civic, Scottish and foreign universities more dominant, if anything, than Oxford and Cambridge.[2] Several had either been educated or brought up abroad or like Ashfield, Austin and Baron had gained success in business or developed as professional managers there first. Ashfield, son of English immigrants, had begun his working life in America as a messenger for a Detroit railway company; he returned to England in 1907. Austin had been apprenticed in engineering in Australia, but had returned in 1895 to manage the Wolseley Co. and eventually to start making cars under his own name at Longbridge. Baron was born of Russian Jewish parents and emigrated to America when a boy. He made one fortune in tobacco manufacture there after starting as a labourer, came to England in the 1890's, bought Carreras in 1903 and made another fortune building it up. Finally, public service, patronage of the arts and charities was a marked characteristic of the group. This again is not easy to assess in the absence of comparative statistics and given the level of affluence of the group as a whole these interests were to be expected; but again it can hardly be discounted in understanding the group as a whole. Mond, Weir, Colwyn, Londonderry, Ashfield, Willey, Davies, Hirst, Humphries, Lee and Stamp had all held government posts or served on Royal and other Commissions and Committees, some of them many times over.[3] Davies and Baron were

[1] Baker, Seddon and Johnston have already been mentioned. See above, p. 274. Hadfields of Sheffield had been noted for their good personnel policies over the years. Sir Robert boasted in an article in *System*, August 1919, of never having had a strike and of introducing the eight-hour day in 1891; Rylands did his best to keep the J.I.C. in the industry afloat in the early 1920's. The *Annual Reports* 1919–20 and 1921–2 are full of his, and the unions', enthusiasm. An M. of L. *Memorandum* (331 883) of 21st February 1919 remarks on the 'goodwill' in the industry.

[2] See below; the Special Note on the Mond group.

[3] Weir's close alliance with Baldwin has already been mentioned (above, p. 265).

famous for their benefactions and Mond, Londonderry and Courtauld were well known for their patronage and knowledge of the arts.

It was then, above all, a group whose range of personal endowment, interests and education or business experience was very wide, a group which might be expected to possess the imagination to tackle new problems courageously and humanely. The sort of task it set itself in 1928 required all these qualities.

SPECIAL NOTE ON THE MOND GROUP

Twenty-one, including Mond, signed the original letter, three more names were added later and twelve more identified themselves with the talks in the next two years, appearing at one or other of the Conferences. Details of all but two (Mr. M. Mannanberg and Mr. G. S. Tomlinson) are given in either *Who's Who* or the D.N.B. Their names, and the companies with which they were mainly identified, are as follows:

Lord Aberconway (Chairman, John Brown)
Lord Ashfield (Chairman, London Traffic Combine)
Sir Herbert Austin (Chairman and Managing Director, Austins Ltd.)
Arthur Baker (Director, Bowaters)
Bernard Baron (Chairman, Carreras)
Henry Bond (Chairman and Managing Director, Richard Thomas (Steel))
Sir H. Bowden (President, Raleigh Industries)
Sir David Brook (Birmingham City Council)
P. Brown (Director, Hadfields (Steel))
Sir John Cadman (Chairman, Anglo-Persian Oil Co.)
Lord Colwyn (Directorships in india rubber, cotton, etc.)
Samuel Courtauld (Chairman, Courtaulds)
David Davies (Chairman, Ocean Coal and Wilsons)
Sir Arthur Dorman (Chairman, Dorman Longs)
Sir Robert Hadfield (Chairman and Managing Director, Hadfields (Steel))
W. J. Hadfield (Sheffield City Engineer)

Mond had held office as Commissioner of Works, then as Minister of Health under Lloyd George, 1916–18 and 1921–2, Ashfield was President of the B.O.T. under Lloyd George, 1916–18, Colwyn was on the Flax Control Committee and the Admiralty Committee on Dockyards in the war, Stamp on numerous Commissions and Committees connected with taxation, Willey Assistant Director of Equipment and Ordnance services, Lee had been on the Samuel Commission, etc. etc.

W. Harrison (Managing Director Harrisons (Agricultural Machinery))
W. H. Hazell (Chairman, Hazell, Watson and Viney (Printers))
Sir Hugo Hirst (Chairman and Managing Director, General Electric Co.)
A. E. Humphries (Chairman, Coxes Lock Milling Co.)
T. B. Johnston (Chairman, Pountney's Bristol (Pottery))
K. Lee (Chairman, Tootal Broadhurst Lee)
Lord Londonderry (Coalowner, Northumberland)
Sir H. McGowan (Director, I.C.I.)
Sir E. Manville (Chairman, Daimlers)
Sir F. Mills (Chairman, Ebbw Vale Steel Co.)
Sir Alfred Mond (Chairman, I.C.I.)
Sir Charles Parsons (Chairman, C. A. Parsons)
Sir W. Peter Rylands (Managing Director, Rylands (Iron and Steel wire))
Sir Joseph Stamp (Director, I.C.I.)
G. C. Vyle (Managing Director, W. T. Avery)
Sir David Milne Watson (Governor, Gas Light and Coke Co.)
Lord Weir (Managing Director, G. J. Weir (Engineers))
Hon. Vernon Willey (Partner in Francis Willey (Wool merchants))

The average age was 58–60, the youngest being Willey (43) the oldest Arthur Dorman (79). The university background of some of the better known or more significant members of the group is as follows: Mond, Natural Sciences (Cambridge and Edinburgh) and Law (Inner Temple); Aberconway, Law (Edinburgh and Lincolns Inn); Baker, Chemistry (Manchester); Bowden, Engineering (Cambridge and Lausanne); Milne Watson, Law (Edinburgh, Oxford and Marburgh); Parsons, Engineering (Trinity College Dublin and Cambridge); Rylands, Law (Cambridge and Inner Temple); Stamp, Economics (L.S.E.); Vyle, Electrical Engineering (Glasgow); Weir, Law (Glasgow); Willey, History (Oxford); Courtauld, Silk Technology (Krefeld); Davies, History (Cambridge); Dorman, Engineering (Paris); Hadfield, Metallurgy (Leeds and Sheffield); Hirst, Chemistry (Munich); and Lee, Law (Manchester). The contributions of Stamp to economics and statistics, of Hadfield to metallurgy (he discovered manganese steel) and Parsons to engineering were outstanding.

19

The Conference and its Joint Subcommittee 1928-9

(i) PURPOSE OF THE CONFERENCE

Consolidating and implementing the contractual co-operation norm

The passage in Hicks' speech to the 1927 Congress,[1] to which Mond responded, spoke of the workers aiming at:

> obtaining a share in the control and administration of industry through the trade unions. Training in management and administration is absolutely essential as a preliminary step towards industrial freedom. Not until the workers fit themselves to deal with the problems of management and the conduct of industry will they be capable of controlling industry. And here I would like to say this. We all know—employers as well as trade unionists—that the vexatious period through which we are passing is a transitional period. Much fuller use can be made under these conditions of the machinery for joint consultation and negotiation between employers and employed. We have not reached the limits of possible development in this direction. It is more than doubtful whether we have seen the fullest possible development of machinery for joint consultation and negotiation between employers and employed. We have not reached the limits of possible development of machinery for joint consultation in particular industries and *practically nothing has been done yet to establish effective machinery of joint conference between the representative organisations entitled to speak for industry as a whole. There are many problems upon which joint discussions would prove of value at the present time. Such a direct exchange of practical views between representatives of the great organised bodies who had responsibility for the conduct of industry and know its problems at first hand would be of far greater significance than*

[1] *Report of the T.U.C. Congress, 1922*, pp. 66–7.

the suggestion that has been made in certain quarters for a spectacular national conference under government or other auspices to discuss vague aspirations towards industrial peace. Discussion on these lines would bring both sides face to face with the hard realities of the present situation and might yield useful results in showing how far and upon what terms co-operation is possible in a common endeavour to improve the efficiency of industry and raise the workers' standard of life.

As Citrine notes,[1] the passage here italicised was drafted by Hicks, Tracey and Citrine himself and it was inserted at the latter's suggestion. In a sense it sits uneasily with that immediately preceding it in which, despite the lack of coherence of one section with another, it would appear that the consultation in question was to be but a preliminary to workers' control. It was at least capable of that interpretation and given Hicks' known views, which he was soon to reassert,[2] the interpretation was not entirely unjustified; it was one which many of the employers showed that they preferred. And not only was Hicks' approach capable of this interpretation; in the debate Citrine at least did not exclude it.[3] Such confusion and contradictions simply reflected the state of flux which existed at the time. But in the light of events it is evident that the operative phrase in Hicks' speech was the last one quoted; 'Co-operation in a common endeavour to improve the efficiency of industry and raise the workers' standard of life' was what was being suggested. This was what the talks were about to explore, the possibility of giving effect to the co-operation norm.

In its response to the invitation, the Mond group[4] made it plain that this is as they saw it: since

> *there appears to us, after investigation, to be no single existing organisation of employers which can take the initiative in inviting discussion to cover the entire field of industrial reorganisation and industrial relations* we desire as a representative group of employers to extend to the General Council of the Trades Union Congress an invitation to meet us to consider the questions relating to these matters. The movement towards industrial co-operation has recently received a great accession of strength and there seems to be general agreement that a useful purpose would be served by consideration of certain fundamental factors in industrial organisation and industrial relations

[1] Op. cit., p. 243.

[2] 'His early Marxian concepts combined with his natural militancy got the better of his judgement,' Citrine, p. 246.

[3] *Report of the T.U.C. Congress, 1928*, p. 413.

[4] *Interim Report of the C.I.R.I.R.*, p. 1.

> with a view to the formulation of definite and concrete proposals applicable to and to be determined in detail by the various industries concerned . . . *industrial reconstruction can only be undertaken in conjunction with those entitled and empowered to speak for organised labour . . . necessity therefore impels us to seek the immediate co-operation of those who are as vitally interested in the subject as ourselves* . . . the common interests which bind us are more powerful than the apparently divergent interests which seem to separate. The prosperity of industry can in our view be fully attained only by full and frank determination to increase the competitive power of British industries in the world markets coupled with the free discussion of the essentials on which it can be based. *That can be achieved most usefully by direct negotiations with the twin objects of the restoration of industrial prosperity and the corresponding improvement in the standard of living of the population.*

Taken as a whole this passage was as much a rejection of the N.C.E.O.-E.E.F. attitude to industrial relations as was the T.U.C. initiative a rejection of any suggestion that it was the overthrow and replacement of the existing system labour intended. In the first instance, the passage did not accept the distinction between the two supposed aspects of employers' interests, labour and trade matters, which could be so separated that decisions in the one field could be made entirely independently of the other. In the second it recognised quite explicitly the right of the unions to take an interest in and be consulted on every matter affecting the interests of the industry on which they too depended for their livelihood. Co-operation based on this recognition of the power and place of the unions, co-operation aimed at working together to solve the industries' problems was the aim, in other words the full contractual co-operation norm was accepted and was to be implemented. The group put an emphasis on the need to restore international competitiveness, a phrase which was much beloved by the men who wished to reduce wages and conditions to the extent they thought that purpose needed. But though they emphasised it, they did not reach the same conclusion. For the Mond group the living standards of the wage-earners were not to be held at risk to meet the 'needs of trade'. The intention was to manipulate policy and improve efficiency through rationalisation so bettering the position of industry and of all who lived by it.

(ii) PREPARATION FOR AND THE RESULTS OF THE FIRST CONFERENCE, JANUARY 1928

The General Council's reply to the trade union critics

Mond's letter was received on 23rd November 1927, but it was 20th December before a special session of the General Council discussed and accepted the invitation.[1] There had been considerable opposition to the talks in some sections of the labour movement. A. J. Cook was the most energetic and persistent opponent; his charges ranged from connivance by the leaders of the T.U.C. in misleading the unions to their being the honest dupes of the Mond group.[2] Emotion rather than reason dictated Cook's attitude and he used any argument, good, bad or indifferent to clothe his opposition to what he felt to be wrong. There was opposition also from the A.E.U. on a technicality; the T.U.C., it held, had no mandate. It was for Bevin to point out that the opposition of the A.E.U. to the talks was curiously akin to that of the E.E.F. and the N.C.E.O.,[3] turning on technicalities but no less bitter and sustained for that. The comprehensive answer to the objections was contained in the *Official Report* on the Conferences and the subsequent defence of its work by Bevin especially.[4] In the *Report* to the Congress in 1928, Citrine had said that the movement had three choices in the light of worsening conditions of trade and industry. They could do what they could to procure the breakdown of the industrial machine so that a revolutionary situation is created; a policy which 'the Trade Union movement has rejected decisively as futile, certain to fail and sure to lead to bloodshed and misery'. They could alternatively stand by and let the employers get on with it but this is a course 'entirely inconsistent with the modern demand for a completely altered status of the workers in industry . . . a confession of failure for unions to say that they are going to take no hand in the momentous changes that are taking place in the economic life of the nation'. The third course was for the movement to see that it had a voice and an influence in new developments. 'The ultimate policy of the movement can find more use for an efficient industry than for a derelict one, and the unions can use their power to promote and guide the scientific re-

[1] *Report of the T.U.C. Congress, 1928*, p. 211.

[2] *Mond Moonshine* and *Mond's Manacles* were titles of two of his pamphlets.

[3] *Report of the T.U.C. Congress, 1928*, p. 446. The correspondence with the A.E.U. is reproduced on pp. 217 ff. of the same.

[4] Ibid., pp. 407 ff., *Report of the T.U.C. Congress, 1929*, pp. 384 ff.

organisation of industry as well as to obtain material advantages from their reorganisation.' This, the Council concluded, was the only possible course to be taken, the course best likely to secure for the members of the trade unions the improvement in standards of living and the conditions of work they looked for.

The Conference and the joint subcommittee

Though determined to enter into the talks with the intent of getting from them the maximum possible, the General Council approached the whole situation very warily: it began by appointing a group to consider procedure.[1] This consisted of Ben Turner of the Textile Workers, who was the Chairman, E. Bevin of the Transport and General Workers, A. Pugh of the Iron and Steel Trades Confederation, T. Richards of the Miners' Federation, J. H. Thomas of the National Union of Railwaymen, William Thorne of the General Municipal Workers and Walter Citrine, General Secretary of the T.U.C. Its recommendations were that the first subject that the talks should concern themselves with was the power of the respective participants; secondly that nothing the Conference did should bypass the existing machinery of negotiation; thirdly that the discussions should be carried on without prejudice to the freedom of action of the parties and finally that the object of the talks should be the review of the general principles governing the economic situation and matters of interest to all engaged in industry in any capacity. On this basis the first meeting between the full General Council and the Mond groups was scheduled to take place on 12th January 1928.

At the meeting[2] Mond was in the Chair and explained that they had issued their invitation because no representative organisation on their side existed which covered all the issues that were relevant. They were not only aware that they could only deal with labour through the trade unions; they wished to assist trade unionism and co-operate fully with it. As an outline sketch of the sort of topics the Conference could deal with he mentioned rationalisation, security of the wage-earner, housing, health and unemployment insurance, education, industry, taxation and rates, works councils, financial participation by the wage-earner, investigation into cases of disputes and the creation of some permanent standing committee. In the discussion at the meeting, Cook took the opportunity to dissociate himself from what

[1] *Report of the T.U.C. Congress, 1928*, p. 211. [2] Ibid., pp. 212–14.

was going on but apart from that the attempt to be constructive was sustained and effective; Tillett brought up the question of the effect of financial policy on industry and both Richards and Bevin stressed the need to do something about victimisation. Milne Watson from the employers' side asked that three propositions be agreed on by the Conference: that industrial prosperity and welfare depended on co-operation; that though the right to strike or lock out existed there should be a more reasonable way of settling disputes; and that as the existing industrial system was only a stage in our economic evolution, changes to be brought about in a constitutional manner. Citrine rejected this approach. The future pattern of industry could look after itself; it was improvements within the present set-up which they wished to explore. Mond also rejected it. The purposes of the talks were essentially investigatory; only through the co-operation of organised labour could anything be done and no aspect of the problem, managerial or otherwise, could be excluded. The employers had already appointed their subcommittee to take part in further discussions. The trade union side had no such committee ready and empowered to indulge in further talks. At a special session of the Council on 24th January, however, it was decided that the talks could continue[1] and the group under Turner's Chairmanship should act for the General Council in a joint subcommittee with the six employers acting in a similar capacity.[2]

(iii) THE ENDORSEMENT OF THE SUBCOMMITTEE'S WORK

By the General Council and the C.I.R.I.R., July 1928 to March 1929

During February the executives of all the trade unions affiliated to the T.U.C. were circularised[3] on what had been done and decided to date; the subcommittees agreed to meet again on 27th February to work out a statement of purposes and an agenda. The statement of purposes[4] asserted that:

> The object of the Conference to discuss the entire field of industrial reorganisation and industrial relations, is to assist the solution of the greatest problem facing the country at the present time namely

[1] Ibid., p. 214. [2] Above, pp. 275 and 284.
[3] Ibid., and *Minutes* of the Industrial Committee Meeting, 28th February 1928.
[4] *Interim Joint Report* cited, p. 5.

the restoration of industrial prosperity and with it the progressive improvement of the standard of living of the population . . . the parties do not intend to interfere with the functions of the existing machinery . . . it is also recognised that the present position of industry is not necessarily final but that it is only a phase in its evolutionary development. . . . Industrial reconstruction can best be undertaken in conjunction with and with the co-operation of . . . organised labour. Every effort will therefore be made to further the co-operation of all those who participate in production and to secure the objective that all those who participate in production should also participate in the prosperity of industry. It is agreed that the most effective co-operation in industry can be obtained by deliberation and negotiation with the accredited representatives of affiliated trade unions.

The Agenda resolved itself into a series of eight topics:

(1) *The organisation of industrial relations:* T.U. recognition, collective bargaining, security and status, victimisation, legal regulation of hours, management and labour, works councils, information, investigation into the causes of disputes, extension of the Industrial Courts, factory legislation, health and unemployment insurance, suggestions machinery, personal relationships.
(2) *Unemployment.*
(3) *Distribution of the proceeds of commodities and services:* High wages, participation in prosperity through shareholding, profit and cost sharing, payment by results, minimum wage principles.
(4) *Organisation, technique and control of industry:* Rationalisation, the effect of unnecessary internal competition, sheltered and unsheltered industries distribution.
(5) *Finance:* Monetary technique, industrial finance, taxation and rates.
(6) *Constitutional:* The National Industrial Council for regular consultation, machinery for continuous investigation into industrial conditions.
(7) *International:* Competition from countries with lower living standards, international agreements and conventions, international economic conferences.
(8) *General:* Housing, health, education, technical education, research.

The statement of purpose and agenda were approved by the General Council and the combined subcommittee met ten times on it in the next few weeks.[1] There was no set order for dealing with it and in fact the first subjects to be considered were questions of Trade Union Recognition and Victimisation. Agreements, statements or memoranda were in addition published on the Gold Reserve, the National Industrial Council, the Prevention of Disputes, Rationalisation and Unemployment. The first six were all prepared before the second full joint Conference on 28th July, which duly approved them. The seventh and last, on Unemployment, was approved by the third and last full Joint Conference on 3rd March 1929.

The agreements on *Trade Union Recognition* and *Victimisation*[2] were full endorsements of the main trade union claims on these points. Trade unions had a right, not only to represent their members within each industry, but the T.U.C. had the right too to speak for the whole movement on any question of national policy affecting that movement. Collective negotiations were not to be confined to wages, hours and conditions but extended to 'other matters of common interest to the trade and industry concerned'. The full co-operation norm was then at the heart of its recommendations on industrial relations.[3] On *Victimisation*: the merits and demerits of the National Strike were deliberately left without comment. That there should be any victimisation as a result of it was pronounced to be a hindrance to the desired improvement of industrial relations. In dealing with the prevention of disputes,[4] the Conference did not wish to interfere with existing machinery in any way or to give any support to ideas on compulsory arbitration and conciliation. The strengthening of organisations on both sides and the recognition of the joint industrial responsibility shared by them was the best guarantee of industrial peace. A *National Industrial Council*[5] 'for the continuous improvement of industrial organisation and industrial relations' consisting of members of the T.U.C., F.B.I. and N.C.E.O. was to meet once a quarter for general consultations on the widest possible range of questions affecting industry and industrial progress and to establish and direct machinery for the continuous improvement of industrial relations. Again the full acceptance of the co-operation norm is here set out. Among other things a Joint Standing Committee of the Council would refer disputes submitted to it to a Joint Conciliation Board whose specific functions

[1] *Minutes* of the Industrial Committee Meeting, 28th February, and *Interim Report*, p. 6. [2] *Interim Report*, pp. 9 and 10.

[3] The phrase 'full recognition of affiliated unions or other bona fide trade unions' caused some heartburn but since the same document had defined bona fide as one affiliated to or recognised by the T.U.C. there was no justification for complaint.

[4] Ibid., p. 11. [5] Ibid., p. 10.

and procedures within general powers to consider all questions affecting the dispute should be determined by the J.S.C. Time limits for reference, hearing and reporting would be decided by the latter. *Unemployment*[1] was dealt with in the wider context of the economic problems of which it was a result. Specific proposals were for raising the school-leaving age, augmenting pensions for the over sixty-fives, helping the older industries to rationalise, increasing government orders, the treatment of mining as a special problem and opening up new public works schemes and development of projects of national importance.

The reports on the gold reserve and rationalisation, as well as those of unemployment and the National Industrial Council, saw the economic and the industrial relations problems as inextricably linked. The document on the *Gold Reserve* underlined the dependence of industry in highly developed countries on the provision of credit and it emphasised that the gold standard was no longer adequate as a basis for that credit. It requested in particular that a full enquiry should be held as soon as possible into national monetary and banking policy. *Rationalisation* was inevitable and beneficial, but steps should be taken to counter the displacement of labour and deterioration of working standards it could involve. It was for employers and trade unions to co-operate in meeting the demands of the new situations and nothing which did not have the full agreement of both parties should be put into practice. In dealing with *Unemployment,* the interaction of monetary policy, world economic conditions and the problems of rationalisation were interlinked and none could be answered in isolation from the other. Specifically a government enquiry into banking and currency policy was an essential concomitant of the attempt to solve the unemployment problem. The National Industrial Council with its wide powers for general consultation should be the means through which industry should keep its eye on all matters which were not normally within the competence of the collective bargaining organisation in individual industries but which affected industrial prosperity.

Throughout the period from February to June 1928 when the subcommittee was meeting regularly to work out these statements, the T.U.C. kept a close watch on its conclusions. On 25th April the proceedings to that time were examined and approved,[2] specifically the agreements on *Trade Union Recognition, Victimisation* and the *Gold Reserve.* There was some opposition to the suggestion that the Conference should turn its attention to the problems of industrial disputes, but at a

[1] *Report of the T.U.C. Congress, 1929,* pp. 188 ff., contains the *Memorandum.*
[2] *Report of the T.U.C. Congress, 1928,* p. 214.

special meeting of the General Council on 14th May the work to date and future plans were again approved. The occasion was the one on which the question of Mond's supposed Fascism was dealt with.[1] A further special meeting to consider the motion that the subcommittee had outlived its usefulness was held on 26th June.[2] The motion was defeated, and a second full meeting agreed for 28th July 1928, at which Turner moved the adoption of an interim *Report* on the work done. He repudiated the views of those within the trade union movement who had attacked the talks and spoke of the advantages of the statements concerning recognition and victimisation and hopes of his concerning the National Industrial Council. If the *Report* was approved by the Congress in September it was hoped that the Conference subcommittee would go on to consider the question of unemployment. Melchett seconded the adoption of the *Report*, pointing out the numerous advances it marked in the handling of the problems that beset industry.[3]

By the Annual Congress of the T.U.C., 1928

At the 1928 Congress, the interim *Report* received an overwhelming vote of confidence. Both Bevin and Citrine spoke in defence of the work done by the Conference and the subcommittee.[4] Far from the talks being a trap for the unwary the results of them so far were such that there would be great difficulty in getting the rest of the employers to accept them. Far from enslaving, the talks were the next 'logical, sequential step in the development of trade unionism'. Bevin[5] pointed out that much union opposition was very similar to that of Allan Smith of the Engineering Employers' Federation, an organisation which had been formed to prevent progressives getting away from the old pattern. Milne Watson had had some difficulty with the N.C.E.O. because he wished to take part in the talks.[6] As for the attacks on Mond, the fact was that there were other employers involved whose approach to industrial relations could not be criticised in any respect. Ashfield's

[1] Though not a Fascist, he was given to expressing strong right-wing views, as Bolitho notes (op. cit., p. 280). Hicks declared himself influenced against the talks by the Rome interview which started the controversy. *Report of the T.U.C. Congress, 1928*, p. 429.

[2] *Report of the T.U.C. Congress, 1928*, p. 215. [3] Ibid., pp. 217 ff.

[4] Ibid., pp. 407 ff. [5] Ibid., p. 445.

[6] Milne Watson was President 1927–8. He also acted in a liaison capacity with the N.C.E.O. for the Mond group. *Minutes* of the C.I.R.I.R. Joint Subcommittee, 20th December 1928.

employees, for example, were practically 100 per cent organised and he was a declared believer in a high wages policy. The Conference had issued a formal statement on *Recognition* and on *Victimisation* and it had done so at trade union insistence. Bevin was ready to state that these two things had done more than anything else to discourage victimisation and company unionism in the difficult times since the strike.[1] On the *Gold Reserve*, the Committee had done nothing but act on the advice of competent labour economists and politicians; so too with *Rationalisation.* The Conference had adopted a definition and an approach to it which had been accepted by the World Economic Conference from a document largely drawn up by Arthur Pugh of the T.U.C. General Council.[2] What the *Report* offered the movement was an intelligent and rational way of exerting the maximum possible pressure for the realisation of its aims. Anyone who hoped that they could lead the British trade unionists any other way than through pressure on constitutional, negotiated lines, was deceiving himself. They were most of them far less belligerent than even the assembled delegates. The case for the continuation of the talks was overwhelming: 3·07 million votes were for acceptance, only 0·56 million against.

(iv) THE ATTITUDES OF THE N.C.E.O./F.B.I., 1927–9

The subcommittee explores the situation

Once it had been made plain that the whole trade union movement was behind the C.I.R.I.R. and the agreements it had reached, the initiative for any further action lay with the official employers' organisations with whom it had been always hoped that the consultation would eventually take place. From the first the auguries had not been good and the N.C.E.O.'s attitude made it highly unlikely that it would even have any serious intention in taking part in the same spirit as the Mond group. The Mond letter had been sent after the first official response of the N.C.E.O. made it clear that it thought no good would come of Hicks' suggestions and that the matters he referred to were best dealt with through the existing negotiation structures.[3] During 1927, the Confederation had been locked in combat with the Minister of Labour, and presumably the government, cautiously trying to do something about the Washington Convention of the I.L.O. The response of the

[1] *Report of the T.U.C. Congress, 1928*, p. 449. [2] Ibid., p. 450. [3] Ibid., p. 210.

N.C.E.O. was to dig its heels in absolutely; it had no alternative suggestions to make, nor would it join with the Ministry in an enquiry on the matter. What had already been said in the early 1920's was sufficient.[1] In Confederation terminology, legislation on these matters was unjustifiable political interference with industry. This being its attitude, the statement in October was not surprising. The question of the reaction of the employers' organisation, however, came up once again when the Interim *Report* of the Conferences was ready for publication in July 1928. The response from the Grand Council of the F.B.I. was most favourable; the N.C.E.O. would decide at its next meeting in October.[2] Meanwhile it was circularising its members and if the response from its most influential affiliate, the Engineering Federation, was typical, the result could not be expected to be hopeful. Protesting their devotion to the beliefs set down in their pamphlet of the previous year, the Engineers doubted the value of any discussion with the T.U.C. Such discussions 'are in grave danger', it said, 'of complicating the industrial situation unnecessarily while giving no hope of useful result'. The Confederation would of course make up its own mind but 'it would appear to be an unusual course to pursue to have these views discussed with the mandatory of the Labour Party without having the corrective of discussion with the other political parties'.[3] It was the old political syndrome again; the desire to keep the unions in their place and refuse to admit that any broader interest on their part was acceptable. The Engineers were to continue to be the centre of opposition to the Conferences.

Though the subcommittee did not meet again until October it then decided to resume regular meetings,[4] fortnightly as against weekly before. At the meeting of 20th December, Turner raised the question of the attitude of the F.B.I. and the N.C.E.O.[5] Melchett expressed the opinion that the F.B.I. would probably be prepared to discuss with the T.U.C. any economic questions arising; the N.C.E.O. was proving more difficult but had not rejected the N.I.C. outright. He and Willey had attended the meeting of the F.B.I. Council to urge the matter and Weir and Milne Watson had done the same at the N.C.E.O. Weir's statement at the meeting of 10th January simply said that the matter was being considered. There followed what the minutes describe as a 'vigorous' discussion and the matter was then

[1] Lab. 2/992/768. Above, pp. 252–3.

[2] *Minutes* of the C.I.R.I.R. Joint Subcommittee, 12th July 1928.

[3] *Report of the E.A.E.F.*, 1928.

[4] *Minutes* of the C.I.R.I.R. Joint Subcommittee, 18th October 1928.

[5] Ibid., 20th December 1928.

dropped.[1] Meanwhile in January the Engineers were making their opposition plainer. The *Bulletin of the British Engineers' Association* attacked the proposal for a National Industrial Council. It repeated its attack in the February edition. The trade unions, it stated, were determined on a take-over of industry and this was the first step towards that end. It was conveniently able to quote the debate at the 1928 Congress, Citrine's words included, to this end.[2] In February 1929 the official reply of the two employers' organisations came: they rejected the *Report* and specifically the N.I.C. Willey[3] remarked that the younger employees took a more liberal view than the older ones, but that it was the older who were in control and made the decisions. With some reluctance the T.U.C. side decided, after consultation with the General Council, to accept the offer of a meeting with the two orgnisations to see what could be achieved in spite of the embargoes on the N.I.C. and the *Report*. Such a conference took place 'without prejudice' on 23rd April 1929,[4] and the old defensiveness of the employers reasserted itself from the start. The F.B.I. representatives said that they could only deal with trade matters and they in any case could only progress at the pace their members allowed them to. The N.C.E.O., which had come into being in 1919 precisely to handle labour matters in view of the Conference of that year, now proclaimed itself incapable of taking any steps which would lead to participation in the proposed N.I.C. and insisted on the separation of trade from labour questions. The pointing out by the T.U.C. members that it was impossible to separate them was of no avail. In a general way the employers were ready to meet to discuss 'current aspects of agreed questions'; beyond that nothing. Citrine had insisted that the T.U.C. reserved the right to continue the talks with the unofficial group if those with the official one were unsatisfactory. Perhaps this likelihood had helped to persuade the employers that they had better make some gesture to keep the thing under control. On 15th May the T.U.C. General Council decided to accept the Industrial Committee's recommendation that the official talks be continued[5] and accordingly, on 27th June 1929, the original group of employers decided to suspend their meetings and on 19th December formally disbanded.[6]

[1] *Minutes* of the C.I.R.I.R. Joint Subcommittee, 10th January 1929.
[2] Twelve individual quotations were made to prove the point.
[3] *Minutes* of the C.I.R.I.R. Joint Subcommittee, 14th February 1929.
[4] *Report* of 1929 Congress, p. 205. [5] Ibid., p. 208.
[6] *Minutes* of the C.I.R.I.R. Joint Subcommittee, 27th June 1929. *Report of the T.U.C. Congress, 1930*, p. 161. *Final Report* of the C.I.R.I.R., December 1930 (published by the T.U.C.).

The official scheme for consultation

As a consequence of its decision of 15th May 1929, the T.U.C. appointed a subcommittee of eighteen, including the Secretary, Milne-Bailey, to consult with the F.B.I. and N.C.E.O. and work out a scheme. Two months later, on 24th July 1929, it met with the employers; the two sides decided, after a general discussion, to appoint a further sub-committee to work out the scheme. The T.U.C. members were Tillett, Pugh, Bevin, Hicks, Citrine and Milne-Bailey. After two meetings, November and December 1929, this subcommittee was able to present the full conference on 29th December 1929, with a scheme under the above title.[1] It was impressive only if read superficially.[2] It began by asserting that any of the three parties—the F.B.I., N.C.E.O. or the T.U.C., could refer to it any matter of common interest to British Industry provided that they did not invade each other's province. It was to have a committee to allocate the subject. There was no provision for permanent organisation, staffing or for regular meetings. The machinery was used on four occasions. In 1930 the T.U.C. and the F.B.I. considered the question of evidence before the Macmillan Committee but in the event each gave its evidence separately.[3] The same organisations discussed the question of Commonwealth trade before the 1930 Imperial Conference and this time a joint Memorandum was issued.[4] In 1931 the F.B.I. and the T.U.C. considered the British Film industry and the Film Quota Act in particular.[5] The only consultation that took place between the T.U.C. and the N.C.E.O. resulted from the initiative of the former; it was on the question of redundancy and reorganisation and it came to nothing.[6]

The fact was of course that once the Conferences were out of the hands of the Mond group the N.C.E.O.'s attitude to industrial relations and to collective bargaining dominated once again and the attempt to introduce co-operative bargaining was alien to it. Nor was the F.B.I.'s attitude any more hopeful. Since the first flush of its enthusiasm in the war and early post-war period it had steadily come under the sway of the older ideas. The N.C.E.O. and the F.B.I., in Bevin's words, 'killed the Mond-Turner Report as far as they could'.[7] The conditions of the slump put paid to any hope of a more optimistic view of the possibilities. The

[1] *Report of the T.U.C. Congress, 1929*, p. 209.
[2] *Report of the T.U.C. Congress, 1930*, p. 160. [3] Ibid., p. 161.
[4] Ibid., p. 162, and 1931, p. 92. [5] *Report of the T.U.C. Congress, 1931*, p. 92.
[6] Ibid., pp. 92 and 218. [7] Ibid., p. 362.

F.B.I. and the N.C.E.O. were leading the chorus of those who were sure that the economic problem could not be overcome until the social service costs, including unemployment pay, had been cut 30 per cent and until the export industries were allowed to control wage levels.[1] While such views dominated in the Councils of the employers, consultation and co-operative bargaining were hardly possible. T.U.C. protests[2] were of no avail. Citrine has kind words to say about the work of the Allocation Committee and its effects in broadening the mind of both sides.[3] Such witness cannot be lightly dismissed and anything which helped to bridge the communications gap was invaluable. But compared with what the Conference helped to achieve it was little enough.

[1] Richardson, pp. 93 and 97. *Industry and the Nation* (published by the F.B.I., 1930).
[2] *Report of the T.U.C. Congress, 1931*, p. 361.i [3] Op. cit., p. 250.

20

The C.I.R.I.R. assessed

(i) AS AN ANSWER TO THE PROBLEMS OF INDUSTRIAL RELATIONS IN 1928–9

The Conference was less a response to an immediate situation of crisis in industrial relations than any of the previous national consultations had been. The pause for reflection provided by the lull after the national strike and the debate that surrounded the passing of the Trade Disputes Act at best provided the occasion for its calling rather than its cause. Inevitably, however, it did concern itself with current industrial relations problems—the trade unions saw to that—though it saw them in the context of the total problem of industry rather than in isolation. The distinctive note of the Conference was that in and through it a group of major employers and the trade union movement represented by the General Council accepted that the problems were inter-related, that no answer which led to a reduction in the wages and living standards of the people was to be tolerated and that in their solution the two sides needed to co-operate. It, therefore, represented a rejection on the one hand of ideas long regarded as self-evident by many employers and on the other of the long-held claim of some that the answer to the problems of industrial relations lay in a change in the system of ownership. Both sides saw themselves as co-existing to their mutual satisfaction for the foreseeable future and not only co-existing but co-operating.

In tackling the central problem of industrial relations in the inter-war years, the problems presented by large-scale unemployment, the Conference showed its orientation. The unemployment problem was a product of world economic conditions, whose effects were aggravated by national and economic and especially monetary policies combined with the slowness of industry to reorganise to meet new conditions. If the problem was to be solved, realistic economic policies had to be formulated at national level and industry had to contribute to their formation. In tackling the problem of rationalisation the C.I.R.I.R. placed the same emphasis on national policy. The problem from an industrial relations point of view was finding more work for the displaced and seeing that they did not suffer because of the needs of change which they, like everyone else, had to accept. Other causes of local difficulty in industrial relations were identified—victimisation, weakness in the collective bargaining structure through non-recognition or insufficient recognition of unions, incomplete dispute procedure. But the fundamental ones were connected with economic conditions and economic policy.

The analysis of the general problem being such, the recommendations about how to solve it were sound also in so far as they went, and as Skidelsky[1] has shown, in their time they were ahead of much contemporary thinking. Practical suggestions concerning organisational changes to improve industrial relations were also to the point, improving procedures and giving the N.I.C. the role of general supervisor of industrial relations—but they too relied upon a general situation of economic growth to have their full effect. Without it, the strain on procedures and structures would be so great as to present a threat to their existence and proper functions.

The failure of the Conference to have any immediate practical effect on any scale was caused basically by a lack of real enthusiasm for it among the employers' organisations, though it is doubtful if, even with the best will in the world, much could have survived the coming depression. The representations of the Conference had some good effect on the Bank Note and Currency Act of 1928; the emphasis in the *Report* on monetary policy and public works was a useful contribution to the current debate. The Macmillan Committee was foreshadowed by the Conference's recommendations. As we have seen, Bevin was of the opinion that the statements on victimisation and trade union recognition stemmed the growth of company unionism and eased the situation at a crucial time. Citrine asserted that the Conference permanently affected the attitude of organised labour and of the employers. After it, the backwoodsmen could never again claim to have reason and common sense on their side; it was obvious to most that collective bargaining should be based on the co-operation norm and should secure certain acceptable minimum standards. Although the depression would give the advocates of a more dismal view further encouragement and make the co-operation norm harder to appreciate, the C.I.R.I.R. remains as a monument to the deeper and more durable

[1] Op. cit., pp. 44 and 117.

tradition of the system, however slow we have been to build that tradition.

(ii) AS A CONTRIBUTION TO THE NORMS AND INSTITUTIONS OF COLLECTIVE BARGAINING

Hicks' invitation, which led by stages to the calling of the Conference, suggested that the employers and the trade unions should seek the terms 'on which co-operation is possible in a common endeavour to improve the efficiency of industry and the workers' standard of life'; Mond's letter repeated this in so many words and the official statement of purposes which emerged from the joint subcommittee spoke of furthering 'the co-operation of all those who participate in production and [to secure] the objective that all those who participate in production should also participate in the prosperity of industry. It is agreed that the most effective co-operation in industry can be obtained by deliberation and negotiation with the accredited representatives of affiliated trade unions.' The elements in the contractual co-operation norm were then present—the mutual acceptance of mutual rights and the readiness, on the basis of these rights, to negotiate co-operatively out of self-interests for the general improvement of industrial relations and individual performance.

It is the fullness of the statement of the norm and the authority with which it was backed which puts the Conference's support of it in a different category to that of its predecessors. The C.I.R.I.R. was not a government-sponsored gathering and in it the trade unions were represented by the T.U.C. which had the full support of the Congress. The employers could not come as a united body but in both what they did and what they represented, the Mond group can claim to have spoken for that element in British management thought and practice which was in line with the soundest tradition and indicative of the most hopeful trend.

In *organisation* the Conference returned to the need for a National co-ordinating organisation for the industrial relations system, an idea which its predecessors had underlined. The same criticism can be levelled at it as could be levelled at them; the basis for the operation of such a body did not exist. But that it once again showed the need of such a National Council as part of the voluntary system of collective negotiations indicates how deeply the need for such an organisation is rooted in the logic of that system. On the other procedural issues, detailed questions of *interpretation* and *codification*, the Conference had nothing to add, though the supervisory role of the National Council would have been in their support.

The contribution of the Conference to the appreciation in depth of what the *minimum wages and conditions* norm meant was as great as its contribution to the serious establishment of the co-operation norm. The Conference did not so much stress the need for decent wages and conditions, it said that these must be taken for granted if industry was to fulfil the role it has to play. Rather it emphasised that without the right sort of monetary and economic policy the industrial prosperity which would assure decent wages and conditions did not exist. The suggestions it made in this respect, though incomplete, were on the right lines as future developments showed. The other substantive norms were seen in this context. The *adjustment norm* is partly dependent on public policy but as such it was only implied. The questions of health, education and research were mentioned in the original topics for discussion but were not in fact dealt with. The Conference did, however, with an insistence on the need for adequate economic policies, provide the context for general productivity bargaining. The Whitley Committee had emphasised the need for improved productivity but it did not concern itself with problems of effective demand. The greater realism of the Conference in this matter is part of its more sophisticated approach.

21

The evolution of the norms and institutions of collective bargaining, 1911-39

The Industrial Council was the occasion of the first nationally significant attempt by trade unions and employers in this country to work out the norms governing their relationship in industry and to improve the institutions for organising it accordingly. The Royal Commission on Labour in the 1890's had examined the system very thoroughly and taken great pains to see that the employers and the trade unions were able to put their points in detail, yet no coherent philosophy of industrial relations emerged, nor did any suggestion for positive improvement, still less a recommendation that the government adopt a policy on these lines. The government was still holding the ring. The main outcome of the Commission was the Conciliation Act of 1896 which gave to the Board of Trade powers already possessed and used by the government, namely the power to intervene in protracted disputes which were assuming national significance. The state could use its powers as conciliator; it could do nothing to remove the causes of disputes or to organise the improvement of collective bargaining. The Industrial Council on the other hand made such recommendations and assumed that the government was able and ready to adopt and apply them. It made these recommendations because it had at least an embryonic philosophy of industrial relations. That philosophy amounted to a rationalisation of the elements in the British system and the recommendations for national policy were aimed at improving it along the same lines. The Council was in fact representative of the men and the organisations which had built the system, and in fact were the system. At a time when there was a tendency to question it on the right and the left they stated their faith in it but also showed that they were aware of its considerable weaknesses.

In the first place they showed, in word and deed, that there was in British industry no ideological conflict between the interests they represented however much difference there was on practical issues. The unions and employers were prepared to accept each other as the legitimate representatives of legitimate interests, having an equal right to exist in industry and to negotiate as equals on matters affecting wages, hours and conditions as they were at that time regarded as negotiable. There were elements in their situation which prevented this negotiation being as equitable as it should have been. Without full employment and the welfare state the hands of the unions were to some extent tied; but the unions themselves showed they had faith that the system itself was capable of providing what they wanted; they did not wish to destroy it in search of a socialist dream. In other words they accepted the contractual co-operation norm of industrial relations with all that it implied; not a unitary concept of the industrial relationship but one based on organised strength of the parties working through well-organised and integrated collective bargaining. In this context co-operation arises out of self-interest.

This organisation was the next point in the philosophy of industrial relations as detectable in the Council's *Report* on agreements. They concluded that, where there was strong organisation which really did represent and negotiate agreements in which those subject to them had confidence, needless disputes were reduced to a minimum. Order they knew existed where there was such trust in the thorough collective bargaining that a sense of moral obligation was generated. It was in considering how best public policy could work in supporting this system that the recommendations of the Council were made. They recommended that where collective agreements existed in a district they should be enforceable by law. This was a dubious means to the right end. But it was in line with voluntarism and it did indicate the need for government policy to support the voluntary system by legislative action if need be.

The Whitley scheme was more authoritative and more significant in practical terms than the Industrial Council. It too was built on the assumptions of the contractual co-operation norm but significantly the *Report* took collective bargaining a stage further to embrace a wider range of interests than would have been acceptable before the war. The *Report* also realised that wages could be linked to productivity, but it failed to see that the problems of effective demand and security had to be solved before this made full sense to the unions. In practice the success of the Councils was in enabling the attitudes which produce and are produced by the co-operation norm to extend their influence. As a result organisations were improved beyond recognition and means were found for resolving the worst of the difficulties over the substantive norms. The contrast between the industries examined in Chapter 9 and those examined in Chapter 10 hinges mainly on this question of the co-operation norm. Where the trade unions and the employers were ready to drop their suspicions of each other and to work together to rebuild wage structures, agree on adjustment norms and work out procedures concerning application, interpretation and codification, the improvement in industrial relations was considerable. Where suspicion remained, improvement was minimal. That attitudes determine organisations was the major lesson of the Whitley scheme. And the attitude which produced the most effective improvement in industrial relations was that summed up in the co-operation norm.

It is in the light of the co-operation norm that the recommendations of the *Fourth Report* of the Committee, relevant here in the procedural context, must be seen. The Industrial Courts were in line with the voluntaristic tradition of the system which Whitley accepted. Like the Industrial Council, the Whitley Committee realised that the logic of the system required some form of national and final court of appeal though like the Council it saw this within voluntarism based on co-operation. Similarly the co-operation norm aided the emergence of the secondary substantive norms. Holidays with pay, redundancy and pensions provisions, safety, health and welfare, training and education, organisation and efficiency for the first time began to be the subject of collective action or agreement on a significant, though very limited, scale.

The Whitley Committee, and the Whitley Councils, had hoped for a positive government policy in support of the scheme. It did not unfortunately develop on any scale after 1919. Negative voluntarism—'do not do anything for industrial relations, let the unions and the employers get on with it'—ruled the minds of the governments of the 1920's and 1930's. What the Whitley Councils wanted was what the Industrial Council had wanted—positive voluntarism, government action to support unions and employers in the improvement of collective bargaining. But collective bargaining was a political issue; there was no strong collective bargaining without strong trade unionism and there was too much suspicion of trade unionism in Conservative Party Councils to make it possible for the governments of the 1920's and 1930's to embark on such a policy.

The National Conference of 1919–21 also came out strongly in support of the co-operation norm—a fact not without significance in the troubled post-war period. But it was not its contribution here which was the most significant though it had much of value to say on the need for a national organisation to oversee industrial relations and underlined the need to improve organisation of collective bargaining. Its main contribution was the emphasis it placed on national policy in support of minimum wages, conditions and security. The means to this end were the wrong ones but the N.I.C. had grasped a nettle that the Industrial Council and the Whitley Report either could or would not grasp. It had insisted that without concern for adequate minima and security the industrial relations system would be unsound. Public policy in support of voluntarism must be more fundamental than simply underpinning the organisation of industrial relations; it must provide the economic conditions in which good industrial relations can evolve.

The Conference on Industrial Reorganisation and Industrial Relations made the most comprehensive contribution to the evolution of norms, just as the Whitley Councils made the most significant contribution to the evolution of institutions in this period. The C.I.R.I.R. did this through the context in which the co-operation norm was reasserted and in its understanding of the context of the minimum wages and conditions norms. It had much else of value to say, for example on the question of a national organisation to oversee industrial relations, but these were not a major contribution.

The C.I.R.I.R. owed less to government initiatives and pressure than its predecessors had done. The Conference was an assembly of trade unionists and employers—an assembly to which the trade union movement was officially committed and in which the more open-minded employers, those who were interested in the present and the future rather than the past, found a voice denied them by the organisation of employers' associations. Because of this, its acceptance of the co-operation norm is of greater significance than that of its predecessors.

It saw also that the context of the minimum wages and conditions norm was a national economic policy for economic prosperity. Minimum wages were not specifically mentioned but adequate wages cannot be secured without economic prosperity and securing that prosperity was very much the Conference's aim. This concentration on economic growth and stability and the need for rationalisation of industry provided the right basis for trade union co-operation in improving productivity. The Conference stressed both the right of the wage-earners to get their share of the increased prosperity and to be secured against the effects of any redundancy reorganisation brought with it.

In and through these Councils and Conferences in the years 1911–39, the framework of a positive philosophy of industrial relations emerged. It emerged through the norms which they accepted explicitly or implicitly and in the assumptions about public policy that they made in their efforts. Through the Whitley Councils this philosophy in part was able to leave a positive mark on the institutions of industrial relations. In summary that philosophy and those norms can be stated as follows. The unions and the employers agreed that they can co-exist within the system and on the basis of strong organisation negotiate their respective needs co-operatively out of self-interest, accepting the moral obligation to observe agreements. This approach demands of public policy two things—the right sort of economic and social policy in its support and that sort and that degree of legal intervention which is in positive support of voluntarism. On the co-operation norm and its voluntaristic presuppositions the other norms of collective bargaining are built: organisation, interpretation and application, codification, minimum wages and conditions, adjustment and the secondary substantive norms; in this context, productivity bargaining develops naturally.

It need hardly be said that these norms remain valid. They meet the human need of the wage-earner in providing him with the means to ensure that his power is organised and his needs represented. They meet the needs of efficiency by leading on to productivity bargaining where this is relevant and so are beneficial to the employer and the nation as well as the wage-earner. They are not in themselves complete; they leave many questions unanswered—the question of the overall supervision of the system and the final court of appeal, the question of the criteria on which wages are to be determined, the question of how to handle requests for adjustment in wages and conditions in an affluent society, especially where increased productivity is not possible. They remain for all that the basis of any answer we find to these problems.

This being so, the question arises of why the system did not continue to develop in its self-understanding as it did in the years between 1911 and 1929 and why in fact some of the norms it established, above all the co-operation norm, are still not fully accepted. If we look at the forty years up to 1911 we see a very considerable development in the industrial relations system. It speeded up from 1911 to 1929, but since then one can hardly avoid the impression that the process has slowed. In 1871 trade unionism was the privilege of a few crafts and favourably placed groups of operatives; it had only recently won legal room to manœuvre. The T.U.C. was in its infancy and the conciliation movement, which led to a considerable improvement in the extent and effectiveness of bargaining, was just under way. By the end of 1911, labour organisation had, through the Royal Commission on Labour, shown itself as a tolerated if not officially encouraged part of the industrial system. It had secured its position legally through the 1906 Act, extended its influence to major groups of unskilled and transport workers and, through the events of 1911, broken the back of much of the old-fashioned libertarian objection to trade unionism. Between then and

1928, the unions and collective bargaining emerged into the full light of day. The war was the great influence here, of course, and much of the wartime experience was embodied in the Whitley Report and Councils. In the Whitley Councils and the C.I.R.I.R. especially it was seen that the government and industry accepted, in its clearer-headed members and moments anyway, the place of the unions in the system and the positive value, the social necessity of effective collective bargaining. It was a bargaining based on voluntarism in the positive sense described and it was bargaining which was open to the more modern development of the productivity agreement. Had these advances been built on and continued, our industrial relations system would surely have developed differently and more helpfully; what went wrong?

It would seem that the answer lies in the events of the 1930's and the effect that this further proof of the capriciousness of the political and economic system had on the thinking of the sort of men who had come together in these Councils. For many on the union side hereafter nationalisation was the only answer; for others the springs of optimism and positive thought so evident in the C.I.R.I.R. had dried up. The main condemnation of the economic system had always been its readiness to put human needs at the mercy of its real or imagined requirements. It was lack of security which had always threatened to undermine the attempts to accept and apply the co-operation norm. The viciousness of the depression and the indications that in the seats of economic and political influence and power there were many who still were prepared to make human happiness an offering to the god of economics made attempts at co-operation unlikely. The hopes of Labour that nationalisation would be the answer have not been well founded. A change of management from private to national does not change the industrial relationship fundamentally, though the industries that were nationalised after 1945 have achieved much in the sphere of industrial relations as in industrial efficiency and organisation. There is no evidence in the meanwhile that there is any real desire among the majority of the wage-earners in this country that they want anything which can be called workers' control. They want what Gosling said they wanted at the 1916 Congress, what Bevin and Citrine reasserted in the 1920's and what the Congress confirmed in the 1930's: the right to negotiate as equals on all matters affecting their daily lives at work. It is because the system has continued to give them this only very inadequately that we have our present troubles and the reasons for this inadequacy are to be found in national attitudes and public policy, reflected in and partly produced by the attitudes of management and unions.

The system of industrial relations developed rapidly between the 1870's and the 1920's. In this time, and during the period we have reviewed especially, it established the outlines with which we are familiar today. But it developed with precious little assistance from anyone outside industry. The policy of the State was that of negative voluntarism. Voluntarism has much to be said for it; it is, in fact, a safe way for a democratic system of industrial relations to develop, putting as it does the responsibility for it where it belongs—on those subject to it and administering it. But the State needs a policy in its support, that is, a policy of positive voluntarism. This we have not had; trade unions and employers' associations, collective bargaining, the essentials of our system were tolerated once established rather than encouraged and given assistance in their work and development. The one genuine chance that government had to support the system effectively through the Whitley Councils was accepted only half-heartedly. The trade unions and the employers had among them until the 1920's and beyond men who were ready to seek the positive improvement of the system. They have had few since. The complacency with which the industrial relations system has been regarded since the end of the 1939 war is one of the most astonishing facts of our time. Now in the 1970's we are faced with the consequences: the harsh evidence that the system is not good enough, the lack of real information on it, the parade of old prejudices and shibboleths in the attempt to reform it. I suggest that the philosophy of industrial relations as it emerges from the efforts of these Councils and Conferences before the disaster of the 1930's, and the interlude when nationalisation seemed an answer or complacency seemed justified, gives us the guidelines we are looking for. The British system developed through the efforts of men who accepted the co-operation norm. The first task of national policy is for us to re-educate ourselves on this. Industrial relations, voluntarism above all, depends on mutual trust, and the co-operation norm—with its realistic basis in self-interest—shows us in what that must consist. Upon that co-operation norm all the rest depends. Given that fundamental acceptance the organisation of industrial relations can go ahead according to a logical and effective plan—the right sort of organisation for collective bargaining, the right sort of procedures for dealing with the interpretation and application of agreements, for codification, for filling out the substantive norms.

The lessons of the Whitley system, that attitudes determine organisations, still remains to be learned. In too many areas of the British system the existing but erroneous and irrelevant illusions of anti-unionism on the part of the employers and their supporters and of comparable attitudes on the part of the unions and their supporters remains. The arguments and the facts recounted in these pages do not justify the view that support of the co-operation norm is an abandonment of the rights of employers, unions or community. Rather it is the framework which allows each to seek his own interest without harming those of others. Whatever else is necessary to improve our system—and much is needed from national economic policy down—it requires a coherent philosophy to hold it together. I suggest that the co-operation norm, and all that goes with it, drawn as it is from the lessons of the British system, provides it.

Sources and works cited

I. SUMMARY NOTE ON SOURCES

The primary sources of information concerning the Councils and Conferences examined are their own minutes, reports and records of their actual activities. These are variously in the Public Records Office (P.R.O.), the Ministry of Labour Library (M. of L.), (now the Department of Employment Library), the records of trade organisations (employers' associations, trade unions and, in the case of the Whitley Councils, the Councils themselves), Sessional Papers (S.P.—Parliamentary Papers, Reports, etc.), and other government papers and publications. Some aspects of consultation and co-operation are dealt with in general works—trade publications, biographies, studies of unions or industrial relations.

(i) *The Industrial Council*

Board of Trade Records (B.O.T.) in the P.R.O.: B.O.T. Establishment Dept. B.T. 20/5, B.T. 21/4 (1911) and B.T. 13/49 (1912).

Notes on the Proceedings of (Industrial Council), 26th October 1911 to 8th June 1912 (M. of L. 331.11).

Ninth and Tenth Reports of the Proceedings under the Conciliation (Trade Disputes) Act of 1896 for 1911 and 1912 respectively. S.P. 1912/13, XVII, and S.P. 1913, XIX.

Enquiry into industrial agreements. Minutes of Evidence and *Report*, S.P. 1913, XXVIII.

The Industrial Council by Sir Charles Macara (London n.d.). Copy in the British Museum Library.

(ii) *The Whitley Committee, Report and Councils*

The Committee

Ministry of Reconstruction Papers (P.R.O.). Under Rec. 1/8, Rec. 1/40, Rec. 1/41, Rec. 1/71 Parts One and Two.

Report of the second meeting of the Committee, dates of meetings and attendance, *Memoranda* of the Committee, etc. U.K. Ministry of Reconstruction Papers (M. of L. 331.883).

Passfield Papers (London School of Economics Library). Reconstruction Papers 1916–1918, Vols. I and II.

The Whitleys of Halifax, Rowland Bretton. Halifax Antiquarian Society 1963.

J. H. Whitley: A Memoir by W. A. Davies, May 1963. Both in the Whitley Family Archives.

The Report

The First Interim Report, S.P. 1917/18, XVIII.

Ministry of Reconstruction Papers (P.R.O.) as in the previous section.

Ministry of Labour Papers, Memorandum by the Ministry on the Scheme, Lab. 2/212. *Memorandum* on the Press reactions, Lab. 2/229/2469.

Cabinet Papers (P.R.O.) G(War) Series Cab. 24/4, Cab. 24/14, Cab. 24/24, Cab. 24/26.

T.U.C. *Reports* 1917 and 1918, the F.B.I. pamphlet *Recommendations on the Whitley Report* 1917.

The Councils in general

Memorandum by the Ministry of Reconstruction and the Ministry of Labour on Industrial Councils and Trade Boards, S.P. 1918, XXII.

Report on the work of the Ministry of Reconstruction until 23rd December 1918: S.P. 1918, XIII.

Report on the Establishment and Progress of the Joint Industrial Councils, H.M.S.O., London 1923.

Ministry of Reconstruction Papers (P.R.O.), Rec. 1/71 part 3, for reactions to and Conferences on the Scheme.

Report on Trade Conferences 1918. U.K. Ministry of Labour Intelligence Section, M. of L. 331.883.

Reports on the attempts to get the Councils established in mining, engineering and railways: Ministry of Labour papers (P.R.O.), Lab. 2/487/13082 and Lab. 2/491/580.

Files which throw light on the relationship between the Ministry and the Councils are mainly those which deal with the National Association of J.I.C.s and the general question of legislation in support of the decisions of the Councils.

Lab. 2/715 (Formation of the N.A.J.I.C.) 1920.

Lab. 2/713 (1925–7 and 1929–30), Lab. 2/1467 (1933).

Lab. 2/775 (1933) and Lab. 2/2012 (1935); Memoranda, deputations etc. on legislation to regulate wages.

Lab. 2/2033 (1935–6), Lab. 10/9 and Lab. 10/11. Cotton (Temporary regulation of Wages) Act 1935–6.

Lab. 2/1309/671 Parts I and II. List of Councils in operation and the question of reviving the scheme; observations of the Ministry on its role regarding the Councils.

The Individual Councils

With a few exceptions where published accounts of the work of the Council in an industry proved adequate, or where records were neither made available to me by the Councils nor were to be found in the Ministry of Labour records at the P.R.O., the account of the J.I.C.s' work has been taken from the Records and Minutes of each.

Building Industry

Report on the Industrial Council for the Building Industry: Garton Foundation (London n.d.)

Proposal for a Builders National Industrial Parliament (London 1917). M. of L. 331.883.

Management and Costs Committee Reports of the Council, ibid.

Annual Reports of the Council 1919, ibid.

The Master Builders and Association Journal, February 1917 to August 1924.

R. W. Postgate, *The Builders History*, London 1923, pp. 440 ff.

P.R.O. Lab. 2/710, Lab. 2/709 and Lab. 2/791.

Boot and Shoe Manufacture

A. Fox, *History of the National Union of Boot and Shoe Operatives* (Blackwell 1928), pp. 400–4.

F. Gannet and B. F. Catherwood, *Industrial and Labour Relations in Great Britain* (New York 1939), pp. 202 ff.

P.R.O. Lab. 2/2043, Lab. 2/915.

Cement Manufacture

N.J.C. for the *Cement Manufacturing Industry*: Approved Working Rules 1921.

Information obtained in correspondence and interview with Mr. Neale and Mr. A. J. Kean, O.B.E.

P.R.O. Lab. 2/811/532.

Heavy Chemicals

N.J.I.C. for the Heavy Chemicals Industry: complete records and minutes do not appear to have survived. I have consulted those known to exist. I also had access to the Chemical Employers' Federation Records.

Address of Mr. Chapman to the Chemical Industries Association on the history of the Employers' Federation (1965): *Address* of Mr. Bottomley to the same on the history of the J.I.C. 1969.

The negotiating Machinery in the Chemical Industry, T.G.W.U. 1961.

P.R.O. Lab. 2/265/116.

Docks

The N.J.I.C. for the Port Transport Industry could not allow me access to its Records and the P.R.O. does not possess them.

Shaw Enquiry (Court of Enquiry concerning Transport Workers—wages and conditions of employment of Dock Labour), S.P. 1920, XXIV.

Ministry of Labour *Port Labour Enquiry* Report 1931 and the Reports of the Standing Advisory Committee on Decasualisation. M. of L. 331.761.

Allan Bullock, *The Life and Times of Ernest Bevin* (London 1966), pp. 237 ff.

Ministry of Labour *Industrial Relations Handbook* 1944, pp. 47 ff.

Electrical Cablemaking

Joint Industrial Council for the *Electrical Cablemaking Industry* Minutes of Meetings, and other records 1919–39. Archives of the Cablemakers' Association, London.

Electricity Supply

N.J.I.C. for the *Electricity Supply Industry*: Minutes and Records P.R.O. Lab. 2/672–3–4 and Lab. 2/911–2.

Flourmilling

N.J.I.C. for the *Flourmilling Industry*: Minutes and Records. Also files of *Milling*, the trade journal.

F. Gannet and B. F. Catherwood, *Industrial and Labour Relations in Great Britain*, pp. 127 ff.

A. Bullock, *The Life and Times of Ernest Bevin*, pp. 95–6.

Unity (National Industrial Alliance Journal) March 1937.

Gas Supply

N.J.I.C. for the *Gas Industry*: Annual Reports 1919–39.

P.R.O. Lab. 2/458.

Heating and Domestic Engineering Industry

N.J.I.C. for the *Heating and Domestic Engineering Industry*: the Minutes and Records.

National Union of Operative Heating and Domestic Engineering, etc. *Workers* (Heating and Domestic Engineering Union.) Annual and Conference Reports 1913–39.

Hosiery and Knitwear

N.J.I.C. for the *Hosiery and Knitwear Trades*: Minutes and Records.

P. A. Wells, *The British Hosiery Trade* (London 1935).

Local Authorities

N.J.I.C. for *Local Authorities* (Non-trading services). Minutes and Records in P.R.O. Lab. 2/278, Lab. 2/279, Lab. 2/280, Lab. 2/851.

Industrial Relations Handbook, H.M.S.O., 1944, p. 32–3.

Paint and Varnish Manufacture

N.J.I.C. for the *Paint, Varnish and Lacquer Industry*: Minutes and Records, company histories.

Papermaking

N.J.I.C. for the *Papermaking Industry*: Minutes of meetings and records of N.J.I.C. and its predecessor the I.I.R.C.

Information and Interview with Mr. Arthur Baker, whose pamphlet *The Employers' Federation of Papermakers and Boardmakers* (London 1953) for private circulation was also made available along with the Minutes of the Executive meeting of the Federation and several company histories.

Pottery

N.J.I.C. for the *Pottery Industry*: full accounts month by month in the *Pottery Gazette and Glass Trades Review*.

P.R.O. Lab. 2/138, Lab. 2/452, Lab. 2/453.

W. H. Warburton, *A History of Trade Union Organisation in the North Staffordshire Potteries* (London 1931).

Printing

The N.J.I.C. for the *Printing Industry* fully reported in John Child, *Industrial Relations in the British Printing Industry* (London 1967), Ch. XVI. Annual Reports of the N.J.I.C. (included in the *Federation of Master Printers' Circular*).

Quarrying

N.J.I.C. for the *Quarrying Industry*: Minutes and Records.

Ministry of Labour, *Report on Collective Agreements,* H.M.S.O. (London 1934), Vol. I.

R.C. on Mines and Quarries *Minutes of Evidence,* S.P. 1912–13, XLI.

Railways

Memorandum on the Railways Bill, S.P. 1921 XXX and *Appendix* to same.

Labour Gazette, July 1921 and February 1922.

Minutes of meetings of the Railway and Sectional Councils. Great Western. B.R. Western Region Archives.

P. S. Bagwell, *The Railwaymen* (London 1953).

C. S. Halverson, 'The Development of Labour Relations in British Railways since 1800', unpublished London University Ph.D. thesis.

Frank Pickstock, *British Railways, the Human Problem*. Fabian Research 142.

Report of the Special Joint Committee on the Machinery of Negotiation for Railway Staff, February 1934.

Silk Manufacture

J.I.C. for the *Silk Industry*: Minutes and Records.

Soap and Candle Manufacture

J.I.C. for the *Soap, Candles* (and later Edible Fats) *Manufacturing Industry*: Minutes of meetings and Records from 1925.

P.R.O. Lab. 2/986 and Lab. 2/2016 contain many of the pre-1925 records and Minutes.

A. E. Musson, *Enterprise in Soap and Chemicals* (Manchester 1964).

Evidence of the Employers' Federation before the Royal Commission on Trade Unions and Employers' Associations (the Donovan Commission) 1966.

Tramways

N.J.I.C. for the *Tramways Industry*: Minutes and Records, P.R.O. Lab. 2/886, Lab. 2/885, Lab. 2/652, Lab. 2/887 and Lab. 2/453.

Report of a Court of Enquiry into the stoppage of London Tramways, etc., S.P. 1924, XI.

Water Supply

J.I.C. for the *Water Supply Industry*: Minutes and Records, P.R.O. Lab. 2/909 and Lab. 2/910.

Tinplate

Transcripts and Proceedings of the Conciliation Board and (from 1919) the J.I.C. in the *Welsh Tinplate Industry*, 1911–39.

W. E. Minchinton, *The British Tinplate Industry* (Oxford 1957), pp. 134 ff. and 213 ff.

Wool and Allied

N.J.I.C. for the *Wool and Allied Trades*: Minutes, Reports and Records, together with the same for the Northern District and some of those for other Districts.

Memorandum on the Working of the Control Board in the *Woollen and Worsted Industry* printed for the use of the Ministry of Reconstruction 1917, M. of L. 331.883.

Woollen and Worsted Industry: *Historical survey of the Building up of the Wage Structure*. W. and A.T.E.C. records.

Report of a Court of Investigation under the Chairmanship of Harold Morris, K.C., 1925. W. and A.T.E.C. Records.

Report of a Court of Enquiry concerning matters in dispute regarding wages in the Northern Counties Wool and Textile industries (The Macmillan Enquiry), S.P. 1929–30, XV.

(iii) *The National Industrial Conference*

(a) *The Conferences*

The Full Report of Speeches at the First Conference (27th February 1919), which was published by H.M.S.O. 1919. Copies in the T.U.C. and the M. of L. libraries. *The Times* also reported the Conference in great detail. 26th February 1919.

The *Report on Conciliation and Arbitration,* etc., S.P. 1920, XIX. Appendix on the Conferences.

The *Report of the Provisional Joint Committee* presented to the Second Conference on 4th April 1919, S.P. 1919, XXIV.

Trade Union Memorandum on the Causes of Industrial Unrest, ibid.

(b) *The Provisional Joint Committee*

Minutes of the Proceedings of the Provisional Joint Committee and the *Reports* of Subcommittees. M. of L. 331.1, and the T.U.C. H.D. 5545.

Confidential Report of the T.U.C. on the P.J.C. (duplicated), 3rd June 1921. T.U.C. H.D. 5545.

The *Report on Conciliation and Arbitration,* S.P. 1920, XIX, summarising the work of the Committee.

P.R.O. Lab. 2/775/1730: Minutes of the Memoranda concerning the Conference.

Lab. 2/556/7809: Conference between the T.U.C. Representatives on the P.J.C. and the Ministry.

Lab. 2/775/204 1927 Historical note on the 1919 N.J.I.C.; Lab. 2/821/615 1921; Lab. 2/891/1034 1919; Lab. 2/981/113 1923: Memoranda, deputations etc. on the subject of legislation on wages and hours recommended by the N.J.I.C. and supported by the I.L.O. Convention.

(iv) *The Conference on Industrial Reorganisation and Industrial Relations*

Minutes of meetings of the Industrial Committee of the T.U.C. General Council (the union side of the Joint Subcommittee of the C.I.R.I.R.) 1928–9.

Minutes of the meetings of the Joint Subcommittee of the C.I.R.I.R. 1928–9.

Interim Report of the C.I.R.I.R. adopted 4th July 1928: *Official Report of Proceedings* of the meeting of 4th July 1928 (duplicated). Archives of C.M.F.

Report of the T.U.C., 1927; the Reports for 1928, 1929, 1930, 1931 give full details of the Conference. That for 1929 also contained the Report on Unemployment issued after the Interim Report was accepted.

Final Report of the C.I.R.I.R., December 1930, published by the T.U.C. for the C.I.R.I.R.

H. Bolitho, *Alfred Mond: First Lord Melchett* (London 1933).

A. Bullock, *The Life and Times of Ernest Bevin*, Vol. 1 (London 1960), Chapter 15.

Lord Citrine, *Men and Work*, London, 1964 (Chapter 13).

Sir Alfred Mond, *Industry and Politics* (London 1927).

2. LIST OF WORKS CITED

(i) *History*: social, political, economic

D. Abel, *History of British Tariffs* (London 1946).

P. Abrams, 'The Failure of Social Reform 1918–1922', *Past and Present*, April 1963.

F. Benham, *Great Britain under Protection* (New York 1941).

W. Beveridge, *British Food Control* (Oxford 1928).

C. Booth, *Life and Labour of the People of London* (London 1902–3).

A. L. Bowley and A. R. Burnett Hurst, *Livelihood and Poverty* (London 1915).

A. L. Bowley, *Prices and Wages in the U.K. 1914–20* (Oxford 1921).
D. Butler and J. Freeman, *British Political Facts* (London 1964).
J. H. Clapham, *An Economic History of Modern Britain*, Vol. 3 (Cambridge 1938).
G. D. H. Cole, *A Short History of the British Working Class Movement* (London 1932).
H. Daalder, *Cabinet Reform in Great Britain*, 1914–63 (Oxford 1964).
G. Dangerfield, *The Strange Death of Liberal England* (London 1936).
A. V. Dicey, *The Law and Public Opinion in England* (London 1905).
R. C. Ensor, *England 1870–1914* (Oxford 1936).
E. Eshag, *From Marshall to Keynes* (Blackwell 1963).
M. P. Fogarty (ed.), *Further Studies in Industrial Organisation* (London 1948).
A. Gleason, *What the Workers Want* (London 1921).
E. Halévy, *A History of the English People in 1905–1915* (London 1934).
H. R. Hikins, 'The Liverpool General Strike', *Trans. Royal Hist. Soc. of Lancashire and Cheshire*, 1961, Vol. 113.
S. J. Hurwitz, *State Intervention in Britain* (New York 1949).
T. J. Kiernan, *British War Finances* (London 1920).
A. W. Kirkaldy, *Credit, Industry and the War* (London 1915).
A. W. Kirkaldy, *Labour, Finance and the War* (London 1916).
E. D. Lewis, *The Rhondda Valley* (London 1963).
E. M. H. Lloyd, *Experiments in State Control* (Oxford 1923).
J. M. McEwan, 'The coupon election of 1918 and the unionist Members of Parliament', *Journal of Modern History*, 1962.
H. Macmillan, *The Winds of Change* (London 1966).
A Marwick, *Britain in the Century of Total War* (London 1968).
A. Marwick, *The Deluge* (London 1965).
C. F. G. Masterman, *The Condition of England.*
Lucy Masterman, *C. F. G. Masterman* (London 1939).
K. Middlemass, *The Clydesiders* (London 1966).
Ministry of Munitions (History of) (London 1922), etc., 12 vols.
B. R. Mitchell and P. Deane, *Abstract of British Historical Statistics* (Cambridge 1962).
E. V. Morgan, *Studies in British Financial Policy 1914–25* (London 1952).
W. A. Orton, *Labour in Transition (1914–21)* (London 1921).
H. Pelling, *A Short History of the Labour Party* (London 1965).
S. Pollard, *The Development of the British Economy 1914–50* (London 1962).
S. Pollard, *A History of Labour in Sheffield* (London 1959).
D. Ricardo, *The Principles of Political Economy and Taxation* (Everyman edition, London 1961).
Romney Street Group, *The Other War* (London 1917).

B. S. Rowntree, 'The Industrial Unrest', *Contemporary Review* (October 1911).
B. S. Rowntree, *Poverty—a Study of Town Life* (London 1901).
J. A. Schumpeter, *A History of Economic Analysis* (London 1963).
R. V. Sires, 'Labour Unrest in England 1910–1914', *Journal of Economic Hist.*, 1955.
R. Skidelsky, *The Politicians and the Slump* (London 1967).
K. B. Smellie, *100 Years of British Government* (London 1937).
J. Symons, *The General Strike* (London 1953).
A. J. P. Taylor, *English History, 1914–45* (Oxford 1964).
C. Watney and J. Little, *Industrial Warfare* (London 1912).
T. Wilson, 'The Coupon and the British General Election of 1918', *Journal of Modern Hist.*, 1964.
H. Wolfe, *Labour Supply and Regulation* (Oxford 1923).

(ii) *Biography*

C. Addison, *Four and a Half Years*, 2 Vols (London 1934).
N. Angell, *After All* (London 1951).
G. Barnes, *Workshop to War Cabinet* (London 1924).
G. Blaxland, *J. H. Thomas: a Life for Unity* (London 1964).
A. Boyle, *Montagu Norman* (London 1967).
M. V. and O. S. Brett, *Journals and Letters of Reginald, Viscount Esher* (London 1934–8), 4 vols.
J. R. Clynes, *Memoirs* (London 1937).
J. C. C. Davidson, *Memoirs of a Conservative* (London 1969) (edited R. R. James).
Lord Devonport (Hudson Kearley), *The Travelled Road* (London 1924).
K. Feiling, *Life of Neville Chamberlain* (London 1946).
W. Gallacher, *Revolt on the Clyde* (London 1936).
H. Gosling, *Up and Down Stream* (London 1927).
M. A. Hamilton, *Arthur Henderson* (London 1938).
D. Kirkwood, *My Life of Revolt* (London 1935).
W. Lee, *Thirty Years in Coal 1917–47* (London 1954).
Lloyd George, *War Memoirs* (London 1938).
M. H. Mackworth (ed.), *D. A. Thomas, Viscount Rhondda* (London 1921).
T. Mann, *Memoirs* (London 1923).
K. Middlemass, *Baldwin* (London 1969).
W. Haslam Mills, *Sir Charles Macara* (Manchester 1917).
E. Nixon, *John Hilton* (London 1946).
R. A. S. Redmayne, *Men, Mines and Memories* (London 1942).
Sir W. Runciman, *Before the Mast and After* (London 1924).
Sir James Sexton, *Sir James Sexton, Agitator* (London 1934).

R. Smillie, *My Life for Labour* (London 1924).
W. Thornex, *My Life's Battles* (London 1925).
J. T. Thorpe, *Friends and Adventures* (London 1931).
D. Torr, *Tom Mann and His Times*, vol. 1 (London 1956).
B. Webb, *Diaries 1912–1924* (edited Cole) (London 1952).
J. Wilson, *My Stormy* Loyage *Through Life* (London 1927).

(iii) *Industry and Industrial Relations*
G. C. Allen, *British Industries and Their Organisation* (London 1958).
V. L. Allen, *Trade Unions and the Government* (London 1960).
R. Page Arnot, *The Miners* (3 vols.) (London 1949–61).
R. Page Arnot, *The South Wales Miners* (London 1967).
Amalgamated Society of Railway Servants, Proceedings, 1911.
G. R. Askwith, *Industrial Problems and Disputes* (London 1920).
P. S. Bagwell, *The Railwaymen* (London 1963).
W. Milne Bailey, *Trade Union Documents* (London 1919).
A. Briggs (ed.), *Essays in Labour History* (London 1964).
British Engineers Association Bulletin, January–February 1928.
E. H. Phelps-Brown, *The Growth of British Industrial Relations* (London 1960).
C. J. Bundock, *The Story of the National Union of Printing, Bookbinding and Paperworks* (London 1959).
C. R. Carter, 'The Triple Alliance of Labour', *Economic Journal*, September 1916.
N. Chamberlain and J. W. Kuhn, *Collective Bargaining* (New York 1965).
D. Chang, *British Methods of Industrial Peace* (Columbia 1936).
J. Chapman (ed.), *Labour and Capital After the War* (London 1918).
J. Child, *Industrial Relations in the British Printing Industry* (London 1967).
H. Clay, *Problems of Industrial Relations and Other Lectures* (London 1929).
H. A. Clegg, *General Union* (Blackwell 1954).
H. A. Clegg, *Labour Relations in London Transport* (Blackwell 1960).
H. A. Clegg, *A New Approach to Industrial Democracy* (Blackwell 1960).
H. A. Clegg, A. Fox and A. F. Thompson, *A History of British Trade Unions Since 1889* (Oxford 1964).
G. D. H. Cole, *Labour in the Coal Mining Industry During the War*, (Oxford 1923).
G. D. H. Cole, *Organised Labour* (London 1923).
G. D. H. Cole, *Trade Unionism and Munitions* (Oxford 1923).
A. J. Cook, *Mond Moonshine* (London 1927).
A. J. Cook, *Mond's Manacles* (London 1928).
P. L. Cook, *The Effects of Mergers* (Oxford 1958).

S. Courtauld, *Ideals and Industry* (London 1949).

Engineering and Allied Employers' Federation, '30 Years of Industrial Conciliation' (London 1927).

D. Evans, *Labour Strife in the South Wales Coalfield, 1910–1911* (Cardiff 1911).

E. W. Evans, *The Miners of South Wales* (Cardiff 1961).

S. Everard, *The History of the Gas Light and Coke Co.* (London 1949).

Federation of British Industries: Annual Report 1918–1919.

The Control of Industry, Nationalisation and Kindred Problems (London 1919).

The F.B.I. What it is and what it does (London 1922).

Industry and the Nation, 1931.

Federation of Master Cotton Spinners Reports, 1895–1911.

A. Flanders, 'Collective Bargaining—A Theoretical Analysis', *The British Journal of Industrial Relations*, March 1968.

A. Flanders, *Industrial Relations: What is Wrong with the System* (London 1965).

A. Flanders, *Trade Unions* (London 1952).

H. Fyrth and H. Collins, *The Foundry Workers* (Manchester 1959).

Garton Foundation. Memorandum on the Industrial Situation After the War (London 1916).

E. Halévy, 'Les Whitley Councils', Rev. d'econ, politique, 1919.

J. R. Haynes, *Coal and its Conflicts* (London 1928).

E. J. Hobsbawm, *Essays in Labour History* (London 1964).

J. B. Jefferys, *The Story of the Engineers* (London 1945).

T. B. Johnston, *Industrial Councils and their Possibilities* (Manchester 1920).

A. E. Kirkus, *British Railway Statistics* (London 1927).

K. G. C. Knowles, *Strikes* (Blackwell 1952).

Labour Magazine, August 1919 to August 1933.

E. C. P. Lascelles and S. S. Bullock, *Dock Labour and Decasualisation* (London 1924).

League of Nations Union, *Towards Industrial Peace* (London 1927).

Liberal Industrial Enquiry Report, *Britain's Industrial Future* (London 1928).

J. Lovell, *Stevedores and Dockers* (London 1969).

C. Macara, *Getting the World to Work* (Manchester 1922).

C. Macara, *Modern Industrial Tendencies* (Manchester 1927).

C. Macara, *Pulling Together in the Industrial World* (Manchester 1928).

C. Macara, *Social and Industrial Reform* (Manchester 1918).

A. Marsh, *Industrial Relations in Engineering* (London 1965).

B. G. de Montgomery, *British and Continental Labour Policy* (London 1922).

W. E. Minchinton, *The British Tinplate Industry* (Oxford 1957).
A. C. Pigou and others, *The Reorganisation of Industry* (London 1916).
L. H. Powell, *The Shipping Federation* (London 1950).
B. Pribicevic, *The Shop Stewards Movement and Workers Control* (Blackwell 1959).
Sir Arthur Pugh, *Men of Steel* (London 1951).
Railway Association *Minutes* August–December 1911 (British Transport Historical Records).
R. C. Rawley, *Economics of the Silk Industry* (London 1919).
R. A. S. Redmayne, *The British Coalmining Industry During the War* (Oxford 1923).
J. H. Richardson, *Industrial Relations in Great Britain* (London 1933).
B. C. Roberts and J. Lovell, *A Short History of the T.U.C.* (London 1968).
B. C. Roberts, *Trades Union Congress 1868–1921* (London 1958).
W. R. Scott and J. Cunnison, *The Industries of the Clyde Valley During the War* (Oxford 1924).
J. B. Seymour, *The Whitley Councils Scheme* (London 1932).
I. G. Sharp, *Industrial Conciliation and Arbitration in Great Britain* (London 1950).
M. Sparkes, *A Memorandum on Industrial Self-Government* (London 1917).
B. Tillett, *A History of the London Transport Workers Strike, 1911* (London n.d.).
Trade Union Congress *Reports*, 1912–1932.
Unity (Monthly) published by the National Alliance of Employers and Employed, 1919–39.
L. Urwick and E. F. L. Brech, *The Making of Scientific Management* (London 1949, etc.), 3 vols.
S. and B. Webb, *A History of Trade Unionism* (London 1920).
S. and B. Webb, *Industrial Democracy* (London 1920).
S. and B. Webb, *A Constitution for the Socialist Commonwealth of Great* Britain (London 1920).
F. A. Wells, *The British Hosiery Trade* (London 1935).
L. D. White, *Whitley Councils in the British Civil Service* (Chicago 1932).
G. E. Williams, *The Derbyshire Miners* (London 1963).

(iv) *Sessional Papers, Parliamentary Debates, etc.*

S.P.	1894	XXXV	Royal Commission on Labour: *Final Report.*
	1908	XI	*Departmental Enquiry on Checkweighmen in Quarries*, etc.
	1910	XX	*Report on Collective Agreements.*

	1918	X	(Whitley Committee) *Second Report on N.J.I.C.s.*
		XIV	*Supplementary Report on Works Committees.*
		VII	*Report on Conciliation and Arbitration.*
		VII	*Fifth and Final Report.*
	1936–7	XXVI	*22nd Abstract of Labour Statistics, 1922–1936.*
S.P.	1909	XLIX	*Report on Strikes and Lockouts* 1908.
	1910	LVIII	*Report on Strikes and Lockouts* 1909.
	1911	XLI	*Report on Strikes and Lockouts* 1910.
	1912–13	XLVII	*Report on Strikes and Lockouts* 1911.
	1914	XLVIII	*Report on Strikes and Lockouts* 1912.
S.P.	1911	XIII	*8th Report of Proceedings under the Conciliation (Trades Disputes) Act of 1896.*
	1912–13	XVII	*9th.*
	1913	XIX	*10th.*
	1914	LXXIX	*11th.*
	1919	XIII	*12th.*
	1920	XIX	*Report on Conciliation and Arbitration etc.*
S.P.	1911	XXIX	*Report on the Railway Conciliation and Arbitration Scheme, 1907.*
	1912–13	XLV	*Minutes of Evidence* of same.
S.P.	1911	XLVII	*Employment of the Military* during the 1911 Railway Strike.
S.P.	1912–13	XLVII	*Report on Present Dispute affecting Transport Workers in the Port of London,* etc.
S.P.	1914–16	XXIX	*Report on the Clyde Munition Workers.*
		LV	*Return to an order . . . for Report and Statistics of Bad Timekeeping in Shipbuilding,* etc.
S.P.	1917–18	XV	*Reports of the Commission of Enquiry into Industrial Unrest.*
S.P.	1917–18	XV	Summary of the Reports
S.P.	1919	XI	*Reports of the Coal Industry Commission* (Sankey Commission).
S.P.	1920	XXIV	*Report of a Court of Enquiry concerning the Transport Workers—wages and conditions of employment of Dock Labour.*
S.P.	1926	XIV	*Report of the Royal Commission on the Coal Industry, 1926* (Samuel Commission).
S.P.	1909	XXXVI–VII	*Report of the Royal Commission on the Poor Laws,* etc.

S.P.	1912–13	CVIII	*Earnings and Hours of Labour Enquiry:* Railway Service in 1907.
S.P.	1914–16	LV	*Ministry of Munitions, Health of Munition Workers Committee.*
S.P.	1916	XIII	*Memoranda* 1–14.
	1917–18	XVI	*Memoranda Interim Report on Industrial Efficiency and Fatigue.*
S.P.	1918	XII	*Final Report of the Committee.*
S.P.	1917–18	XIV	*Royal Commission on the Housing of the Industrial Population of Scotland.*
S.P.	1924–5	XIV	*Report of the Ministry of Labour,* 1923–4.
S.P.	1937–8	XII	*Ministry of Labour: Report on Holidays with Pay.*
S.P.	1918	XIII	Ministry of Reconstruction: *Report of the Committee on Trusts* and *A Study of Trade Organisations and Combinations in the U.K.*
S.P.	1918	IV	*Report of the Select Committee on Transport.*
S.P.	1918	VII	*Reports of the Committee on Currency and*
	1919	XIII	*Foreign Exchanges after the War* (Cunliffe Committee).
S.P.	1920	XXI	*Report on the Working of the National Maritime Board* 1917–19.
S.P.	1922	IX and XI	*Reports of the Committee on National Expenditure* (Geddes Committee).

Industrial Court Decisions, 861–1003 1924 vol. VI.

Industrial Councils Bill, Bills Public 1924 (II).

Industrial Councils Bill, Bills Public 1929–30 (II).

Cotton Manufacturing (Temporary Regulation) Act: Public and General Acts: 1933–4 Ch. 30.

Parliamentary Debates. House of Commons, 29, 35, 41, 95, 112, 115, 121, 142, 174, 205, etc. H.C. Deb. 5S.

Census of Production 1924, 1935.

Census of Population 1921, 1931.

Committee on Industry and Trade (Balfour Committee) Survey of Metal Industries H.M.S.O. 1928.

Royal Commission on Trade Unions and Employers Associations Research Papers 1, 2 (Part 1), and 4, 1967 etc.

Index

www.ingramcontent.com/pod-product-compliance
Lightning Source LLC
LaVergne TN
LVHW020644300926
849161LV00004B/802
* 9 7 8 1 0 3 2 8 4 6 4 8 4 *